Kathy Cha...

P9-DNZ-255

OUTSTANDING REVIEWS FOR
LOVE'S BLOOD:

"An absolute spellbinder."

—*Library Journal*

"Vivid, captivating."

—*Publishers Weekly*

"A gripping 'Why-dunnit.'"
—Lucy Freeman, author of
The Beloved Prison and *Fight Against Fear*

"A powerful story of self-deception and sexual enslavement—riveting, chilling and above all, authentic."
—Barbara D'Amato, author of
The Doctor, The Murder, The Mystery

"Excellent . . . A fine piece of investigation from true crime's gutsiest author."
—Elliot Leyton, author of
Hunting Humans and *Sole Survivor*

St. Martin's Paperbacks Titles
by Clark Howard

BROTHERS IN BLOOD
LOVE'S BLOOD

LOVE'S BLOOD

**The Shocking True Story of a Teenager
Who Would Do Anything
for the Older Man She Loved—
Even Kill Her Whole Family**

CLARK HOWARD

ST. MARTIN'S PAPERBACKS

Chicago Tribune photographs © 1993 Chicago Tribune Company. All rights reserved. Used with permission.
Daily Herald photographs used by permission of the *Daily Herald*, Arlington Heights, IL.

Published by arrangement with Crown Publishers, Inc.

LOVE'S BLOOD

Library of Congress Catalog Number: 92-15915

ISBN: 0-312-95301-1

Printed in the United States of America

Crown hardcover edition published 1993
St. Martin's Paperbacks edition/August 1994

St. Martin's Paperbacks are published by St. Martin's Press, 175 Fifth Avenue, New York, NY 10010.

10 9 8 7 6 5 4 3 2 1

*To the memory
of a good friend
and a special lady,
ELEANOR SULLIVAN*

CONTENTS

PART TWO: THE TRIAL

PART THREE: AFTERMATH

AUTHOR'S NOTE

The tentacles of a murder reach out to touch many people, some in a consuming embrace, others with barely a brush. However brief the contact may be, no one forgets it. The people, events, and conversations depicted in the triple murder about which this book is written have been reconstructed from comprehensive research, which is described to the reader as the story progresses. Much of what is related came from public records and the investigative files of the dedicated police officers who solved the case, while other information was gleaned from the memories of people who stood anywhere from the very center of the tragic crime to its farthest fringe. Some details, such as confidential therapy sessions between one of the principals and her psychologist, have obviously had to come solely from the patient, although in some instances the information could be corroborated through outside sources. As with any work of nonfiction, there are times when, in the interest of logic and continuity, the author has been required to interpret and even extrapolate the known facts. Also, to safeguard the privacy and whereabouts of certain individuals, the author has changed their names and other identifying characteristics. But essentially, the following story is, I believe, as true and complete as it will ever be told.

PREFACE

In this book, the reader is going to be introduced to the details of one of the strangest and most senseless multiple murders on record. It is a crime that was rooted in love and lust, a crime that was swept along by sexual energy in its broadest range.

Because the crime is nearly two decades old, and because one of the principals is telling her story for the first time, it has been necessary, in the first part of the book, to structure the story in a way that takes the reader back and forth in time. Some of the details in this section came from the principal herself; some have been corroborated by research, some not. Interspersed are sections designated with the author's initials—"C.H."—which are personal recollections as well as a chronology of the extensive research done. Gradually, all of it comes together—the principal's story, the known facts, the perversity of the people who advanced the murders—to create the first complete picture of *a crime that did not have to happen*.

By the time the reader reaches the second part of the book, which narrates the trial, an opinion will probably have been formed about the woman whose story this book essentially is. That opinion may or may not be changed by the trial and its aftermath. But whether or not one's opinion changes, at least the reader, having decided what to believe—and what not to—will have had, for the first time, the benefit of many heretofore unknown aspects of the story, including facts never brought out at this long and very strange trial.

And that, after all, is what a book like this is all about.

Part One

The Crime

C.H.
May 1976

I was in Chicago doing some final research on a book that I would eventually call Six Against the Rock, *about the big escape attempt at Alcatraz in 1946. I had been snaking all over the country interviewing old-time outlaws who had been on the Rock during the siege.*

It had been a long, tiring research trip and I drove on up to Chicago for a couple of days of rest and to put all my notes in order. That's what I told myself. The truth of the matter was, Chicago periodically drew me back to its concrete bosom. I hadn't lived there for nearly twenty years, but every once in a while I had to go back and prowl its lower West Side streets like a specter in a graveyard. Maybe it was because between the ages of eight and fourteen I had spent a hundred years on those streets searching for an ex-convict father who was already dead; or because my mother had overdosed on heroin there; or because my earliest real friends had been street kids like myself and had all been sucked into the sump of killings, crime, prison, drugs, alcohol—and I had not. My only "time" had been done in a euphemistically named "state training school" for boys—read reformatory— and my only killing had been sanctioned by the Marine Corps. I had long ago made my own break from my own prison, and it had been successful. The other kids hadn't escaped. Maybe that was what drew me back now and then. Wondering: why me?

I was dug in at a little hotel on Rush Street, just across the river from the Loop, the first time I saw Patricia Columbo's picture. It was in the Tribune *and showed a pretty but strained nineteen-year-old girl with a jungle of streaked dark blondish hair entering a funeral home with a handsome man referred to only as her unidentified escort.*

The Tribune *story was written by a reporter named Mitchell Locin. A nice piece of writing, I thought.*

She summoned the strength to kneel at the three caskets—her entire family.

Patricia Columbo was the only one left of the Frank Columbos of Elk Grove Village, a family that was described as "ideal neighbors."

The nineteen-year-old entered the Galewood Funeral Home, 1857 North Harlem Avenue, and greeted relatives, friends, and acquaintances with a weak smile. Asked if she was ready to go into the chapel, she said quietly, "I don't want to, but I have to."

She knelt at the matching slate gray coffins that held the remains of her father, Frank, forty-three; her mother, Mary, forty; and her brother, Michael, thirteen.

The three were slain sometime last Tuesday in their home at 55 East Brantwood, but their bodies were not discovered by police until Friday afternoon. Authorities say they had been bludgeoned, stabbed as many as forty or fifty times, shot in the head, and had their throats slit. Mrs. Columbo was raped.

"Patty looks like Mike," murmured one relative watching the grim procession proceed from casket to casket.

"I don't know. I don't know," muttered many of the men.

The Rev. J. Ward Morrison, pastor of the Queen of the Rosary Catholic Church in Elk Grove Village, said he knew of no occasion that was sadder in his thirty-two years in the priesthood. The Columbos had attended his church for eleven years.

Meanwhile, police continued their search for the killers. Elk Grove Village investigators were stationed inside and outside the chapel, checking with acquaintances for any strangers that may have been present.

The latest theory is that a gang of professional home invaders may have been high on narcotics when their robbery turned into the torture and killing spree.

Home invaders? When had insanity like that begun? Burglars I knew went into homes to steal, not slaughter. And they never used drugs while they were working.

Later that evening, I caught a television news update on the story:

> . . . bodies were discovered late Friday afternoon on a routine police call regarding a missing automobile. The cause of death of the three victims, which was not immediately apparent, has now been determined as gunshot wounds to the head, although all three also had their throats cut and were badly mutilated about the body. Investigating officers told reporters that the interior of the home looked like a slaughterhouse at Chicago's South Side stockyards. Widespread speculation among law enforcement personnel is that the killings are the result of a home invasion type of crime such as the Manson cult began in 1969, and the murders of Green Beret doctor Jeffrey MacDonald's family a year later. Such crimes are becoming less and less uncommon in America, having been reported in recent years in Oklahoma, Georgia, California, Virginia, and Texas . . .

I looked at the Trib *picture again, at the pretty young face under the jungle of hair, the wide, dark eyes, the discernibly tall, slim figure . . .*

Nineteen years old, I thought. You're lucky you weren't there, kid.

1
May 1976

The little poodle's name was Gigi.

It huddled close to the body of the dead woman. Occasionally it shivered uncontrollably, although the temperature inside the house was a comfortable seventy-one. Now and again, the poodle would whine for a few minutes; sometimes it turned its head to lick the woman's still arm. It would not lick her face because there was too much blood on it.

The little dog was constricted with fear. It hadn't moved its bowels or urinated in nearly three days. The food in its feeding dish had grown hard and stale.

Daylight came and then nightfall, and then daylight again. Sometimes the little dog would go to one of the other dead bodies and stand there for a while, whining, begging. Or it would go to the front door, which was not quite closed, and whine through the narrow opening that looked onto the front porch. Invariably, however, it returned to the body of the woman and huddled against her again.

Another nightfall, another daylight.

The little dog kept whining.

On Friday afternoon, May 7, 1976, Chicago police officers Joe Giuliano and Eddie Kozlowski answered a call to investigate a suspicious automobile parked at 140 South Whipple, on the city's West Side. They parked behind a maroon Thunderbird at the curb, called in their location, and got out to investigate. Giuliano talked while Kozlowski made notes.

"Okay, it's a 1972 Thunderbird, maroon, license number EG 5322, right-front window broken out, and the ignition pulled," Giuliano said, indicating that the car's entire ignition system had been removed. This was commonly accomplished, particularly on Ford vehicles, by car thieves using a special tool called a "lockpull." It made for quick and easy starting of cars without keys. "Interior of car littered with broken glass," Giuliano continued, moving around the vehicle. "Hubcaps missing, trunk locked." He walked back to the front of the car. "It's got an Elk Grove Village tax stamp on the windshield." He rubbed away some dirt to look at the vehicle identification number on the dashboard. "The VIN is ZY87N111090."

Giuliano radioed the VIN to the police computer staff. In minutes it was back negative; the car had not been reported stolen. Running the registration, they discovered that the car belonged to one Frank P. Columbo of 55 Brantwood in the western suburb of Elk Grove Village.

Several times that afternoon, Joe Giuliano attempted to telephone Frank P. Columbo to advise him of the whereabouts of his car. There was no answer. Finally, toward the end of their shift, Giuliano gave the information he had to a police communications clerk and asked that it be sent to the

Elk Grove police department for a notification call: an Elk Grove officer to personally contact the individual and request that he get in touch with the Eleventh District police in the city.

The two tac officers closed out their shift.

At 4:45 that Friday afternoon, Officer Kenneth Kvidera of the Elk Grove Village Police Department was on routine patrol along Arlington Heights Road when his dispatcher radioed the notification request from the Chicago officers. A routine call. On this day the dispatcher didn't even tell Kvidera what the notification was for; it usually made no difference because Elk Grove was rarely involved except as messenger.

Kvidera, in uniform and driving a black-and-white patrol car, jotted down Frank P. Columbo's name and the 55 Brantwood address as he waited for the light to change at John F. Kennedy Boulevard. Then, pulling to the side of the road across the boulevard, he got out his map. Elk Grove Village, a township of about twenty thousand people, lay immediately west of Chicago's massive O'Hare International Airport. It was composed of a confusing complex of similarly named streets that twisted in every direction. Brantwood, for instance, might be Brantwood Avenue or Brantwood Lane or even Brantwood Court.

Studying his street map, Kvidera saw that he was practically on top of the west end of Brantwood Avenue; it looked to be no more than three blocks away. He eased back into traffic. At Lonsdale, the officer turned left for a block, at Lancaster right for half a block, then left on Brantwood; and—how lucky can you get—there was number 55, third house from the corner, on the right. Even though the driveway was empty, Kvidera parked on the street.

The house was typical for this upper-middle-class suburban neighborhood. Mostly in the sixty-five-thousand-dollar price range, some of the houses were split-level, some partially brick, all easily upgradable, all on lots just a tad too small; they were occupied primarily by midlife couples with adolescent or grown children. Most of the homeowners had worked long and hard to get there and had left behind inner-city neighborhoods that were deteriorating, less than ideal for families. Out here in Elk Grove Village, life was more secure.

Kvidera got out of his patrol car and walked the twenty or so feet along the driveway to the porch. As he approached the front door, he suddenly felt wary and broke stride hesitantly. Something about the place wasn't right. There was too much mail sticking out of the mailbox. At his feet on the porch lay three daily issues of the *Elk Grove Herald*. Behind the storm door, he could see that the front door to the house was ajar. From inside, he heard a dog crying pitifully. Very quietly, Kvidera tried the handle of the outside glass storm door; he found it unlocked. He knocked and waited. No answer.

Back off, his instinct told him. *Look around a little.*

Kvidera moved slowly off the porch and walked around the outside of the house, scrutinizing doors and windows. Everything *looked* all right. Still . . .

Returning to his patrol car, Kvidera called his dispatcher. "Request assistance at Fifty-five Brantwood."

"The notification call?" the dispatcher asked incredulously. "Is this a joke, Kvidera?"

"Negative," Kvidera replied quietly, holding the mike very close to his mouth. "There's something funny about this place. It doesn't look right and it doesn't feel right. Request assistance."

"Ten-four," the dispatcher confirmed soberly. There was something about Officer Kenneth Kvidera's voice . . .

In his patrol car, the young officer, then in his third year as a policeman, waited for help with increasing tension.

In less than two minutes, a second Elk Grove Village police car pulled up in front of 55 Brantwood and Officer Jerome Maculitis got out. He had been on traffic patrol only two blocks away.

"What's happening?" he asked, walking back to Kvidera, who got out of his own unit.

"I'm not sure. Front door's open, dog's whining inside, three days' newspapers outside, mailbox crammed with mail. It doesn't feel right."

"Let's take a look," Maculitis said.

On the porch, Kvidera quietly opened the storm door and motioned for Maculitis to hold it. Then he slowly pushed the inner door farther open and peered inside. Immediately beyond the door was a small foyer with two short flights of stairs, one leading up to the main level of the house, one leading down to the lower level. At the bottom of the steps going down, a little poodle barked up at them. Kvidera moved into the foyer, hand now on his gun, and motioned for Maculitis to follow him. Quietly letting the storm door close, Maculitis came in behind him. Both officers now drew their guns and began to ease up the stairs that led to the main level of the house. Not even halfway up, Maculitis heard Kvidera mutter, "Holy Christ—"

Maculitis looked past Kvidera through a wrought iron railing into a living room and saw the body of a man, lying on his back, wearing trousers and socks, his face and stomach grotesquely swollen, head and chest caked with dried blood, in a state of early putrefaction. There were large smudges of blood on the foil wallpaper at the top of the stairs. A blood-soaked chair cushion lay on the floor near the body. As the officers stood staring, they became aware for the first time of the putrid stench of death that was becoming decay.

Maculitis moved up two steps to get a better view. When he turned to go back down, he saw a second corpse.

"Jesus, there's another one—"

Lying partly in a hall off to the right was the body of a woman, also on her back, her blond hair bloodied, her robe open, nightgown around her waist, panties down around her knees.

As steadily as they could, the two officers retreated from the house. Because his car was nearest, Maculitis called the dispatcher. He reported an apparent double homicide or possible double suicide and requested an investigative team and evidence technicians.

So Kvidera had been right, the dispatcher thought, he *had* needed backup.

Shortly after five o'clock that afternoon, Raymond Rose, an eight-year veteran of the Elk Grove Village Police Department, was returning to his headquarters from the state's attorney's office in Niles, another near-western suburb of Chicago. Most of Elk Grove's felony cases were prosecuted through that office, just as most suspects who were formally charged were arraigned in one of the departments of the Niles courthouse.

Earlier that day, Rose had taken a rookie officer, Gary Keeno, over to Niles to introduce him around and walk him through the procedure for obtaining a search warrant. It was Rose's first day back on routine duty after a five-month assignment as part of an interagency undercover drug enforcement operation. A quietly direct man with black hair and a drooping black mustache, he was frequently thought of as intense, when in reality he was calmly competent and thorough. The son of a policeman, he was unconditionally dedicated to law enforcement.

As the two officers drove toward Elk Grove, a radio call came through for Ray Rose. It was Deputy Chief William Kohnke.

"Ray, get over to Fifty-five Brantwood—right now."

"Right," Rose replied. "What's up?"

"Just get over here," Kohnke repeated, and cut him off.

It took Rose seven minutes to get there. Three patrol cars were already at the scene. Two uniformed officers, Kvidera and Maculitis, were standing between their units and the driveway. Deputy Chief Kohnke was near the porch with Lt. Fred Engelbrecht, the watch commander, and another plainclothes investigator, John Landers. A reporter from the *Elk Grove Herald* was just driving up, and neighbors were beginning to gather on both sides of the house at number 55.

As Rose walked up, Kohnke said, "We've got a man and woman dead inside. You're in charge of it, Ray."

Rose nodded and looked at Landers, who bobbed his chin at Kvidera and Maculitis. "The two uniforms say it looks pretty violent. Blood everywhere. There was a little poodle in there but we got it out."

"Okay. Ready to go in?" Rose asked.

"Yeah."

The two investigators looked at Deputy Chief Kohnke and Lieutenant Engelbrecht. Both nodded assent. Together, Rose and Landers entered 55 Brantwood.

Inside the house, Ray Rose and John Landers found a scene of carnage unlike anything either had ever seen before.

On the upper, main level of the house, in the living room, they found, lying on his back, the dead body of a man they would later determine to be Frank Columbo. The trained

minds of both officers immediately began to record vivid details of the scene, like human video cameras with eyes for
lenses. The corpse was dressed in plaid slacks, a white
T-shirt, and socks, no shoes. The T-shirt was soaked across
the top and down the right side with putrefying blood. The
man's face was covered with the same. The wounds readily
apparent were two markings, almost black from decomposition, across the throat, and several deep, block-shaped lacerations that went two inches or more into the skull. All around
the body were numerous pieces of glass: shards, slivers,
chips. Some of the glass was green, some clear. A lamp
shade, ripped and bloody, lay nearby. Both investigators
glanced around the room at the same time, looking for the
same thing.

"Not here," Rose said quietly.

Landers nodded silent agreement. There was no lamp to go
with the shade. But while they were looking, they found
something else on the blood-soaked carpet: four human teeth.
Overhead on the ceiling were blood splatterings in two distinct patterns, indicating separate upward swings of the
bloody instrument used to bash in Frank Columbo's head. On
a glass coffee table, on the *under* side of the glass, were more
splatters, which had to have come up from the floor where
the body lay, indicating that Columbo had been cut or shot or
otherwise traumatized after he had fallen helplessly to the
floor.

The officers moved into a nearby hallway and found the
body of the woman that would prove to be Mary Columbo,
wife of the dead man. She was lying in front of an open bathroom door, an inch-wide wound cut all the way across her
throat, below a face covered with congealed blood. In the
center of the bloody mask was a neat round hole where she
had been shot between the eyes. Her head, like her husband's,
appeared to have been bashed in with a block-shaped blunt
instrument. A white nightgown and red housecoat were
pulled up to her waist; a pair of white panties were down just
below her knees.

Rose noted a large diamond ring on the corpse's left hand.
Not robbery, he thought. Not a good one, anyway.

The bathroom had a second door, opening into a bedroom,
and in there they located the source of a muted buzzing

sound: a clock radio next to the bed. The alarm was set for
nine o'clock, with no indication whether it was A.M. or P.M.
Rose used one finger to carefully shut it off.

As the two officers moved about the house, they noted that
blood appeared to have been smeared over several walls and
both sides of one door. On that section of the stairs leading
down to the lower level, Rose observed an empty clear plastic
sheath with a foldover top, obviously made for scissors. In
another place there was a white leather purse on the floor, its
contents strewn about. In the kitchen, the telephone was off
the hook; strange, because Officer Joe Giuliano had tried
three times to call the number that afternoon to advise Frank
Columbo that his Thunderbird had been found. Each time
Giuliano got a ring but no answer. If the receiver had been
off the hook, he should have heard a busy signal.

Next to the telephone, a personal telephone book lay open.
On the floor was a small pile of garbage. In the closet of a
downstairs room they discovered a large wall safe; it was se-
curely locked and did not appear to have been tampered with.
On that same level, some drawers were standing open, their
contents, some of it sewing accessories, strewn around. On an
arrangement of three shelves laden with bowling and other
athletic trophies was a rectangular pattern in the dust, from
which something had been removed. Upstairs, loose jewelry
was scattered about the top of a dresser. Chair cushions
were lying about on the floor; one chair had blood on it. In
one bathroom was an *Elk Grove Herald* dated Tuesday,
May 4—three days earlier.

Finally the two policemen got to the last bedroom in the
house, on the upper level—and it was there that they discovered the body of an adolescent boy, eventually to be identified as thirteen-year-old Michael Columbo. The corpse was
dressed in a white T-shirt and blue sweat pants, and was barefoot. Its head, like those of the other two victims, was covered with congealed blood. Lying next to the body was a
bowling trophy: a silver figure mounted on a marble base.
The figure was bent, its base covered with blood. Rose and
Landers exchanged silent glances again; the block-shaped
blunt instrument had been found. The body was lying on its
back, but from a matching bloodstain about eighteen inches
from the head, it was apparent that the boy had at first been

lying face-down, and had been rolled over; on one forearm was a bloody handprint, badly smeared, apparently made when he was moved. The dead boy's chest was peppered with numerous small slashes, cuts, and puncture wounds. Rose pursed his lips in a silent whistle. "How many you figure?"

Landers shook his head uncertainly. "A lot. Twenty-five, thirty maybe." The officer was less than half-right; they had not seen the boy's back yet.

The officers continued looking around the room. Near the dead boy's head was a key case with two keys exposed. On a metal closet door was a small indentation that looked like a scar from a bullet ricochet; if it was, the bullet was probably somewhere in the deep shag of the room's carpet. On a nearby desk, there was a pair of gold-colored sewing scissors—with blood on them.

Rose and Landers exchanged a final look, the kind that only two police officers could understand. Both were damned glad that this was the last room they had to check at 55 Brantwood.

Back out on the porch, Rose said to Deputy Chief Kohnke, "We've got three bodies, Bill. Man, woman, and a teenage boy."

Although Rose spoke very quietly, several neighbors gathered on the next-door driveway overheard him. A wave of shock rippled through them. One woman bit her lip tentatively and said, "My God. Who's going to tell Patty?"

The woman to whom she spoke shook her head. "Her whole family . . ."

On the porch, Ray Rose turned to brief the next two men who would enter the murder house: Christopher Markussen and Robert Salvatore. Both were highly experienced evidence technicians for the Elk Grove police department. Markussen had thirteen years' experience in the field of collecting evidence at crime scenes, Salvatore nine years.

"Watch out for blood on the carpet," Rose cautioned them now. "There are places where it's soaked through down to the pad, and it's hard to see because of the lighting. Also, there are four teeth you need to watch for, two near the top of the stairs and two others closer to the man's body. And be careful of broken glass all over the living room and in the hall—"

Even as he spoke, Ray Rose knew it wasn't really necessary to give instructions to these men, professionals of the highest caliber. But two things were making him ultracareful tonight.

The first was the simple statement by Deputy Chief Bill Kohnke as Rose had walked up to 55 Brantwood a little while earlier: "You're in charge of it, Ray."

The other was the fact that the butchered young boy lying inside the house was about the same age, with the same kind of adolescent features, as his own son.

Ray Rose was being ultracareful tonight because this was one case he badly wanted to solve.

Markussen and Salvatore entered the house and began what would become five excruciatingly tense hours of processing the murder scene.

The critical pieces of evidence were collected first. Markussen recovered the metal-and-marble bowling trophy near Michael Columbo's body. Although bent, it remained in one piece, intact except for a small chip broken off an edge of the base. There was blood on the base and also, to a lesser extent, on the metal bowling figure.

"Somebody used this baby for a club," Markussen remarked to his partner.

Salvatore, also in the dead boy's bedroom, carefully collected from his desk the pair of gold-plated scissors. In addition to being stained with dried blood, they also appeared to be sprung. The points of the two cutting blades, which should have aligned, overextended; that created, instead of a common single point, two separate points approximately one-quarter inch apart. This defect caused the finger holes at the handle end to overlap.

"I think these were used to hack that kid up," Salvatore said. Markussen, looking closely at the pair of scissors, nodded.

The technicians noted also that Michael had two very clear gunshot wounds in his head: one just left of the left eye, the other at the right side of the temple. In the blood around the former could be seen slight traces of black powder. "I think we've got a bullet around here somewhere," Markussen said. "It looks to me like the slug went in one side of his head and out the other."

They started looking for it. On the metal sliding door of the closet, they found the same ricochet scar that Rose and Landers had seen a few minutes earlier. "Yeah," Salvatore said, "the kid was standing up when he was shot. The bullet came out the right side of his head, hit the door, and ricocheted." They got down on their hands and knees and started working their fingers into the shag of the carpet like two bakers kneading dough. After several minutes, Markussen straightened up. "Got it."

Moving cautiously about the slaying scene, the officers began painstakingly to obtain both patent (visible) and latent (invisible) fingerprints. One came from a handrail on the stairs; one from a doorjamb; a partial palm print was secured in the utility room, another from the handset of the telephone. Following the print search, they collected blood samples: on numerous pieces of carpet; a section of chair cushion; three pieces of wallpaper; a fourteen-inch square of kitchen linoleum; and anything else they could find that had blood on it. Some of the items they collected had no blood on them, but were possibly significant to the crime in other ways: quantities of prescription drugs, for instance, from the medicine cabinet, which included four tablets of Maleen, forty-six tablets of Permathene, and an undetermined quantity of Valium; a pair of black woolen-and-leather gloves, which could have been left by the killer; and a black leather key case containing a dozen keys. Both evidence techs wondered why the latter had been lying near the dead teenage boy's head.

Markussen went about patiently collecting numerous pieces of broken glass around the bodies of both Frank and Mary Columbo, while Salvatore began to double-check and list what was now approaching nearly one hundred separate items of evidence.

It was almost ten o'clock at night, into the fifth hour of their work. They both felt as if they had been in the house for a week.

Outside, John Landers reported back to Ray Rose on the front porch.

"There's another Columbo family car missing besides the Thunderbird they found down in the city," he reported. "A seventy-two Olds Ninety-eight, black vinyl over green, four-door."

"Put out a bulletin on it," Rose said.

Chris Markussen and Bob Salvatore came out of the house.

"Finished?" Rose asked.

"Finished," Markussen confirmed.

"This is the worst one I ever saw," Salvatore said.

On the lawn near the front porch, Deputy Chief Bill Kohnke was being interviewed by the news media. "It's a very brutal, weird, senseless murder," he would later be quoted as saying. "It doesn't have any rhyme or reason."

"Do you know how many killers were involved?" asked one reporter.

"Was it a gang of some kind?" asked another simultaneously.

"There must have been at least two intruders," Kohnke replied to both. "There was tremendous resistance; there are many wounds in the hands and arms, indicating that the victims tried to defend themselves."

"Was the woman raped?"

"She appears to have been."

Two hearses arrived from a local funeral home and attendants carrying body bags approached the house. Chris Markussen and Bob Salvatore looked at each other. One of them had to go back into the house, back into that carnage, and supervise the removal of the bodies.

"I'll do it," Salvatore said finally.

On the upper level of the house, one of the body bags—rubberized, with a full-length zipper, waterproof and odorproof—was laid out next to Michael Columbo. As the attendants were about to reach for the dead boy, Salvatore suddenly said, "Wait a minute—!"

He knelt and looked closely at the body. The evidence technician's trained eyes had seen something, with the body now on its back. In one of the bloodstains encrusting the shirt material, at approximately mid-torso, was a single hair. Michael's own hair? Probably. But also, *possibly*, a hair from the killer's head.

Very carefully, Salvatore rolled the T-shirt up to the dead

boy's armpits, preserving the hair within the rolled portion of the shirt.

As the bag with Michael's body was being carried out to the hearse, Salvatore said to Ray Rose, "I'll have to go with the kid. There's a hair on his body and I don't want to break the chain."

Rose nodded his permission. Salvatore was referring to the legal chain of evidence that would be required if he ever had to testify in court about finding the hair. He had to physically remain with that strand of hair until it was removed from the body and marked as evidence. If he let that body bag out of his sight, even for a moment, the evidence chain would be broken and Robert Salvatore wouldn't be able to swear under oath that a hair present in court as evidence was the *same* hair he had first observed. The rule regarding the chain of evidence was very specific, the law very strict.

While Salvatore went with Michael's corpse, Chris Markussen oversaw the removal of the bodies of Frank and Mary Columbo. Mary was put into the hearse with her dead son; Frank's body was put into the second hearse.

"You ride with the man's body," Ray Rose said to Landers. "See you over at the hospital."

The two hearses carrying the three murdered members of the Columbo family were driven away from 55 Brantwood shortly before 11:00 P.M. Within ten minutes they were turning into the emergency room driveway of Alexian Brothers Medical Center, a five-story red-brick hospital facility that served Chicago's western suburbs.

One by one, the rubber body bags were unzipped for the emergency room doctor on duty, and one by one he examined the three murder victims for any sign of life. While this was going on, Father Ward Morrison, a heavyset, gray-haired Roman Catholic priest, approached Ray Rose.

"Good evening, Ray," he said.

"Hello, Father," said Rose. "Were the Columbos in your parish at Queen of the Rosary?"

"Yes," Father Morrison said. His face was starkly sad. "What's to be done with them now, Ray?" he asked.

"They have to go to the county morgue, Father," said Rose, almost apologetically. "To be autopsied."

"I see." Father Morrison looked at the two hearses, their doors standing open. "Would you have any objection to my performing the last rites on them here? I'd like to do it before the bodies are further desecrated by the autopsies."

"Of course, Father," said Rose. "Go right ahead, please."

As the emergency room doctor finished declaring each victim dead, the priest came along behind him and performed the ritual of extreme unction: from a small bottle of holy water, he anointed each one of the bodies and said a brief prayer for the salvation of that person's soul. When both the doctor and the priest were finished, and Frank, Mary, and Michael Columbo were officially dead and spiritually saved, the doors of the two hearses were again closed.

Now the officers involved began their last ride with the victims. Into the city they went, into Chicago, some fifteen miles to the Fishbein Institute of Forensic Medicine—more commonly known simply as the Cook County morgue.

When the hearses arrived, Frank Columbo was about twelve city blocks away from his maroon 1972 Thunderbird, still parked in the 100 block of South Whipple Street. Since it was now known that the car belonged to a homicide victim, four Chicago policemen, positioned at various places on the block, had it under close surveillance, in case someone returned to see if it had been found yet.

Ironically, Frank Columbo's killer didn't even know the car was there.

2
May 1976

A tearful, trembling Patty Columbo sat in an interview room at Elk Grove police headquarters and tried to help investigating officers with as much information as they asked for.

"Where was your father employed, Miss Columbo?"

"At the—the Western Auto supply terminal down in Chicago. It's at 525 West Forty-seventh Street." She tried to smile. "When I was a little girl, he used to take me to work with him sometimes and the ladies in the office would pretend to let me help them."

The officer cleared his throat. "Did your mother work?"

Patty shook her head. "No, she never worked. Dad wouldn't let her."

"How old was Michael?"

"Thir—thirteen. He was—thirteen last month."

"Can you tell me about any valuables that were kept in the house?"

She shook her head again. "I don't know. I haven't lived at home for over a year. I know my mother had a few diamond rings and some diamond earrings. For pierced ears. And she had a gray fox stole."

"Did your father keep large sums of money in the house?"

"I don't think so. He never talked about it if he did. Any money would have been in his safe, I guess. It's in a downstairs closet, right at the end of the hall."

"Yes, we saw it. Do you have the combination?"

"No."

"We'll have to force it open then. Were there any guns in the house?"

Patty shrugged. "Just Michael's BB gun is all I know of."

"When did you last talk to your parents?"

"It was either Monday or Tuesday night, I'm not sure. Dad called me to talk about my wedding plans. We'd been on the outs for a while; he didn't approve of my boyfriend because he'd been married before. My dad is"—her voice broke, her words faltering—"I mean, my dad *was*, real old-fashioned, you know, and I'm his only daughter. But he finally came around and accepted my boyfriend, and he and my mom were actually looking forward to the wedding." Before the investigator could frame another question, Patty asked, "Can I tell you about the crank calls I've been receiving?"

"What crank calls?" This was interesting.

"It's been going on for two or three weeks now. I'll answer my phone and some guy will say, 'Is this Pat?' Then he starts breathing real heavy, almost like he's panting. I didn't think much about them, but now that this—this thing has happened—"

"They may or may not have anything to do with what happened to your family, Miss Columbo, but we can place a tap on your phone line to find out where the calls are coming from."

"Yes, I'd like you to do that, please. And can you tell me when you're going to force my dad's safe open?"

"Why? Is there something in it that particularly interests you, Miss Columbo?"

"I think there's a letter indicating what kind of funeral arrangements they wanted. My Uncle Mario, my father's brother, is trying to take charge of everything, but I think the letter says for me to do it."

The officer cleared his throat again. "If we find a letter like that, Miss Columbo, we'll see that you get it right away."

After the police interrogation, Patty was interviewed by reporters from the Chicago and suburban newspapers. Asked if she had any personal suspicions about her family's murder, she shook her head. "I don't know. The only thing I can think of is that whoever did it must have been high on drugs or something. Or else they're very sick people."

"Miss Columbo, the police have a personal phone book taken from your family's home that contains several names that may be Chicago crime syndicate figures. Do you have any knowledge of your father having underworld connections?"

"No, I don't," Patty asserted firmly, "and that is the most terrible thing anyone could say about my dad. He was so honest he wouldn't even tell a lie."

"Do you fear for your own life, Miss Columbo?"

"Yes, I do. I've had the locks changed on my doors. I also keep a large German shepherd in my apartment now."

It sounded as if she had just gotten the dog, but in fact she had owned it for six months.

As they questioned the slim, shapely nineteen-year-old with her pert baby face, flawless complexion, and mountain of Farrah Fawcett hair, even the crime reporters, jaded as they were toward violence and carnage, realized that this was one very fortunate young lady. One of the headlines that morning had read:

MURDER VICTIMS TORTURED BY KILLERS

How much more horrible that headline would have been if this pretty young woman had been a fourth victim.

* * *

Licensed to practice medicine in the state of Illinois for more than twenty years, Dr. Robert Stein possessed impressive credentials: bachelor's in biology, master's in pathology, doctor of medicine. On this day he was employed as director of forensic pathology by the Cook County coroner's office. He was on his way to perform his hundredth forensic autopsy of 1976. Over the years, he had completed more than one thousand such postmortem operations.

At the morgue, on lower Harrison Street, Dr. Stein parked in his reserved space and, walking briskly, without even stopping in his office, went directly to the locker room downstairs and changed into surgical scrubs. In the autopsy theater, he found his assistants waiting, along with Investigator Robert Salvatore of the Elk Grove Village Police Department, the official police witness to the autopsy proceedings. This was Salvatore's second visit to the morgue on the Columbo murders. Having accompanied Michael's body there early Saturday morning, he had, before the three victims were stripped to be photographed, personally removed Michael's T-shirt, careful to keep in place that part of the shirt he had rolled up to preserve the single hair he had noticed at the crime scene. The rolled-up portion intact, Salvatore had sealed it in a brown paper evidence bag and marked it for later identification.

"Good morning, gentlemen," Dr. Stein said upon entering the operating room. "Officer"—he addressed Salvatore—"anything special we need?"

"Yes, sir. Contents of the stomach, if possible, Doctor," said Salvatore. "We need to know the food items of their last meal. We're trying to determine when they were killed."

"All right." Dr. Stein turned to his assistants. "Let's proceed. Microphone on, please."

Stein stepped to the nearest operating table, where an assistant removed the cover sheet from a male corpse. The doctor looked at the tag attached to one big toe of the body.

"This is case number one hundred. Body has been identified as Frank Peter Columbo, a Caucasian male measuring seventy-one inches in height and weighing one hundred eighty-two pounds. The hair is dark brown, balding slightly; eyes are also brown. There is marked evidence of decomposition, early putrefaction, and skin slippage. Indication of considerable gas production in the body. Marked swelling of the penis and scrotum. External examination further reveals obvious marks of violence characterized by lacerations, apparent bullet wounds, and a number of incised wounds," the latter being the medical term for cuts made by a sharp instrument. These wounds, the doctor reported, were around and across the throat area. The lacerations were all on the top, side, and front of the head, and had been caused by striking with a blunt instrument of some kind. In addition, Stein found on the left side of the neck a number of round, brown areas resembling burns—such as might have been made by a lighted cigarette.

Dr. Stein proceeded to open the head. "There are four bullet entry wounds and no bullet exit wounds," he said. "Bullet number one entered the head on the right side of the face and is being retrieved from the sphenoid," the middle bone of the skull. "Bullet number two entered the mouth and is being retrieved from inside the sinus. A number of teeth are missing from the upper and lower gums. Bullet number three entered the left side of the face and is being retrieved from immediately behind the left cheekbone, which is fractured. This bullet is in a deformed condition. Bullet number four entered in back of the left ear and is being retrieved from the temporal bone. This bullet did not enter the skull." An examination of the brain revealed no tumor or other injury except those caused by the bullets.

Opening the torso, Dr. Stein examined the lungs and heart; then the abdominal organs: liver, gallbladder, pancreas. From the gastrointestinal tract, he removed 250 cubic centimeters, approximately one-half pint, of meat particles, green vegetable particles, and fragments of potato, all intermixed with body liquid.

Meat, a green vegetable, a potato: that had been Frank Columbo's last meal.

Perfect, Robert Salvatore thought at these findings. In the thirty-two hours since the bodies reached the morgue, Ray Rose and his investigative team had, through a thirteen-year-old friend of Michael Columbo's named Glenn Miller, who lived next door to the murdered family at 53 Brantwood, determined that the Columbo family had eaten dinner on Tuesday night, May 4, at the Around the Clock Restaurant in Arlington Heights. The Miller boy had seen the family driving back home from the restaurant. And a waitress at the restaurant, Judy DiMartino, remembered serving them bell peppers stuffed with hamburger, with Frank and Michael also eating baked potatoes. If Mary and Michael had similar contents in their stomachs, then Tuesday night's dinner would have been their last meal also.

At this point, Dr. Stein supervised the taking of hair and blood samples, as well as fingernail scrapings, and oral and rectal swab specimens, as requested by the Elk Grove Village Police Department.

"The cause of death of Frank Peter Columbo, case number one hundred," Dr. Stein concluded when he completed the autopsy, "was one or more bullet wounds to the head."

The community of Elk Grove Village, particularly the neighborhood that was in close proximity to the murder house at 55 Brantwood, was in a state of alarm bordering on terror. The violence that most of the first-generation suburbanites thought they had left back in the inner city had suddenly, shockingly, come out of nowhere to fall on their quiet little township like the breath of evil. From a relaxed, active little village, Elk Grove became for a while a subdued place. Where there was activity, it was conducted at a more hurried pace, with cautious glances. Children were more carefully watched, door locks checked and double-checked.

At Lively Junior High School, special assemblies were held for Michael Columbo's seventh-grade classmates. Elk Grove's mental health center provided counselors to try to help the youngsters overcome a feeling of helpless grief that the murders had generated. There was also a keen sense of fear that the same thing could happen to them and their families. Many of the students had slept badly since learning of the horrible crime.

News reporters networked the little suburb. No opinion, theory, or rumor escaped unquoted. The "home-invasion" hypothesis, expounded by Elk Grove's deputy police chief, William Kohnke, remained the favorite. Either three or four invaders had entered the home by expanding the rear doorjamb or picking the side door lock. Kohnke's conclusion was that Frank Columbo, in the process of getting ready for bed, had heard noises downstairs and had gone down to investigate. There, he was overpowered, stabbed, bludgeoned, and shot to death. His wife was then raped and murdered. The teenage son was killed in his bedroom so that there would be no witnesses.

One story stated that the family's Lincoln Continental had provided police with a number of fingerprints believed to have been left by the killers. Another credited the discovery of the bodies to Frank Columbo's co-workers, who telephoned police because of his unexplained absence from work. Deputy Chief Kohnke believed that the crime had begun as a robbery, then escalated into a torture-killing spree when the robbers got high on narcotics.

Every one of these theories would be proven wrong. Even the make and model of the car was wrong.

While the home-invasion rumor was saturating Elk Grove, another possibility was quietly coming to life. County law enforcement investigators, already interested in several names in the family's personal telephone directory—names like DeStefano, DeBartoli, and others, which had in the past been associated with organized crime in Chicago—now began to scrutinize Frank Columbo's financial interest as a "silent partner" in two Chicago businesses that did a considerable amount of contract work for Columbo's employer, Western Auto.

When Columbo's interest in the two firms, which weren't immediately identified, came to light, Deputy Chief Kohnke allowed that "there may be a connection" between those business dealings and the murders. He indicated that records in Columbo's safe, which the police had now opened, showed that as much as seventy thousand dollars at a time was kept there. Copies of income tax records also showed that Columbo failed to report the money he received from the two firms. Kohnke, in a rare display of reticence, declined to identify the two companies, but said the state's attorney's office was preparing to subpoena their financial records as well as the officers of the firm.

The deputy chief's new theory, based on this latest information, was that three or four intruders had gained entry to the house by activating an automatic garage door, then forcing the lock on a door connecting the garage to a lower-level family room. The torture of Frank Columbo was now believed to be an attempt to force him to open his safe.

Kohnke said his department had now drawn up a list of suspects in the case. There were nineteen names on the list. None was made public.

In the autopsy theater of the morgue, Dr. Robert Stein turned to the second operating table.

"Case number one hundred and one," he said, "identified as Mary Columbo, is a Caucasian female measuring sixty-six inches in height and weighing one hundred and thirty-seven pounds. The hair of the body is artificially blond with dark brown roots; the eyes are green."

Again, he included a report on stages of decomposition.

"Further external examination," he continued, "indicates marks of violence characterized by a laceration of the head, compatible with being struck by a blunt instrument, and an entrance bullet wound at the bridge of the nose between the eyes. There are also numerous incised wounds of the neck, compatible with being cut by a sharp instrument. These incised wounds are superficial, having severed only the blood vessels." Before opening the head to probe for the bullet, Dr. Stein looked deeply into each eye with a powerful ophthalmoscope. "Extremely severe ecchymosis in both the right and left eyes," he reported. The single bullet had ruptured enough blood vessels in Mary Columbo's head to flood her eyes with blood.

And Mary's eyes were wide open, their pupils grossly dilated. Mary Columbo had known what was about to happen to her; she had seen death coming and was staring at it in horror.

When the doctor reached Mary's lower torso, he carefully examined the perineal area and found a grayish white liquid matter that had since dried. He was aware of news stories that the woman had been raped; nevertheless he reported, "This appears to be a natural excretion," concluding that it was probably the result of vaginitis or some other minor vaginal condition. He found no visible indication of rape or other sexual offense. Aside from her urinary bladder being devoid of urine, the remainder of her examination was unremarkable.

In Mary Columbo's gastrointestinal tract was found the same kind of meat and green vegetable particles that had been found in her husband's body. There were no fragments of potatoes. It now appeared certain that waitress Judy DiMartino had indeed served the family their last meal on Tuesday night.

A surgically repaired colon, which Mary Columbo had, was not mentioned in the autopsy report. Preexisting conditions in a murder victim are not relevant. That Mary Columbo had survived colon cancer and then been murdered could weigh heavily against her accused murderer; likewise, if she had a brain tumor and would have died in six months *anyway*, a juror might use that fact to mitigate an accused's guilt. Such conditions therefore are not admissible evidence.

"The cause of death," Dr. Stein once again concluded, "was a single bullet wound to the head."

Blood and hair samples, fingernail scrapings, and oral, rectal, and vaginal swab specimens, all requested by the Elk Grove Village Police Department, were taken.

Sunday morning was almost over. Two down, one to go.

The two mystery firms in which Frank Columbo was alleged to be a silent partner were identified as a local trucking firm that did delivery work on a contract basis for Columbo's employer, Western Auto, and a day-labor firm that furnished dockworkers to Western Auto to load those trucks. As a grand jury prepared to look into Columbo's conflict-of-interest position, the executive management of Western Auto voted to offer a five-thousand-dollar reward for information leading to the arrest and conviction of the family's killers.

Patty Columbo telephoned the Elk Grove police the day after the bodies were found. She spoke with Sgt. Ron Iden. "I just talked to my aunt," Patty said, "my mom's sister. She told me something, I don't know if you'd be interested in it or not—"

"What was it, Miss Columbo?" Iden asked.

"Well, you know my dad and my brother were real CB nuts. They had citizens band radios all over the house, and they belonged to a CB club there in Elk Grove. Well, my aunt said she thought maybe some CBers had been involved in what happened, because Dad recently had something to do with the disciplining of a member who was giving the club problems. I didn't know anything about it myself; my aunt thought you ought to know."

"We definitely should, Miss Columbo," Iden assured her. "We want to know anything like that; anything at all. Sometimes things that seem very insignificant become major leads."

"Okay. I wasn't sure if I should bother you—"

"Please call us anytime," Iden urged, "with any information you consider important. We appreciate the help."

It was an interesting possibility. Ray Rose and his team of investigators knew that an expensive CB radio, missing from the murder house, had been sold by a black man at the Maxwell Street open-air market in Chicago two days after the bodies were found. The buyer had come forward with the radio after discovering the name *Columbo* etched on the metal underside.

This development added still another dimension to the case: black robbery gangs. There were two notorious outlaw crews of young black men operating in the Chicago area at that time: the Myrick-Williams gang and the Gilmore gang. The former was led by John Myrick and Anthony Williams, both wanted for murder at the time; their gang had a known modus operandi of stabbing with scissors. The other gang, the Gilmores, comprised five young men, all born between 1949 and 1956, whose specialty was the invasion and robbery of homes in well-to-do white neighborhoods. Another, albeit weaker, gang suspect was the Royals; it was on their "turf" that Frank Columbo's abandoned Thunderbird was found.

The day after Patty Columbo telephoned Sergeant Iden about the CB club, she called him again. "Hi. I just talked to my aunt again and she told me something else I thought you ought to know. She said that a cousin of hers named Mickey Dunkle called and talked to my mom last Wednesday morning."

"Oh?" Iden knew that the current consensus of evidence was that the family had been murdered on Tuesday night. Wednesday morning's newspaper was still on the front porch,

Wednesday afternoon's mail still in the mailbox. "Is he sure about the day?" Iden asked.

"She says he is. He picks up and delivers school buses for a living, and he was down at the Chicago Greyhound station Wednesday morning on his way to pick up a bus somewhere. He called my mom about six o'clock in the morning."

Patty went on to say that her mother, according to Dunkle, had sounded "relaxed and normal." She then informed Iden that her aunt was severely distressed over the rape and murder of her sister, and suggested that the police not call or visit her unless it was absolutely necessary.

"If you have any questions for her," Patty offered, "you can ask me and I'll ask her for you."

"We appreciate the help," Sergeant Iden said.

So much erroneous and confusing information had been given to the press in the wake of the discovery of the bodies that Elk Grove Chief of Police Harry Jenkins finally issued everyone, including Deputy Chief Bill Kohnke, a gag order. Kohnke, who had been officially appointed to his position almost concurrent with the murders, had been quoted as being responsible for extensive misinformation, and the press was beginning to feel put upon. Chief Jenkins clamped a tight lid on the release of further information related to the case, and issued a mea culpa statement saying, "There has been too much information which has been erroneous, purely speculative, and otherwise ill advised—although well intentioned—reported to the media." It went on to say what Dr. Robert Stein had already determined: there was no evidence to support any supposition that Mary Columbo had been sexually assaulted.

Through all this confusion and commotion, Investigator Ray Rose, in charge of the case, moved his team doggedly forward in a probe that had already dismissed drugged-out home invaders, crime syndicate hit men, and black youth robbery gangs, and was moving steadily toward the real killers of the Columbo family. His inquiry was now far afield of any theory previously offered, and his team of officers, who had put in more than three hundred hours of overtime, most of it without pay, were now focusing on two men whom no one—not even Deputy Chief Kohnke with his boundless imagination—had even remotely connected with the crime.

* * *

At the morgue, Dr. Robert Stein moved to an operating table where the corpse of a young boy lay uncovered.

"This is case number one hundred two, identified as Michael Columbo, a Caucasian adolescent male measuring sixty-five inches in height, and weighing ninety-four pounds. His hair is black, his eyes are brown. The body appears to be in a state of early putrefaction with notable skin slippage and with general overall decomposition. External examination reveals multiple contusions and lacerations of the scalp, plus what appears to be the entrance and exit wounds of a single bullet. The entry wound is at the outer aspect of the left eye, and the exit wound is on the right side of the temple. There is definite stippling around the entry wound." Stippling was unburned gunpowder from the bullet, an indication that it was fired very close to Michael's face, anywhere from three to ten inches away.

Dr. Stein proceeded to the boy's torso. "I find numerous punctures on the trunk of the body. On the right side of the chest, I count"—he paused, tallying silently to himself—"forty-eight incised wounds. In the back, on the posterior chest wall, I find an additional"—again he paused to count—"thirty-six wounds. Of the thirty-six in back, eight are deep, penetrating wounds, while the remaining twenty-eight are incised wounds." The victim, then, had been stabbed deeply eight times, and cut or sliced seventy-six times. "There are no defense wounds," Dr. Stein added. Defense wounds, usually found on the hands, wrists, and forearms of a victim, are sustained when a person attempts to defend against attack. Death came so suddenly to Mary and Michael that they had no opportunity to defend themselves; Frank Columbo died very hard, but with two bullets in his head at the outset, most of his struggle was probably instinctual rather than reactive.

In the stomach of Michael was found a quantity of fine meat particles, similar to those found in the stomachs of his parents. The only unusual finding in Michael's autopsy, aside from his criminal wounds, was the weight of his brain. One school of medical opinion holds that the larger a person's brain, the more nerve interconnection possible; thus, the greater *capacity* for intelligence. Although there is no automatic correlation, many persons of conspicuous ability have had brains of larger than normal size. The average adult male's brain weighs 1,409 grams, or slightly less than 50 ounces, and achieves its prime weight by the twentieth year. Michael's brain, six years before its full development, already weighed 1,540 grams. He may nevertheless have been nothing more than an average teenage boy. But the world will never know.

The cause of Michael's death, as with his father Frank, and his mother Mary, was a bullet wound to the head. A blood sample was taken, fingernail scrapings collected, and oral and anal swab specimens secured, as requested by the Elk Grove police.

No hair sample was taken from Michael.

"That concludes the autopsies of cases number one hundred, one hundred one, and one hundred two," Dr. Stein said. "Microphone off, please."

After Dr. Stein, his autopsy assistants, and Investigator Robert Salvatore left, two attendants came in to put the cadavers back into refrigeration. One of the attendants shook his head woefully.

"Brother, I would hate to be the mortician who has to work on these three."

"I don't think they're going to have to be worked on," said his partner. "There was a call out in the office a little while ago from a crematorium. They're going to be cremated."

The first attendant looked at the tag on Frank Columbo's toe. "But the guy that identified the bodies—Mario Columbo, it says his name is, a brother—put down that they was Catholic. I didn't think Catholics got cremated."

The other one shrugged. "I didn't think so either. But these are."

C.H.
August 1977

In August 1977 I was back in Chicago, researching material for a book about several generations of prison wardens, the "keepers." A sense of déjà vu threaded through the research, because as a kid I frequently hid out from truant officers at that same library. I had learned early on that truant officers always staked out poolrooms, movie houses, penny arcades, and the like for scholastic delinquents, but never the public library. No street kid in his right mind was going to hang out in a place with all those books. Me, though, I never claimed to be in my right mind. I never got caught by a truant officer, either.

Dug in at the same little hotel over on Rush Street, I had just ordered the Tuesday-night special in the coffee shop and opened my newspaper when I saw a familiar name: Patricia Columbo. It was under a photo of a pretty, pensive, dark-haired, full-figured woman in a two-piece culotte outfit, stalking down a corridor handcuffed to someone. The caption read: "A sullen Patricia Columbo walks from the Cook County Criminal Courts Building Monday, after a judge sentenced her and her pharmacist lover, Frank DeLuca, thirty-nine, to two hundred to three hundred years in prison for the May 4, 1976, slayings of her Elk Grove family."

I stared in total disbelief at the woman in the photo. Convicted of three murders? A lover twenty years older?

Was this the same person I had read about sixteen months earlier? Was this the grief-stricken kid who had forced herself to go from casket to casket at her family's wake? I remembered thinking then: You're lucky you weren't there, kid.

Now I thought incredulously, it looked like she hadn't been so lucky, after all. And apparently she had *been there.*

Twelve jurors thought so, anyway.

Over dinner I read the accompanying story.

Patricia Columbo and her pharmacist lover, Frank DeLuca, had each been sentenced to serve two hundred to three hundred years for the murders themselves; Patricia received an additional twenty to fifty years, and DeLuca ten to fifty years, for solicitation to commit murder.

At the sentencing, Patricia had stood with her eyes down-cast. "There is one thing," she said, when asked, "the court cannot take away from me, and that is that my father and my mother and my baby brother know that wasn't us in the house that night or that morning, or whenever it was, and that's all that matters."

DeLuca made a shorter statement: "Patrish and I are inno-

cent. I will stand on my testimony . . . because that was the truth."

The sentencing had been held in a sweltering, eerie atmosphere, because an early-morning thunderstorm had caused a power failure in the criminal courts building, knocking out the lights and the air-conditioning. Murky light came in from the courtroom's single wall of windows, but not much because they faced the overcast sky to the west.

Patricia's lawyer contended that he had found seventy-one points of error in the trial, and DeLuca's attorney cited forty-eight others affecting his client. The trial had been marked by explicit sexual references, including one by a police officer to a photograph of a naked Patricia with her German shepherd. Testimony also indicated that the convicted couple had tried to persuade others to commit the murders, and that Patricia engaged in sex acts with persons representing themselves as hit men.

Before I put the paper aside that evening to go out and walk off my dinner on the old streets, I noticed in a recap of the trial that Frank DeLuca had testified, as part of his alibi, that he and Patricia had taken a drive into Chicago to visit the West Side neighborhood around Damen and Chicago avenues, where Patricia had been born. He also stated that at one time he himself had lived on the West Side at 608 South Albany Avenue. The prosecution had elicited the testimony in an attempt to connect him with one of the murdered family's cars, the Thunderbird abandoned at 140 South Whipple Street.

The addresses seized my memory like eagle talons. I knew those areas like I knew the lines that were starting to show in my face. Between where Patricia Columbo had been born and where Frank DeLuca had lived as a boy, there were thirteen blocks from east to west, and eleven blocks from north to south. When I was growing up, I lived in five different buildings in that thirteen-by-eleven-block area, and at various times attended five public schools, one of which was Brown Elementary, six blocks from where Patricia Columbo was born; another was Calhoun Elementary, seven blocks from where the DeLuca family lived when Frank was a boy.

There was, of course, no way I could have known Patricia; by the time she was born, I was already back from the Ko-

rean War. But her lover DeLuca and I were only three years
apart in age. Maybe our paths had crossed.

The possibility began to intrigue me.

When I went walking that hot August night, I started west on
Chicago Avenue. When I got to Ashland Avenue, I knew I
wasn't far away. The paper had said Patricia Columbo was
born at 1803 West Ohio Street. Four more blocks. I walked
on to Wood Street, halfway, picked up a newspaper from a
corner stand, and went into a neighborhood tavern. The sign
on the door said MEMBERS ONLY, but that didn't bother me; I
was white, and that's what the sign meant.

The bartender looked like Rocky Marciano, reincarnated
from the plane crash that had killed him eight years earlier.
"What'll you have?"

"Pabst Blue Ribbon. Tap." I put a twenty on the bar.

As I sipped my beer, I pretended to glance through the paper, the one I had already read. There were eight other people in the tavern, all of them sitting at the bar, three of them
women, Slavic looking, no makeup, the kind that could do
heavy lifting next to any man in the place. One of the men
had a newspaper on the bar as I did, and occasionally
pointed to something in it as he talked.

I finished my first glass of beer and ordered another, and
while the bartender was drawing it I folded my newspaper
and laid it on the bar with the picture of Patricia Columbo
faceup. When the bartender brought my second beer, I
pointed to the picture.

"Paper says this Columbo girl came from around here. I
didn't know that."

He nodded. "Yeah. The fam'ly lived a couple blocks from
here. They moved away eight, nine years ago. I knew the father, the one she killed."

"No shit?" I acted impressed.

"Oh, yeah. Knew him, his brother Mario, guys they hung
out with, Phil Capone, Joe Battaglia, Gus Latini. Yeah, they
lived in the neighborhood for ten, twelve years."

"Know her?" I asked, tapping Patricia's picture.

"Naw, not really. Seen her once in a while. Pretty little
girl, always dressed just so: ribbons, lace, that kind of shit.
Seen her down at Wrigley Field with her old man from time

*to time. He was a real Cubs fan, that guy; used to get really
pissed at the umpires sometimes. I remember one time . . ."*

*The bartender talked about the Columbo family off and on,
between serving customers, for an hour, and at one point was
joined by one of the Slavic women, who came walking up to
where I sat, beer mug in hand.*

*"Hell, I remember Patty like it was yesterday," she said.
"Her and my little girl used to play together." She laughed a
throaty laugh. "They had to play together; they was the only
two little girls on the block!"*

*I bought her a couple and she kept talking, and the bar-
tender kept coming back with something new, and between
the two of them I got a word picture of a respectable,
working-class, Italian-American family with a baseball-loving
father, a mother who stayed at home to take care of the house
and kids, an almost-textbook set of children: one girl, one
boy, six years between them in age; a family that eventually
followed the inner-city American dream to a house in the suburbs.*

*"And then this," said the Slavic woman, whose name was
Vera, as she shook her head at the newspaper photo of
Patricia.*

And then this.

*A little while later, I left the tavern and walked those last
two blocks to look at the building at 1803 West Ohio Street
where Patricia Columbo had been born. It was a two-flat, as
common as tap water in that part of the lower West Side. It
stood on the corner, and across the street down the block was
Talcott Elementary, where she had gone to school, and on the
corner was a candy store where she had probably gone to
spend the quarters that her daddy gave her when she was a
good girl. She had played up and down this block like any
other city kid: hopscotch in chalked squares on the sidewalk;
jacks on the front steps; Mother, May I? I had played those
games myself until I moved on to Ringolevio, Buck-Buck, and
the bloody Knuckles.*

*For a while I stared at that two-flat building, my mind
shooting out thoughts like an automatic weapon. She was
conceived in that building, with her father Frank and her*

mother Mary coupled in a passionate naked embrace. In that building she was an infant, a toddler, a preschooler, a kinder-gartner, a little girl "always dressed just so: ribbons, lace . . ."

And then this. *Father, mother, brother—slaughtered.*

Was she the proverbial bad seed? Or was she driven to it, as many killers are, by an overpowering desperation?

Maybe no one would ever know. Murder was like that.

It was getting late. I walked back over to Chicago Avenue and sat on a doorstep to wait for the number 66 bus to take me back down to Rush Street. I should have been thinking about the book I was working on, but I couldn't get Patricia Columbo off my mind.

How, I wondered, did this pretty little girl in ribbons and lace grow up to butcher her family?

And how had they found out she did it?

3
May 1976

In the seven days immediately following the discovery of the bodies, Chief Investigator Ray Rose and the men assisting him in the probe of the crime had found themselves searching for clues and evidence in scores of directions. The second Columbo car, an Oldsmobile, had been located in a nearby suburb, and both it and the Thunderbird found down in the city were being thoroughly processed. While this was going on, Rose and his men worked day and night following even the remotest leads developed.

Rose himself, with Investigator Edward Kuehnel, began backtracking the last few days of Frank Columbo's life. At Western Auto, where Columbo was in charge of a huge con-solidation warehouse operation, they talked to his assistant, Jack McCarthy, who related that Columbo had not come to work on Monday, May 3, because he had taken his son, Mi-chael, to the dentist. The following day, he returned to work, driving the Thunderbird, as usual; McCarthy recalled only two occasions when Frank Columbo had driven the family

Oldsmobile to work. Columbo had appeared to be in good spirits that day.

"Tuesday was the last time I saw him," McCarthy recalled. "He didn't come in Wednesday the fifth or Thursday the sixth. But it wasn't all that unusual because Frank was the head man; he took days off when he wanted to. Finally, when he didn't come in on Friday the seventh, I tried calling him about two-thirty in the afternoon. I got a busy signal."

A busy signal at two-thirty in the afternoon? The same afternoon that Officer Joe Giuliano was getting a ring with no answer three times? The Columbo telephone was becoming a thorn.

Jack McCarthy's information fit perfectly with other facts being developed that indicated that the killings had occurred late Tuesday night, May 4.

When Rose asked if McCarthy knew of any problems Frank Columbo might have been having, the murdered man's assistant recalled that Columbo had seemed somewhat irritated by his daughter, Patty, recently. "A couple weeks ago, he said she'd told him that she was planning to get married soon and wanted a big wedding. But he didn't really think she was serious. He said he'd believe it when he saw it."

Investigator Russ Marinec, meanwhile, also developed information regarding a pending marriage for Patty. Richard and Ann Nyquist, former neighbors of the Columbos in Elk Grove Village, now lived in another nearby suburb, Itasca. They had run into Frank and Mary on Sunday morning, May 2, at a restaurant when they went out for breakfast. During conversation between the two couples, it was mentioned that Patty would be marrying Frank DeLuca within "the next couple of months." Mary Columbo at that time stated she wasn't going to the wedding. According to the Nyquists, Frank had said, "Oh, Mary, you're just upset now. When the time comes, you'll go." Mary then adamantly insisted that she would *not* go.

Investigator Gene Gargano, representing the Cook County Sheriff's Office, was assigned the task of interviewing both Patty Columbo and Frank DeLuca for the purpose of obtaining from each of them a day-by-day itinerary of their movements during the week of the murders, Monday, May 3, through Friday, May 7. The resulting statements were almost identical, containing nothing that would have cast suspicion on either the surviving member of the Frank Columbo family or her fiancé, with whom she lived.

In Patty's version of the week, she indicated that upon arriving home at their apartment from a Kentucky Fried Chicken at 6:00 P.M. on Tuesday, May 4, she'd found her telephone ringing. She said it was her father and she claimed she spoke with him for about thirty minutes. Frank DeLuca stated that he had received a telephone call from Frank Columbo on the previous evening, Monday, May 3, at 10:30 P.M., and a second call about twenty minutes later at 10:50. Those were the last times Patty and DeLuca claimed that either had spoken to the murdered man.

Investigator Gargano also interviewed Gloria Rezzuto, Frank Columbo's sister, another resident of Elk Grove Village. Mrs. Rezzuto had last spoken to her brother and his wife on the phone on Sunday, May 2. Mary Columbo at that time said she and Frank hadn't seen Patty for a month. She told Gloria that Patty was "flaky" and that whenever she spoke with her daughter, she always became "terribly upset." Gloria Rezzuto said she tried to encourage her brother to communicate with Patty, to "smooth things out," because Mary never wanted to make the effort. But as of that Sunday, the family hadn't "made up." Mrs. Rezzuto felt that Frank would have reconciled with his daughter only if Mary wanted him to.

"There was nothing my brother wouldn't do for Mary," she told Gargano. "He always wanted to keep Mary happy."

Regarding Michael, Mrs. Rezzuto said Patty had a "very close relationship" with him.

One other interesting point emerged in the Gloria Rezzuto interview. Her grown son Bobby knew from having personally seen it that Frank Columbo carried a gun in the glove compartment of his car, and Frank had told his nephew that he also owned a second gun, which he kept under the bed.

Gargano next interviewed Carolyn Tygrett, a sister of Mary Columbo's, who lived in Cary, Illinois, about thirty miles farther out of Chicago. Mrs. Tygrett had last seen Mary at the Columbo home on Saturday, May 1, when she stopped in after a shopping trip to a nearby mall. It was about two o'clock in the afternoon and Mary was home alone. According to the sister, Mary said she had "been in touch" with Patty and that her daughter and Frank DeLuca were planning to be married on June 5, exactly five weeks away. The couple purportedly was planning a trip to Italy and Greece in September. Mrs. Tygrett indicated that Mary was much more bitter toward Patty than her husband now, but was "starting to soften a little."

Another piece of information elicited in that interview was that Frank Columbo was considering leaving his longtime job at Western Auto and starting a trucking business of his own.

Eyewitness information, although very scant, also began to surface. Ann Charleville, who lived at 70 Brantwood, had observed a vehicle backing out of the Columbos' driveway about nine o'clock Tuesday night, May 4, almost striking another vehicle that was passing at the time. She agreed to help a Cook County sheriff's artist, Ronald Coakley, create a composite of the male driver as she remembered him.

Lynette Rowley, whose parents lived farther down the block at 85 Brantwood, was leaving their house earlier that same day, around 4:45 in the afternoon, when she observed a dark blue, full-size car parked in the Columbos' driveway. The car, she recalled, did not have a vinyl top, as did the Columbos' Oldsmobile, and she noticed it because it was the first time she had ever seen the car in the Columbos' driveway.

When Ray Rose learned that Frank and Mary Columbo had taken a vacation to South Carolina two months earlier to visit some of Mary's family, he had his men begin conducting telephone interviews with those relatives on the off chance that something useful might turn up. Something did—interesting, if not exactly useful. Phillip Niville, a nephew, recalled that Frank Columbo told him he had purchased a .25-caliber automatic for Mary, and that it was kept in the glove compartment of the family Thunderbird for her protection. That was odd, since other information indicated that Frank almost always drove that car himself. Michael, who was also along on the trip, later told Niville that his father also had a second gun, a .32-caliber nickel-plated revolver. Another relative, Harry Cheeks, a brother-in-law of Mary's, observed on this same visit that Mary Columbo was carrying a .25-caliber automatic in her purse. It was already known to Elk Grove police that the Columbos had been killed by a .32-caliber pistol, but the weapon had yet to be found.

By now, Ray Rose had begun to suspect that Patty Columbo was somehow personally involved in the killings. Patty herself had ignited the slow-burning fuse of that suspicion the very day the bodies were discovered. Supposedly, Patty had learned of her family's death from Frank DeLuca. One of his employees at Walgreen's, Joanne Emmer, who lived near the Columbo home, had left work at 5:00 P.M. on Friday, May 7, and on her way home had seen the police activity going on around 55 Brantwood. Learning what had happened, she telephoned DeLuca and informed him of the crime. DeLuca had another employee, Barbara Cooper, drive him home. When Patty arrived at their apartment a short time later, DeLuca allegedly broke the news to her. Instead of becoming hysterical and rushing to her family home to see if the shocking story was true, Patty remained in the apartment with DeLuca until later that evening, then went with him to the Elk Grove Village Police Department, where they offered to "help" with the investigation any way they could. Hardly, Rose thought, the reaction of a nineteen-year-old girl who had just been told that the rest of her family was murdered. Rose was suspicious of Patty and her lover so early, in fact, that he had Sgt. Ron Iden take mug shot photos of them that same evening, ostensibly for identification purposes only. Although Patty wasn't *acting* bereaved, the photograph shows her looking all but wasted.

DeLuca, on the other hand, was almost smiling, as if he was thoroughly enjoying the attention.

The first big break of the case came on Monday night following the discovery of the bodies. Ray Rose and his men had been working practically around the clock for four days, going home only to shower, shave, and change clothes, perhaps sleep two or three hours but no more. Rose himself *couldn't* sleep; every time he closed his eyes, he saw Michael Columbo's hacked-up young body. Had it not been for continuous ingestion of caffeine, Rose—and most of his men, as well—would have collapsed already.

At ten o'clock that Monday night, Rose was at his desk staring at the telephone, practically trying to *will* it to ring.

There had been two anonymous calls earlier that night, both from a discernibly nervous young man who claimed to have important information about the Columbo murders, but who did not want to be seen coming into the police department. They could have been crank calls, but Rose felt otherwise; something in the young man's voice made the chief investigator feel that *this* one was for real. So he stared at the phone as if giving it a mental edict to ring again.

It finally did, at 10:50 P.M.

"I still want to give you the information," the apprehensive voice said. "Can you meet me somewhere?"

"Anywhere you say," Rose told him easily.

"You know where Denny's Restaurant is?"

"Yes, I do."

"Okay, I'll meet you there at eleven-thirty. I'll be in a booth by myself."

"Fine," Rose said, keeping his voice calm and conversational. "See you then."

As soon as he hung up, Rose turned to his men and said, "Okay, I want Denny's Restaurant completely surrounded as soon as we can get out there. Cover every door, every window; have cars in place to seal off the parking lot; I want everyone extra alert for this: the caller could be a weirdo of some kind, he could be an innocent citizen who actually has some information, or—he could be the Columbo killer. Let's keep in mind that the second most important thing we have to do is take this guy. The first most important thing is to protect the other people in Denny's." Rose looked at his watch. "Let's get going."

This was going to be it, Ray Rose thought. His police officer's instinct made him *feel* it.

The precautions turned out to be unnecessary.

Ray Rose sat down in the Denny's booth opposite a young man of about twenty, not markedly different from any other young man Rose might have passed on the streets of Elk Grove Village. As the police officer's adrenaline began to slow down, he eliminated in his mind two of the possible three categories into which he had earlier put the young man: this was not the Columbo killer, and he was not a weirdo. This kid had something.

"You the one who called?" Rose asked.

"Y—yeah."

"Okay. I'm Investigator Ray Rose and I'm in charge of the Columbo case. What's your name?"

"Uh, Glenn. Norman Glenn."

"Okay, Norman. I want to thank you for coming forward. It's the right thing to do and I hope you can help us. Now, what did you want to tell us?"

"My—my sister," Norman Glenn said in an unsteady voice. "She—she knows a guy that Patty Columbo tried to hire to kill her parents."

"Who's your sister, Norm?"

"Nancy Glenn. Her and P—Patty used to be best friends. They went—went to high school together."

"And who's the guy she knows?"

"His name is Lanny something. He's a c—car salesman. Nancy knows his last name."

"Okay. Do you know anything else about him? Where he sells cars, maybe?"

"He used to work at Franklin-Weber Pontiac over in Schaumburg. Nancy bought a car from him last year and then dated him for a while. She introduced him to Patty. Then I guess he got married or something and him and Nancy stopped seeing each other. But he called her up a couple of months ago and took her to dinner. That was when he told her that Patty had been trying to get him and a friend of his to kill her parents."

"Where does your sister live?" Rose asked the young man.

"With my parents. On Kendal Road, about a block from the Columbo house," Norman Glenn said.

"Is she at home now?"

"Yeah."

"Okay, Norm. Let's go talk to her."

On the way to the Glenn home, Ray Rose was glad that he'd had the forethought to call Joanne, his wife, earlier in the evening to tell her he might not be home until morning. Joanne was the total opposite of the cliché cop's wife so often portrayed in movies and novels: the wife who constantly complains about her husband's long hours and dedication to his work. She was, and always had been, totally supportive of Ray—"The best wife a career police officer could ask for," her husband said—but she worried nevertheless. Rose tried to alleviate as much of that anxiety as he could by keeping in close touch when he wasn't at home. It had been a rough five months for Joanne already: first Ray's undercover narcotics assignment, and then a major murder case dropped in his lap on the first day back.

Rose's thoughts turned again to Patty Columbo. In spite of his underlying suspicions, it seemed almost incredible to him that a nice, middle-class suburban girl would actually hire someone to murder her parents. And not only her parents, but her thirteen-year-old brother as well. One of the other officers had said Patty had the "face of an angel." That may have been true, but Rose was now convinced that she didn't have the *heart* of one.

Patty was involved, he had no doubt of that. Right then, he had one objective firmly in mind—to find out how *deeply* involved. Maybe then he would begin to learn exactly what her "angel face" concealed.

4
June 1956 to June 1962

Patricia Ann Columbo was born on June 21, 1956, a Thursday, the first day of summer, in the Norwegian American Hospital at 1044 North Francisco Avenue in Chicago, delivered into the world by Dr. Vincent Coletti.

Frank and Mary Columbo thought she was the most beautiful baby they had ever seen: a mass of curly hair already, big dark eyes, perfect little hands and feet—perfect everything. When he got to work the next morning, Frank Columbo, who was a loading-dock foreman at the Western Auto shipping terminal, told everyone who would listen to him how beautiful his little girl Patty Ann was. He kept it up all week.

Frank and Mary lived in a rented second-floor apartment in a two-flat building at 1803 West Ohio Street on the lower West Side of Chicago. Once upper-middle-class, the neighborhood had gradually depreciated first to middle-class, then further down to lower-middle-class, then working-class, or what more and more people were beginning to call a "blue-collar" neighborhood. In mid-1956 it was still all white, reasonably safe, and as clean as could be expected for the city. Frank and Mary, like many other young married couples, coveted a home of their own out in one of the many western suburbs springing up around the airport, O'Hare International, which had opened the previous year. The city had been acceptable to the generation of which Frank and Mary were a part, and people like Frank, who had grown up on the West Side, often recalled how great it had been to be a kid back in the "old neighborhood." But times were changing fast.

Areas had once been fixed, *firm*. Now, in the decade since World War II ended, flexibility had arrived, and someone *different* moved in down the street, and from that point on the neighborhood was no longer sacrosanct; it was "mixed."

The two-flat in which the Columbos lived when little Patricia Ann was born was owned by two sisters, Janet and Marilyn Gower, who had inherited the building back when the neighborhood had been mostly Ukrainian, and had remained there with the advent of the Italians. The unmarried Gower sisters were only slightly older than the Columbos, and when they learned that Mary was pregnant, they were thrilled. Months before the baby came, Janet and Marilyn knew that one of them would be asked to be the child's godmother; the sisters and the Columbo couple had grown that close. To be fair, it was decided that if it was a boy, the godmother would be Marilyn; if a girl, Janet. When Patricia was born, Janet Gower was almost as happy as if she had borne the child herself.

"I saw my little goddaughter last night," she told the other women at Illinois Bell, where she was an office worker. "She is *gorgeous*! A mop of black hair like you wouldn't *believe*! And her eyes! This one is definitely going to drive the boys crazy someday."

As godfather, the Columbos chose a close friend of Frank's named Phil Capone. That too had been the luck of the draw; if the Columbo baby had been a boy, the godfather would have been another of Frank's close friends, Joe Battaglia, who ran Carmela's Grocery across the street. Another close friend, Gus Latini, might have been in the running also, except that he was so nonchalant and easygoing that Frank and

Mary somehow thought that he might not take the responsibility seriously enough.

Mary Columbo, who at one time had desired a nursing career, was, from the birth of her first child, destined to spend the rest of her life as a homemaker. It was a time when two-income families were coming into vogue, when child-care centers were opening, freeing mothers to pursue occupations of their own. To have dual incomes was considered the wise thing by young couples, for whom the new house in the suburbs was not only a goal, but an urgent lure, something they wanted *now*. Not so Frank Columbo.

"You stay home and keep house and cook meals and raise the baby," he said firmly when Mary carefully broached the subject of working. "I'll earn us a living."

"I just thought we could get our own home quicker with both of us working," she suggested.

"We'll get our own home soon enough, don't worry," he assured her. "I'm next in line for promotion. Soon as I'm a superintendent, I got a couple of things I'm gonna get going to bring in some extra cash. We'll make it okay, don't worry."

So Mary stayed at home with her daughter. Her days were filled with grocery shopping, preparing meals, cleaning their apartment, taking care of the baby—who soon became known as Patty Ann, or simply Patty—and in general being the old-fashioned housewife that Frank Columbo wanted. Not the most exciting life, but certainly not a *bad* one, and Mary Columbo adjusted to it without any significant problems. She was Frank's attentive, loving wife, and Patty's attentive, loving mother—in that order, *always*.

As little Patty grew from infant to toddler to preschooler, she found herself living in a mostly adult world. Around her were her mother and father, her godparents, her daddy's friends Gus and Joe, aunts and uncles from both sides of the family—with an occasional cousin who might not be an adult but was invariably older—people who came over to play cards, members of the bowling teams, her dad's friends from work. The little girl played alone a lot, but it never seemed to bother her or her mother. Her father occasionally showed some concern. He wished there were more kids on the block.

But in a couple years, he knew, she would start kindergarten and have all the kids to play with she wanted.

Their building was almost directly across the street from the district public school, Talcott Elementary. Frank Columbo had decided early on that no child of his was going to be sent to Catholic schools. He himself was a product of the Chicago parochial school system and often recalled what he considered harsh and humiliating treatment by the nuns, who, in those days before the advent of lay teachers, had exclusive control of the classrooms.

"I will never, *ever* send any kid of mine to Catholic school," he vowed.

As far as Mary Columbo was concerned, it did not matter. She wasn't Catholic.

When Patty was old enough to play outside, close to their own building, with Frank or Mary or Janet Gower sitting on the front steps to watch her, she at last found a playmate when a Polish family with a little girl Patty's age moved in down the block. It wasn't much of a family: the father, it quickly became known, was a laborer who drank heavily, and the mother was grossly overweight and never looked clean. Not exactly PTA material.

Patty, of course, was delighted to have a friend her own age at last. The other little girl's name was Paula, and she, like her mother, never looked clean. Besides her clothing being shabby and her shoes usually having a floppy sole or pitifully worn-down heels, her dishwater-blond hair was stringy and uncombed, her face was seldom washed, and her fingernails were always dirty. It was only after Patty had been allowed once to go play at Paula's house, and noticed the filthy condition of the place, that she seemed to become aware of Paula's own pathetic personal appearance.

Patty also began to pick up snippets of conversation regarding Paula, usually between her own mother and godmother.

"Honest to God," Mary Columbo said, "the way they let that kid run around. I swear to God you could plant vegetables in her ears, they're so dirty."

"You don't suppose Patty Ann could catch anything from

her, do you?" Janet Gower asked. "I mean, like body lice or something?"

While her mother and godmother fretted and worried, Patty devised steps to try to improve her new playmate's lot. "Mom, when you do my nails, will you do Paula's too?" she asked. "We want to play like we're going to the beauty shop." After some serious preliminary scrubbing with a fingernail brush and soapy water, Mary Columbo complied with her daughter's request and gave both little girls manicures. *The kid's mother,* Mary Columbo thought when she sent Paula home, *will probably come down here and raise hell with me for ruining her fingers.* But nothing was ever said.

When Paula came to play at Patty's house, which was far more frequent than the other way around, Patty would always wait a few minutes and then say, "Come on, let's go in the bathroom and wash our hands and faces, then I'll ask my mom if we can have some cookies." While they were washing, Patty would try to help Paula get as clean as possible without being too obvious about it. For a child not yet in kindergarten, Patty displayed an advanced capacity for identifying the hygiene problem her little friend had, and finding a subtle but effective way of helping solve it. She wasn't a precocious child; in most ways, Patty's conduct was consistent with her age. But every once in a while, due probably to her overexposure to adults, she would say or do something that seemed far beyond her years. Sometimes the adults would notice it, sometimes not. When they did, it was usually, "Listen to that. God, this child is bright. We've got a scholar on our hands, people."

Patty Columbo was maturing very rapidly. But she wasn't really growing up. Not the way she should have been.

Although Patty was not to attend parochial school, she was nevertheless being raised in the Roman Catholic faith. Frank seldom went to mass, and Mary was, if anything, a Baptist. But godmother Janet Gower was a devout, rosary-carrying member of Saint Carmichael's parish, and each Sunday morning at eight-thirty, from the time she was four years old, a ruffle-and-lace-dressed little Patty, bonnet on head, purse on arm, would come downstairs and, taking Janet's hand, walk with her the six blocks to the old gray stone church where they always sat as far up front, as close to the altar as they could get, for nine o'clock mass. Many of the nuns who taught at Saint Carmichael's parochial school attended the same mass and Patty would watch them in awe, all sitting in a row in their black habits and spotless starched white cowls.

"I know your father isn't going to send you to Catholic school," her godmother, whom she called Auntie Janet, told her, "but I'm going to see to it that you get signed up for catechism lessons twice a week. You'll probably go to Saint Carmichael's, and some of those nuns we see at mass might be your teachers. You'll have so much fun learning about the church."

Patty, observing that none of the nuns ever seemed to smile, wasn't all too sure.

When the time finally did come for Patty to start school, she could have taken or left it. The prospect of joining a seething herd of children, such as she had observed from the living room window almost all of her life, held little excitement. She was a fastidious little girl, unusually fussy about her appearance, scrupulously careful not to get dirty—at least not *very* dirty—at whatever games she played. She imagined that most of the children in that writhing, noisy throng on the Talcott Elementary playground were probably more like Paula.

If Patty had been able to think of a way to avoid starting school altogether, she probably would have seized it. But no escape presented itself. So eventually little Patty Columbo, with all the other five-year-olds in the district, trooped off to kindergarten.

Patty liked school. Because of her unusually close association with a lot of adults, she already knew most of the things being taught—numbers, letters, shapes, colors, how to use scissors, paste, ruler—but it was interesting to observe those things being taught in this new environment instead of at the kitchen table. And she particularly enjoyed helping other, slower children who were unable to grasp these new concepts as easily as she. When she recognized a classmate as languorous or indifferent, she made a point of sitting by that child and trying to help him or her improve. Sometimes in the evening, she would complain to her amused parents and others,

"I don't know what I'm going to do with Freddie; sometimes he just won't listen to me."

Before she was halfway through kindergarten, little Patty Columbo had decided that when she grew up she wanted to be a teacher.

In the first grade, just as godmother Janet had predicted, Patty began going to Saint Carmichael's on Tuesday and Thursday afternoons for catechism instruction. She offered some feeble resistance at first, telling her parents, "I don't want to go to the sisters. I see them at mass on Sundays. They never smile."

The ploy almost worked with her father, with his long memory. "If she don't wanna go for catechism, why should she?"

Mary, as usual, didn't care one way or another. It ended up being Frank and godmother Janet one-on-one. And where Frank normally could intimidate a woman without half trying, when it came to Patty's welfare, Janet Gower brooked no nonsense.

"Look, Frank, she's *got* to take catechism lessons," Janet insisted sternly. "If you didn't intend to raise her in the Catholic church, what the hell did you have her baptized for? Why'd you pick me for her godmother if you were going to pull something like this?"

Frank finally relented, and under Janet's patient direction Patty was gradually convinced to study under the sisters without further fuss.

From her very first class with the nuns, Patty saw that she had been mistaken in her original appraisal. Not only did they smile—a lot—but they spoke in soft voices and bestowed gentle touches of approval where appropriate. They weren't at all like the terrible ogres she had heard her father describe. If anything, she found them to be nicer than her teacher at Talcott Elementary, who sometimes, toward the end of the week, seemed to run out of patience with the children. Because the nuns alternated classroom assignments with other duties, the sister doing the teaching always seemed to be in a good mood.

It was sometime during her first or second year of catechism that Patty modified her ambition to become a teacher, and decided she wanted to be a nun—a teaching nun. When she mentioned it to her father, he shook his head and said she was too young to make up her mind about things like that. Her mother shrugged and said that was nice. Only Auntie Janet listened to her with real interest.

"That is a wonderful thing to want to be, Patty!" she praised. "You not only serve God and the church, but you also help all the children you teach get a good start in life." She gave her little goddaughter a loving hug. "If that's what you really want, I'll bet that's what you'll get. And I'll be very proud of you!"

Always in the wake of any disapproval from her father, any disinterest from her mother, came her godmother's enthusiastic support. It was unequivocal and it was enduring.

And that became a matter of great importance to little Patty Columbo when her parents announced that a new baby was on the way.

5
April 1963

It had never occurred to Patricia that she might someday have to share her world with a little brother or sister. All her life the adults around her had been hers exclusively: her parents, her godmother, her godmother's sister Marilyn, her godfather Phil Capone, whom she called "Uncle Philly," and her father's friends, "Uncle" Joe and "Uncle" Gus. When they were around, singly or in a group, Patricia was usually the only child present; she got all the attention, all the candy, all the quarters, all the pats and praises and whatever other amenities there were to be had. She was always the one who got to *go*. If Uncle Philly was running out for beer during a Cubs game on television, she got to go. If Auntie Janet went shopping for new shoes, she got to go. And she seldom came home empty-handed.

"You're spoiling this kid rotten, Janet," Mary Columbo would say.

"Who else have I got to spoil?" Janet would retort.

Mary sometimes complained to Frank about it. "They're

spoiling her rotten, Frank. All of them: Janet, Phil, Gus, Joe.
They treat her like a little princess. Jesus, Gus gave her a
Timex watch last week. She's probably the only kid in her
class who wears a watch."

"What's the difference?" Frank would ask. "They love her,
so they treat her good. What do you want me to do, tell them
don't love my kid no more?"

There was some talk, very quiet talk among friends, that
Mary might be just a hint jealous of the pampered little princess. Some talk that maybe she had even let herself get pregnant again on purpose in order to give little Patty some
competition. A threatened Mary Columbo, feeling insecure,
may have decided that with a new baby in her arms she
would once again take center stage, not only in her husband's
life, but in the lives of their close friends as well.

Patricia was no trouble to Mary while she awaited the birth
of her second child. Always self-reliant when it came to
amusing herself, playing alone, the little girl rarely bothered
her mother. She had her favorite television shows: "My
Friend Flicka," "Rin Tin Tin," "Sky King," "Fury." And she
had her own dog, Mike, to care for and take for walks. When
she had originally asked for a dog, Frank Columbo was dis-
inclined to get one.

"Dogs are a lot of trouble, honey," he said.

Eventually, it was Auntie Janet who got her the dog. Janet
had accompanied a neighbor to the animal shelter to look for
a lost dog, and while there had observed an Old English
sheepdog waiting in a cage all alone near the back door.

"How come that one's over there all alone?" Janet asked
the attendant.

"Waiting for the transfer truck," he replied.

"The transfer truck, what's that?" she asked.

"That's the truck that takes them to be put to sleep. We can
only keep them seven days; on the eighth day, if nobody has
claimed them, they go on the transfer truck."

An hour later, Patricia had a sheepdog.

All the people around Patricia asked her whether she wanted
a baby brother or a baby sister. She consistently said she
wanted a little sister. She did not think a little brother would
be much fun; the boys at school weren't: they played rough

and made a lot of noise and got dirty. But most of the girls were cleaner and quieter than most of the boys, and Patricia decided that if she *had* to share her little-girl world with somebody, it might as well be another little girl.

"So, you want a baby sister, huh?" Uncle Gus said one night, taking her up on his lap and unwrapping a Tootsie Roll for her. Uncle Gus drove a wholesale candy delivery van; he never came over without bringing a pocketful of samples. "What do you think she ought to be named?" he asked.

Patricia didn't know, or care. The name didn't matter, just so the baby was a girl. But Uncle Gus kept pressing her until finally Patricia came up with the first name that entered her head.

"I think she should be named Susie."

From that point on, Mary Columbo's unborn child was referred to by Patricia and Uncle Gus as Susie.

During the third trimester of Mary's pregnancy, when she began to grow heavy and uncomfortable, Gus Latini often came by in the afternoons when Patricia got out of school and took her off Mary's hands by letting her come along on part of his candy delivery route. It was a great little-girl adventure, that candy van, and Patricia loved it. It was like a big pantry, with shelves along both sides with screens in front of them to keep the cartons of candy bars from falling off. The smell inside the van was sweetly intoxicating, as if a chocolate bomb had exploded.

The van had bucket seats with an accordion door behind them that closed off the back. When the door was pulled all the way, the little front cab was a warm and cozy place to be, especially in the wintertime. The floor heater kept the cab warm, Uncle Gus had a tape deck so they could listen to music, and always there was that exhilarating, mouth-watering Hershey-Nestlé-Brach-Mars aroma. Like cigarette smoke, it eventually permeated even one's clothes; Gus Latini always smelled like a candy bar.

Patricia loved going on the route with Uncle Gus. They drove to a different part of the city every day, and one day they went into the near-north suburbs. Patricia particularly enjoyed the suburban run. Outside the city, people lived in houses instead of apartment buildings, and had lawns instead of front stoops. The neighborhoods were open, airy places, with lots of clear sky and trees and light colors; unlike Ohio Street, over which there was usually an industrial sky—smoky, sooty—and the dominant color was a weary and worn gray stone so dingy its only salvation lay in sandblasting.

From candy store to cigar store to soda shop, Uncle Gus would take Patricia in with him and introduce her to the proprietor as his "helper." Patricia would watch with great interest as Uncle Gus inventoried the store's candy supply; then she would accompany him back out to the truck where he opened the double rear doors, climbed inside, pulled Patricia in after him, and let her hold his clipboard while he filled a big plastic tray with boxes of restock candy to be taken inside.

At some point in the afternoon, Uncle Gus and Patricia would take their "break," usually at one of the soda shops, where Gus would have his coffee and Patricia a soda or float or whatever she wanted. She also got to buy comic books, trinkets, puzzles, games, other things from the variety of inexpensive wares that most of the stores carried. There were times when Patricia felt like the luckiest little girl in the world having Gus Latini for an "uncle." Next to her parents and Auntie Janet, he was easily her favorite person, and she unabashedly gave him her affection.

Now, Uncle Gus would start off each trip with Patricia by saying, "Well, sweetheart, I wonder if little Susie will be born today while we're gone."

"I hope so," Patricia would invariably reply. "I want to start playing with her and teaching her things."

Then Uncle Gus would suddenly pretend to be worried. "I hope you're still gonna love your Uncle Gus after that new baby sister gets here."

"Uncle Gus, I'll *always* love you," Patricia would solemnly reply. She would throw her arms around Uncle Gus's neck and kiss his sandpaper cheek, and they would happily continue on "their" delivery route.

One morning when Patricia woke up, Auntie Janet was there instead of her mother. The new baby had come during the night, on April 10. A little brother. He had been named Michael. Already Auntie Janet was calling him "little Mike."

Patricia could not believe it. She had planned for months

on a sister. And why name him Mike? That was her doggy's
name.

A very disenchanted little Patty Columbo went to school
that morning. This was not fair, she fretted. She and Uncle
Gus wanted a girl; they had never talked about anything *but*
a girl.

In class that morning, Patricia began wondering if it might
all just be a big mistake. Maybe her mom and dad only
thought it was a boy; it was probably hard to tell with little
babies. Or maybe, she imagined further, her daddy was playing a joke on her and Uncle Gus. Maybe it really *was* a little
sister, and he was teasing them, making them worry that it
was not. Her daddy sometimes liked to play jokes on people.

Patricia went home for lunch grimly determined to find out
if this was a joke, a mistake, or exactly what. Her father was
home by then, but asleep; Auntie Janet, who had taken off
work that day, fixed lunch for them in her apartment downstairs. After extensive close questioning of her godmother
during that lunch hour, little Patty finally became convinced
that she did indeed have a new baby brother.

Patricia returned to school that afternoon determined to do
something to right what she considered a great unfairness.

In class, during their show-and-tell period, Patricia raised
her hand.

"Yes, Patty?" her teacher said.

"I have something to tell," Patricia said.

"All right, come up to the front of the room. Class, Patty
has something to tell as part of show-and-tell. Pay attention,
please."

Standing at the front of her class, Patricia very determinedly said, "I got a new baby sister last night. Her name is
Susie."

She marched back to her desk, thinking: *There*.

During the three days that Mary Columbo and the baby
stayed in the hospital, it was Gus Latini who was first able to
break through the wall of Patricia's disappointment and subsequent unhappiness.

"You know what?" he said that first night after Michael
was born. "I don't really care if it *is* a boy." He sat down
with her on the floor where she was halfheartedly playing

with her dolls—all girl dolls. "As a matter of fact, I'm even glad that the new baby is a boy," Uncle Gus continued. "Wanna know why?"

"Why?" Patricia grudgingly asked, barely mumbling the word.

"Because," Uncle Gus said, "I'm glad you're gonna be the only little girl around. Now I get to keep paying all the attention to you, see? You'll still be my best girl, my *only* girl. We can still go on our route together and everything. If there was another girl, she'd probably wanna come with us. But this baby boy, when he gets older he's gonna wanna do stuff like play baseball and build model airplanes and dig up worms to go fishing."

"Uggh," Patricia said, intentionally shivering.

"He won't wanna do nothing like go on the candy route with me, 'cause it won't be exciting enough for him. So that'll leave just you and me, like always. Way I see it, we're getting the best of the deal."

Uncle Gus was gradually able to bring Patricia around, coaxing her out of the lethargy of disappointment, slowly manipulating her around to joining him in a new attitude and position: We don't care if it *is* a boy. We're *glad*. Like the old song said: We've got each other.

Patty Ann and Uncle Gus, two against the world.

As it turned out, of course, from the moment Mary Columbo walked through the door with Michael, he became Patricia's baby. It was love at first sight; her "We don't care" alliance with Uncle Gus went right out the window. And Mary Columbo, in the softness of new motherhood again, was so tearfully delighted by Patricia's praises—"Oh Mommy, he's so beautiful!"—that she happily shared her son with her daughter without reservation. Mary sat Patricia on the couch and let her hold Michael at once.

"Hey, what is this?" Frank Columbo asked in mock chagrin. "I haven't even held the kid yet!"

"You'll get your turn; after all, Patty Ann *is* the big sister."

"I see," said Frank. "And I'm only the father, huh? Well, I guess I know my place."

It was all good-natured, the adults—Auntie Janet, Auntie Marilyn, Uncle Gus, Uncle Joe Battaglia, a few relatives, the parents—smiling in the mutual joy of bringing this new little miracle home to become a part of them and what they were. Patricia was euphoric. Her attention was divided between the tiny sleeping infant in her arms, and snatches of conversation that she kept picking up:

"—looks exactly like Patty Ann when she was born—"

"—such a big help to you, Mary. Look how she loves that baby already—"

"—actually better off having a daughter first and then a son, Frank. I mean, lookit, if anything should happen to Mary in a few years, God forbid, then you'd have Patty Ann to help raise Michael, right? She could, like, take Mary's place as the woman of the house—"

"—if nothing else, you'll have a built-in baby-sitter in a few more years—"

All of the adult conversation, which Patricia had long since become accustomed to tuning in and out, served to reestablish her bond to these grown-ups of her world, and to eradicate the sense of betrayal she had felt at first. She was restored to her position as pampered little princess, a place no longer unique now that there was also a little prince, but as Uncle Gus had pointed out, and indeed continued to emphasize to her, she was still the only *girl*—which was a very special status. *And*—she was the oldest, the significance of which had barely entered her mind as yet, but upon which everyone, especially Auntie Janet, seemed to place great importance.

"Remember, you're the big girl now. Michael's the little baby. You must try to help your mommy all you can. Promise me you will."

Patricia decided that she was going to try to please everyone, try to be the perfect little girl in every way. But now that she was so happy about her baby brother, she couldn't help feeling guilty about Uncle Gus. And he seemed to feel her stroke of conscience.

"Hey"—he pulled her onto his lap when they were alone in the kitchen—"I thought you and me had a deal about this baby. I thought we wasn't gonna care, we was just gonna let everybody else be crazy about him, and you and me were gonna be crazy about each other. You let me down."

"Oh, Uncle Gus, I'm sorry!" Patricia pleaded. "I didn't

think he would be so *sweet*! Anyway, we can still like each
other the best, can't we?"

"I dunno." Uncle Gus shrugged and looked away, as if he
were hurt. "I guess we can try, if you still want to."

"I do! We can!" Patricia exclaimed.

Patricia gave Uncle Gus a big bear hug and kissed him
loudly and squarely on the lips. Auntie Janet walked in at that
moment.

"What are you guys up to in here?" she asked.

"We're having a little business conference, Patty and me,"
Gus said self-importantly. "After all, she's a partner in my
candy route, you know."

Patty smiled in delight. Uncle Gus made her feel so good.

C.H.
September 1981

*In 1981, Jay Robert Nash, whom I considered to be the fore-
most chronicler of crime and criminals, published a book entitled* Look for the Woman, *a narrative encyclopedia of
female criminals from Elizabethan times to the current year.
While thumbing through his latest collection of crime facts, I
found, on page 91, a full-page photo of a familiar person:
Patricia Columbo. Nash had devoted three and a half pages
of text to "Patricia Columbo—Murderer." His account went
beyond what had been reported in the Chicago area newspapers, augmenting those articles with details of which I had
not previously been aware—details, I thought as I read, that
made the story even more interesting. Two years after starting
her prison sentence, for instance, Patricia had been accused
of organizing sex parties by procuring attractive inmates for
two high-ranking prison officials. The two officials were subsequently suspended. There was no indication, however, that
any charges were ever filed against Patricia. Had she done
anything or hadn't she? The article went on to say that
Patricia was taking college courses offered by Northern Illinois University, working toward an associate of arts degree.*

*Now I really became curious. Was Patricia Columbo orga-
nizing sex parties for prison officials and trying to earn a*

college degree? Busy, busy. Or, since she apparently hadn't been formally charged, was the sex-party rap a setup of some kind? Patricia Columbo would not be the first high-profile inmate to take some heat for nothing more than proximity to a prison beef.

But another, more compelling thought was also lurking in my mind: were there two Patricia Columbos—a split personality?

Once again, as on two previous occasions, the case—and the woman—began to intrigue me. I seemed to sense that someday, somehow, I would become involved in it.

Whether I wanted to or not.

6
May 1976

While Ray Rose was talking with Norman Glenn at Denny's Restaurant late on Monday night after the Columbo bodies had been discovered, Norman's sister Nancy was pacing nervously back and forth in the kitchen of the Glenn family home. Agitated, she said to her mother, "Patty was responsible for it. I *know* she was."

Mrs. Glenn remained calm. "No," she quietly pointed out, "you may suspect it, but you don't know it."

"Mother," Nancy all but pleaded, "she told me herself one time that she'd like to find somebody to kill her parents so she could be Michael's guardian and raise him. She's even been trying to get these two guys I know to kill them for her!"

"What two guys?" Mrs. Glenn asked.

Nancy became vague. "Just two guys, Mother. You don't know them." *Careful, Nancy,* she warned herself. There were some things a girl did not tell her mother.

Nancy Glenn was nineteen years old, the same age as Patty Columbo. They had been best friends in high school, but afterward had kept in touch only on an infrequent basis. After graduating, Nancy worked as a nurse's aide at the Alexian Brothers hospital in Elk Grove Village, while Patty worked at the big Walgreen's drugstore several blocks away. From time to time they would run into each other, maybe have lunch, occasionally gossip on the telephone. They still considered themselves friends, maybe not as close. Until about eight months earlier, that is, when Nancy called Patty to go on a blind date.

That, as Nancy thought about it now, was probably when the whole goddamned nightmare had begun—the nightmare that might have led to murder.

That was as much as Nancy could bring herself to tell her mother. And that was as much, she was sure, as her mother would want to hear. To tell her mother about the relationship she and Patty had with the "two guys," was mortifying and unthinkable. But she had to make her mother understand that what she was saying about Patty was anything but frivolous.

"Mother, this one guy—his name is Lanny; I bought my Camaro from him—told me Patty had been trying for months to get him and his friend to kill her parents."

"She couldn't have been serious," Mrs. Glenn said easily.

"Mother, she *was* serious, I'm sure of it!" Nancy insisted. "Lanny said she was having sex with this friend of his to try to get him to do it for her."

Just then Nancy and her mother heard the front door open and close. A moment later, Norman Glenn came into the kitchen, followed by a man whom they had never seen before.

"Nancy," her brother said, "this is the policeman in charge of the Columbo murder case."

"I'm Ray Rose, Miss Glenn," the chief investigator introduced himself. "I understand from your brother that you have some information that we should know."

Nancy's shoulders slumped as she sighed. Blinking back tears, she said, "Yeah, I guess I do."

"Can we talk about it?" Rose asked.

"Okay," Nancy said. "But not here. I don't want to wake my father. I haven't told him anything about this."

"I understand," Rose said. "Why don't you and I go somewhere and get some coffee. You don't have to make a formal statement or anything like that right now. We'll just have a little talk, all right?"

Nancy swallowed dryly and took a deep breath. "Okay."

* * *

Rose took Nancy Glenn to the all-night Frontier Restaurant, where they sat in an out-of-the-way booth and the police officer listened quietly to her story.

"His name is Lanny Mitchell," she said. "It's really Lanyon, but he likes to be called Lanny. The first thing I noticed about him was that he had a real nice smile. A sincere smile. And he was kind of cute. A little short, but then so am I. He was a real sharp dresser: always wore leisure suits with an open-collar shirt. And he had a really pleasant way of making conversation and putting people at ease . . ."

"So, this is your first car, you say?" Lanny Mitchell commented as he was filling out the state license form.

"Yes, it is, Mr. Mitchell," Nancy answered politely.

"Hey"—he flashed her his best smile—"what's with this 'mister' stuff? Call me Lanny."

They were in a small sales office just off the main showroom of Franklin-Weber Pontiac, a big, glitzy automobile dealership in Schaumberg, the next suburb west of Elk Grove Village. Nancy, feeling her independence with a regular income from her nurse's aide job, had just bought a nice little blue '73 Camaro—on time payments, at the usual outrageous interest rate charged young, single buyers. Nancy wasn't concerned about the payments, however; she had a *car*—and this really cute guy, whom she now called Lanny—had told her it was a "real cherry." Nancy had blushed and looked down when he said it, and Lanny had immediately apologized, explaining that the term had slipped out from force of habit because he so seldom had the pleasure of dealing with someone as nice as her.

"This really isn't my regular job," he confided. "I'm really a police officer, but I got in a little trouble and was suspended. I'm just doing this as a kind of fill-in, you know?"

"That's too bad," Nancy commiserated. "Your suspension, I mean. Do you think they'll take you back?"

"It's hard to say," Lanny shrugged. "I was set up on an armed robbery beef."

"That sounds serious," Nancy said. Her eyes had widened with the look of adolescent awe on her face. Suspended policeman, armed robbery—this was heady stuff; it might have come right out of "Police Woman," one of her favorite television shows.

"It's serious, all right," Lanny allowed. Now he gave her his confident look. "But it's nothing I can't handle. I've got some connections that are helping me out. One friend in particular is very heavy with the Chicago mob. I've been doing a little work for him and he's going to take care of me. I'm kind of on probation with him and his people, which is why I have to fill in my time with a crummy job like this."

"Somehow I didn't think you were just a used-car salesman," Nancy said. Lanny charmingly raised his eyebrows.

"Is that right? Why not?"

"I don't know," Nancy hedged, averting her eyes, slightly embarrassed. "You just look—well, *nicer.*" She felt herself blush. "I must sound really dumb."

"You do not," Lanny told her in what he considered his most earnest tone. "You sound very sweet. It's a pleasure just to talk to someone like you, after the kind of people I usually have to deal with." He tilted his head in a kind of inquisitive, little-boy manner. "I guess a girl like you must have a steady boyfriend?"

"Uh, no." Nancy shook her head.

"No?" Lanny feigned surprise. "Well, listen, would you like to go out sometime? We could go dancing, have a few drinks, get to know each other a little."

"Sure, I guess so."

"Hey, swell!" Now he gave her the Lanny Mitchell deluxe premium smile, which—she would later come to know—was a matchless dazzler that he bestowed only on those who gave him his way without question and pleased him without reservation.

Nancy went out with Lanny the very next night, and within a week had become intimate with him. They dated several times a week and it became routine for them to end the evening in bed in Lanny's apartment. Nancy was a smart girl; she enjoyed sex and she knew how to take care of herself. Lanny was the first "real man" she had gone out with; her dates up to that time had been with gawky adolescents who had no poise or polish. Lanny had both. And he knew how to please a girl in bed.

It was about six weeks into their relationship that Lanny

mentioned his friend again. "You know that guy I told you about? The one who's heavy with the mob and is helping me out of my jam? You think you could find a date for him and we could all go out together?"

"I don't know." Nancy hesitated. "What's he like?"

"A great guy," Lanny said unequivocally. "Little older than me, about thirty. Nice looking, sharp dresser, doesn't mind spending the bucks to have a good time. You got any girlfriends you think would like that kind of guy?"

"Let's see," Nancy pondered, playing for time. She wasn't altogether sure about this. She knew, of course, exactly what Lanny was asking for: someone to have sex with his friend, someone to "party" with. She wanted to keep dating Lanny—he was so *cute*—but finding a date for this other guy, this—well, *hood*, she guessed he was—was something else. It could get sticky. She didn't want to involve any of her girlfriends at the hospital with him, at least not until she found out what kind of person he was.

Then she thought of her old friend Patty Columbo. She'd had lunch with her not long before, and Patty had told her all about the problems she was having in a relationship with an older man. Maybe, Nancy thought, Patty could use a night out just to have a little fun, no strings attached. And one thing was sure: Patty could show the guy a good time.

"I do have this one friend," she said to Lanny, "I don't know if I told you about her or not. She's tall and very pretty, got a great bod. Only thing is, she's living with this guy, see, and her father's really giving her a bad time because the guy's older than her, and he's married, that kind of thing. They're Italian, you know; she even thinks her father has put a contract on her boyfriend's life. Wild, huh?"

Lanny seized on the information like a piranha. "Listen, this friend of mine might be just the guy for her to meet. Like I told you, the man's heavy; if your friend is nice to him, he might be able to do something in the way of a favor for her."

Lanny gave her a quick kiss and handed her the telephone.

"Here, why don't you give this girlfriend of yours a call . . ."

* * *

In the booth at the Frontier Restaurant, Nancy Glenn's expression, after she had told Ray Rose the rest of the story, was drawn.

"That was how Patty got involved with Lanny, and with his friend," she said, almost having to wring the words out. "Through me. But I swear to God, I had no way of knowing that it was going to lead to—to—something like this—"

Ray Rose empathized. "At this stage we don't *know* that it did lead to anything. What was Lanny's friend's name?"

"Roman something," Nancy said. "I only met him twice and he never mentioned his last name either time. But I think he was a cop."

Rose felt his stomach jerk. "Did he tell you he was a cop?" he asked as conversationally as he could.

"Not really," Nancy admitted. "And Lanny had told me he was a hood. But he carried a gun, like Lanny did, and they both talked about the sheriff's department. I just had a feeling he was a cop, like Lanny said *he* was." She shrugged. "Maybe I was wrong."

Ray Rose hoped she was. The second-worst scenario he could imagine in this case would be a couple of cops turning hired killers.

The only worse thing he could imagine was if Patty Columbo had actually done it herself—as opposed to *having* it done.

"Where can we find Lanny?" he asked Nancy.

"He's married now and lives out in Lake Villa," she said, taking a wallet from her purse. "I've got his phone number here somewhere . . ."

Ray Rose drummed his fingers softly on the tabletop. His expression was more solemn than it had been since the night they discovered the bodies.

Please, God, he silently prayed, *don't let these guys be policemen.*

7

February 1989

Late in the afternoon on a frigid but snowless February day in 1989, an older-model but immaculately maintained

Chevrolet drove onto the visitors' lot at Dwight Correctional
Center on the flat plains of Illinois, seventy-five miles south
of Chicago. An almost petite older woman emerged from the
car and faced icy wind as she marched—that was the only
word for it, *marched*—toward the visitors' registration office.
She carried an old-fashioned briefcase, the kind with two
handles, that looked too heavy for her; unlike others on the
same path, she did not bend her head to the wind but faced
it directly. Anyone seeing her would have known instinctively
that she gave little thought to either the weight of the briefcase or the rawness of the wind opposing her.

At the counter in the visitors' registration office, the
woman said, "I wish to see Patricia Ann Columbo, please."

"Have you visited her before?" the officer asked.

"No."

The officer looked up at a wall clock. "Visiting hours will
be over in half an hour—"

"I have permission to stay after visiting hours end," she
told him. "You may check with your superiors to verify that.
My name is Sister Margaret Burke."

The officer handed her a form. "Fill this out, please, Sister." As she sat down at a table with the form, the officer
picked up the telephone.

An overweight black inmate was mopping the floor of the
visitors' registration office. She unobtrusively worked her
way over to the table. "Hey, Sister Burke," she said quietly.

"Why, hello, Nettie," Sister Burke replied, smiling slightly.
One got the impression that she did not smile much. "How
long have you been down here?"

" 'Bout a year now. I'm on the cleaning detail."

"Yes, I see." Vocational training, she supposed they called
it. "How are your children, Nettie?"

"They fine, Sister Burke, just fine. I never got a chance to
thank you for going to see them when I was in the county
jail. It helped a lot, them and me both, for you to talk to
them."

"I'm glad it did, Nettie. You take care of yourself now.
God bless."

When Sister Burke finished filling out the form, she returned it to the officer at the counter. There was a second of-

ficer there now, a young woman. "Will you come with me, please, Sister?" she said. "We have to search you. I'm sorry."

"Don't apologize," Sister Burke said easily. "I've been in jails and prisons before; I know the routine."

In a tight little inspection room, Sister Burke removed her heavy coat, her shoes, her belt. She was not wearing a conventional nun's habit, but was dressed instead in a dark blue wool skirt, simple white blouse, and dark blue sweater. Her hair was cut medium-length in back and on the sides, combed away from her forehead in front; it was still dark brown but gray was beginning to show. She resembled a smaller, prettier Maureen Stapleton.

When the search routine was completed, including an examination of her briefcase, the back of Sister Burke's right hand was stamped with an ultraviolet ink mark and she passed through a metal detector to a large metal-and-glass door. It buzzed loudly as its lock electronically disengaged, and Sister Burke pushed it open to enter a very large room furnished with numerous tables and chairs. Only a few visitors were still there; daylight ended early in winter, and most people liked to get back on the road before dark. Inmates and their visitors could purchase coffee, soft drinks, snack food, and microwaved pizza at a screened-in counter along one wall. A Polaroid camera was set up in a corner in front of a bench with a painted backdrop behind it, where photos could be taken for one dollar. Along another wall were several glassed-in rooms for attorneys and other private visits. They were all unoccupied at the moment.

Another female officer approached Sister Burke from a desk that was positioned to view the entire room. "You can use any of the private rooms, Sister," she said. "Columbo is on her way over."

"Thank you."

Sister Burke chose the room farthest from the guard desk. As she said, she had been in prisons and jails before.

Margaret Burke had been a nun in the Society of the Sacred Heart for forty years. A farm girl from Morris, Minnesota, she had earned a bachelor's degree in education at Duchesne College of the Sacred Heart in Omaha before taking her vows, and then began her teaching career at a Catholic academy in Lake Forest, Illinois, an affluent suburb near Chicago. At the same time, she pursued her own higher education at Loyola University. Ultimately, she earned first a master's, and then a doctorate, in psychology, and subsequently became chairwoman of the psychology department at Barat College of the Sacred Heart in Lake Forest. A strong advocate of higher education for women, she was ultimately named president of the college.

At the same time, Sister Burke was also fostering women's rights in a variety of other ways, serving with such groups as the American Bishops Committee on Ecumenism, and the Chicago Archdiocesan Committee on Human Rights. Yet Margaret Burke still felt a need to do even more, particularly in areas not as privileged as a Lake Forest college campus. Soon she was on the advisory board for Chicago Legal Aid to Incarcerated Mothers. From that point on, her life's work was inextricably linked to jails and prisons.

In May 1976, Sister Margaret Burke retired as president of Barat College after heading it for twenty-two years. Still only in her early sixties, she now had the time to pursue the work that had replaced education as closest to her heart—working with deprived women: the homeless, the battered, the incarcerated. She became head psychologist and counselor at the Maria Shelter for Women on Chicago's South Side. After a lifetime in suburban Lake Forest, Sister Burke moved all the way to the other end of life's spectrum: the ghetto.

After establishing herself at the shelter, the tireless nun also began counseling women at the Cook County Jail. That same month, a nineteen-year-old girl named Patricia Columbo was remanded to the jail to await trial for murdering her father, mother, and brother.

The Cook County Jail women's division was a morass of despair, desperation, and danger. Six tiers of mostly black and brown faces, its occupants ran the gamut from slack-jawed recovering junkies to strutting dykes who carried a bar of soap in a sock to dent a person's face if the spirit moved them. Between these two extremes were the shoplifters, hookers, child abusers; desperate women who shot or stabbed their husbands, boyfriends, pimps, or did the same to the "other" woman who had tried to *steal* their husbands, boyfriends, pimps. There were receivers of stolen property, drug peddlers, accomplices to boyfriends who were over in the men's jail awaiting trial for robbery, burglary, car theft, forgery—anything that was against the law.

Some of the women in the jail had already been convicted and were serving county jail time; most of the others knew they would *be* convicted and either stay there or be shipped to one of the minimum security prisons for women or, worse, to Dwight, the maximum-security joint. That realization kept a lot of nerves teetering on the edge. It was like a pit of vipers; one little brush could start some serious hissing.

Putting Patricia Columbo in the women's jail, after her arraignment on three counts of murder, was like putting a pampered, overprotected house cat out into the jungle with *real* cats. Cook County Jail was the last place on earth that a suburban white girl needed to be. Patricia immediately got sick—physically ill; everything she ate, which consisted mainly of cold cuts, Velveeta cheese, and Kool-Aid, she promptly threw back up. Between bouts of regurgitation, she cowered on her bunk like a trapped animal. Whenever she looked up, there was usually a black or brown face looking curiously in at her, unable to resist the temptation to see what a person looked like who was accused of butchering her father, mother, and younger brother. It was the latter element of the crime that seemed to touch the most nerves: "Thirteen? That boy on'y thirteen? Good God almighty! That be *cold*, baby."

When Patricia's weight dropped enough to cause concern among her jailers, and following a psychiatric evaluation that indicated she was possibly suicidal—and no doubt also considering that she was a very-high-profile prisoner—they took her off the tier and put her into the jail hospital. Part of her condition was due to a sudden withdrawal from high doses of Valium; when her body had abruptly been deprived of the tranquilizer, it had rebelled against everything else: food, such as it was; rest; composure. She developed a bad rash, diarrhea, irregular heartbeat. The hospital staff set about stabilizing her for return to the tier.

"I won't go back to that place," Patricia vowed. "I'll kill myself first."

A black woman named Darcy asked wryly from the next bed, "Oh, yeah? How you figure to do that, girl?"

"I'll find a way," Patricia declared. "I'll do it somehow. I don't have anything to live for anyway."

"Ever'body got *somethin'* to live for, honey," the black woman said.

A couple of days later, Darcy said, "You Patty Columbo, ain't that right?"

"Yes."

Darcy chuckled. "I bet them women on the tier gave you plenty room to walk!"

"What do you mean?"

"I mean, I bet they got out of your way, didn't want to hassle wif' you."

"They came around to my cell and looked at me like I was some kind of freak," Patricia told her.

Darcy was surprised. "They did? Well, what did *you* do then, girl?"

Patricia shrugged. "I just tried to ignore them."

"Wrong," Darcy said emphatically, shaking her head. "You got to eyeball them right back, honey. Look"—she sat up on the side of her bed—"you gonna be in that place a long time, Patty; hell, you prob'ly won't go to trial for six months. You can't let them bitches on the tier back you down like that; you do, baby, and next thing you know you be eating pussy just to stay alive. Now look, far as all them other women is concerned, you a triple murderer, see? It don't mean shit whether you *really* guilty or not; until you get let off, you a triple murderer, period. Now you got to *act* like one. One of them bitches eyeball you, you eyeball the bitch right back. And you act just a little bit nuts, see? You talk to yourself, you walk back and forth, or around in a circle, like you fixin' to blow up. Breathe real heavy, like you 'bout to have a fit. You gonna find it make your life a whole lot easier . . ."

Darcy was right.

Within minutes after Patricia was returned to the tier, a smartass little Puerto Rican girl said, "Hey, wow, look who's back—Tinker Bell from the suburbs."

There were half a dozen women loitering on the cell walk, all of them wearing similar expressions of gang smugness.

Patricia stood up from straightening personal belongings on her bunk and went over to the cell door, which was racked open. Staring at the Puerto Rican, she asked quietly, "What did you say?"

"I said Tinker Bell from the suburbs is back," the girl repeated, smiling at her friends.

Patricia's large brown eyes fixed on the girl without blinking. She moved one step out of the cell. "What did you say?" she asked again, even quieter this time.

"I said—" The Puerto Rican girl's words faltered when two of the women with her abruptly walked away. "Hey, where the fuck you going?" she asked.

"Tell me again what you said," Patricia repeated. She compressed her lips and made her nostrils flare. Two more women ambled away. "Tell me again what you said." She was like a record with the needle stuck. Her eyes were wide and wild looking.

The little Puerto Rican girl bit her bottom lip briefly and shook her head. "Nothin'. I didn't say nothin'." She walked away too.

The remaining inmate, another Puerto Rican named Leta, studied Patricia for a long moment, then reached in the pocket of her dress and pulled out a candy bar. "Want half of a Baby Ruth?" she asked.

"Shit, yes!" Patricia said. "I haven't had any candy since I don't know when. Come on in."

Leta went into Patricia's cell, breaking the Baby Ruth in half.

Darcy had underestimated the length of time Patricia would remain in the Cook County Jail, Division 3, the women's section. She would not stand trial for the murders of her family for one year and three days after her arrest. It would be a long, long year.

Patricia's secondary family—aunts, uncles, cousins—completely abandoned her after she was charged with the murders. Supposedly, they all believed her to be guilty. According to newspaper reports, they were busy involving themselves in the probate of the family's will, as well as considering a possible libel suit based on alleged statements

by officials that Frank Columbo had been involved in the
Chicago crime syndicate.

The only people who did not desert Patricia were her godmother, Auntie Janet, married and now Janet Morgan, and her
parish priest, Father Ward Morrison, pastor of Queen of the
Rosary Church in Elk Grove Village. Auntie Janet saw to it
that Patricia always had fifteen or twenty dollars in her inmate account at the jail, and Father Morrison made the long
trip into the city to visit her at least once a week.

Two public defenders had been appointed to represent
Patricia at the murder trial, and there were numerous attorney
conferences and other legal maneuverings that required her
presence or attention. But those activities took up only a fraction of the time, and for the rest of the days and nights
Patricia was faced with the aspects of incarceration that are
the most grueling: monotony, tedium, mind-numbing bore-
dom that sowed the seeds of utter despair. To keep from losing her sanity, Patricia desperately sought some avenue of
mental release.

"What's this Institute of Women Today all about?" she
asked Leta one morning. "They have some kind of classes
here in the jail?"

"Yeah, some nuns run it," Leta said. "I think it's, like, a
writing class or something."

Patricia decided to check it out. When the next IWT class
assembled, she showed up and stood at the rear of the mul-
tipurpose room that the jail had assigned for the activity.
While she was standing there, a mature woman in a plaid
blazer came over to her.

"Hi, kid," the woman said.

"Hi." Patricia scrutinized her for a moment. "You a nun?"

"Yeah, but don't hold it against me." The woman held out
a hand. "I'm Sister Margaret Traxler. Are you interested in
the workshop?"

Shaking hands, Patricia shrugged. "Maybe. What's it all
about?"

"It's a journal-writing workshop," Sister Traxler explained.
"We try to show the women who participate how to acknowledge their fears and other feelings by writing them down in
a personal journal and then analyzing what they have written.
They can either share it with other participants or keep it to

themselves—it's up to the individual. The important thing is
to get it out of your head and down on paper. When you can
look at your problems on a piece of paper, they aren't so
overwhelming." Sister Traxler tilted her head an inch. "Think
you'd like to try it?"

"You don't have to show what you write to anybody?"

"Not a soul. You can write it down and then burn it if you
want to." The nun winked. "I'll even supply the matches."

Patricia enrolled in the workshop.

When she had been in the IWT journal-writing class for a
few weeks, and had time to further observe Sister Margaret
Traxler, Patricia commented to one of the volunteer aides,
"Traxler sure isn't like any nun I've ever seen before."

"She's not what you'd call your average sister," the aide
allowed. "She's been a member of the School Sisters of Notre Dame since she was seventeen years old—more than
thirty-five years. Her entire life has been spent in service to
others. She was a freedom marcher in Selma, Alabama, in the
sixties. She set up workshops on race relations for the National Catholic Conference on Interracial Justice. She was a
protester against the war in Vietnam. And just last year,
Prime Minister Golda Meir gave her the State of Israel Medal
for years of work she's done encouraging understanding between Christians and Jews. She founded the Institute of
Women Today, which isn't just this," the aide said, indicating
the journal-writing workshop. "It also has classes to teach
women their legal rights. And it has vocational classes to
teach job skills. Sister Traxler has all sorts of projects going
on." The aide smiled. "There's a saying about her. Sister
Traxler is like rust. She never rests."

When Sister Margaret Burke, the psychologist, began counseling women in the county jail, she and Sister Traxler sometimes compared notes on their respective endeavors, as well
as on individual inmates. Patricia Columbo was a natural
topic of conversation for them.

"When I first read about her," Sister Traxler admitted, "I
was appalled. What she was accused of doing was beyond
belief, beyond reason."

"Yes," Sister Burke agreed. "The savagery of the crime is difficult to get past."

"Very honestly, I thought I could probably never forgive such a person, if she were proved guilty," Sister Traxler admitted. "If it happened to my loved ones, I don't know whether I could deal with it. Has Patty requested any counseling?"

"No," Sister Burke said. "I wish she would; I'd like to try and help her. If she is guilty, she is bearing an almost unimaginable burden right now."

"Would you like me to encourage her to seek some counseling?" Sister Traxler offered. "We're not close, but she is in my journal-writing workshop. We sometimes chat."

Sister Burke declined. "I'd rather you didn't. In her case, I don't think it would be wise to suggest that she needs help; she would probably balk and throw up every defense mechanism she has. This is something she must initiate on her own. She must first admit to herself that she *needs* help; then she must ask for it."

"Do you think she will?" Sister Traxler asked.

"Yes, I think so," Sister Burke replied after a moment's pondering. "It might take her a while."

It took thirteen years.

When Sister Burke saw Patricia Columbo walking across the visiting room at Dwight Correctional Center in 1989, she didn't recognize her. It was only after Patricia opened the door to the small, glass-windowed private room that Sister Burke knew who she was. The girl back at the county jail had been a baby-faced kid; this was a woman in her thirties who had convict eyes: flat, hard. When she came in, Sister Burke smiled and offered her hand.

"Well, Patty, we meet at last. How are you?"

"I'm fine, Sister, thank you. Would you mind not calling me 'Patty'? I prefer 'Trish.' "

"Of course. When did you stop going by 'Patty'?" The gentle probing had begun.

"A few years ago."

"Didn't you like the name 'Patty' anymore?"

"No, I can't stand it. I don't let anybody call me 'Patty' if I can help it."

"I see." Was this because Patty had committed murder and Trish didn't want to accept responsibility for it? The judge who sentenced Patricia had called her a "Dr. Jekyll and Mr. Hyde." Perhaps his evaluation had been valid. Time would tell. "Well"—Sister Burke changed the subject—"I've heard some very good things about you over the years, Trish."

Patricia's eyebrows went up. "Oh? Who from?"

"Just the prison grapevine, the county jail grapevine," the nun replied, a little twinkle in her eyes. "I'm not exactly one of the natives, but I do hear the drums."

"What's been said about me?" Patricia asked.

"Just how well you're doing, how you've adjusted, how you're educating yourself—and especially how you're tutoring some of the younger ones here, ones who can't even read. That's very praiseworthy."

"I don't do it for praise," Patricia told her evenly.

A little tension was building, so Sister Burke cut the small talk and got to the purpose of her visit.

"I understand," she said, "that you're interested in examining your childhood and adolescence to try and determine how you came to be the person you were in 1976."

"Yes. I've tried to do it myself, but I can't seem to get a grip on it. I thought maybe a professional could help me along."

"I see. Have you taken the matter up with the prison psychologist?"

"No, I won't talk to a DOC shrink." She meant Department of Corrections.

"May I ask why?"

"First, what an inmate tells a DOC shrink isn't confidential. Everything you say goes into your prison record; it can be read by the staff, guards, inmate office help, everybody. Secondly, the whole DOC structure, including the psychiatrists and the psychologists, is male dominated. One thing I do *not* need is another man helping me try to solve my problems."

"I take it then that you've had no psychological evaluations since you've been here?" Sister Burke asked.

"Just the intake evaluation the first week I was here. It lasted about five minutes."

"Do you know the results of it?"

"Sure. It was decided that I was a sociopathic personality, and there was no possibility of them rehabilitating me."

"How do you feel about that?"

Patricia shrugged. "They were right about rehabilitating me; *they* couldn't have done it in a million years. I've rehabilitated myself."

"Why do you need me, then?" Sister Burke asked quietly, without challenge.

"To find out how I got into the situation, or condition or whatever, where I *needed* rehabilitating. I want to know what happened to me as a child, and why it happened, and what it did to me."

"Is there some specific element of your childhood that you're referring to?"

"Yes, there is. I was sexually abused as a child. I—I've just started remembering it—"

"I see." Sister Burke nodded. "By whom, Trish?"

"By my—my father."

In the split instant that Patricia's words faltered, in that infinitesimal blink of time, Sister Burke detected in Patricia's voice the scantest hint of uncertainty.

Uncertainty about what, Sister Burke did not know. She was not sure Patricia herself knew.

"Do you want to tell me about it?"

"I'd—like to try, Sister—"

8
June 1970

The Columbo household, when Patricia was fourteen years old, was for the most part placid and relaxed. Frank Columbo had a notorious temper, which could be displayed even in the home, though it was never directed at his wife, daughter, or son. Toward his family, Frank was the epitome of patience and restraint. As far as he was concerned, the world was divided into three places: inside his home, outside his home, and the ballpark at Wrigley Field. Inside his home was where he was most at peace with his existence—except during Cubs games on television, which usually agitated him, or when a neighbor had done something to irritate him. Generally, at home, Frank Columbo was mellow.

It was an uninhibited family atmosphere. Frank and Michael ran around the house in their underwear: Frank in boxer shorts, Michael in briefs. Patricia, though filling out more and more all the time, lolled about in nightgowns. Mary Columbo was the most conservative; usually, if she had on a nightgown, she wore underwear beneath it or put on a robe over it. No one in the house really paid much attention to how anyone else was dressed. It was people *outside* the household who eventually expressed displeasure with the informality.

"Mary," a friend or relative had been known to say in private, "don't you think Patty's getting too old to show off everything she's got like that?"

Mary would shrug. "It's just in the house here." Later, she might mention it to Frank. "So-and-so says she thinks Patty's too old to run around the house in her nightgown."

"Too old? She's just a kid, for Christ's sake," Frank would reply irritably. "Besides, it's just in the house. What the hell's the matter with people anyway? They gotta look for problems?"

Sometimes the comments were about Frank instead of Patricia. "Mary, why don't you buy him some pajamas? At least then he could button his fly. Boxer shorts weren't made for leisure."

"Frank won't wear pajamas," Mary said.

"Well, he ought to wear *something*, Mary. It's not decent."

Mary would shrug again. "It's just in the house." After fifteen years with Frank Columbo, she had absorbed many of her husband's principles, much of his philosophy. If it was in the house, Frank felt, it was all right.

Patricia had her first nightmare when she was fourteen.

The Columbo split-level home had four bedrooms, two up and two down. Frank and Mary had their bedroom on the upper, or main, level. Michael was on that level also; he had been too young when the family first moved in for his parents to feel comfortable having him sleep on a different level. Patricia's bedroom was one of the two on the lower level; her mother used the other room for closet storage or an occasional guest.

It had never bothered Patricia to sleep on the lower level alone. Actually having her bedroom down there gave her a modicum of privacy that the other members of the household did not enjoy; after she went down to bed, it was rare to have anyone else down on that level. And she wasn't afraid down there, or anywhere else in the house; she never felt safer or more secure anywhere in her life than in the house at 55 Brantwood.

Never in her recollection had Patricia experienced a nightmare of any kind—not even one of the spooky dreams experienced by little children; her sleep had never been disturbed by bad dreams. So she was not at all prepared for the frightening experience the first time it happened.

What struck her was its clarity. It was like watching a television picture, or a movie . . .

The man was standing next to her bed, looking down at her, trousers unzipped, flopping a flaccid penis around and calling her name very softly: "Patty, honey. Patty, wake up—"

In her dream, Patricia opened her eyes and stared up at him in revulsion. She didn't speak, but her thoughts in the dream were as clear as the man's words: *He can't do this in my bedroom—*

"Patty, honey, it's me. I love you, Patty. Do you love me, honey?"

Still she did not speak. With a feeling of utter repugnance she watched his limp member begin to thicken and grow, the man rotating his hand on its head now like someone working a throttle.

"Would you like to do it with me, honey?" he asked.

She refused to answer him, her lips in the dream compressed tightly. Her eyes shifted to his face and glared at him in defiance; then they looked back down at his penis, now fully erect, vein laced, throbbing—

"I want to go all the way with you, Patty," the man said, his voice soothing, urging. "Come on now, honey, like a good girl—"

Patricia scrambled to the far side of the bed, close to the wall, turning her back to him. She began to yell.

"No! No! I won't! Nooooo—!"

Then she felt his hand on her shoulder . . .

* * *

"Patty! What's the matter? Patty, wake up!"

Opening her eyes, Patricia stared at the wall inches from her face, not certain whether she was awake or still in the dream. The hand on her shoulder seemed very real. Raising on one elbow, she looked over her shoulder. Her father was there, lying up against her on the bed; it was his hand on her shoulder. She half turned toward him. Her nightgown was up very high, and her long bare legs were bent slightly at the knees. The fly of her father's boxer shorts was parted in front, and his penis, flaccid like the man's had been at the beginning of the dream, was touching her bare thigh.

"Patty, honey, what's the matter?" her father asked. "Are you okay?"

Patricia jerked away from him, away from the touch of his terrible—awful—*thing*. Scrambling to a sitting position, she snapped, "Get away from me!"

"Patty, it's okay, honey," her father soothed. "You must have had a bad dream—"

"Leave me alone!" Cowering, she backed off the foot of her bed and stood, pushing her nightgown down to cover herself. Like a terrified animal she started backing out the door. Suddenly there were footsteps on the stairs coming down from the main level. When Patricia backed into the hall, her mother, in nightgown and robe, was hurrying toward her.

"What's the matter?" Mary Columbo asked urgently. "What's going on down here?"

"Make him leave me alone!" Patricia cried.

In boxer shorts and undershirt, Frank came out of Patricia's bedroom. "She must've had a nightmare or something. I heard her yelling and came down to see what was wrong—"

Patricia turned from both of them and ran upstairs. Frank and Mary followed her. On the main level they looked for her—living room, kitchen, bathroom. They finally found her in bed with Michael, huddled up against him as if he were the older sibling, she the younger. Michael, oblivious to it all, was sleeping as only young boys and the dead sleep.

Looking at his daughter, Frank Columbo sighed wearily and shook his head.

Mary Columbo, waving a hand in exasperation, said, "Leave her." The parents returned to their own bedroom.

* * *

The next morning, after Frank had gone to work and Michael was out in the backyard, Patricia came into the kitchen and poured herself a glass of orange juice. Her mother was at the table with a cup of coffee and the morning paper.

"What was that all about last night?" Mary Columbo asked.

"Nothing," Patricia mumbled.

"Did you have a nightmare?"

"I don't know." She wasn't being evasive. She *thought* it had been a nightmare, but after she woke up and found her father there, with his—his—

"Well, either you had one or you didn't," Mary said impatiently. "Do you remember anything about it?"

"No." She couldn't bring herself to tell her mother about the man in the dream because she knew her mother would ask who the man was. Patricia did not want to bring his face back into her mind.

"Your father said you were yelling 'No, no, no.' Do you remember that?"

"I think so."

"Well, what was that all about?"

"I don't know."

Mary shook her head. "For somebody who woke up the whole house, you don't remember much."

"I didn't wake up the whole house," Patricia retorted. "I didn't wake up Michael."

"An earthquake wouldn't wake up Michael."

Patricia finished her orange juice and put two frozen waffles in the toaster. While she waited for them, she said, "I want to sleep in Michael's room from now on."

"Don't be ridiculous, Patty Ann."

"I'm not being ridiculous. I'm scared down there by myself. Michael's got twin beds. I want to sleep in his room."

At that moment, as if knowing he was being talked about, Michael came in, slamming the back door. Without a word to either of them, he went to the refrigerator, opened it, and stood critically studying its contents.

"Michael," his mother said, "your sister wants to sleep in your room from now on. She says she's scared to sleep downstairs."

"Okay," Michael said. He selected two plums from the fruit drawer and slammed the refrigerator door.

"You don't mind your sister sleeping in your room?" Mary asked in amazement.

"No," Michael said, shrugging. As he started out of the kitchen, Patricia grabbed him, hugged him, and kissed him on the cheek. Michael twisted and squirmed away from her. "Cut it out, Patty!" he cried, wiping off his cheek as if she had put lye on it. That was Michael: he didn't mind his big sister sleeping in his room if she was afraid to sleep downstairs, but no way did he want her *kissing* him.

Patricia tried every way in the world to convince herself that she *had* experienced a nightmare, that it *had* been the man in the dream whose erect penis was exposed to her, and that her father *had* got into her bed only to help her because he had heard her yelling "No, no, no!" She did, in fact, remember actually yelling that—whether partly in her dream and partly in reality, she wasn't certain. Unfortunately, what she *was* certain of was that it had been her father's penis against her bare thigh—that had been *real*.

How much, she wondered, of what seemed like the dream had also been real? How much of the man in the dream had been her father, and how much of her father had been the man in the dream?

The incident tormented her. Vigilantly, she watched her father for some indication, some sign, that would confirm some impure motive on his part. She wasn't sure exactly what she expected: a look, a gesture, a touch perhaps. But as the days and weeks passed following the incident, there was nothing. Frank was no different than he had ever been before the nightmare; he was the same father she had always known.

Still, she refused to go back down to the lower level and sleep alone.

Patricia thought initially that when her father heard about her wanting to sleep in Michael's room, there would be some resistance to the idea on his part. Mary Columbo, of course, predicted an immediate veto of the plan by her husband. Later that first morning, after Michael had said he didn't care, Mary had warned Patricia not to count on it.

But Frank Columbo surprised both of them.

"What does Michael think about it?" he asked that evening.

"He doesn't seem to care, Frank, but that's not the point," Mary said. "The point is, Patty has her own bedroom and she should sleep in it."

"Yeah, but if Michael don't care, what's the big deal?" Frank shrugged. "It'll probably only be for a few nights, until she gets over that nightmare thing. I don't see nothing wrong with it, Mary."

Once Frank had expressed his opinion, Mary didn't protest the matter any further. Mary Columbo now had many years' experience in her role—and knew it well. If Frank thought it was all right for Patty Ann to sleep in Michael's room instead of her own, Mary wasn't going to argue about it.

Beginning the night following her nightmare, Patricia began sleeping in her brother's room.

9
February 1989 and October 1973

Sister Burke pursed her lips in thought for a moment after Patricia finished telling the story. Then she said, "You had a thought during your dream that I think we should explore. You said that, regarding the man in the dream, you thought: He can't do this in my bedroom. *In my bedroom.* Did you feel when you had that thought, that it would have been all right for him to do it someplace else?"

"No, I don't remember feeling that," Patricia replied.

"Did you have a sensation that the man in the dream had been intimate with you before?"

"Yes, very much so."

"Did you have that feeling before he said, 'I want to go all the way with you, Patty'? Or did the feeling come only after he said that?"

"I—I don't know. I'm sorry."

"Don't be sorry," Sister Burke counseled. "It's never our fault when we don't remember something—never." She tapped a forefinger soundlessly on the tabletop. "Now then, you had the sensation that the man in the dream had been intimate with you before. Many times?"

"I—I think so. Back when—I was just a little kid."

"Younger than fourteen?"

"Yes."

"How young?"

Patricia shrugged. "Twelve." She thought about it for a moment. "Ten. Eight." She shrugged again. "Younger even."

"Trish, was the man in the dream your father?"

"I—don't know. I'm not sure—"

"Can you remember any other specific time when your father ever physically touched you like he did when you had the dream?"

"I remember once he kissed me," Patricia said.

"Fathers kiss daughters all the time," Sister Burke pointed out.

"This wasn't a father-daughter kiss," Patricia said. "Nowhere near."

"Tell me about it," Sister Burke said.

One night when she was seventeen, three years after the nightmare incident, Patricia came home later than usual from her part-time job at Walgreen's and found her father slumped in his chair in the living room. He had an open can of beer in one hand and a slack-jawed expression on his face.

"Where the hell you been, Patty Ann?" he asked. His tone was oddly devoid of anger.

"I worked overtime and then went to get something to eat with a couple of the other girls," she said. "I'm sorry, I should have called."

She started past him, hoping he would let it go at that, but knowing with a sudden dread that he would not. Yet, since he was not acting mad at her, she thought she might be wrong. Just let me get to my room, she silently prayed.

"Your mother's in the hospital," Frank Columbo said before Patricia could get away.

She stopped and turned to look back at him incredulously, momentarily speechless.

"The doctors think she might have cancer. Of the colon. They haven't told her that yet, but they told me. They're gonna give her some tests tomorrow to find out for sure."

Patricia was dumbfounded. "But, how—I mean, when—"

"She's been having bad stomach pains for about a week—cramps, like. And diarrhea that was black. And she was losing weight—a pound a day since last Friday. At first she thought it was food poisoning like that—what do you call it, that bad food poisoning?"

"Salmonella?"

"Yeah. At first she thought it was that. But the stomach cramps kept getting worse and worse. So finally tonight I took her over to Alexian Brothers to the emergency room. They examined her and did a blood test, and then they said she had to stay. I sat with her until she went to sleep; then I came home."

"I didn't even know she was sick," Patricia said, as much to herself as to her father.

"How the hell could you know?" Frank Columbo asked accusingly. "You're never home, you're never around." He drank a swallow of beer and studied her sullenly. "For your information, I called Walgreen's from the hospital. They said you wasn't working."

"Well, I—I was working back in the stockroom. Maybe whoever you talked to didn't know I was there."

"Yeah. Maybe. I asked to speak to the store manager—what's his name again?"

"Uh, Mr. DeLuca. Frank DeLuca."

"Yeah, DeLuca. I asked to talk to him but he wasn't there either."

Patricia didn't know whether his remark was an insinuation or not. Probably not, she thought. Hoped. Her father was obviously very upset, very worried; it was only natural for some of what he said to be disjointed. He needed comforting, understanding. Patricia took his hand.

"Come on in the kitchen, Dad. I'll fix you something to eat."

"I'm not hungry."

"Coffee then?"

He shook his head. "No."

"When do you have to go back to the hospital?" she asked.

"They're gonna give her some tests early in the morning before she has anything to eat. By ten o'clock or so, they might know what's wrong."

"I'll stay home tomorrow and we'll go over there together," Patricia said. "Does Michael know?"

Frank Columbo shook his head. "He knows she's in the hospital but he don't know how bad it is."

"Well, let's don't tell him yet," Patricia decided. "We'll say it's probably appendicitis. His friend's mother had her appendix out and came back home in a couple of days, so he knows it's not anything to be afraid of."

"Okay," her father said. "Whatever you think's best."

She still had hold of his hand and tugged it gently. "Come on, let's get you to bed. The best thing for you is a good night's sleep. In the morning I'll fix us all breakfast and get Michael off to school. Then you and I will go to the hospital. How's that sound?"

"Good. That sounds good, Patty." He allowed her to lead him to the bedroom he and Mary shared. At the door to the bedroom, he patted her arm.

"Thanks, honey. I'll see you in the morning."

At the Alexian Brothers hospital the next day, Patricia and her father learned that Mary Columbo had undergone a barium enema examination that morning and definitely been diagnosed with colorectal cancer—but that the doctor felt they had caught it in time and that surgery in the form of a colostomy was recommended, as soon as a few more tests had been done.

"We want to do an intravenous pyelogram to get a good fix on the condition of her kidneys. And a colonoscopy to look at the overall inside of her colon. These are primarily safety precautions to keep the surgical team from being surprised in the middle of the procedure by some condition that wasn't expected."

Frank Columbo grew sullen after the talk with the doctor. "He's lying to us," he said to Patricia as they left the hospital late that afternoon.

"Dad, that's silly," Patricia said. "Why would he lie?"

"He's checking her kidneys because he thinks there's cancer there too. And if she's got it in more than one place, she's not going to make it." He swallowed dryly. "We're gonna lose her, Patty—"

"We are not!" Patricia began to cry. "Don't say that and

don't think it, Daddy! Mom's going to get through this! We're all going to get through it!"

When they got home, they retrieved Michael from a neighbor's house and then Patricia fixed spaghetti for them for supper.

Michael suspected that something other than appendicitis was wrong with his mother, so part of their supper hour was spent pretending to him about her condition and assuring him that she would soon be back home and getting well again. Michael, as usual, kept his own counsel, and gave the appearance that he was accepting his father and sister at their word, but they both knew that it was only a matter of time before the strong-willed boy would demand the truth.

Late at night on the eve of Mary Columbo's surgery, Patricia, back to sleeping in a bedroom of her own again, was awakened by a noise she could not identify, and got up to see what it was. Earlier, she had become aware that Michael was tossing and turning in his bed, and had gone in and sat on the side of his bed and gently rubbed his back for a while until he settled down again. She knew it had to be uneasiness caused by knowing that his mother's operation was imminent; otherwise, as usual, he would have been like a mummy.

When she heard the unfamiliar noise later on, Patricia at first thought it was Michael again, but when she checked in his room he was as still as a statue. Then she thought it might be her father, in the kitchen. It was Frank Columbo, all right, not in the kitchen but sitting in his chair in the living room, staring at the other chair, where Mary usually sat. In the shadowy glow of a nightlight coming from the hall, Patricia was surprised to see that her father was still fully dressed, even though he had gone in to bed two hours earlier.

"Daddy, what are you doing up?" she asked, going over to him. "Why haven't you gone to bed?"

"Why go to bed?" he said. "What for? I couldn't sleep."

"Well, at least get into bed," Patricia said, kneeling in front of him. She put her hands on his knees. "Read for a while; you might get sleepy. At least you'll be resting. You can't just sit there in the dark all night—"

Her father suddenly stood up, almost knocking her backward. She got on her feet to face him.

"I'm scared, Patty—"

She had never heard his voice tremble before, and it both
surprised and touched her. She put her arms around him.
"Oh, Daddy—"

Suddenly he was holding her tightly, desperately, his strong
arms enfolding her, pressing his body against hers with consuming urgency. Bending forward, he buried his face against
her neck and shoulder.

"I'm so scared, Patty—"

"I know you are, Daddy. I am too—"

He straightened and with one hand held her head against
his chest. His arms were like manacles around her body.

"Patty—Patty—"

She felt Frank's hand under her chin, tilting her face up,
and then she felt her father's lips on her lips, kissing her ar-
dently, passionately, not like a father at all, more like—

Patricia's mind reached back more than a decade to the
apartment on Ohio Street, the day her mother had brought
Michael home from the hospital, with the place full of friends
and relatives, and little Patty holding her new baby brother on
her lap, playing with him as she picked up snatches of adult
conversation. Someone had said, "*. . .good that Patty is the
oldest because if anything, God forbid, should ever happen to
Mary, she can help raise Michael and be the woman of the
house . . .*"

Her father's lips were still on hers, Frank Columbo kissing
her like a lover would kiss her—and she remembered the
night of the bad dream, her father's penis against her thigh—

No! her mind screamed. *No! No!*

She wanted to scream the word with her voice, not just her
mind, but her lips, her mouth, and her tongue were all captive
to her father's sudden compulsion, just as the rest of her was
a prisoner of his powerful arms.

Patricia began to struggle and make gnawing, choking
sounds, and as abruptly, as suddenly, as he had taken hold of
her, her father took his lips from hers and dropped his arms
from around her body. Then she could scream at him with her
voice, but she did not. Instead, she backed away, a step at a
time, and said, as she had the night of the terrible dream,
"No. No. No—"

Her father shook his head in despair and confusion. "Patty
Ann, I—I—"

But she refused to listen. All she did was step back and say, "No," and step back again and say, "No," and continue like that until she was in the hall, out of his sight. Then she hurried to her room and locked the door.

And she thought: *I was right about him all along.*

10
May 1976

Exactly one week after the discovery of the Columbo bodies, Ray Rose and a team of his men had under surveillance the home of Lanyon Richard Mitchell at 837 Hilda Lane in Lake Villa, a suburb some twenty-five miles north of Elk Grove Village, and only about five miles south of the Wisconsin state line. Rose was thankful that the twenty-four-year-old suspect hadn't moved any farther away; if he had crossed the Wisconsin line, where Rose had no authority, the investigation could have become mired in interstate paperwork. That sometimes gave people time to put together alibis.

The officers had been waiting for a couple of hours when a 1974 Chevrolet Vega pulled into the driveway, a man driving, a young woman in the passenger seat. "Run the plate," Rose said to one of his men. "RDM seventy-four, Illinois."

Ray Rose got out of his surveillance car, a signal to the other officers to do the same. All coats were unbuttoned, all service revolvers ready to be drawn; none of the officers knew whether this man was a hired killer or a total fraud.

"Lanyon Mitchell?" Rose asked, cautiously approaching the Vega.

"Uh, yeah," the man emerging from the driver's side said tentatively. He suddenly became aware that there were other men around also.

"Investigator Raymond Rose of the Elk Grove Village Police Department," Rose identified himself. "Do you know a woman named Patty Columbo?" he asked.

Lanny Mitchell's face turned as white as field cotton. A fraud, Ray Rose's instinct told him at once. This guy might *carry* a gun, but he would never have the nerve to use it.

"We're investigating the Columbo murders, Mr. Mitchell,

and have reason to believe that you're involved in that crime," Rose told him bluntly.

Lanny Mitchell almost fainted.

Lanyon Mitchell had not, as Ray Rose dreaded, ever been a police officer. For a short time he had been a civilian employee of the Cook County Sheriff's Department, hired under a federal government work program. He *wanted* to be a police officer, or at least *somebody* with stature, but he ended up selling used cars out in the suburbs.

Within twenty-four hours after Ray Rose had found him, Lanny Mitchell had confessed to the following:

He had met Patty Columbo in the fall of 1975.

Patty Columbo had asked him to get her an "unmarked" gun.

Patty Columbo had requested of him that he kill her parents and brother.

Patty Columbo had agreed to pay ten thousand dollars for each of the three members of her family whom she wished to have murdered.

Payment for the murders was to be made by Patty Columbo from the proceeds of the insurance and the estate.

Patty Columbo wanted the killings to occur near a holiday as a present to her family.

Patty Columbo wanted to be present at the time of the killings.

Patty Columbo and her boyfriend, Frank, wanted the killings to occur as soon as possible.

Patty Columbo told Lanny that a door leading from the garage into the house was kept unlocked.

Patty Columbo told him that among the valuables that could be taken from the house were furs and a twenty-three-channel CB radio, but that diamonds shouldn't be taken because she would inherit them.

Finally, Patty Columbo instructed that a family automobile should be taken to give the appearance during the days following that no one was home, which would delay discovery of the bodies.

Mitchell also admitted that he had actively engaged in planning the murders with Patty Columbo, telling her at one point that he would be able to gain entry to the Columbo house by opening the electric garage door, and that once inside the house he could hide, kill the family when they returned, and take certain valuables to give the appearance of a robbery.

He further admitted accompanying Patty Columbo to the house to reconnoiter the premises, but failed to do so because Mary Columbo was unexpectedly at home.

And he admitted having—and turned over to police—photographs and handwritten descriptions of each victim, diagrams of the Columbo house, and other information about the routine habits of the family. Patty Columbo, he claimed, had given him all of it to aid him in the killing of her family.

But Lanny Mitchell stated emphatically that *in fact he had not committed or participated in the Columbo murders.*

Mitchell voluntarily agreed to take a lie detector test. At the Elk Grove Village Police Department, beginning at one o'clock in the morning, Saturday, May 15, the test was administered by polygraph examiner Steve Theodore.

The primary thrust of the examination was to determine whether or not Lanny Mitchell was telling the truth when he claimed he was solicited by Patty Columbo to kill Frank Columbo, and that he did not participate in the killings. That issue was profiled by four questions and answers:

Question: Did you shoot Frank Columbo? Answer: No.

Question: Did you ever actually enter the Columbo house? Answer: No.

Question: Were you solicited to kill Frank Columbo by Patty? Answer: Yes.

Question: Do you know who actually shot Frank Columbo? Answer: No.

Five polygraph tests were administered. The examiner found no significant emotional disturbances indicative of deception, and in his opinion Lanny Mitchell had given truthful responses to the four key questions.

Ray Rose had been right again. Lanny Mitchell was no killer.

With the information given by Lanyon Mitchell, Ray Rose was now ready to move against Patricia Columbo. He dictated a seven-page complaint requesting a search warrant based on two elements of probable cause: first, a statement

from Nancy Glenn that she had "conversations" with Patricia
Columbo in which Patricia Columbo "repeatedly" told her
that she desired to have her parents killed; and second, the
admissions of, and physical evidence turned over by, Lanny
Mitchell. The complaint asked the court's permission to
search apartment 911 on the ninth floor of a building at 2015
South Finley Road in the suburb of Lombard, Illinois, the residence of Patty Columbo and Frank DeLuca.

In the search warrant request, Rose asked for permission to
seize the following:

> a Midland citizens band radio, serial number 04109709;
> a Johnson citizens band radio, serial number
> 023F045-46737;
> a glass lamp with a glass base containing glass circular
> rings;
> a man's wallet containing identification of Frank P. Co-
> lumbo;
> identification of Mary F. Columbo;
> a light brown mink cape;
> two sets of keys containing automobile and house keys
> to the residence at 55 Brantwood;
> an opal necklace with matching earrings;
> all clothing containing apparent bloodstains;
> a garage door opener set to a frequency of 305.20;
> any and all firearms and ammunition;
> a blue T-shirt with a surfer motif; and
> both male and female footwear.

Those, except for the footwear, were the items the investigative team had determined were missing from the murder
house. The footwear was to be seized because two bloody
footprints had been found in the kitchen.

Rose had the search warrant complaint approved by
Gino L. DiVito, an assistant state's attorney, and it was taken
to Judge Marion J. Peterson.

Lanny Mitchell's friend Roman was now also identified—and
much to Rose's chagrin, he *had* once been a policeman.

Eleven years earlier, Roman Iganatius Sobczynski, age

thirty-three, had served as a Cook County deputy sheriff for fourteen months, carrying star number 776. He had left that job and moved up to his current position of recruiter for the Cook County Civil Service Commission.

A records search also showed that Sobczynski was a petty thief. He had been a shoplifter for at least thirteen years, both before and after becoming a deputy sheriff, and had a record of arrests in suburbs of Chicago dating back to 1960. Rose was astonished. How Sobczynski had ever been given a badge and gun was completely baffling to him. But Rose was relieved that at least Sobczynski had been out of the department for more than a decade.

Ray Rose planned eventually to use Roman Sobczynski to substantiate Lanny Mitchell's story, but for now the chief investigator put the ex-cop on hold. Rose had to devote himself to a more pressing matter: the search warrant complaint he had submitted was now approved by a judge.

Ray Rose was ready to confront Patty Columbo.

11
February 1989 and May 1963

When Sister Burke returned to Dwight Correctional Center the following week for their second session, Patricia sought to reassure herself of the confidentiality of their relationship. At the table in the private visiting room, she asked, "Everything we say in here is strictly between us, right? I mean, you don't give information to the DOC or anybody?"

"Definitely not." The nun smiled slightly. "I do not work for the Department of Corrections. I have a different employer altogether."

Patricia was unable to suppress a smile. *Not bad, Sister,* she thought.

"Would you mind talking a little about your mother today?" Sister Burke asked.

"My mother?" What the hell was this? It was her goddamned father who had done those filthy things to her. "What about my father?" Patricia wanted to know, her words just short of a challenge.

"We'll get back to him, of course," Sister Burke assured her. "But if you want to know what influences on you, as a child, helped shape the adolescent personality you became, then we mustn't restrict ourselves just to your father. Weren't there other people in your life?"

"Sure, there were a lot of people in my life. But they didn't all sexually abuse me."

"I'm sure they didn't," Sister Burke allowed. At this point, she apparently suspected that Patricia's father had not abused her either—but she had to determine why Patricia *thought* he had. Sister Burke had seen cases where the mother, for reasons of her own, had convinced her daughter that the father had molested her. It was a good place to begin probing. But with Patricia resisting, Sister Burke reversed her approach.

"If you don't want to talk about your mother, we don't have to."

"I don't *mind* talking about her," Patricia quickly asserted. "What do you want to know?"

"Whatever you want to tell me. Did the two of you get along when you were a child?"

"Yeah, I guess so." Patricia shrugged. "I got along better with my godmother Janet, but I don't think my mother and I had any real problems. She *was* unreasonably hard on me sometimes. Like the time I told the lie at school about having a baby sister—"

Mary Columbo had been terribly upset when she learned that the teachers at Talcott Elementary thought she had given birth to another girl, and that the baby had been named Susie. It was an unreasonable feeling: not quite anger, but more than indignation. Perhaps it was caused by mixed emotions of pride at having given her husband the son he wanted, plus the natural postpartum depression that is sometimes accompanied by feelings of aggressiveness toward other family members.

Whatever the reason, Mary called Patricia a little liar and told her she had done a terrible thing. Her daughter was dismayed by her mother's confrontation; she had all but forgotten the story she had made up for show-and-tell.

Janet Gower tried to pacify Mary, after Patricia ran crying to her about the incident, but the new mother was decidedly beside herself. She not only intended to tell Patricia's father about the deception, but Patricia was also going to have to admit to her classmates that she had deliberately lied to them. The latter stipulation, Mary Columbo asserted, was not her idea; it was the decision of Patricia's teacher.

With Patty bawling loudly and Auntie Janet pleading fervently, Mary Columbo eventually relented and agreed not to tell Frank Columbo—but there was nothing she could do about the school part; that was up to the teacher. Patricia would simply have to do it.

At school the next day, when it was time for show-and-tell, Patricia rose, eyes downcast, and walked purposefully to the front of the room. When she turned and looked up, her gaze swept the faces of her classmates, who were staring at her expectantly. When she had looked at them all, she raised her eyes slightly and fixed them on a set of multiplication tables on the rear blackboard.

"I lied about my mother having a baby girl and naming her Susie," she said clearly, almost studiously. "My mother really had a baby boy. His name is Michael." She glanced at the teacher, then back at her classmates again. "I am a liar," she said evenly. Then, to her teacher, "Is that enough?"

"Are you ashamed that you lied?" the teacher asked.

"I am ashamed that I lied," Patricia told the class. She stood waiting for further instructions.

"All right, Patty, you may return to your seat."

Head held high, eyes no longer downcast, Patricia walked back down the aisle.

With the show-and-tell lie behind her, and her discovery that the presence of a baby brother was not only acceptable but enjoyable, young Patty Columbo looked forward to settling into a routine where she would be, as Auntie Janet had urged, a "big girl" who would help her mother with the baby all she could.

Patricia loved little Michael so much that it was all she could do to wait until three o'clock when school let out so she could rush to the corner, wait patiently for the crossing guard to stop traffic, and hurry home to begin her daily duties.

It was Patricia's job to see that Michael's fresh diapers from the semiweekly diaper service were stacked neatly on the shelf of his changing table; that he always had his little blue blanket over him when he was asleep in his bassinet; and that there was a clean baby towel and washcloth hanging on the end of the Bathinette when Mary got ready to give Michael his bath.

It was all very new, very exciting for the little girl. When Frank Columbo came home after work, he always asked, "Well, did you help your mother take care of little Michael today?"

Patricia would always smile, say yes, and climb onto her daddy's lap to tell him everything she had done to help. She was very proud of herself in the role of big sister, beaming when her mother would exclaim, "Patty Ann is such a big help. I don't know what I'd do without her."

Where she was her mother's "helper" during the day, Patricia became her father's "scholar" in the evening. Frank Columbo couldn't get over how intelligent his daughter seemed to be. He was forever bringing home sets of flash cards, with which he would first test and then teach Patricia. On cold winter evenings they would often sit together until her bedtime, close to the radiator, and go through one or another set of cards: arithmetic, spelling words, state capitals, U.S. presidents—Frank bought them all. And like Mary, he constantly bragged about his daughter. In Carmela's Grocery, he boasted to Michael's godfather, Joe Battaglia, "We went through a set of flash cards last night that were for *twelve*-year-olds, an' she only missed four of them. I hope your godson Michael turns out as smart."

Patricia enjoyed the praise from both of her parents. She loved being the perfect little girl.

One afternoon when Patricia hurried home from school, she saw the familiar red candy truck parked at the curb and found Uncle Gus sitting on the front stoop waiting for her.

"Patty Ann, honey," he said, "your mom took Michael to the doctor; nothin' serious but she said if she wasn't back by the time you got out of school, for you to ride on the rest of the route with me."

Patricia climbed into the bucket seat she had ridden in so many times before and put her schoolbooks on the floorboard. "Where are we working today?" she asked matter-of-factly.

"Logan Square," Uncle Gus said.

It wasn't Patricia's favorite route, but it was okay; a lot of neighborhood candy stores, smaller grocery markets like Royal Blue, and a few cigar stores. At some stops, Uncle Gus could service two or three customers from one parking place in the middle of a block.

"I'll wait in the truck and study," Patricia said. She had been into all of the stores many times; there was nothing new about them anymore. Besides, she had spelling words to memorize.

Whenever they parked anywhere, and Patricia opened a schoolbook on her lap to study, Uncle Gus would conscientiously lock the doors to the cab of the truck and remind her, "Remember, never let nobody in the truck while I'm gone."

"I'll remember," she promised.

Patricia studied her spelling assignment off and on for two hours that afternoon while Uncle Gus restocked his customers in the Logan Square section of the city. Patricia knew the route by heart, so when he came out of the last stop and didn't turn around to start back the other way, Patricia was immediately curious.

"I thought we'd do something a little different today," he told her.

It was late in the afternoon now, the lull just before the evening traffic rush began. Uncle Gus drove to the Logan Square el station and turned into a one-way street that ran parallel to the train tracks. On one side of the street was the back of a row of small office buildings, and on the other a block-long unimproved dirt lot where city commuters parked their cars to take the el downtown. Uncle Gus drove the van over the curb and parked it at the far end of the lot, in the deepening shadows of the el tracks.

Locking the cab doors, Gus opened the accordion partition into the rear and stepped back between the two bucket seats.

"Come on back, honey," he said. "I want to show you something."

Patricia went into the back of the van and Uncle Gus then closed the accordion door and turned on the van's inside ceiling light. It cast an eerie yellow glow over everything. Uncle

Gus spent a moment making sure the accordion door was closed flush with the wall, then he opened a cabinet under the wire-cage candy shelves and pulled out a rolled-up length of carpet and a surplus army blanket.

"How's this for a cozy little setup?" he asked Patricia, unrolling the carpet to lay it on the floorboard between the facing shelves, and spreading the blanket over it. "When I get tired, I can just pull over and take a little rest." He smiled his best Uncle Gus smile. "I think I'll take one right now. Wanna take a little rest with me?"

Patricia shrugged. "Okay." This was kind of funny, she thought. But it must be all right. It *was* Uncle Gus.

They lay down on the carpet side by side, and Gus pulled the blanket partway over them.

"We don't have to go to sleep, do we?" Patricia asked.

"No."

"Good, because I'm not sleepy."

Patricia became aware that Uncle Gus's hands were moving under the blanket, like he might be scratching himself. Presently he reached over and took one of her hands.

"I want you to feel something," he said. Under the blanket, he curled her fingers around something rigid and warm. "You know that little thing Michael's got between his legs," he explained. "Well, I've got one too, only mine is lots bigger. Do you have one of those things?"

"Uncle Gus! You know I don't!" Patricia vaguely remembered times when Uncle Gus leaned in the bathroom doorway and watched her mother giving her a bath. "Only boys have those," she said.

"Sometimes little girls grow them too," Uncle Gus told her. "Are you sure you don't have one?

"Uncle Gus, I *don't*!"

"Well, I wanna check and make sure," he said. "Hold still—"

Patricia felt his hand on her stomach, fingers working their way under the waistband of her skirt, the elastic of her panties, tickling slightly. It was not an unfamiliar experience having Uncle Gus touch her, handle her even; he frequently pulled her onto his lap, picked her up into his arms, patted her head, buttoned her blouses, tied her shoelaces; she was *accustomed* to him. When he put his hand where he was putting it now, she wasn't frightened.

Uncle Gus's hand urged her legs apart a little and his fingertips began touching the soft, smooth folds of her vulva. The contact was not harsh or probing; it was gentle, loving, the way she herself touched Michael; there was nothing alarming about it. It was almost—pleasant.

While Uncle Gus was checking with one hand to see if she had grown a "thing," Patricia could tell by the movement of the blanket that with his other hand he was still scratching himself, very fast now—and breathing heavily—and then he did the funniest thing: he took his hand out of her panties, held his fingers to his nostrils for a brief moment, then put his fingers in his mouth and sucked them like Tootsie Rolls.

Presently Uncle Gus's knees went up, pulling the blanket off Patricia entirely, and the still concealed hand kept scratching furiously as Uncle Gus, eyes closed, sucked and sucked on those fingers that only seconds earlier had been exploring her little-girl femaleness. Patricia stared at him with wide-eyed curiosity. After a moment, his expression tensed, eyes opened and rolled up slightly, and Uncle Gus took his fingers out of his mouth, shoved the hand under the blanket, and seemed to be struggling with something in his back pocket. Then he locked his knees together, catching part of the blanket between them, groaned softly, and abruptly went limp.

For several moments Uncle Gus lay still except for his heavy breathing, and when that slowed he rolled up onto one elbow and smiled at Patricia. "I'm glad you haven't grown one of those things," he said, and gave her one of his winks. When he tossed the blanket aside, she saw that he held a crumpled handkerchief in one hand. His trousers were unzipped too, but the "thing" he had put her hand on was not in sight. "Well, that was a nice rest," he said, getting to his knees and folding the blanket. He had Patricia stand to one side while he put the blanket and carpet back into the cabinet.

Uncle Gus cracked the accordion door to the cab an inch and peered out. When he was satisfied that no one was nearby, he folded it open all the way and they both got back up front.

Driving home, Uncle Gus said, "I don't want you to tell

your mom or dad or Auntie Janet or anybody else about the little rest we took."

"Why?" Patricia asked.

"They might get mad at us. Everybody knows that you're my favorite little girl, and that I'm your favorite uncle. They might get mad at us because we like each other so much. Grown-ups call that being jealous of somebody. You ever heard that word, 'jealous'?"

"No," Patricia said, shrugging.

"Well, that's what they call it: getting jealous. If you was to tell them, they might get jealous—if they believed you. But they might not even believe you."

"Why not?" Patricia asked, puzzled. This was all new, and confusing.

"They might think you was lying," Uncle Gus said easily, "like when you lied in school about having a baby sister."

Patricia turned red and looked out the window. *How did he know about that?* Her mother wasn't supposed to tell.

"Sure, your mother told me," Uncle Gus said, as if reading her thoughts. "She told your father too; he just promised not to say nothing to you about it." Uncle Gus reached over and squeezed her knee. "I'm the only one you can trust to keep a promise, honey. And I'll always believe you, no matter what. But let's don't tell them nothing. What we do in the candy truck will be our secret, okay?"

Patricia did not answer at once. She was still embarrassed, still looking out the side window, watching the lighted stores of Milwaukee Avenue go by, each one of them like a flash-bulb exploding in some dark recess of her ever more cluttered young mind. Somewhere in the swirl of thoughts was an urgent repetitious question: *Am I in trouble?*

She wasn't able to answer herself.

"Okay?" Uncle Gus cajoled.

"Okay," she said.

Patricia would not tell.

Not until years later, when her life was a tragic disaster.

In the little visiting room, Patricia, realizing what she had been saying, stopped speaking and stared almost in shock at Sister Burke.

She had begun the session by telling the nun about the

show-and-tell admission—and before she knew it, was relating something about Gus Latini that had been buried in her mind for years.

"It—wasn't my father," she muttered. "It was Uncle Gus. He was the man in the nightmare. I—don't understand—"

"When the mind doesn't want to deal with something," Sister Burke explained, "it sometimes buries it deeply in the subconscious. Later in life, things that happen can stir up what's buried, stimulate it back to the surface of the mind. When that occurs, the two levels, the two different times, often get mixed up. When the minor incidents with your father took place— and it seems as if that's all they were, Trish, minor incidents— they brought all the buried memories of this Uncle Gus back up. And because your father was there and Uncle Gus wasn't, your mind substituted one for the other."

"My god," Patricia said quietly, slowly shaking her head. "All those years—"

"Time means very little to the human mind," Sister Burke said. "It's very common for children to bury their bad memories for twenty years, even longer. In the case of abused little girls, they frequently don't even begin recalling details until they're women in their thirties. How old are you now, exactly?"

"I'll be thirty-three in a few months."

Sister Burke nodded. Almost textbook perfect.

Patricia stared into space. "No wonder I hated them—"

"Hated whom?"

"My mother—my father—"

"Why do you think you hated them?"

"Because of what Uncle Gus did to me. They should have known. They should have stopped it—" She turned to look at Sister Burke, her eyes and expression charged with bitterness. "It went on for *years*—"

12
May 1964 to June 1966

For a long while, Uncle Gus did nothing more to Patricia than what he had done that first time, except he became more overt. The blanket slipped off his raised knees once, and as she watched what he was doing, almost hypnotized, Gus in turn watched her, seeming to derive even more enjoyment from it. The little girl watched to the end when the "juice"—that's what Uncle Gus called it—came out of the big pinkish-purplish head. That, she found out then, was what the handkerchief had been for.

After that day, Gus never bothered with the blanket, not as a cover; he only spread it out on the carpet so they could lie on it. From then on, he just stretched out beside her, unzipped, and began to masturbate.

It was not until Patricia was eight, going on nine, that Gus began to tire of the routine. One day in the spring, a couple of months before her ninth birthday, when the weather was warm, Gus took off his trousers and undershorts altogether, and Patricia got her first real look at a mature male penis.

At first it frightened her—the big hairy pouch and all the other black hair around his thighs and up his big belly; he looked like an ape, and there he was, looming over her, giving her the frightening feeling that he might come down on her face and suffocate her. She began to whimper.

"Hey, what's the matter, honey?" Uncle Gus asked, his tone genuinely concerned.

"You—s-scare—me—" Patricia sniffed.

"Aw, honey, I'm sorry, I didn't mean to." He dropped to his knees and took the little girl in his arms to calm her. His erection was prominent between them. "I don't ever mean to scare you, Patty Ann. Uncle Gus loves you, you know that." He kissed her on each cheek, then held her at arm's length. "You know Uncle Gus's thing won't hurt you, don't you?" he asked with a smile. "It never has, now has it?"

"N-n-no—"

"There, you see. I just took off my pants because it's so warm today. You can too if you want to."

"I don't—want to," Patricia said.

"Then you don't have to, honey," he cooed. And, suddenly: "Hey, I've got an idea! Instead of me making my juice come out today, why don't you do it?"

"Me?" Patricia frowned at him. "How?"

Gus guided both her little hands down and taught her how to masturbate him.

* * *

If there was any change in Patricia because of what Gus was doing to her, no one appeared to notice it. When Gus was visiting, he acted the same way he always had, and Frank and Mary Columbo treated him with the same conviviality. If Auntie Janet was there, or Uncle Phil, or anyone else who was considered a regular in the Columbo household, they too seemed exactly the same around Gus Latini, and he around them. Nothing had changed, Patricia thought, except with her. Somehow, that didn't seem right, though she wasn't sure why.

At school no one had noticed a change in her either. She had a teacher, Miss Robin, whom she liked better than any teacher she'd had, public or parochial. Miss Robin seemed a lot younger than most of the teachers at Talcott Elementary. She was pretty, with short dark hair and an engaging way with the children in her class. Patricia thought several times about talking to Miss Robin about Uncle Gus; she considered asking her whether it was all right to do what he wanted if he was a friend of her mom and dad, and if he said he loved her. Patricia even fantasized that Miss Robin would smile and say, "Of course it's all right, Patty, dear! Don't you worry your little head about it another minute." How nice that would have been, to tell *someone*, to have anyone, a grown-up, say what she was doing was okay.

But she never got up enough nerve to say anything to Miss Robin. She kept remembering that Uncle Gus had said not to tell *anybody*.

As the years went by on Ohio Street, Frank Columbo, as he had promised, was striving to get ahead in order to improve his family's means. The dream of a house in the suburbs was still theirs, and as the lower West Side continued to deteriorate, the more essential it became to Frank that he move his family out.

At the big Western Auto distribution terminal, Frank had climbed steadily up the ladder of responsibility. Well regarded personally by bosses and union alike, with a solid fifteen years of seniority behind him, and a reputation for steady, efficient performance, he had been pegged by management as the employee to oversee the entire warehouse someday. He was already running the unloading and loading operations, and had built up a tight and loyal little group of subordinates, including secretary Geraldine Strainis, who gave him dedicated, competent support.

Frank Columbo knew that if he worked hard for Western Auto, the company would take care of him in return. But he also knew that what he got back from the company would be what the *company* considered enough, not what *he* considered enough. Frank Columbo did not intend to have his family live on what someone else thought was enough—not when there was other money to be made.

Shortly after Frank took over the unloading and loading operations, he went to see Tom and Ed Machek, the brothers who owned Mulvihill Cartage Company, the trucking firm contracted by Western Auto to redistribute locally the volume merchandise received in its terminal.

"I got an idea for a new business," Frank told the brothers.

His idea was to form a small company to furnish loading-dock laborers for Western Auto. The men who unloaded the big highway rigs and reloaded smaller quantities onto local delivery trucks were hired only as day workers. The firm Frank Columbo had in mind could hire them by the week or longer, and assign them to work the Western Auto docks on a regular schedule.

"Two things would be accomplished," Frank told the Macheks. "First, I'd have better help on my docks because the workers would be steadier and they'd get to know the routine better. Second"—he sat back and smiled—"we'd all make some money."

The Macheks liked the idea. A company named Dock Help, Incorporated, was formed. Edward Machek was president, Thomas Machek secretary, and Frank Columbo and two other investors were principals. Frank Columbo immediately began contracting laborers from the new firm.

A close friend of Frank's suggested that he had to be careful in the new arrangement, since his position might be considered a conflict of interest. Frank shook his head. "It's not that at all," he stated emphatically. "Western Auto ends up with better workers and it doesn't cost them a nickel more. And I make some extra money for me and my family. We're

both better off. That's not conflict of interest, it's free enter-
prise."

Frank was receiving $250 a week from Dock Help. He and
Mary began to drive around on weekends looking at houses
in the suburbs.

The adult influences in Patricia's life when she was nine and
ten years old were distinctly three. First was the familiar influence provided by her primary extended family: father;
mother; little brother, Michael; and godmother, Auntie Janet.
Second was the formal, structured influence provided by the
teachers at Talcott Elementary and the catechism nuns at
Saint Carmichael's. Third was the secret influence of Uncle
Gus and the candy van. And it would be this influence that
weighed heaviest on her young mind, because it was the one
burden in her life that she had to bear alone.

The routine with Gus Latini had progressed far beyond its
awkward, fumbling original effort. Now there was no preliminary talk of taking a "rest," no references to Gus's penis as
his "thing," no necessity for the man to guide her hesitant
hand to his eager erection. Patricia knew her role, knew what
was expected of her as naturally as she knew she had to do
her best with her father's flash cards. So she got right to it.
After all, the quicker she did it to him, the sooner he would
take her home so she could play with Michael.

It usually took Patricia only a minute to make Uncle Gus
ejaculate. Because she did it by rote, with no sense of passion, no understanding of foreplay timing, Gus waited until
he had what preliminary enjoyment he wanted, knowing that
when the little girl's hands touched him, it was almost over.
Both the grown-up and the child had the drill down perfectly.

As far as Gus Latini was concerned, Patricia was *his*. She
belonged to him. He no longer even cautioned her about telling their "secret" to others; if she had not told in all this time,
he was sure she never would. And who would believe her if
she did?

Shortly after Patricia's tenth birthday, Frank and Mary Columbo found the house they wanted. It was in a new section
of Elk Grove Village, a northwestern suburb just past the new
airport. A nice split-level at 55 Brantwood, with two bed-

rooms up and two down, an attached two-car garage, and backyard with a patio, it was situated only a block away from Norton Park, which had a playground; just three blocks or so from Salt Creek Elementary School; and a couple of blocks from the new Grove Shopping Center, which had the convenience of a supermarket, dry cleaners, a variety of small shops, and a big Walgreen's drugstore.

It was a close little community: the fire station and police department were just behind the Grove mall. A medium-size hospital, Alexian Brothers, was only a few blocks down the street. There was a library nearby, a community center, several more parks—Lions Park, Jaycee Park, Burbank Park, Appleseed Park, Audubon Park, and others—nearly all with playground equipment; this was obviously a place meant for families with kids.

One entire boundary line of the township was a forest preserve, another was the western fence of O'Hare Airport, so 50 percent of its perimeter was protected from encroachment of any kind. The other half was taken up by two suburbs to the south: Wooddale and Itasca, both quiet, middle-class communities; and the Salt Creek Country Club, situated on the bank of Salt Creek, a meandering stream that made its way through five Elk Grove Village's public parks before reaching that point. This was the suburbia of the sixties, mainstream America's dream come true, the best of both worlds: employment in bull-shouldered, bustling Chicago, and family life out in the country, a halfway return to small-town living, where the streets were safe, the schools were decent, and people mowed their lawns every Saturday.

When the elder Columbos took Patricia and Michael out to see the house for the first time, it was a toss-up as to which child was the most excited. Michael, of course, was overwhelmed by such expectations as his "own room" and a playground nearby with real grass, not gravel like in the city. Going on four, he did not have to deal with changing schools or other complex emotional problems.

With Patricia, it was a different kind of excitement. Like Michael, Patricia was delighted at the prospect of her own bedroom, decorated as she wanted it to be, and kept private and neat from the sometimes less-than-tidy younger brother with whom she was now sharing a room. The thought of transferring to a new school didn't bother her; she was not especially attached to anyone at the school on Ohio Street, and had really liked only Miss Robin throughout the five years she had attended. But the main thrill for Patricia, the absolute biggest deal of all, was that she would be getting away from Uncle Gus and the now dreaded red candy truck.

Aside from the fact that she didn't like being with him, and that she sensed, despite Uncle Gus's assurances to the contrary, that what they did together was wrong, there was also the enormous burden of having to keep it entirely to herself. It was such a *secret* secret: she could never mention it to anyone. Confiding a demanding problem to someone else, an understanding person, being able to talk about it, to rationalize with another's help, is often one of the most therapeutic antidotes available to a troubled person, and it is one of the most commonly sought and applied. When that avenue of emotional relief is blocked, it can turn the mind into a dungeon in which secrecy, guilt, deception, and shame all vie, singularly and in force, to taint everything else. At ten years of age, Patricia Columbo was trying to cope with a sexual problem, sexual torment, that might have driven someone more mature over the brink.

To be out from under the clandestine oppression of Gus Latini in an escape so unexpected, so simple, seemed like a miracle. She was moved at once to include special words of gratitude in her prayers at catechism and Sunday mass, even though—and this suddenly occurred to her—she had never prayed for help in the three-year sexual straits she had suffered. Maybe, she thought, now that the end was in sight, she had refrained from talking to God about it because it was so—dirty. That was another new admission, that single, simple word: *dirty*. She had never allowed herself to think of what she was doing in that particular term before; Uncle Gus had always told her it was all right to do the things they did because they loved each other so much. Only when there was no love between two people, he had once told her, was it considered "nasty" and "bad."

Patricia had often wondered whether her father or mother would help her if she told them what was going on. She wondered first if they would *believe* her; if so, how would they have helped her? Now, without even knowing it, they *had* helped her: they were eliminating her problem unwittingly, by buying the house and taking her away from the city. At last, she thought with immense relief, she would be free of Uncle Gus and would never, ever, have to admit to anyone the repugnant things she had done in the red candy truck.

That, to ten-year-old Patricia Columbo, was the most wonderful thing of all.

Years later, in the prison visiting room with Sister Burke, the nun would say to Patricia, "So your parents eventually did help you resolve the problem of Uncle Gus, even though they didn't know it. When you say you hated them for *not* helping you, do you mean not helping you purposely, or sooner, or what?"

"I mean," Patricia replied evenly, "that they should have paid enough attention to me to sense that something was wrong. I was their *daughter*, Sister Burke. How could a situation like that have gone on for three years without one of them at least *suspecting* something?"

Sister Burke nodded. "I understand your point, Trish. But I don't think it's accurate to say they didn't discover your problem because they didn't pay enough attention to you. From what you've told me, it seems that you received an abundance of attention from both of them. Even after Michael was born, you were obviously still your father's favorite. As for your mother, she apparently didn't give you the same degree of focus as your father, but she certainly didn't ignore you."

"Then why didn't they see what was happening?" Patricia adamantly pressed.

Sister Burke sighed quietly. "I wish I could answer that, Trish. I wish I had a pat explanation that would satisfy your mind and alleviate your hostility over it—but I don't have. You never mentioned it to them—"

"I couldn't. I didn't know how."

"I understand that. It is far from unusual in these cases. And apparently you had enough composure at that age to also *act* as though nothing untoward was going on. Your Uncle Gus also obviously played his role well enough not to arouse suspicion. And like many in-family child molesters, he was

careful enough to go only so far with you, so that there was
never any physical evidence on your body." Sister Burke
shook her head. "To be fair about it, Trish, there was really
no reason for your parents to suspect anything."

"Maybe not during that first period of abuse there wasn't,"
Patricia grudgingly allowed, "but there was plenty of reason
to suspect it when it started again."

The psychologist stared at Patricia, trying to conceal her
surprise. "Are you saying the abuse resumed?" she asked in
the calm, neutral tone she had taken years to perfect. "After
the move to the suburbs?"

"Yes, it started all over again—and this time I gave my
parents, especially my mother, plenty of reason to be suspicious."

"All right. We'll get into that. But I want you to tell me
first how the molesting resumed. Was it the same as before?"

"It was worse," Patricia said.

13
September 1966

The first thing of any import that Patricia noticed about her
new home was that there were no girls her age on the block.
There were plenty of boys; and there were plenty of girls and
boys who were about Michael's age. But as for the availabil-
ity of playmates of her own gender, Patricia might as well
have stayed on Ohio Street. At least there she had Paula for
a friend. If she wanted to play with girls, she would have to
settle for younger ones.

For a time she tried that, more in acquiescence than by
conscious choice, because the little girls on the block seemed
naturally to gravitate to her; and their mothers, impressed by
Patricia's fastidious appearance, her politeness, and her
demeanor—which was that of a much more mature, responsible youngster—gladly released their little daughters to her
care during the day.

"I can't get over how *grown up* Patty is," was a common
remark heard often on Brantwood Avenue. "She's such a lit-

tle *lady*. I hope my Cindy"—or Nancy or Heather or Tina— "turns out as well."

Playing with the younger girls was a way for Patricia to pass time, but it wasn't really fun. She had already lost interest in many of the things to which they were just beginning to relate. Consequently, Patricia usually ended up not so much playing with them as mothering them. With infinite patience she taught them how to tie shoelaces, color inside the lines, properly enunciate words with which they were having difficulty, sing the lyrics to children's songs. Sometimes it must have seemed to Mary Columbo, looking out at their back patio, that Patricia was running a preschool nursery. And sometimes at dinner, Patricia would say, as she had back on Ohio Street, "I don't know what I'm going to do with Cheryl. She doesn't remember her ABC's from one day to the next."

Michael, meanwhile, had fallen in with Brantwood's male preschool crowd, a boisterous, constantly moving group of little boys who seemed to live by the creed that to be still or quiet was to die. When Patricia had her little friends on the patio, and the boys came into the Columbo yard making their airplane, dump truck, or machine-gun sounds, Patricia would simply tell the girls to ignore them, and she would keep on with whatever activity she was overseeing at that moment. If the boys became too rowdy, or for some other reason disrupted Patricia's "class," she quickly made them aware of their folly. Confronting them with her best teacher-nun impression, she would say, "Don't you *dare* butt into what we're doing! Get out of this yard right now or I'm going in the house and call your mothers!"

She rarely had to threaten twice.

During this period, Patricia once again changed directions in her juvenile ambition. One night at the dinner table she told her parents, in solemn words that made her seem much older, "I think I was born to teach."

It was something she really believed.

In that first summer at the new house, Patricia would also help her mother, or play games with Michael if her brother wanted to stay in, or simply find things to do to amuse herself. Having been so much in an adult world during the years on Ohio Street, she had learned to devise solitary pastimes. Patricia was always so quiet, never a problem, that there were times when Mary Columbo had to call her name to determine whether her daughter was even in the house.

Patricia discovered a new pleasure in Elk Grove Village: the public library. In the city there had been the Damen Avenue branch library, some twelve blocks from where she lived—too far to walk by herself; and none of the adults in her life had ever suggested taking her. Nor had she asked. She had seen the inside of the place only once, on a field trip with her Talcott Elementary class, and she hadn't been impressed by the musty smell, cramped book stacks, and seemingly endless litany of rules recited to them by the librarian in charge. She derived all the more pleasure therefore from discovering the Elk Grove Village library.

The library stood at the intersection of Brantwood and JFK Boulevard. Completely different from the inner-city branch, it was housed in its own rambling single-story building set against a backdrop of park greenery and trees. Inside, Patricia found large windows affording lots of natural light, widely spaced and airy book stacks, pleasantly colored tables and chairs of modular plastic, and an inviting checkout counter tended by librarians who looked cordial rather than stern.

Patricia spent so much time in the Elk Grove library on her first visit that when she got home Mary Columbo scolded, "Where in the name of God have you been, Patty Ann? I was almost ready to call the police!"

"I'm sorry. I was at the library; it's down around the corner at the end of the park. You should see it—it's the neatest place. I brought home an application for a library card—"

For a time after that, the library was the most important thing in Patricia's life. She spent hours there, browsing, reading, occasionally straightening shelves of books if she found them disarranged. Sometimes she was waiting at the library when it opened, stayed all morning, walked home to eat lunch, and returned to spend most of the afternoon there. Then, when she was ready to leave, she would check out a book to take home for the evening. More often than not, the book she selected to take home was one that she could read to Michael at his bedtime. Michael thought it was wonderful to have a big sister who not only had access to all those books but who would read them to him until he fell asleep. Before long, he was conveying requests to Patricia before she left the house.

"Bring home a book about boats, Patty," he would ask, or, "Patty, see if they have any books about cowboys."

For some reason it began to bother Mary Columbo that Patricia was spending so much time at the library. She knew her daughter *was* there, because she dropped in several times to check on her, to make sure Patricia wasn't using the library as a subterfuge, perhaps to meet some of the neighborhood boys in the park. Although only going on eleven, Patricia was tall and beginning to show indications of the woman she would become: she already had shapely legs and a nice little bottom. In another couple of years, when Patricia filled out on top, Mary could foresee the problems there would be with boys; it was something, because of her husband's temper, to which she did not look forward.

Any suspicions she had about Patricia proved to be groundless, however; three times Mary drove over to the library, ostensibly to ask her daughter if she wanted to go somewhere with her, and each time she found her exactly where she was supposed to be, alone and quite innocent.

Mary Columbo should have been relieved, but she was not. It perturbed Mary that Patricia was content to spend her days in such solitary activity. She felt that Patricia should be *doing* something: something more active, something that required some effort, some vigor.

"I swear to God, she's going to turn *into* a book," Mary said more than once to her husband.

To Patricia she would say, "Don't you get tired of going to that library all the time?"

Patricia would answer guilelessly, "I like the library." She saw nothing wrong with what she was doing. A couple of the older boys on the block started calling her a bookworm, but she quickly put a stop to that by calling them assholes, a word she had picked up from her father and on the playground at Talcott Elementary.

Mary Columbo could not be distracted from her nagging misgivings, however; she pestered her husband about it more and more. To calm his wife, Frank started taking Patricia to work with him a couple of times a week. He turned her over to his longtime secretary, Geraldine Strainis, and Patricia was her "helper" for the day. Frank had taken Patricia to work on occasion when she was younger, before Michael had been born. Now, however, an entirely new problem arose: little Michael regularly threw a fit because he couldn't also go along.

"My God, the trouble Patty Ann can cause sometimes," Mary Columbo said. It was a comment she frequently made in front of her daughter. Frank Columbo apparently never pointed out to his wife that she was the one causing the problem in the first place.

Frank also took his daughter—Michael was too little—to an occasional Cubs game at Wrigley Field. That was the year Frank Columbo bemoaned the end of baseball as he had known it; the last year before the old National and American leagues divided into East and West divisions and expanded from eight to twelve teams in each league, bringing in new ball clubs such as Atlanta, Houston, San Diego, and Montreal.

"Montreal, for Christ's sake!" Frank lamented. "It ain't even in America! Next thing you know they'll have the Cubs playing in Mexico or someplace!"

He remained a steadfast fan nevertheless, finding something good to say about the most error-prone player, but never, *ever*, allowing that the team management included anyone above imbecile level.

Patricia enjoyed the Wrigley Field outings with her father. Mary did not care for baseball, and although occasionally one or more of Frank's cronies from work would accompany them, frequently it was just father and daughter. They had club-level seats, ate hot dogs and drank Cokes, and Patricia listened attentively as Frank gave her his personal evaluation of each player who came up to bat. Patricia was aware that her father's passion for the Chicago Cubs was intense; she knew that at no time was his temper more volatile than when he was holding forth on the subject of baseball. An example of that combustibility could be generated by the mere mention of Leo Durocher, the controversial manager of the Brooklyn Dodgers and later the New York Giants. Frank Columbo hated Leo Durocher with a hair-trigger wrath; Patricia had once seen him actually drive his fist through a plaster-board wall over something Durocher had done that infuriated him. His temper might also focus on a neighbor, an auto me-chanic, a politician, or some other outsider, and Frank could still be reasoned with to some degree; but the three members of his household were careful never to challenge him on mat-ters about which he had irreversible opinions, such as the fact that Leo Durocher was not a member of the human race.

But Patricia still spent what Mary Columbo considered an inordinate amount of time in "that damn library." It was as if the mother had made up her mind about the library much as the father had about Leo Durocher. Her arguments sometimes approached absurdity.

When Patricia thought about her mother's attitude years later, from the perspective of the tragedy, she still could not entirely understand it. Was it simply a need on Mary's part to control her daughter, to be in charge of this other female in the household who was moving inexorably through the stages that led to womanhood—and equality with Mary? Was it a matter of status, Mary competing with the only other female love in Frank Columbo's life? Or was it simply a matter—far more common an occurrence than generally admitted—of a parent simply not *liking* the "person" her child was growing up to be, and becoming over-critical as a result?

As Mary became more determined in her efforts—whatever their motive—to control her daughter, and her com-plaints against the library became more farfetched—Patty wasn't getting enough fresh air, Patty was ruining her posture with all that sitting—she eventually hit upon a final desperate argument and a cruelly ironic, and terrible, solution. Mary Columbo decided that the library was a place where sex per-verts lurked to lure little kids away. She decided to curtail some of Patricia's time there by sending her into the city now and then to spend the weekend with Auntie Janet.

"Gus said he'd take her on Friday afternoons," she told Frank. It seemed he had a new route, closer to the suburbs. "He said it won't be no trouble at all to come by and get Patty."

When Patricia heard the news, it was all she could do to keep from screaming.

*   *   *

"Did you tell your mother you didn't want to start riding in the truck with Uncle Gus again?" Sister Burke asked, when Patricia finished telling her the story.

"I didn't put it that way specifically," Patricia replied. "But I made it clear to her that I didn't want to go visit Auntie Janet once a month."

"That's not exactly the same thing," Sister Burke pointed out. "Did you indicate to your mother at all that you had a reason, a *good* reason, for not wanting to ride in that truck?"

"I—no, I guess I didn't." Patricia stared off into space, biting her lower lip.

"What about your father?" the nun asked. "Did you complain to him?"

"A little. Not much. Gus was one of Dad's best friends; I'd never have had the nerve to tell him what Gus was doing."

"Why not, do you suppose? Don't you think he would have believed you?"

"Yes, I think he would have believed me. It's just that I would have been too ashamed to tell him."

"Why would you have been ashamed? What was happening wasn't your fault."

"I—I was afraid somebody—my mother—might think it was." A slight tremor rose in her voice. "And, dumb as it may sound, I couldn't get past that promise I made to Gus. What we were doing was *our* secret; I wasn't to tell *anybody*. I took that very seriously."

"That was natural," Sister Burke assured her. "In spite of what this man was doing to you, he was nevertheless a figure of affection and authority. And you trusted him, I presume."

"Oh, yes." Patricia nodded emphatically. "I know it's strange, but there were times when he was the only real dependable person in my life."

"Yet you were relieved to be rid of him when you moved out of the city," Sister Burke reminded her.

"Yes. Because I didn't like what I was doing in that truck."

"Which is why you resisted reestablishing the relationship, correct?"

"Yes. I didn't want to start all that again."

"But your efforts failed?"

"Yes."

"When the association started again, did you resist Gus himself?"

"I—I think I did. I tried to." Patricia shook her head in uncertainty.

"Tell me," Sister Burke gently probed, "about how it was when the relationship started again."

"I'm not sure I can," Patricia said. She turned in her chair, shaking her head at the wall.

"Eventually you will need to."

The room was completely silent for a long, heavy minute. Then, haltingly, Patricia started telling her visitor what she wanted to know.

"I was—very tense—the day it started again . . ."

14
September 1966 to May 1968

Patricia sat board-straight in the passenger seat of the candy truck, staring straight ahead through the windshield.

"How have you been, honey?" Uncle Gus asked.

"Fine," Patricia barely mumbled.

"Have you missed going for rides with your old Uncle Gus?" He glanced over at her, smiling.

Patricia merely shrugged.

"I sure have missed you," Uncle Gus said after a moment. "It's been real lonely doing the route by myself all the time."

Patricia sat stolidly, determined not to respond. She knew what he intended to do to her; she was trying desperately to think of a way to prevent it.

"A lot of the people on the route have missed you too, you know that?" he said. His voice was ingratiating, almost fawning. "They're always asking me, 'Hey, Gus, where's that pretty little helper of yours? How can you work the route without her?' "

Patricia said nothing.

As they now drove along a street that took them past the forest preserves, Uncle Gus said, "Boy, this sure is nice out here, huh, Patty? Sure beats living in the city, with all the noise and dirt. Just look at the woods, all those trees. You ever go into the woods to play?"

It was a direct question, so she had no choice but to answer. "No."

"You know what I think would be fun?" Uncle Gus said cheerily. "Let's take a drive through the woods. We've got plenty of time; your Aunt Janet don't get off work for another couple hours—"

Patricia clenched her jaw and blinked back tears. She knew exactly what was coming.

In the back of the truck, Uncle Gus took off his trousers and shorts.

"Remember this?" he asked, fondling himself, flipping his stiffening penis up and down like a length of hose.

Patricia looked away and said nothing. Uncle Gus sat down on the blanket and took her hand.

"Hey, come on, what's the matter? This is your Uncle Gus. Don't you love me no more?"

She did not reply.

"I asked don't you love me no more?" he repeated. There was the slightest hint of harshness in his tone this time.

"Yes, I still love you," Patricia said, shyly, reluctantly.

"Hey, that's my girl!" Uncle Gus said happily. He drew her to a sitting position next to him. Casually, he lay his left hand on her leg, just above the knee where the hem of her skirt reached. "You know, Patty Ann, I knew I could count on you. I mean, why shouldn't I be able to, right, after all we been through together? Remember, it was always you and me whenever things got bad at home or at school. I was always there for you, any time you needed me."

As Gus spoke, he began moving one hand up and down Patricia's leg, the other up and down his now rigid erection.

"You want to help Uncle Gus feel good, don't you? Show me that you love me?"

"I guess," Patricia allowed.

"Come on and give me a great big kiss then." He leaned toward her, moving his hand up and squeezing her thigh, and kissed her on the lips. Then he said, "How about letting me kiss you in the other place too—"

"I don't want to today," Patricia said, trying very hard to

sound like her teachers had always sounded, like she herself sounded when she conducted her make-believe classes with the younger children on Brantwood. "Maybe I'll let you kiss me there next time."

"Aw, honey," Gus said, pulling a long face, sounding terribly disappointed. "I've been looking forward to it all week. It's all I've been thinking about, just being with my little sweetheart that I love so much, and kissing her in our secret way. Now you're going to let me down." He paused a beat for effect, and added, "I don't think you really love me at all."

"I do so, Uncle Gus," the girl declared. "You know I do!"

"Well, then, let me kiss you there," he coaxed. His hand slid smoothly up her dress until his fingers reached the fabric of her panties and pulled them down. He buried his face in her lap.

"Oh, that's good, Patty," he said between movements of his lips and tongue, "that's so sweet—it tastes so good, Patty—oh, honey, tell Uncle Gus you love him—"

"I love you, Uncle Gus," she dutifully replied.

When she said it, Gus held her tightly against his face and groaned into her flesh. He tensed, shivered, and finally was still.

Patricia knew then that it was over.

Patricia started attending Salt Creek Elementary, about three blocks from her new home. It was a typical, newer, more attractive school than the gray-concrete-and-red-brick-factory kind of building that Talcott had been; its architecture was modular; its rooms were convertible, expandable; its windows let in lots of light; its hallways were wide and uncluttered.

Patricia liked the school. Her reading habits all summer had put her well ahead of her peers and it became apparent almost at once that she was the brightest student in the class. Shortly after the semester began, her teacher asked, "Patricia, were you a grade ahead in the Chicago school?"

Patricia had not been, nor had she taken any special classes, which was the teacher's next inquiry. But she had, with her previous teacher's approval, helped slower students when she completed her own assignments. Her current teacher found that very interesting. Several days later, Patricia was offered the opportunity to become a teacher's aide in the kindergarten class a couple of hours a day, providing her own studies were complete. Patricia enthusiastically accepted.

Her new schedule began at once. Now she didn't have to sit idly in her own classroom waiting for others to finish; she handed in her completed assignment at once, and was given the next one immediately; in this way she accumulated up to an hour of free time in both the morning and afternoon, which she was allowed to spend helping kindergartners. As admirable as the idea appeared to be, it was, in reality, one more instance in which the girl was removed from the company of her peers and put into another environment, placed on another level, where she was required to function almost as an adult—because to the kindergarten children, she *was* an adult.

Neither Patricia nor the teachers involved saw a disadvantage in the routine; Patricia really relished the work. At eleven, she was the perfect mother hen, teaching her little chicks their numbers, letters, colors, shapes; patting little heads, tucking in little shirts, tying little shoelaces.

Patricia was maturing all the time—but she was not really growing up the way a young girl was supposed to grow up.

Throughout the first school year in Elk Grove, Mary Columbo continued to insist that Patricia spend one weekend a month in the city with Auntie Janet.

"It's good for Patty," Mary said to her husband. "Gives her something different to do."

Little did Mary know. The visit meant taking a ride with Uncle Gus, who always came by for her in the candy truck on the appointed Friday afternoon. And always stopped to park somewhere on the trip in. After a while, it just seemed to Patricia the price she had to pay, and it was something she was powerless to change.

Patricia knew she was beginning to change physically. Where once her chest had been as flat as Michael's, there were now two buds starting to swell and puff a little; her examination of herself in the bathroom mirror at home told her that she would soon have "boobs" like some of the girls in the upper grades.

Of course, Uncle Gus noticed them too.

"You're gonna have great tits, honey," he would tell her. "They're gonna be nice and big and round, and have the kind of nipples that get real hard and stick out nice. Don't ever tell anybody I told you so, now; that's part of the secret we've got, you and me. But one of these days, honey, you're gonna have a wonderful set of jugs."

Uncle Gus had begun talking to her now as if she were more of an adult. He asked her lots of questions, most of them boy-girl related, often embarrassing.

One time Uncle Gus asked, "Do you know what it means for a boy and girl to go all the way?"

"I'm not sure," Patricia replied very quietly. She *thought* she knew, but she didn't savor the idea of discussing it with Uncle Gus. Why did he have to *talk* to her about such things?

"When you're a little older, you and me will start going all the way," he told her, as if promising her some special gift. "You're gonna really enjoy that."

Patricia sat in the passenger seat, staring straight ahead, saying nothing, frozen. Inside, she felt frightened and sick.

A spot of resentment suddenly developed in Patricia's young mind. It was a tiny dot that, like the pupil of an eye abruptly subjected to a lesser light, dilated immediately to compensate for the darkness. One moment it was only a pinpoint speck on her consciousness, something that vaguely troubled her from time to time; then without warning it enlarged and spread—and became a scourge of which her mind could not rid itself.

Why were they letting this happen to her?

Her mother.

Her father.

Auntie Janet.

Her godfather, Uncle Phil.

Why hadn't someone realized what was going on and done something about it?

Each time it happened now, after each monthly incident, for several days Patricia would try to think of *some* way to tell *someone*.

Invariably she started with her mother. Girls were supposed to be able to talk to their mothers; in school, in girls' hygiene lectures, they preached, "Share your problems with your mother, get advice from your mother, remember that your mother can be your best friend—and that she has already gone through everything that you are going through at your age."

Mary Columbo was eliminated almost as quickly as she was considered. First of all, Patricia was certain that her mother had *not* gone through what she herself was going through. Second, she knew instinctively that Mary Columbo wouldn't believe her.

"I'm wise to you, young lady," she could hear her mother say. "You're just trying to get out of doing something you don't want to do. Shame on you for saying such an awful thing about your Uncle Gus!"

Next, her father. Patricia knew Frank Columbo's short-fuse temper, his inclination toward violence. If he believed her, and she thought he probably would, he would most likely go after Uncle Gus and kill him, beat him to death with his bare fists, as he had frequently said he would like to do to Leo Durocher. No, telling her father was out of the question; it would cause more trouble than it would solve.

Her godfather, Phil Capone? Patricia really didn't see him as a defender or a protector. He was just a big, burly, likable Italian, in the restaurant-supply business, who came around to visit the family quite often. Definitely not a knight in shining armor.

Auntie Janet herself was the closest Patricia could come to having a confidante. But what prevented her from telling her godmother about the situation with Uncle Gus was the fear that Janet Gower already *knew*—or at least suspected. Patricia didn't see how Auntie Janet *couldn't* know. Janet was always the first person to see her after it happened. Surely she could tell by Patricia's face, by what was on the outside, how Patricia felt on the inside. It might be understandable that her parents, who wouldn't see her until Janet took her home on Sunday, or Uncle Phil, whom she didn't see that often, might not recognize any signs, pick up any clues—but why didn't Janet detect something?

In her confused but rapidly maturing mind, Patricia vacillated from one conclusion to another. Janet *knew*—and was doing nothing about it. Janet *didn't* know—but should have. Sometimes she thought it would drive her crazy.

Months passed.

The school year ended. Another summer came and went. Another school year began.

Patricia continued to develop physically: breasts, buttocks, thighs, hips. Downy pubic hair appeared. Strange things began to happen to her body; new feelings manifested themselves. She was twelve, nearly a teenager. A bright, exciting future of learning and teaching awaited her in junior high school. But her outlook for what lay ahead, instead of being eager and positive and sunny, was filled with trepidation.

Patricia knew with each passing day that she was getting closer and closer to the time when Uncle Gus would go all the way.

"That was the first time I ever thought about suicide," Patricia recalled in prison two decades later. "I thought if that man put his cock in me, I'd never be able to face another human being. For some reason, I had it in my head that people would *know*, that they'd be able to look at me and *tell*. I don't know if I thought my eyes would change color or I'd break out in a rash or what. I just knew I wouldn't be able to stand it; I'd have to kill myself."

"Even with that increasing fear," Sister Burke asked, "you still could not bring yourself to tell anyone about Gus?"

"No, I couldn't. I tried not to even think about it. I only had to put up with it once a month at that time, so I just accepted it. When that one weekend a month was over and I got back home, I'd just lose myself in school and other things, knowing it would be a whole month before I had to go through it again. I think I could have gone on like that indefinitely if Gus hadn't started talking to me about actual intercourse. Going all the way. That was what terrified me, what started me thinking about killing myself."

"How far along did that thought process take you?" Sister Burke asked. "Did you think about *how* you would kill yourself?"

"I was thinking about slashing my wrists with a razor blade in a tub of water. That was the only way I knew of; I had read that in a book. I was going to do it on one of the weekends I was with Aunt Janet. I was afraid if I did it at home, Michael might see me dead like that. I knew it would scare him."

"You were twelve years old then," Sister Burke said. "Had you intended to leave a note to anyone, explaining why you had killed yourself?"

Patricia shrugged. "I don't think so. If I did, I don't remember it."

"Thinking back, if you *had* decided to leave a note, who do you think you would have written it to?"

"Auntie Janet," Patricia replied without contemplation. "I think she would have been the only one, besides Michael, who would have been sad; who wouldn't have been mad at me for doing it."

Dear Lord, Sister Burke commented to one of her colleagues after that visit, the conclusions we sometimes cause our children to reach. Monstrous.

"When did you stop thinking about suicide?" Sister Burke asked later in the session.

"When I was saved from Uncle Gus the second time," Patricia replied. "Auntie Janet saved me—without even knowing it . . ."

15
May 1976

At 7:00 A.M. on Saturday, May 15, in a cool drizzling rain, four cars of officers drove quietly up to the high-rise apartment building at 2015 South Finley Road in Lombard. It was eleven days after the Columbo family had been murdered.

Ray Rose technically was in charge of the officers, because he was in charge of the Columbo case, even though the group included his deputy chief, William Kohnke, and Lt. Frank Braun of the Cook County Sheriff's Office, as well as assistant state's attorneys Colin Simpson and Terry Sullivan. Others in the group were sheriff's deputies Gene Gargano, Roy Fiske, and Glenn Gable; investigators Michael Severens and John Landers, and evidence technicians Chris Markussen and

Robert Salvatore, all of the Elk Grove Village Police Department. Several officers from the Lombard police had also joined them.

One of the state's attorneys, Simpson, remained by the building's front door; Gene Gargano and John Landers also remained downstairs. Rose and the rest of the men rode the elevator to the ninth floor.

"I wish she lived in some other apartment," one of the men cracked. There was some soft chuckling. The number of Patty Columbo's apartment was 911, which was the emergency police number then coming into use across the nation.

On the ninth floor, the officers proceeded to the apartment door and Lieutenant Braun knocked. He knocked several times before a male voice inside finally asked, "Yeah? Who is it?"

"Police officers," Braun announced. "We have a search warrant legally authorizing us to search the premises. Open the door, please."

There was no immediate response from inside. Braun knocked again.

"Open the door, please. We have a search warrant."

"Wait a minute," the male voice said. "I want to make a phone call before I open the door."

"We're police officers," Braun said. "I'm holding my identification up to the peephole in the door for you to see. We have a search warrant and you must open the door immediately."

Now the officers heard a female voice inside yell, "You motherfuckers aren't coming in here!"

"If you don't open the door," Braun advised, "we'll have to kick it in."

"You guys are fucking animals!" the female voice yelled back.

Ray Rose now motioned to two of his men, Mike Severens and Bob Salvatore. "Kick it in," he ordered.

The other officers moved aside and Severens and Salvatore began kicking at the apartment door. They took turns kicking for five minutes. The door did not budge.

"Check the hallway and stairway," Rose said to several men. "See if you can find a fire ax. We'll chop it down."

The men looked but found only fire extinguishers, no axes. Finally Rose turned to the Lombard officers.

"Can you get a couple of firemen over here from the Lombard Fire Department? With axes?"

"Sure." One of them had a field radio. He began communicating a request for fire department assistance. Meanwhile, Severens and Salvatore resumed kicking. Finally the male voice inside the apartment conceded.

"Okay, okay. Wait a fucking minute! I'll open the door!"

The apartment door opened to reveal Frank DeLuca, barefoot, bare chested, wearing only trousers. Behind him, Patty Columbo, also barefoot and clad in a black jumpsuit, was holding on to the collar of a large, agitated, black German shepherd.

Ray Rose entered the apartment and handed DeLuca a folded sheet of paper. "This is a copy of our legally authorized search warrant," he told him.

Sheriff's Deputy Roy Fiske stepped past Rose toward Patty. "You'd better put that dog somewhere before it gets hurt," Fiske said.

Patty started dragging the dog toward the bedroom. "Come on, Duke, come on," she said.

"Not in there," Fiske said. The bedroom had to be searched too. "Put him out on the balcony."

Rose walked farther into the apartment. On a table he saw an open notebook. Its paper looked exactly like the sheets of paper he had obtained from Lanny Mitchell, on which were written the daily routines of Frank, Mary, and Michael Columbo, as well as a hand-drawn sketch of the house at 55 Brantwood. Rose motioned for one of the evidence technicians to bag the notebook.

Lieutenant Braun meanwhile had come in and was scrutinizing the small living room. On an end table he saw an ashtray containing several cigarette butts that he recognized immediately as being the brown-wrapped More brand cigarettes. Braun recalled that similar cigarette butts had been found in Mary Columbo's abandoned Oldsmobile, which had been found and which one of Braun's men, Gene Gargano, had processed. Braun had an evidence technician collect and mark the contents of the ashtray.

On a kitchen counter, Braun also saw a small stack of

snapshots. The top one showed Patty Columbo, naked, performing fellatio on a naked man whose head was not visible
in the photo. Braun had the photos collected also.

At this point, the officers decided to take Patty Columbo in
for serious questioning. Glenn Gable and Roy Fiske were assigned the task. Gable went over to her.

"We're taking you in, Miss Columbo," he said. "Would
you like to get your shoes and coat?"

Gable went with her into the bedroom where she got a pair
of black strap shoes and a rose-colored trench coat. Gable
then handcuffed her wrists behind her, and he and Fiske took
her down in the elevator.

Outside, it was still drizzling. Patty had not put her shoes
on, merely held on to them, and now she was carrying them
behind her back; the trench coat was thrown over one shoulder. Gable recited her Miranda rights to her and put her into
the rear seat of a police car. He got in with her, leaving Fiske
to drive.

The last time Patty had been in a police car was when she
was a juvenile and had been arrested for using a credit card
that wasn't hers. She had burst into tears and asked to call her
daddy.

This time she had no daddy to call.

16
May 1968 to May 1971

Janet Gower, the person Patricia thought should have rescued
her from Gus Latini, finally did—in a way Patricia never
would have foreseen.

Janet Gower got married.

Her groom, Bill Morgan, was, like Janet, a longtime employee of Illinois Bell. For Patricia, the marriage was totally
unanticipated; she didn't even know Mr. Morgan—and suddenly he was "Uncle Bill." At this point, the honorary title of
"Uncle" might well have been abhorrent to her, enough to
make her dislike Bill Morgan just on general principles. But
that wasn't the case. If anything, Auntie Janet's new husband
almost filled the role of cavalier hero by the simple act of

moving Janet away from the old Ohio Street address. They
moved out to the far West Side, much nearer to Elk Grove
Village than before. Patricia didn't think she would ever forget Mary Columbo's statement: "Well, you'll be able to see
Auntie Janet a lot more often than once a month now that
she'll be living closer. And your Uncle Gus won't have to go
out of his way to drive you in anymore."

It was over.

Just like that, without fanfare or celebration, Patricia knew
instinctively that her long intimacy with Gus Latini had come
to an end. She would never, no matter what, have to get back
into that terrible candy-delivery truck again.

It was over. Period.

And Gus Latini never had gone all the way with her. Too
bad, *Uncle* Gus.

Patricia was secretly joyful. That night in bed, she cupped
both hands between her legs and softly cried tears of happiness.

Adolescence now began for Patricia Columbo without conscious blight. As she moved on to Grove Junior High School,
she felt good about herself for the very first time, as if she
had shed an awful impurity. She was just like everyone else
now; there was no hidden taint, no dirty little secret she had
to keep. No longer did she have to look down at the floor
when she talked.

In junior high school she thrived. There was so much more
to *do*. In addition to classes, the school was bristling with social life: study groups, clubs, teams, cliques, circles—every
get-together had a name. There were unscheduled but regular
caucuses before school, during lunch, after school, anytime;
interminable note passing; conversations on the run, between
classes; constant planning—especially among the girls: it was
like a hive filled with queen bees. And most of their gatherings, when analyzed, were simply to plan other gatherings.
But it was so much *fun*.

And then there were the boys.

Shooting up in height in their teens, beginning to sprout
traces of facial hair, walking around red-faced half the time,
too loud, too awkward, discovering crudeness, forever fixing
hungry eyes on newly expanding bustlines, most of the boys

were not—in the opinion of the girls—cool. There were occasional exceptions: a football team captain, a basketball team center, a class president, someone who owned a motorcycle, someone who had been "crushed" by a brief "affair" with an "older woman"—read *senior* high school; these were the anomalies, the ones who were surreptitiously watched, studied, discussed, analyzed. All the rest of the boys were jerks with a capital *J*.

Patricia was not at all preoccupied with boys, but you couldn't have proven that to Mary Columbo.

"Patty, why don't you come right home from school like Michael does?" she would ask suspiciously.

Patricia would shrug. "I just have things to do."

"What kind of things?"

"I don't know. Just *things*."

"Are you meeting boys after school?"

"No," Patricia would answer with exaggerated exasperation, "I'm not meeting boys."

Mary wasn't keen about some of Patricia's clothes either.

"My God, if that skirt was any shorter, you'd get arrested for indecent exposure! Where'd you get that skirt anyway?"

Patricia, patiently: "At Yorktown Mall, Mother. You were with me when I bought it."

"I didn't realize it was so short. I think you ought to get longer ones."

Patricia rolled her large brown eyes. "They don't *make* them any longer, Mother. This is the style."

"Some style. You better hope your father don't see you in that."

Patricia felt that her mother didn't "understand" her. She was not alone; most of her friends at school felt the same way.

"Mothers," one of them said with a learned air, "don't like it when we start growing up. They've always dealt with us as kids; now they have to start dealing with us as young women. Most of them don't know how to handle it."

To Patricia, that was *deep*. She gave a lot of thought to it. Eventually, she decided that her friend was absolutely right.

To Sister Burke, years later, Patricia would reflect, "I think the relationship with my mother was probably pretty normal at that point. At least, it seemed normal, based on what my girlfriends were saying about *their* mothers. I mean, all of our mothers sounded as if they were pretty much alike; one of us would say something about her mother and halfway through it the rest of us would find ourselves nodding, you know, like, yeah, we had all been through the same thing she was talking about."

"So your life," Sister Burke observed, "pretty much settled down at that point, would you say?"

"Definitely. When I was sure—I mean, *absolutely* sure— that the thing with Gus was over and done with, I made up my mind to forget it entirely. Looking back, I think I actually programmed myself to do that; whenever a thought or a memory of what he did would pop into my head, I had this trick I'd use to purge it. There was this song that was real popular at the time, called 'Raindrops Keep Falling on My Head,' that B. J. Thomas made a record of, so every time the thing with Uncle Gus would pop into my mind, I'd get rid of it by singing that song to myself. If I could, I'd sing it out loud—it nearly drove Michael crazy at home; if I was in class or somewhere like that, I'd just concentrate real hard and sing the words in my mind. That's the way I got rid of Gus Latini for good."

"That's the way you put him into your subconscious, you mean," Sister Burke corrected. "Unfortunately, we never rid our minds completely of undesirable thoughts; if we could do that, there'd be no need for people like me." The little nun-psychologist smiled one of her brief, rare smiles. "I imagine you're thinking: What a blessing *that* would be."

Patricia smiled back. "You're finally wrong about something, Sister. As difficult as these sessions have been, I'm really very glad to have met you." Her smile faded and she turned her eyes away in embarrassment. "You're the first person from the free world who's meant anything in my life in a long time—" She swallowed dryly. "I—I'm not sure I'll ever understand myself—but whatever understanding I do achieve will be because of you."

"Only partly, Trish," the nun said. "We're in this together. I couldn't help you a bit if you didn't *want* to be helped, and if you weren't willing to help yourself in the process. Getting to know ourselves, coming to terms with all our strengths and weaknesses, addressing our own flaws directly—that's the real rehabilitation." She smiled again—twice in one session, a new indoor record. "Now then, that is sufficient mutual praise for today; let's get back to work—"

Sister Burke now moved the counseling sessions toward learning how Patricia's life—the life that Patricia called "normal" following the end of her defilement by Gus Latini—had derailed again. The psychologist believed the cause could be Patricia's nightmare, which they now knew had been about Uncle Gus, but which Patricia thought was about her father.

"Your 'Raindrops' song apparently served you very well," Sister Burke concluded some five or six months after their sessions had begun. It was summer now and they were allowed to stroll the grounds instead of being confined in the little visiting room. "The song worked so well, in fact, that when you dreamed that you were being abused in your own bedroom, you weren't certain who the man in the dream was. What Gus had done to you was by then so deeply buried in your subconscious that the molester in the dream was unidentifiable. You didn't put a face on him until you woke up and saw your father's face. It was incredibly unfortunate that you also saw your father's penis, and that it touched you. All those things combined to convince you that your father was the man in the dream. And because the man in the dream was associated with your past molestation, your mind simply blamed your father for all of it. Just as I thought months ago."

"What made you suspect it that soon?" Patricia asked.

"Your voice, at first," Sister Burke told her. "It faltered; you weren't quite sure yourself, even though you thought you were. But when I really knew was when I was driving back to Chicago that night and something suddenly dawned on me. Something we both should have realized."

"Which was?"

"When you woke up and found your father lying next to you, he had no erection. He was there to comfort you. As a father."

They went beyond the trauma of the dream.

"Let's talk about how the household functioned *after* you

had the nightmare," Sister Burke said. "Your mother was opposed to you sharing Michael's bedroom, but your father saw nothing wrong with it?"

"Yes. I learned later that Dad only let me do it because he thought it wouldn't last long; he thought I'd get tired of the arrangement and go back to my own room downstairs. He had no idea how frightened of him I was at that time, or how suspicious I was of his motives. I watched him like a hawk whenever he was around, looking for some little sign to reinforce what I thought he was trying to do to me."

"Was there tension in the household, do you recall?"

Patricia shook her head. "Just with me, I think. Maybe with Mom, a little. Dad, no. Michael, never."

"Michael didn't resent you intruding on his privacy at all?"

"No." Patricia smiled slightly. "He *tried* to from time to time, but he couldn't quite bring it off." In spite of the smile, her eyes welled with tears. "Michael loved me more than anyone ever loved me—"

Sister Burke sat quietly to allow Patricia to compose herself. This was the first time Patricia had made any direct reference to her relationship with Michael. She had never publicly commented on the death of her brother or her feelings toward him prior to that time.

"That year," she told Sister Burke after she had regained her composure, "the year I was fifteen and Michael was eight, was when both of us really learned what it meant to be brother and sister. In spite of the fact that he was my little brother and was seven years younger, he helped me through a really bad time that year."

"Do you want to tell me about it?" Sister Burke asked. "Are you ready to talk about Michael?"

There was desolation in her expression. Her voice was haunted as she said, "As ready as I'll ever be, I guess . . ."

17
Summer 1970

Contrary to Frank Columbo's prediction, Patricia's wanting to sleep in Michael's room did not end a "few nights" later as he thought it would. A week passed, another, several more. Patricia showed no inclination toward returning to her own bedroom on the lower level. Her father began to fidget about it.

"I didn't think it would last this long," he admitted to his wife when she reminded him, "I told you it wasn't the right thing to do."

Frank pondered the dilemma. He considered moving Michael downstairs, but decided that wouldn't be fair to his son; Michael loved his room and had it fixed up exactly as he wanted it. The problem was to get Patty *out* of there; Frank simply didn't feel it was an acceptable enough arrangement to continue indefinitely.

He finally came up with a solution: he and Mary would move downstairs and give Patty the master bedroom. In presenting the plan to Mary, he emphasized that it would give them, the parents, privacy from *both* kids: they would have the entire lower level to themselves at bedtime, because there would be no reason for either kid to come down there. Mary, still shapely and attractive in her late thirties, and a woman who enjoyed intimacy with her still quite virile husband, liked the idea at once.

The change in sleeping accommodations was made.

"Now," Frank explained to Patricia, "you don't have to be scared of being downstairs all alone. You'll have Michael up here with you."

On the one hand, Patricia liked the idea; having Michael close by, even though he was younger and smaller, nevertheless gave her a sense of security. On the other hand, she could not help being suspicious of the move, particularly after she heard it mentioned in casual conversation that it had been her father's idea. That gave her pause for thought. Why had he done it? To make it *look* like he was moving her to a less isolated section of the house? When she analyzed it, she decided that it might be—*could* be—only a ploy. He now had her mother downstairs, out of the way. And while before, when Patricia was downstairs, he had to have an excuse, a reason, to go down there, now he had all the reasons in the world to go *upstairs*. The kitchen was up there, the phone was up there, the front and rear doors were up there; if he said he heard a noise and came up to investigate, who would challenge him? He could wander around her bedroom at will with complete impunity. And Michael, in the other bedroom, would really be no deterrent at all; everyone knew he slept as if he were drugged.

Patricia could not help it: she still felt vulnerable. Each night, after she heard her parents go downstairs to bed, she quietly left her own room and went in to sleep with Michael.

The summer she was fourteen, the big thing for Patricia and her classmates was the municipal swimming pool. It was *the* place: to meet, to be seen, or observe others, to lie in the sun, occasionally even to get into the water and swim.

When Patricia walked around the pool toward the vending machines, she got plenty of looks from the boys. Growing taller, still slender, she was now as well or more developed than any other junior high school girl at the pool. Gus Latini had been correct about one thing: her breasts showed promise of perfection, and her hips and buttocks were already in excellent proportion with her long, slim legs and tiny waist. Add her shoulder-length dark hair and deep, dark eyes, and she was a comely young girl indeed. Her two-piece patterned swimsuit was not a bikini—but it didn't have to be.

At home that summer, Patricia endured much the same kind of hassle from her mother about the municipal swimming pool as she had earlier about the library.

"What's the big attraction at that pool anyway?" Mary wanted to know. "You go there every day of the week."

"Everybody goes there," Patricia said. "It's fun."

Once Mary had the audacity to say, "Instead of going to that pool every day, why don't you go to the library for a change?"

Patricia could only stare at her mother in disbelief.

Patricia met Jack Formaski in the casual way most teenagers meet. She had seen him around a lot and knew he lived nearby. Jack was a year ahead of her in school; she knew that because he played on the junior varsity football team. She thought he was "cute." And she sensed that he liked her looks too, because he began to say hello to her when they saw each other at the pool. And she caught him staring at her at odd times, showing up on her block to "hang out" with some of the older boys who were Patricia's neighbors.

Before long, they found things to talk about: mutual acquaintances; the junior high school they would both be attending in the fall; singer John Denver; the television show "Hawaii Five-O"; "Peanuts" in the comics. At some point they began to ease away from others in the group just to talk, just to be together.

Finally, Jack asked her out. "Uh, would you like to go for a drive sometime? I got my license and my dad lets me take the car a couple nights a week. I could come by your house and pick you up."

"I don't think my parents would let me go for a drive," Patricia told him. "But I could tell them I was going to the movies. *Airport* is playing at the Cinema Two; I could say I was going to see that. You could pick me up in front of the movie."

They made the date.

When Jack picked Patricia up that night, he asked, "Where do you want to go?"

"I don't care," Patricia said, then immediately decided, "Let's go to Pizza Hut; we can get pizza by the slice. And don't worry about money; I've got some."

"I'm not worried about money," Jack said, slightly embarrassed. "You don't have to spend yours."

They went to Pizza Hut. In a little booth, they each ate a slice of pepperoni pizza and drank ice-filled Cokes. There was a coin-operated record selector right in the booth, and Patricia played "Bridge Over Troubled Water."

"I just love this song," she said, dropping in a quarter and pressing the same button three times.

When they finished eating, it was close to eight o'clock. Jack asked, "Uh, you want to go for a drive?"

"Sure."

Jack drove down Arlington Heights Road, toward Higgins Road. Patricia didn't have to ask where they were going; everyone in junior high knew where boys with cars took girls when they went for a ride.

At Higgins, Jack turned left into Busse Woods, a section of the forest preserves. The road cut through an area of tall pine trees belting the deep woods on each side. Patricia had heard a lot about Busse Woods. In the ninth grade, a girl had left school suddenly and it was later rumored that she had gotten pregnant on a picnic table in these very forest preserves. Some boys, she had heard, carried blankets in the trunks of their cars, just in case they "got lucky."

They passed a number of places to pull in and park, but Jack seemed to know where he was going so Patricia said nothing. Presently he turned into a narrow lane leading to a small parking area at the beginning of several hiking trails. One other car was already there. Jack parked well away from it and checked to make certain the doors were locked.

"Have to be kind of careful out here," he said.

In more ways than one, Patricia thought.

They turned to each other in the front seat and Jack put his arm around her. Although it was Patricia's first normal experience as a teenager petting in a car, she slipped effortlessly, naturally into Jack's arms and they began to kiss. Jack's technique was awkward, his embrace clumsy. He was not inept, merely unskillful; he fumbled a lot. Patricia had to unbutton her own blouse and let him feel one of her breasts in its cotton brassiere. When he squeezed too hard, she whispered, "Easy—"

She was wearing a midiskirt with snaps up one side that opened a slash up to her thigh, so it was an uncomplicated matter for him to slip his hand all the way up to the crotch of her panties and feel the heat intensifying there. He did not rub or knead, merely cupped his hand there and held it in place.

Jack's hand presently went back to her breast, his fingers exploring hungrily. "Undo your bra," he whispered.

"No," Patricia said. "Not this time."

"Jesus, Patty," he moaned.

He became more energetic, desire mounting, and they began to French-kiss, their mouths wet, young tongues trying to fuse. His fingers went up her exposed leg again and she could feel his fingers trying to work under the taut hem of her panties. She didn't want to say no again, but she didn't want him to go any further, either.

Patricia knew exactly what he wanted her to do—whether from subconscious memories of the candy van, or simply through natural assimilation of information in her maturing process. And somehow she seemed to know too just how to terminate the growing passion she was encountering. She rested one hand on the bulging erection in Jack's pants and began to rub it back and forth.

A moment later he ejaculated in his pants.

18
September 1970 to September 1971

Patricia went steady with Jack Formaski for nearly a year without letting her parents know about it. She knew she would meet resistance from both of them, so rather than try to cope with that, she simply kept the relationship to herself. Perhaps she was accustomed to secrecy by now. At any rate, because she was smart enough to see him only before the curfew hours set for her, Patricia's parents did not become suspicious.

Michael found out, of course; Michael seemed to find out everything through his network of little friends who eavesdropped, as he did, on older sisters and brothers. He didn't inform on Patricia, however, preferring instead to extort small gifts—whistling yo-yos, baseball cards—in exchange for his silence.

To get out of the house to see Jack, Patricia used various excuses such as going to a girlfriend's house to study, or going to a basketball game at school. On weekends she said she was going out with her girlfriends to the ice rink to skate, or shopping, or to a movie. Once she was out, Jack would pick her up at Grove Shopping Center, several blocks away, and they would go to one of the parks or to Busse Woods if the weather was warm, to one of the big indoor shopping malls in another suburb if it was cold. Often they ran into other couples they knew and went somewhere for Cokes and fries, or just hung out in a public place where they could loiter and talk.

Those were fun times, innocent times, the kind of times parents frequently seemed not to understand.

Times that Patricia had to lie about.

Busse Woods, with its quiet, even eerie privacy, was their main sanctuary when they wanted to be strictly alone. The dark forest was a place where they could unabashedly hold, touch, caress, and kiss each other without fear of a sudden adult reprimand, a harsh word, a disapproving look. They could be what they felt like being: silly, brazen, audacious, shameless, passionate. No need to blush or to be afraid, or maintain the dull reserved behavior that parents seemed to expect of them.

Patricia and Jack adjusted to each other after a few outings and compromised on a physical routine they could both live with. Jack, of course, unaware that he was stirring memories in Patricia, wanted to "go all the way," but Patricia would not agree to *that*. Nor would she give him the "head" he yearned for. She didn't deprive him of ejaculation, but she had made up her mind that he was not going to deposit his semen any-where *in* her. Little packs of Kleenex became a staple in her purse.

Jack was pretty much free to do as he pleased otherwise. She allowed him to range with his eager hands wherever he chose. Between her legs, inside her panties, he could rub, tweak, cup, tickle, whatever, as long as he did not attempt to penetrate, even with a finger, beyond her labia. Jack usually did not try to assert himself beyond what he knew to be Patricia's prohibitions, because other than momentarily, he wasn't frustrated by her treatment; as soon as he unzipped and took it out, she always got him off with her hand.

As far as Patricia's own satisfaction was concerned, she had never climaxed and didn't realize what she was missing. Her pleasure lay in having a steady boyfriend, and letting others—not her parents—know about it.

After Patricia had secretly dated Jack Formaski nearly a year, she decided to present him to her parents. It was ridiculous, she felt, to continue walking up to Grove Shopping Center so that Jack could pick her up. He got his own car toward the end of the school term that spring of 1971, a neat little Camaro, and Patricia saw no reason why Jack shouldn't come to the house to pick her up. They wouldn't be going to the same school together the following semester; Jack would be entering Elk Grove High, and Patricia would have to transfer for one year to the newly opened Lively Junior High, whose district would include her block on Brantwood. So her time with Jack was going to be limited strictly to evenings and weekends; there would be no more eating lunch together, no more quick kisses and touches during the commotion between classes, no more holding hands following the afternoon junior-varsity football games, in which Jack, becoming brawny and muscular, always looked so sexy in his jersey with the big number on the back of it.

It was going to be a fun summer: get-togethers at the muni pool, now made up of couples instead of girls on one side, boys on the other; movie dates; baseball games; jaunts down to the Loop; Sundays on one of Lake Michigan's beaches; a *really* fun summer. And Patricia saw no reason why it should be tainted by her having to sneak around. Anyway, she was tired of having to bribe Michael; the mercenary little bandit had worked his way up to getting a percentage of her allowance every week. Patricia couldn't wait until *he* got a girlfriend; she wasn't going to blackmail him—instead, because she knew how embarrassed boys became when initially stricken by the opposite sex, she intended to tease him relentlessly.

After making up her mind to tell her parents about Jack, Patricia, who by now was practically incapable of doing anything in a direct manner, went about planning it. Needing a story that made sense and at the same time offered a course of action that both her father *and* her mother would consider at least acceptable, she finally came up with something.

For eons, her parents had been drumming into her head to associate only with "nice" kids. So, she decided to tell them that some of the not-so-nice boys at school had been giving her a hard time. It was nothing all that serious, nothing really physical, and *certainly* nothing her father needed to consider going to see the class counselor about; it was just adolescent stuff—pestering, annoying; a lot of girls went through it at school. But in her case it was all over now; this one guy had been *really* nice to her and started walking to class with her so that the bullies wouldn't bother her.

This guy—his name was Jack—was a junior-varsity football player, really nice looking, a nice dresser, nice reputation; everything about him was nice, nice, nice. Well anyway, he had his own car, a Camaro, and he had asked if she would like to go to a movie sometime, and she had said she would ask her parents and let him know. He would come by in his Camaro to get her and they could meet him and see for themselves how nice, nice, nice he really was.

It sounded good, she thought.

Patricia practiced the story in front of her mirror. Presentation, she had learned, was important. She drilled herself, striving for sincerity without eagerness, plausibility without perfection, credibility without creating suspicion.

When Patricia felt the time was right, and after making certain her extortionist brother was not in the house, she cornered her parents in the living room and laid it on them. They listened attentively. When she finished, she was both surprised and delighted to find that there was no significant resistance. Her father put his sports page aside to ask a few perfunctory questions.

"What's his last name?"

"Uh, Formaski."

"Polack, huh?"

"I guess so." She shrugged.

"What's his old man do?"

"I'm not sure. Something in the building trades."

"Those Polacks are usually handy with tools," Frank Columbo allowed. He looked at his wife. "What do you think, hon?"

Mary shrugged. Whatever Frank said, as usual.

"Okay," her father consented, "have him come around. Only nothing serious, understand?" He pointed an intimidating finger at her.

"Nothing serious," Patricia agreed innocently. She went into her bedroom and grabbed the handiest notebook she saw. "I have to run over to the library," she said.

Jack was parked over there waiting to hear how it turned out.

"How did your parents take to Jack when you introduced him?" Sister Burke asked in one of their sessions.

"Dad liked him," Patricia replied. "Jack was the kind of kid that fathers want their sons to grow up to be: he was well built, athletic, nice looking, clean, polite; if he'd been Italian instead of Polish, I think Dad would have started thinking seriously of him as a potential son-in-law."

"How did your mother feel?"

"The same." Patricia grunted softly. "Mom *always* felt the way Dad felt."

"And Michael?"

Now Patricia grunted aloud. "Jack and Michael were crazy about each other. Jack didn't have any younger brothers and he kind of adopted Michael. We took Michael with us on half of our dates; we took him to movies, ball games, to the beach. Dad started calling Michael our chaperon." Patricia sighed a melancholy sigh. "We had a great summer that year, the summer of seventy-one. It was the last good summer of my life—eighteen years ago."

"That," Sister Burke recalled, "was about a year after you had the nightmare. How were your feelings toward your father at that time?"

"Pretty normal, I guess. I don't think I was afraid of him trying to molest me anymore; that had kind of gradually faded away—and the incident when Dad kissed me so passionately hadn't occurred yet. I still had the bedroom upstairs, but I hadn't gone into Michael's room to sleep in a long time."

Sister Burke referred to some notes she had. "It had now been about three years since the sexual abuse by Gus Latini ended. Do you recall what your feelings or thoughts were about him?"

Patricia frowned. "I don't think I had any. I didn't consider him a part of my life anymore."

"Did he continue to be a friend of the family and still come around?"

"Not as much. Once in a while my parents would mention something about his work keeping him busy, that kind of thing. When he did come over, if I knew about it ahead of time, I'd manage not to be home. My mother and I got into it one time about that; she said I was going to hurt his feelings."

"Did you ever think about the things he did to you when you were younger?"

"Never," Patricia replied emphatically. "My only feeling was that I wanted to stay away from the man. I knew I didn't like him, but I wouldn't let myself even *think* about why. I was having a perfect summer and I tried very hard to avoid anything that would spoil it."

"Is this the same period," Sister Burke asked, "you were referring to when you said Michael helped you through a really bad time?"

"It was right after that. Summer vacation was over and school had started again . . ." Patricia's words trailed off and she stared down at the tabletop.

"Do you want to tell me what the really bad time was, what brought it on?" Sister Burke asked, possibly wondering if it had something to do with Gus Latini again. But it did not.

"It was Jack," Patricia said. "Jack caused it . . ."

19
October 1971

One Saturday a month or so into the new school year, Patricia went shopping with her mother. Jack had called to break a date to go roller skating that afternoon, saying his father wanted him to stay home and help with some chores—mostly yard work, which Jack hated and which he complained bitterly about.

"I told him we had a date to go skating and he didn't even care," Jack said glumly.

"Oh, it's all right," Patricia assured him. "Just go ahead and do it. We'll go skating next weekend. Are we still going to see *The French Connection* tonight?"

"Sure. I'll pick you up at seven—that is, if my dad doesn't decide we should paint the house or something."

Toward midafternoon, Mary Columbo asked Patricia if she wanted to go out shopping for a while. "I've got to get Michael some jeans and there's a sale on today."

In the car, when they were driving past a hospital, Patricia said, "I've been thinking about becoming a candy striper. My counselor at school handed out an information sheet about it yesterday." Candy stripers were high school girls who helped the floor nurses in hospitals, so named because they wore red-and-white striped uniforms, like candy canes.

"Really?" Mary Columbo said, smiling at her daughter. "Did I ever tell you that I once wanted to become a nurse?"

"No!" Patricia replied, surprised. She had never imagined her mother having any ambition at all except to be a housewife.

"Sure," Mary confirmed. "When I was a little girl, that's all I ever played: being a nurse, with my dolls for patients."

"No kidding?" Patricia was amazed; she had never thought of her mother as a little girl with dolls either.

That day in the car was one of the rare instances in which mother and daughter learned they had something in common. They had never been close, these two. For years it had seemed to them that if they could just live in the same house without confronting each other in serious—really *major*—conflict, it would be significant accomplishment enough. Their minor discords, they both came to realize, were trivial and quick to pass, seldom resulting in anything but the most short-lived bad feelings—which, like the problems themselves—were quickly forgotten. Mary, of course, knew nothing about Patricia's now deeply buried feeling that her mother should have recognized what was happening to her at the hands of Gus Latini and done something about it. That notwithstanding, it was a delightful surprise to both of them that day when the subject of nursing bonded them together for a few minutes in a common dialogue.

They had been talking with such enthusiasm that Patricia paid no attention to the direction they were traveling, and presently was surprised to find them leaving Elk Grove Village.

"Where are we going anyway?" she asked.

"Town and Country Mall," her mother said. "In Arlington Heights."

"Why are we going all the way up there?" Arlington Heights was one of the suburbs several miles north of Elk Grove Village.

"Because that's where the sale is," Mary Columbo said. "The way your brother goes through jeans, I want to buy them as cheaply as I can."

At the mall, they did the necessary shopping first, then just browsed. It was when they were walking between stores that Patricia suddenly stopped and stared incredulously at a table just inside the railing of one of the mall's several snack shops. Jack Formaski was sitting there with a pretty blond girl. They had burgers and drinks in front of them. On a chair next to the girl was her coat and a pair of roller skates with white leather uppers. The girl herself was wearing a fuzzy white turtleneck that perfectly complemented her rosy cheeks and flaxen hair.

"Oh, Christ," Mary Columbo muttered to herself when she saw what Patricia was staring at. She took her daughter's arm. "Don't make a scene, Patty Ann."

"I wouldn't dream of it," Patricia replied, fuming but in control. Removing her mother's hand from her arm, she walked over to the railing that bounded the snack shop's table. "Hi, Jack," she said sweetly. "Get all your yard work done?"

"Oh, hi, Patty." He stood up, turning scarlet. "Yeah, I did. Oh, I tried to call you but you weren't home. Oh, Patty, this is Lorene Roberts; she's in my homeroom. Lorene, this is Patty Columbo."

"Hi, Patty." Lorene had a Debbie Reynolds smile.

"Hi, Lorene," Patricia said. "You guys been skating?"

"Yeah." Lorene kept smiling. "Had a really neat time."

Jack looked past Patricia and waved at Mary Columbo, still standing where Patricia had left her. "Shopping with your mother, huh?" he said. Patricia had never seen him turn quite so red.

"Yeah," she replied, keeping her voice as pleasant as she could. "Trying to get Christmas ideas for my dad and my boyfriend. We sure didn't expect to run into anybody we knew way out here." For a split instant she locked eyes with Jack. "Bet you didn't either." Patricia glanced at her mother. "Well, better run, Mother's waiting. Nice to meet you, Lorene. Bye, *Jack*."

In the car, before she started the engine, Mary Columbo tried, in her own way, to ease some of the hurt and anger she knew her daughter was feeling. "Listen, Patty, you can't take a thing like this too hard. He's not worth it."

Patricia, staring straight ahead through the windshield, was not to be consoled. "Leave me alone, Mother, please," she said tightly. "Just leave me alone."

Mary Columbo left her alone.

Patricia and Jack did not go to see *The French Connection* that night. He called for her at seven, as scheduled, and she left with him, and they even drove to the theater where the new movie everybody was talking about was playing; drove there in stony silence, Patricia staring straight ahead in Jack's car as she had in her mother's on the way home from the mall. Jack parked in the theater lot and turned off the headlights, but neither of them made any move to get out.

"Okay," Jack said at last, "I guess you're mad at me, right?"

"Yeah, I guess I am," she replied. "Wouldn't you be if it was the other way around?"

He did not answer.

"Well, wouldn't you?" Patricia demanded.

"Sure, I guess so," he said grudgingly.

"Guess so, hell!" Patricia snapped. "You know goddamn well you would! You flipped out that time I took a handful of popcorn from another guy's box at a football game! And here I catch you *out* with another girl! You took her skating, didn't you?"

"Not exactly. I met her over there."

"Did you know she'd be there?"

He shrugged. "Yeah, kind of. She told me she went every Saturday."

"And you didn't really have to do all that work for your dad, right? I mean, that whole song and dance about being pissed at your dad was all bullshit, right?"

"Look, Patty," he said evenly, "I've been trying to find a way to tell you something, but I just haven't been able to figure out how. I think we ought to start going out with other people. Both of us. We've been getting too serious about each other—"

"*We?* You're the one who gets too serious! You've been trying to fuck me for a year, Jack! If I'd left it up to you, I'd probably have a goddamn kid by now!"

"All right, maybe it is me," he allowed. "Whoever's at

fault, I think we've gotten too serious and I think we ought to date other people."

"Are you telling me we're breaking up?" Patricia asked flatly.

"Not exactly." He shrugged again. "I just think it would be, you know, better if we didn't just date each other."

"I see," Patricia said. "And this Lorene that I met today, I suppose she's one that you want to date?"

"Well, we're in the same homeroom and—"

"What the hell has that got to do with it?" Patricia demanded angrily. "Are you going to date every girl in your goddamned homeroom?"

"I might, if I feel like it!" Jack retorted, suddenly as angry as she was. "You don't own me, Patty!"

"Right! I don't own you!" Patricia folded her arms and stared straight ahead again. "Take me home, please."

"Look," he said, slipping an arm around her shoulders, "we don't have to spoil the night. We can still go to the movie—"

"Sure!" she exploded. "Then we can go park in the woods and I can jack you off, right? Well, fuck you, Jack! Jack *yourself* off tonight, *Jack*! Now—*take*—*me*—*home*!"

Red-faced, Jack started the engine and screeched out of the parking lot, laying down rubber in his wake.

Patricia couldn't believe the relationship was over. After all the fun they'd had together; there had been so *many* good times: football dances, the municipal pool, school parties, the beach, hayrides, skating. Not to mention the hours of intimacy they had shared parked in the forest preserves— intimacy that was not only physical, not only sexual, but, Patricia believed, also based on deep affection that each had for the other, on mutual devotion. She and Jack had been in *love*.

And it was *real* love, too, she thought; she had loved Jack sincerely. True, Patricia had told her parents—practically *promised* her father—that her relationship with Jack would not become serious; but that had been an idle vow, like assuring your mother that you would never let boys touch you in certain places. It was a pledge asked for and given out of personal obligation; no one expected it to be kept. Patricia *had* become serious about Jack Formaski, and she knew in her heart that he felt the same way about her.

So it was not over; it couldn't be.

When Jack had brought her home after their argument on the theater parking lot, Patricia had marched into the house, gone directly to her room without a word to her family, and slammed the door.

For the rest of the weekend Patricia brooded, and all through the next school week. After school she came directly home every day and would not go back out for any reason, in case Jack called to apologize. Every time the telephone rang, she all but jumped out of her skin—but she refused to answer it, instead urgently telling her mother and brother what to say if it was for her: "Just a minute, I'll see if she's home," and then tell her who it was.

But Jack's call never came.

As each day of the week passed, Patricia became more dejected and downcast. She began to regret the angry things she had said, to censure herself for having been so harsh. After all, no one was perfect, she reasoned—and all she had to do to confirm *that* was look in the mirror. If Jack truly loved her, he was probably so devastated by her ugly words that he didn't know *how* to apologize; he was probably afraid to come near her. Poor guy, she finally convinced herself, she really had been too hard on him.

By the time the weekend rolled around, Patricia had all but made up her mind to apologize to *him*—with a disclaimer. She would tell him she was sorry for all the nasty things she had said, if he would agree that it had been his fault she had said them. He would have to admit that he had been the one who triggered her outburst. And, most important, he had to apologize for lying to her.

The latter condition was very significant to Patricia. As a consummate liar herself, it was essential to her that Jack realize the magnitude of his deed because *she had never lied to him*. She prided herself on that. He was the *only* person she could say that about; she lied, when she felt it was necessary, to everyone else. That was the reason it had hurt so bad to see him there in the mall. Not so much that he was with another girl, but that he had lied to Patricia to be there.

But she was willing to meet him halfway, to end what she was certain was their mutual misery. She would wait most of the day Saturday, a full week since their argument; if Jack didn't call her by five o'clock, she would take the initiative and call him.

As it turned out, neither of them ever called the other again.

At two o'clock Saturday afternoon, Michael stuck his head in the door of Patricia's room and said, "Jack's driving up and down the block. He's got a girl in the car with him."

Stopping in the middle of cleaning her room, Patricia looked at him suspiciously. "Michael, are you joking with me?" she asked sternly. "If you are, it isn't funny."

"I'm not joking!" Michael declared indignantly. "If you don't believe me, go see for yourself!" He stalked down the hall, muttering, "Nobody ever believes anything I say! I'm gonna quit telling people things!"

Patricia went to the living room and looked out the window. She stood there several minutes without seeing Jack drive by. Her mind began to generate thoughts like, "That little savage Michael, wait until I get my hands on him—"

Then the Camaro appeared, coming around the corner off Lancaster, moving slowly down her side of the street.

It was Jack, all right.

And he did have a girl in the car: Lorene, the blonde he had been with at the shopping mall.

"See, didn't I tell you?" said Michael, coming up beside her.

"I'm sorry I doubted you, Michael," said Patricia, swallowing to control her voice. "Please accept my apology."

"Sure," Michael said, shrugging. He walked away.

In the next few minutes, while Patricia still stood there, Jack drove by three more times: once again in the same direction, and twice in the opposite direction, so that the driver's side was closest to the house. Both those times he slowed and studied the house intently. Patricia knew he couldn't see her in the window unless she opened the sheer drapes—but that was obviously what he was trying to do. He wanted to make sure she saw them. It was his way of telling her they were through.

Patricia's lips compressed and she thought: *All right. If it's over, it's over. Let's end it. I'll give you what you want.*

After he passed by the fourth time, Patricia went outside and stood in the middle of her driveway, hands on hips, waiting. Michael, who had already gone outside, tossed a football to one of his friends and came over to her.

"What are you doing?" he asked.

"What does it look like I'm doing? I'm standing here."

"I know, but what are you standing like that for?"

"Like what, Michael?" she asked impatiently.

"Like you're mad at somebody."

"Because I am. Now leave me alone!" Her brother shrugged his habitual shrug and turned away. Patricia immediately regretted snapping at him. "Michael, I'm sorry," she said, reaching out to briefly touch his arm. "Someday you'll be older and you'll understand."

Several moments later, the Camaro cruised by again. Patricia locked her eyes onto it and held them there, following it all the way toward her and all the way away from her. As it passed directly in front of her, she looked unblinkingly at Jack and he looked back at her. There was a slight smirk on his face, but it was met with nothing that would increase his gratification; Patricia's expression was as inscrutable as a death mask. Her head turned slowly and her eyes never left his face, but she might as well have been looking right through him.

Satisfied now? she asked him silently as he drove on down the street.

Patricia let him go all the way around the curve in the street, out of sight, before she turned and marched back into the house.

She made it into her bedroom before she began sobbing.

By the time Frank Columbo was due home from playing golf with one of the members of his bowling team, Patricia was almost hysterical. Her sobs had become wails; she ranged about her room, door closed and locked, tears streaming, bemoaning what she had by then decided was the end of her life.

In the kitchen, Mary Columbo paced nervously, waiting for her husband. Michael had told her what had happened; she had gone at once to her daughter's room to try to console her, but Patricia had refused to let her in.

"Go away and leave me alone!" she had yelled, bawling loudly. "I want to die! I just want to die!"

Back in the kitchen, Mary wrung her hands in anguish, needing her husband to handle the situation, but dreading his coming home.

"Your father will not put up with this," she said ominously to Michael. "Quick, help me close all the windows so the neighbors can't hear your sister."

"Some of them already heard her," Michael said matter-of-factly.

"What did they say?"

"Nothing. I told them she was going nuts."

"Michael, for God's sake!"

When Frank Columbo walked in the door and heard the terrible sounds of agony coming from somewhere in his house, the color drained from his face. "For Christ's sake, what's happened?" he asked urgently.

"Patty's going nuts, Dad," Michael said before his mother could speak.

"Michael, go to your room!" Mary ordered. "Right now!"

As Michael skulked from the kitchen, he heard his father ask, "What does he mean, Patty's going nuts?"

"Frankie, sit down," Mary urged. "I'll explain the whole thing."

Several minutes later, Frank Columbo went down the hall to his daughter's bedroom, Mary a few steps behind him. Michael, technically obeying his mother, was two inches across the threshold of his own room. Frank knocked heavily enough on Patricia's door for her to hear it above the sounds of her wailing.

"Patty, honey, it's Daddy," he said loudly. "Open the door, sweetheart. I want to talk to you."

There was no response, just the unremitting din generated by Patricia's broken heart.

"Come on now, honey," Frank tried to coax her, "open the door and let Daddy talk to his little girl. Daddy just wants to help his Patty."

"Leave me alone!" Patricia shouted from the other side.

"Trying to be nice to her is not going to work, Frank," his wife advised.

"Patty"—Frank Columbo now introduced a hint of impatient authority into his tone—"I'm not kidding around. Open this door."

Again there was no response. Frank banged on the door with the side of his fist.

"Patty Ann! Open this goddamned door! Right now! If you don't, I swear to God I'll kick it in!"

Tense seconds passed. Patricia did not open the door.

"I'm warning you!" her father threatened. "If I have to kick this door in, I'm not replacing it! You won't have a door on your room, Patty!"

The potential peril of *that* prospect got through the terrible hurt that was consuming her, and before Frank Columbo could speak again, there was a sharp click as Patricia unlocked her door. Both Mary and Michael started toward him, but Frank held up a hand, palm out, to check them.

"Just stay put. I'll handle this."

Frank found an absolutely wretched Patricia. Her eyes were red and swollen, nose red and running, cheeks tear-streaked and beginning to roughen from being repeatedly wiped by her hands. Her hair was a disaster, looking as if she had been pulling at it hysterically with one hand while sticking a finger in an electrical socket with the other. Her overall appearance was one of emotional wreckage.

"Patty, honey," Frank said, moving to her side, his voice soothing again, "come on now. Nothing can be this bad. The guy's not worth it—"

"He is so!" Patricia exploded. "He's the only person that ever really loved me!"

"Honey, that's not so and you know it." Frank glanced at the doorway; Mary and Michael had moved cautiously over to look in. "Your mother and Michael and I love you. Lots of people love you: your aunt Janet, Uncle Phil, Uncle Joe—"

Patricia found that she was girding herself for something.

"—your Uncle Gus loves you—"

"Stop it!" she stormed at her father. "You don't know what you're talking about and you don't know what I'm talking about!" Turning away from him, she sat on the side of her bed, praying: Please, please, please—*don't* sit down next to me.

He did not. Instead, her father stood before her, trying to apply the salve of reason to her wounds of love. "Patty, honey, don't do this to yourself. You're too good for that Polack punk. He don't deserve a girl like you. Look at how he cheats on you. He's a bum. Best thing for you is to forget him, find yourself another boyfriend, maybe a nice Italian boy this time—"

"I don't want another boyfriend," Patricia sobbed. "I want Jack. If I can't have him, I want to die!"

"Patty, honey, don't say a terrible thing like that," her father said.

"I—want—to—die!" she screamed at her father.

Frank Columbo slapped her solidly across the face and sent her reeling sideways on the edge of the bed, and then off the bed onto the floor. She tumbled into a heap, but rolled quickly to a half-sitting position, looking up at him, her cheek flaming red. Beyond her father, she could see her mother hurrying into the room to her, see Michael's stunned expression in the doorway; and then her father staring at his own hand as if he could not believe what it had done.

Frank Columbo looked down at his daughter, his eyes filling with remorse.

Patricia looked up at her father, defiant expression locked in place. She still wanted to die.

20
May 1976

Laura Marie Komar received a telephone call from her employer shortly after seven-thirty on the morning that the Columbo-DeLuca apartment had been searched and Patty Columbo was taken into custody.

"Laura, can you come in?" the police dispatcher asked. "I know it's your day off, but we've got an emergency and really need you."

"Sure, I guess so," Laura said. "Be there in a few minutes."

When Laura arrived at Elk Grove Village police headquarters, she saw Patty Columbo sitting in the squad room with her right wrist handcuffed to the chair.

"We need you to search her and stay with her, maybe all day," the watch commander told Laura. "She's probably going to be charged with the murders of her family."

My God! Laura Komar thought. She had to take a deep breath to keep her composure.

Laura went over to the prisoner. "Hi, Patty."

"Oh, hi, Laura," Patty said, looking up. "What are you doing here?"

"I work here. I'm a community service officer for the department. Uh, Patty, I'm going to have to search you."

"Okay," Patty said, shrugging.

Glenn Gable came over to remove the handcuffs he had put in place earlier, and Laura took Patty gently by the arm. "I'll use a juvenile-detention cell," she told the watch commander. "There's more privacy."

The juvenile-detention cell had a solid door except for a twelve-by-twelve-inch window, but there was no one else in that section of the building so Laura had the necessary seclusion for her search.

"You'll have to take off all your clothes, Patty," Laura told her. "This is going to be a full strip search, and I also have to examine your body for bruises or any other marks of possible mistreatment."

As Patty was undressing, she said, "I don't think we've seen each other since I quit high school, have we?"

"I don't think so," Laura said. "Not to talk to, anyway. I saw you a couple of times at Walgreen's, but you were busy so I didn't say hello."

Laura carefully examined Patty Columbo for anything she might have concealed on, or *in*, her person, then went over each separate article of clothing before handing it back to her and allowing her to get dressed again.

"I don't know how long we'll be in here," Laura said. "Want some coffee?"

"God, yes! And a cigarette." As Laura was about to leave, Patty said, "Laur, will you do me a favor?"

"If I can. What is it?"

"I'm worried about Duke, my dog. I put him out on the

balcony of my apartment. I'm afraid if they bring my boyfriend in too, the dog will just be left there."

"I'll see what I can find out," Laura said. She locked the
detention cell door and left.

A few minutes later, Laura returned with coffee and cigarettes, and said, "Your dog's okay. It's been taken to an animal shelter for holding."

"Oh, good." Patty sounded genuinely relieved. "Thanks,
Laur. I had these terrible visions of him starving to death out
there on that balcony."

Patty sat on the single cot in the cell, and Laura propped
the door open and sat just inside it on a chair. They made
small talk and reminisced about their high school days, which
weren't all that far behind them. Patty did not mention the
killings and Laura did not ask her about them. A person's arrest and the immediate period of detention following it made
for constitutional thin ice on which Laura Komar did not
skate unless it was absolutely necessary.

For more than two hours, they talked about everything except why they were there.

Shortly after 10:30, Deputy Chief William Kohnke came back
to the detention cell with two plainclothes officers whom
Laura did not know.

"You're relieved for a little while, Laura," Kohnke told her.
"But stay close. We'll call you when we're finished."

Kohnke and the two officers remained with Patty for
nearly an hour, during which time Laura observed that she
was brought out of the cell several times and allowed to go
into a nearby bathroom. Around noon, Kohnke summoned
Laura back, and he and the two officers left. Laura asked
Patty if she wanted something to eat and Patty said no. She
did ask for a Coke, which Laura got for her.

A while later, Gene Gargano of the sheriff's office walked
past the open door of the detention cell with John Landers,
the Elk Grove investigator who had assisted Ray Rose in sur-
veying the murder scene the day the bodies were found. Co-
incidentally, Landers had also been one of the officers
involved in an incident ten months earlier when Patty's father,
Frank Columbo, had attacked Patty's lover, Frank DeLuca, in
the parking lot of Walgreen's, smashing him in the face with

a rifle butt as a warning to stay away from his daughter. Patty had come to know Gargano slightly in the week during which he had worked on the present murder case.

"I know those two guys," Patty said to Laura Komar as the men went by.

"Do you want to talk to them?" Laura asked.

"God, no," Patty replied, turning away. "I'm too ashamed to face them."

But a little while later, apparently reconsidering, Patty said to Laura, "See if Gargano and Landers are still around, will you? Tell them I'd like to talk to them."

Gargano had left by then, but Landers came back to the detention cell with Glenn Gable.

"Hi, guys," Patty said when they came in. "What's going on?"

"Pat," said Landers, "it looks like you might have some serious problems. But before we talk any further, I want to advise you of your constitutional rights."

"That's already been done twice," Patty said.

"We'll do it again anyway," Landers said, and proceeded to recite to her the rights she had, which were to remain silent and to have an attorney present when questioned.

When Landers was ready to let her talk, Patty said, "John, you know about the problems I've had with Dad. Most of them have been caused by the relationship between my mother and me. My mother had a very strong influence on my father."

"Pat, before you go on," Landers said, "do you want to make a telephone call?"

"You mean call a lawyer?" she asked.

"Yes."

Patty shook her head. "No, I don't need no fucking lawyer."

Landers talked to her a while longer, then brought her out of the detention cell and, with Laura Komar, took her to a rear squad room.

"You can stay in here with Laura," the officer told her, "while I make arrangements for a steno to take down your statement. Make your phone call now if you want to."

Patty sat at a desk and picked up the telephone. Her mind would not respond to what she needed. She had to call the information operator to ask for the number of Janet Morgan, her godmother, in Chicago. There was no listing. She tried again, this time asking for Bill Morgan, and was given a number. Presently, Laura Komar heard her say, "Hi, Auntie Janet . . ."

At that point, Landers returned to the office. Laura and Landers heard Patty say, "They have me here for the murder of Mom and Dad and Michael." After a pause, she said, "No, I don't need a fucking attorney; they're all full of shit anyway. I'm going to give them a statement. They've got Frank down here and the only way they'll release him is if I sign a statement. I know what I'm doing."

One has to wonder at this point where Patricia got the notion that if she signed a formal statement, DeLuca would be released. The most logical assumption is that John Landers told her so; he was the last one to speak with her in private before she agreed to sign a statement, and also the investigator she had known the longest and was obviously the most comfortable with. Nineteen years old, clearly not functioning at full mental capacity, Patricia had by then been in custody, without a lawyer, for some nine or ten hours. If Landers *did* encourage a statement in this manner, it was a shabby way to do it.

When Patty completed her call to Janet Morgan, Deputy Chief Kohnke came into the room and had Laura Komar take her back to the juvenile-detention cell, left them there, and returned a short time later with a civilian whom Laura did not know—but whom Patricia did: it was Lanny Mitchell.

"Do you recognize the person in there?" Kohnke asked Lanny.

"Yes."

"Who is in there?"

"Patty Columbo," Lanny Mitchell replied.

Then Lanny looked in at Patricia and with a forefinger made a cutthroat gesture across his neck. It could have been his way of telling her that the murder game they had been playing was over.

Except that he smiled when he did it.

Lanny was probably letting her know, in his inimitable fashion, that he was cutting *her* throat.

* * *

While Patty was being held in the juvenile-detention cell, Frank DeLuca, who had been transported separately to Elk Grove police headquarters, was in interview room 1, being questioned by Ray Rose and Frank Braun.

After being advised of his constitutional rights, DeLuca was asked if he had any knowledge of the Columbo murders. He answered that he had "no knowledge of who the killers were." *Killers*—plural.

DeLuca went on to say that he did not think Patty Columbo had committed the murders because Patty and he were together at a shopping mall until nine o'clock the night of the crime, then were together in their apartment all night after that. (It is interesting to note that DeLuca did not adamantly, indignantly assert that he *knew* Patty had not committed the crime, but simply did not "think" she had done it.)

His and Patty's last contact with Frank Columbo, DeLuca said, had been telephone calls received from him on Monday night, May 3, and Tuesday night, May 4.

He was, DeLuca stated, in the process of divorcing his present wife, the mother of his five children, so that he and Patty could be married in June. During his interrogation, DeLuca took every opportunity to refer to Mary and Frank Columbo as "Mom and Dad." He said that "Mom and Dad" had finally "accepted" him and that a "good relationship" had begun to develop among "Mom and Dad" and Patty and himself.

Questioned about the photographs found in his apartment, he said that he had taken "most" of the shots, and that he and Patrish had sent pictures and ads to a swingers magazine in an attempt to swap sexual partners with other couples.

Like Patty herself, DeLuca appeared curiously unmoved by the recent tragedy that had befallen the Columbo family. He gave lip service to grief, but might as well have been talking about the weather.

At around 9:30 that Saturday night, after having her in custody for fourteen hours, Ray Rose was ready to take Patty Columbo into Chicago to the Women's Detention Center and formally charge her with murder and conspiracy to commit murder. Deputy Chief Kohnke decided to accompany them, and a now very tired Laura Komar would also go along as the final duty of her long "day off."

Prior to leaving, Patty asked if it would be possible for her to see Frank DeLuca before being taken to jail. Somebody said okay, why not, and DeLuca was brought to the juvenile-detention cell. He and Patty were given cigarettes and left alone together for fifteen minutes.

Laura Komar both heard and saw Patty sobbing during the brief visit.

No one at Elk Grove police headquarters knew what transpired during the few minutes of privacy between the lovers, and Patricia Columbo did not talk about it for fifteen years. But it was at that point in their relationship that Frank DeLuca resumed total command again.

In the beginning, when Patty had been fifteen and Frank thirty-four, she had become his protégée; he was her teacher, adviser, mentor, master. Slowly then, as their affair deteriorated; as their sexual activity became more bizarre; as their unconventional pairing began to affect both their families; as stress, anxiety, violence, and fear began to permeate their every waking hour; and as their consumption of alcohol and drugs steadily increased, eventually Patricia became the couple's strength, DeLuca its weakness.

In the weeks immediately prior to the killings, DeLuca retreated more and more into their little apartment with the fortified door, where he could lose himself in whiskey, pills, and increasingly grotesque and pixilated sexual fantasies. It was left to Patty, now all of nineteen but commonly feeling older than Frank, to take care of their everyday needs, face the world for them, solve their problems. While Frank went to work like a zombie every day, and returned each night like a hunted—and haunted—man, Patty was running on adrenaline, increasing panic, and her own absurd, ludicrous belief that things would still come up roses for her and "the only person she had left" in the world. That the fabric of her entire life was now a tissue of lies did not once occur to her. She had become as sociopathic as the person who had taught her.

So now, in police custody, she assumed his weaknesses, and he became the strong one again.

"You've got to keep me out of it, Patrish," DeLuca coaxed his overwrought young lover. "As long as I'm out of it, they can't get you for anything. I'm your alibi, okay? You were with me all night, okay? Whatever they charge you with, I'll testify that you couldn't have done it. You keep me out of it and we're home free, Patrish. It'll be just you and me. We'll get a sailboat and go away and never come back . . ."

Patty wept and listened and wept some more. It was so easy now to revert back to a time when whatever Frank said was gospel, whatever Frank did was faultless, whatever Frank wanted was unchallenged. Patty knew that in a couple of hours she would be charged with the murders of her father, her mother, and her brother, and she would be locked up in jail. She never expected to be free again—nor at that moment did she want to be.

So why fight it?

"All right, Frank," she told him tearfully. "Whatever you say, Frank."

It was so easy.

21
October 1971 and April 1989

Following the slapping by her father after Jack Formaski's betrayal, Patricia slipped into a lethargy that drew her inextricably down. She became listless, mentally uninterested in anything, physically tired most of the time; she had little appetite, little energy, shunned all activity except that specifically required, such as school—and even then she sat in class as if in a stupor, doing nothing but passing time until she could get back to the privacy of her bedroom and the solitude of an inertia with which she grew to feel quite comfortable. The more languorous she became, the less she felt threatened—by anything. It was as if her condition were a cocoon.

No one accepted her new state except Michael. He had been the first one to commiserate with her after she was slapped. Her mother had run to her where she lay on the floor, instinctively, and tried to help her up, but Patricia had writhed away, shaking her head, pleading, "Leave me alone, please, just leave me alone . . ."

Her father had already walked out of the room; when her mother followed, she made Michael return to his own bedroom. Patricia's door was still open and it was only a minute or two before Michael reappeared, slipping in and closing the door, coming to sit beside his sister on the bed.

"He shouldn't've hit you," the boy said solemnly.

"It's all right, Michael," Patricia sniffed.

"Your face has got a handprint on it," he said, looking closely at her. Patricia saw tears welling in his eyes.

"It'll go away, Michael." She put an arm around him and pulled him against her. "Anyway, it doesn't hurt," she lied.

"I bet it does so," he contradicted, as he himself began to sniff now. "You're just saying it doesn't." Michael made a small fist. "I'd like to hit *him* and see how *he* likes it."

"Don't say that," Patricia half scolded.

They sat that way together for several minutes until Patricia finally patted Michael's head and said, "You'd better go back to your room now."

The boy got up and trudged sullenly to the door. Before he left the room, he looked back and said, "I won't never charge you to keep secrets again. From now on, I'll keep 'em for free."

For Michael, this was the definitive expression of affection. Patricia would have smiled if her face had not been throbbing so.

Frank Columbo made an awkward attempt to say he was sorry—but he qualified it in much the same way as Patricia had planned to qualify her apology to Jack. Patricia was sorry for all the terrible things she had said— but it had been *Jack's* fault that she said them.

That was how Frank Columbo felt.

"Look, Patty Ann," he said the next day, "I know I shouldn't have smacked you like I did, but you gotta admit, you really drove me to it, you know? I mean, I kept telling you to knock off saying that stuff about wanting to die. You were upsetting your mother and brother. You were upsetting me. And you wouldn't listen to me, you know? You know?"

"Yes, I know," Patricia answered quietly.

"If you had just listened to me and done what I was telling

you to do, you wouldn't have got smacked. You understand what I'm saying?"

"Yes, I understand," she replied respectfully.

She kept her eyes directly on him as he spoke, but her father would not reciprocate; he only glanced at her now and then, fleetingly. Mostly his gaze flicked here, there, everywhere—anywhere but on the unsightly bruise that colored the flesh above her cheekbone an ugly purple.

"And you gotta admit," her father further pleaded his case, "that's the first time, right? I mean, tell the truth, I never ever smacked you before, did I? You know, except for swats on the butt when you were a little kid. Right?"

"Right," she agreed, her tone as impersonal as possible without showing disrespect.

"Okay, good," her father said, "let's forget the whole thing then and we won't let it happen again. Believe me, pretty soon you'll have a new boyfriend and you won't remember that this Polack punk ever existed. Okay?"

"Okay."

He patted her on the arm and left the room. In the hall, Patricia heard him say to her mother, "Keep her in the house until that bruise goes away. I don't want her going to school looking like that. First thing you know, we'd have some child-welfare cop at the door asking for an explanation."

Patricia stayed home from school for a week, the excuse being that she had the flu.

Evidently Frank and Mary Columbo wrestled with the problem of Patricia day and night.

"She's like a zombie," Mary complained to friends.

Frank attempted more than once to talk to her. She listened to him very politely, answered him very politely, then resumed her sullenness, as if she hadn't heard a word he'd said. Frank became convinced that his daughter hated him for slapping her.

Mary Columbo rejected that idea. It had been the first time Frank ever slapped her—and as guilty as he felt about it, she was certain it would be the last. Besides, Mary had her own opinion: Patricia hated *her*.

"I've never been able to talk to her," she told friends.

Eventually both parents took the easy way out, using the

age-old explanation that would exempt them entirely from accountability or obligation to act: they decided that Patricia was going through a *phase*. In time, they were sure, she would grow out of it. All they really had to do was ignore her depression and wait.

It would turn out to be the worst decision they ever made.

"So," Sister Burke said of the entire incident, "you lost Jack, became closer to Michael, and—how did you feel about your father after that?"

"I didn't hate him, if that's what you're getting at," Patricia said. "I wasn't even mad at him. *Michael* was angrier at him for smacking me than I was." She shook her head. "To be honest, I can't remember having any feelings at all, about anybody. All I remember is that my life suddenly seemed to be playing in slow motion.

"I was over the initial hurt of it all, and I didn't have any more thoughts of committing suicide; the desperation was gone. But it wouldn't have bothered me a bit to know that when I closed my eyes at night, I'd never open them again. I just plain didn't *care*." She grunted softly. "Fifteen years old and I thought my life was over."

"That," Sister Burke commented, "is not as uncommon as you might think. The midteens are a difficult time." The nun silently drummed her fingertips for a moment. "Trish, we are almost at the point, I believe, where your codefendant, Frank DeLuca, entered your life. Weren't you sixteen when you met him?"

"Not quite," Patricia replied. She put her head back and looked up at the ceiling. "We met on May 26, 1972. People who fall in love real hard remember things like that. It was a little less than a month before my sixteenth birthday, and a little more than a month before Frank's thirty-fourth." She looked back at Sister Burke and smiled wryly. "Of course, he thought I was older and I thought he was younger. Talk about surprise later on."

"I can imagine. What I'm getting at, however, has nothing to do with your respective ages. In the thirteen-plus years that you've been in prison, you have declined all direct comment about your guilt or innocence—although through your attorney you *have* taken responsibility for the deaths of your family. DeLuca, on the other hand, has steadfastly denied being involved in the crime at all. I have to know whether his continued position of innocence is going to influence your ability to open up to me about that critical part of your life. What do you think?"

"I—don't know," Patricia replied hesitantly. "I'm not real sure I understand the question."

"I'm wondering if you feel any obligation to support DeLuca's position, to protect him in any way?"

"I don't feel anything at all toward Frank," Patricia said, "and I haven't in a long time." She tilted her head an inch. "You and I have been talking to each other for a year and a half, Sister Burke, and you've never mentioned my guilt or innocence. Why is that?"

"It hasn't been necessary. That first trip I made down here to see you, Trish, do you recall what you said to me? You said you wanted to find out how you got into the situation where you needed rehabilitating. *Needed* rehabilitating. You voluntarily began a process of internal self-examination because you wanted to know what flaws and weaknesses within yourself led you here to prison. I can draw only one conclusion from that. If I am wrong, please tell me so."

Patricia never told her so.

Sister Burke explained to Patricia what it would be like when they began to discuss DeLuca and the murders.

"It must be a very careful process," she stressed. "For years now, I've likened this type of analysis to the peeling of a grape. We must very slowly cut away the thinnest strips of the outer skin, and only remove one strip at a time. When we have examined the fruit under one thin strip, we must put that strip back in place before removing another one. To peel the entire grape at once would leave all its fruit exposed and prevent us from replacing its protective layer of skin. That would destroy the grape. That grape is your conscious and subconscious mind, Trish; we must be careful to preserve and protect it while we're examining it." Sister Burke paused a beat, then emphasized again, "That's why if there is any reservation at all in your mind about discussing DeLuca, then it would be best not to attempt it at all."

"There's no reservation in my mind that I know of, Sister," Patricia told her.

That I know of. Was that a subconscious defense mechanism latching into place? Maybe, maybe not. Sister Burke apparently couldn't tell at that stage. The only way she would be able to find out was to proceed with the peeling and see what happened. Risky—but necessary in this case, she must have felt.

"So, you were approaching your sixteenth birthday when you met Frank DeLuca . . ."

22
November 1971 to April 1972

One Saturday, a couple of months after Patricia and Jack broke up, Frank Columbo went out shopping by himself. When he returned home, he had a large box in the backseat of his car. It was, he announced, a new family hobby.

The surprise was one of the new citizens band radio sets that many people, particularly those in the suburbs, had recently taken such a keen interest in. Frank Columbo had given a lot of thought to something that his whole family could do together. There was a CBers' club right there in Elk Grove that they could all join. It was called the Spirit of Seven Club, because all its members broadcast on CB channel seven.

Apparently Frank hoped the excitement of the new hobby would bring his daughter out of her lethargy and restore some tranquillity to the household. But when he gathered his little family together to present the new hobby to them, Patricia exhibited no interest at all in it. She made it clear that she would participate only if *required* to. Her father declined to exert any authority in the matter; he wanted her to join in because she wanted to, for the fun of it; he wasn't about to *make* her do it.

Michael, of course, was all enthusiasm, and Mary went along with it for her own reasons—perhaps because Patricia *didn't*, or perhaps because she understood how much it meant to Frank and saw how hard he was trying. Frank and Michael eventually became very active in the CBers' club, and Mary to a lesser degree. Frank chose "Crazy Dago" as his CB handle—the name by which he broadcast.

"I get called that often enough," he frequently boasted.

Michael picked "Blue Mule" for his handle; typically, he refused to tell anyone why. Mary, who mostly listened, rarely transmitting, was "Moon Beam," which she said she took from an old song she liked.

Patricia never chose a handle, because she never participated.

The more involved her parents and brother became in their CB activity, the more alienated from them Patricia felt. She didn't try to place blame on anyone but herself. The more she mulled everything over in her melancholy, the more she realized that she had greatly overreacted to her breakup with Jack Formaski, which caused her to become irrational and hysterical; which in turn caused her father to hit her for the first time ever; which made her distance herself from him, and consequently also from her mother. Michael, at first, had not been included in the disaffection, having allied with his sister the instant she was slapped. But, about to turn nine, Michael's understanding of this kind of intra-family stress was limited to his attention span, just as his fidelity was given, like that of a puppy, to the status quo. If any physical abuse of his sister had been prolonged or repeated, he would have aligned himself with her again. But because it was not repeated, the act of violence itself gradually diminished in his mind to something of lesser import than, say, what was for dessert that night. When Michael, then, slowly withdrew from Patricia, as Patricia was withdrawing from their parents, it served to leave her isolated in her own home. It was at that point that she sought to find a new environment for herself.

At school, they offered a distributive-education course called Work Release, which provided credit for part-time employment after school. Since she was no longer socializing to any degree with her former clique of girlfriends, all of whom still had steady boyfriends while she did not, and she was weary of going home after school every day to face the strained relationship with her mother, she hit upon the alternative of going to work.

The distributive-education counselor was happy to get someone like Patricia. Pretty, poised, well spoken, nicely dressed, with a good grade point average, she could easily have been placed in a high-profile public contact job such as relief receptionist, hospital admittance clerk, even desk clerk assistant at one of the numerous hotels and motels cropping up around the ever-expanding airport. But it was midsemester; all the cushy jobs were gone.

"About the only thing I've got right now," the counselor told her, "is a counter-girl position at a little sandwich shop."

"Where is it?" Patricia asked.

"Corky's. It's in Grove Shopping Center."

"Sure, next to Walgreen's," Patricia said. "I've been in there."

"It's not much of a job, really, for someone like you," the counselor pointed out. "Just making sandwiches, serving customers—"

"I'd like to try it," Patricia said.

"All right, but I'll want to find something more suitable for you next semester. Okay?"

"Sure," Patricia said.

Next semester seemed like a lifetime away.

Grove Shopping Center was one of those large corner conglomerates of smaller businesses clustered together at the rear of a big parking lot, merged geographically for the purpose of luring shoppers, particularly those who lived nearby, away from the glitzy new indoor malls. These independent combines usually had one main anchor store, either a food outlet or major drugstore. Walgreen's was the anchor store for Grove Shopping Center, occupying the prime location nearest the corner of the parking lot.

Corky's was a sandwich shop adjacent to Walgreen's, with a large sliding door that was open during business hours to allow customers to pass back and forth without having to go outside, a convenience during the icy winter months. It wasn't a large place; a row of tables against one wall and a few booths. Set up like a lot of burger shops, it had an automatic broiler grill that moved meat patties through at a pace slow enough for them to come out the other end cooked; a microwave for hot apple pie and other quick-heat dishes; a blender for milkshakes. Nothing on the menu was very fancy: tuna salad already made, ham on rye, roast beef, uncomplicated fruit bowls, iced tea, coffee. Simple and quick, for store clerks with fifteen-minute coffee breaks, half-hour lunches, limited budgets.

Patricia liked it—the place, the work, the variety of people. She wore a little red apron over a starched white uniform that set off her coloring, eyes, and hair beautifully. There was absolutely nothing to learning the ropes—who the hell couldn't take a cooked burger off the automatic grill and put it on a bun? You used an ice cream scoop for the tuna salad, trimmed the crust off the bread, served potato chips with every order, and cut through a metal guide to slice the pies into perfectly sized and shaped wedges. An average eight-year-old, she thought, could have done it.

Eunice was Patricia's boss, a plump, easygoing, wise-cracking woman of forty with bleached blond hair, a husband who drove a beer truck, and no kids. "Never wanted any," she said when she and Patricia gabbed about family life. "I'm not the diaper-changing type. We've got a camper; we like to drive up to Wisconsin on weekends and commune with nature. We cook out, things like that. For a guy who drives a beer truck, Ed is real outdoorsy; he can tell what kind of tree a tree is just by looking at it. We're gonna buy a mobile home someday and live in the country."

Patricia liked Eunice. She was common as tap water, not an ounce of pretension in her body. And she let Patricia know right away that there were certain perks connected with the job. "You got a boyfriend wants to come in for a sandwich, that's fine, just forget to write him a check. The same with your little brother or your parents. Just don't abuse the privilege."

"I don't have a boyfriend," Patricia told her, "and I doubt if my parents will ever come in. My little brother, maybe; he's a born scrounger."

Eunice was surprised about the boyfriend status. "A cute kid like you, I can't believe it."

"Well, I just broke up with a guy," Patricia explained.

"Oh, so you're just *between* boyfriends. That's different. You'll probably have a new one in a week. Lots of nice-looking young guys come in here."

If I last a week, Patricia thought. She still had to tell her father about the job.

Frank Columbo put his fork on his dinner plate and looked skeptically at his daughter.

"A job? What do you mean, you've got a job? What job?"

Patricia explained it to him. Her father shook his head. "No, no, no. Tell the school you don't need to work. You come home after school. What kind of a deal is this anyway? I send you to school to learn things, not to go out and work. I don't understand this."

It was called Work Release, Patricia patiently explained, and its purpose was to teach young people how to handle responsibility and meet the public. Lots of girls, Patricia stressed, went out on their own when they were eighteen, and for her that was less than three years away.

"Three years is a long time," Frank Columbo said. "I don't want you working." He resumed eating dinner.

Patricia had turned pleading eyes to her mother. Mary pursed her lips for Patricia to stop arguing and be quiet. Several minutes later, when Frank and Michael were talking about baseball, Mary subtly brought the subject back into the conversation.

"Corky's—that's that nice, clean little place right up here by Walgreen's, isn't it?"

"Right next door," Patricia said.

They only wanted her to work three hours a day during the week, and eight hours on Saturday. And she would, she emphasized, get *two* credits at school: one for working, and one for attending the distributive-education class twice a week. And lots of kids were doing it. Two boys in her home room worked at Jewel Market, one girl worked at Osco Drugs, and there was another girl who was even a file clerk at city hall.

Eventually Mary Columbo said, "Frank, let's have our coffee out on the patio. I want to talk to you about this. Patty, you do the dishes tonight. Michael, help your sister clear the table."

The parents retired to the patio.

Twenty minutes later, Mary came into the kitchen where Patricia was finishing up. "Your father has agreed to let you keep your job for a while, on a trial basis," she told her daughter. "But you've got to keep your grades up—*and*," Mary said, shaking an underscoring finger, "you've got to improve your attitude around this house. We're all sick and tired of your moping around. I want to see it stopped, understand?"

"I understand," Patricia promptly agreed. "I'll do better. I promise."

"See that you do." Mary started out of the kitchen.

"Thanks, Mom," Patricia said.

Mary kept going without responding. Patricia never knew if she heard her or not.

C.H.
September 1979 to October 1990

As the years went by, I kept up with the Patricia Columbo story through a news clipping service. I don't know if it was just the general professional interest I have in crime and criminals, or if somewhere deep inside me I felt that I would write about her someday. I know that the image of a pretty little girl dressed just so, in ribbons and lace—an image created by a Chicago bartender who looked like Rocky Marciano—always came to mind when I read a current clipping about her.

The business of Patricia's being "involved" in a "sex scandal" a year or so after beginning her two-hundred-to-three-hundred-year sentence oddly was never fully resolved. The story broke in the Chicago Sun-Times *on September 10, 1979, in a piece headlined:*

COLUMBO TIED TO SEX SCANDAL IN PRISON

The story related that the two highest-ranking guards at Dwight women's prison had been accused of intimidating inmates to perform "deviate" sexual acts for them in groups. According to unnamed sources, the women had been procured for the prison officials by convicted murderess Patricia Columbo. At least six women inmates at the prison had complained that they were forced to perform sexual acts by the

*two prison officials. Two of the women were said to have
taken and passed lie detector tests regarding the incidents.
Maj. Denver Weakley, the highest-ranking guard at the
prison, had been suspended for refusing to take a lie detector
test, and Dennis Klosteroff, the prison's chief of internal security, had also been ordered to take one and placed on a leave
of absence until he did so.*

*Following that story, the coverage was curiously lax. Noth-
ing further was reported on the "scandal" for two weeks.
Then, on September 25, 1979, the* Sun-Times *filed a short
piece headlined:*

PATRICIA COLUMBO PLACED IN SOLITARY

*Convicted murderess Patricia Columbo, the story read, had
been placed in solitary confinement pending investigation of
charges that she recruited women inmates for sexual relations
with guards at Dwight Correctional Center. An investigation
was being conducted at the women's prison into allegations
by some inmates that they were recruited for sex parties with
male prison officials. The FBI had also initiated its own
probe, looking for possible civil rights violations of inmates.*

*Columbo had been put into solitary for thirty days during
the investigations. She was secretary to Dennis Klosteroff,
forty-nine, chief internal affairs investigator at the prison.
Formerly the prison's assignment officer, he had originally
detailed Patricia Columbo to work for him. So far, four
women had reportedly passed lie detector tests regarding the
sex parties.*

*Despite its somewhat incriminating headline, the story said
absolutely nothing except that Patricia Columbo was being
isolated during an investigation of "charges" against her.
Readers interested in more on this "sex scandal" would be
sorely disappointed. Following this piece, people who bought
and paid for news in Chicago were not even to be told when,
or if, Patricia Columbo was ever released from solitary confinement, much less the disposition of any "charges" against
her. The story was summarily dropped.*

Well, after all, the main story was that she had been put

into solitary. That certainly meant she had done something wrong.

Didn't it?

The next story mentioning Patricia Columbo to make the Chicago papers was in mid-1980, nine months later. The Sun-Times headlined on July 11: -

FORCED INTO SEX, INMATE CHARGES

This story related that a Dwight inmate named Debra Huddleston, twenty-four, serving ten years for aggravated kidnapping, had filed a fifty-thousand-dollar suit in the U.S. District Court against Dennis Klosteroff, forty-nine, for forcing her to commit deviant sex acts with other females and upon his person. Denver Weakley, forty-seven, was similarly charged. The suit also sought damages from State Corrections Director Gayle Franzen; former Dwight warden Charlotte Sutliff-Nesbitt, who resigned shortly after the original story had become public; and Mike Lane, the temporary warden who replaced her.

The story again reiterated that Patricia Columbo, nine months earlier, had been "charged" by several inmates with procuring them for "sex parties."

If the news story was accurate, apparently Debra Huddleston was not accusing Patricia of anything, only the prison official for whom Patricia had worked, and other officials. As for the accusations made against Patricia nine months earlier, there was no follow-up information as to what the results of those "charges" were, if any. The current story made it clear that the warden resigned, and one of the earlier accounts reported that suspensions, involuntary leaves of absence, and lie detector tests were disrupting the lives of the two top male guards being sued. But again there was nothing but innuendo and apparently unsubstantiated charges against Patricia Columbo. Patricia maintains to this day that she was approached, but declined involvement.

In 1984, Patricia Columbo was routinely considered for parole the first time, and routinely denied.

In March 1987 she was considered again, and it was

pointed out for the record that she had taken "some college courses" during her seven years at Dwight Correctional Center, and had "designed a computer program to help basic education students (at the prison) learn how to read."

Nic Howell, a spokesman for the Illinois Department of Corrections, issued a statement that Patricia was "doing fine" in prison and was writing for the prison newspaper.

At neither of these hearings was any mention made of the "sex scandal."

Later in the month, parole was denied. The Prisoner Review Board issued a statement through its chairman, Paul Klincar, that Patricia would become eligible for consideration again in March 1990.

When the press reported the second denial, it again reminded the public of the "sex scandal" by relating that in 1979 Columbo had been the center of a controversy that led to the resignation of the prison warden. Other female inmates had charged at that time that Columbo organized sex parties with male guards at the prison.

At best, this was extremely careless reporting. Now Patricia was the "center" of the scandal, and had "organized" the sex parties. All this, remember, had been eight years earlier. And still no follow-up information, not even a clue as to the disposition of these "charges," not a hint of how the "center" of the scandal, the "organizer," had been punished. Presumably, this inmate had, at worst, committed a felony, and at best, seriously breached prison regulations. Either requires disciplinary action—and a record of it.

But time had not improved the newspaper coverage. Readers got absolutely no further information. They were never even told the outcome of Debra Huddleston's lawsuit.

Based solely on what the newspapers had reported, coupled with my personal knowledge of prisons, I formed at least a tentative conclusion of my own. Patricia was a high-profile convict; she was a "name," a headliner. And she worked for one of the guards named in the suit. Think how much weaker the story would have been if it had said HUDDLESTON TIED TO PRISON SCANDAL. Nobody knew who Debra Huddleston was; everybody knew the name Patricia Columbo. Throw in the word "sex" and you have a definite attention getter.

It began to look more and more like Patricia Columbo, this

*time at least, had simply been in the wrong place at the
wrong time.*

*Because of some confusion in the Illinois statutory law,
Patricia did not have to wait three years for her next parole
hearing; it was scheduled nine months later, in December
1987. Mother Nature intervened, however, in the form of a
monumental snowfall that all but isolated Dwight Correctional Center, where the hearings were held. The new date
was set for a month later, January 19, 1988.*

*Even before the third hearing, however, a new and surpris-
ing element was introduced into the case. Through a Chicago
attorney, Margaret Byrne, who now represented her without
fee, Patricia Columbo was going to "publicly acknowledge
responsibility" for the murders. That was part of the wording
of a statement that attorney Byrne was going to read into the
record of the next hearing. The press, however, took the statement a giant step further, with one headline reading:*

COLUMBO TO ADMIT KILLING HER FAMILY

That was not what the guarded statement said.

*The story itself did accurately report the exact content,
which was: "Basically, she takes responsibility for the deaths
of her family members, and she is not offering any excuse or
justification."*

*The press again used what had by now apparently become
a stock statement for any Patricia Columbo story: Columbo
was the center of a scandal at Dwight prison in 1979 that led
to the resignation of the warden there. Other female inmates
charged at that time that Columbo organized sex parties with
male guards at the prison.*

*Unfortunately, the nine-year-old "sex scandal" story con-
tinued to ferment.*

*Probably the most interesting element of this latest story
about Patricia Columbo was a comment that attorney Margaret Byrne made to the press that Patricia had, at age thirty-
one, now remembered being sexually abused by her father.
Byrne further stated, "She has begun an internal process of*

*examining the facts and also of examining her own childhood
and adolescence (to see) how she came to be the person she
was at that time."*

That statement hit the bull's-eye for me; it was exactly the
same question that had originally struck a nerve in me more
than a decade earlier.

How did a pretty little girl in ribbons and lace grow up to
butcher her family?

*Patricia's hearing in January 1988 resulted in her third pa-
role denial early the following month.*

*She eventually had a fourth hearing, at which it was
pointed out that she was now editor of the prison newspaper
and studying for a college degree. However, Richard M.
Daley, Illinois state's attorney and a candidate for mayor of
Chicago, told the Prisoner Review Board that "there will
never be enough reason to release this cold-blooded killer."
The board unanimously agreed and parole was denied for the
fourth time.*

*In reporting this latest denial, the press did not include any
mention of the "sex scandal." Several years later, I would
find out that Patricia had been personally involved with one
of the high-ranking guards who himself had been part of the
sex ring—but that she had not been part of the procurement
of others.*

*The Prisoner Review Board, I was later to learn, divides its
parole consideration into three areas of inquiry—past, present, and future: the inmate's life before and at the time of the
offense; the inmate's life in prison following conviction; and
future plans if parole is granted. The board has the inmate's
prison record, of course, and is aware of all that has transpired in the convict's life since arrival at the prison. The
prisoner is asked to explain any breach of prison rules, any
trouble with staff or other convicts, any internal problems at
all. At a parole hearing for Frank DeLuca, for instance, held
at Stateville Correctional Center on September 8, 1984,
DeLuca was asked about some trouble he got into at Pontiac
prison, where he began his sentence, which resulted in his being transferred to Stateville. Under oath—all prisoners are
sworn when they appear before the board—DeLuca testified
about being suspected of involvement in having three men*

stabbed over an extortion or protection-racket plot. This was prison trouble that DeLuca was factually involved in, it was on his prison record, and the Prisoner Review Board asked him about it.

At none of Patricia Columbo's four hearings had she been asked anything about the "sex scandal." Nor was she ever charged.

And the "sex scandal" had been included in newspaper stories about her for nine years—while DeLuca's prison trouble and transfer to a tougher institution was never reported in the press.

There seemed to be little doubt that it was Patricia Columbo who sold the newspapers.

It was some time after Patricia's fourth parole denial that an old friend came back into her life: Sister Margaret Ellen Traxler, the nun who, like rust, never rested. It was now twelve years since Sister Traxler had received the State of Israel Medal from Golda Meir, and during that time she had almost been defrocked. In 1984, along with a number of others, Sister Traxler had endorsed a major New York Times advertisement that challenged the Catholic church's official teaching against abortion. The church retaliated by threatening to remove her from her order, the School Sisters of Notre Dame, to which she had belonged for more than forty years.

Ultimately, the church did nothing drastic—perhaps because of the continuing work of the then decade-old Traxler-founded Institute of Women Today. The latest success of the Institute was Sisterhood, a shelter on the West Side of Chicago for recently paroled women. Now, four years later, Sister Traxler was working to open a new shelter, for the increasing number of homeless and/or mentally ill "bag ladies" that she was seeing on the streets of Chicago.

It was in conjunction with this latest project that Sister Traxler thought of Patricia Columbo. She had seen Patricia over the years in passing when at Dwight on other matters, and was aware of the rehabilitative and educational progress Patricia had made in prison. She also knew that Patricia was in therapy with Sister Burke, and through the psychologist was beginning to discuss and understand the convoluted series of events that had brought her to prison.

Sister Traxler began to visit Dwight specifically to see Patricia, to talk with her, observe her, evaluate her. What she saw looked promising to the crusading nun. So she did an extraordinary thing—she went to the Prisoner Review Board and asked it to release Patricia to her custody, to live and work with her and the other nuns at the new shelter for homeless women. To the board Sister Traxler cited Patricia's accomplishments in prison as a student, a teacher, the prison newsletter editor, and an honor prisoner who had earned and been given many special privileges. And she gave what in her opinion was the reason for Patricia's awful killing rage a dozen years earlier: the fact that Patricia was sexually abused as a child.

"Any young girl who has been sexually abused is not a whole person," Sister Traxler told the board in a moving plea. "Twenty percent of the women in our prisons today were abused children. Most of them, like Patty, hide the abuse deep within themselves, and don't even consciously remember it for years. And when they do, what? Are they going to want to talk about it in the presence of strangers? Of course not. Not even if to do so would help them win release from prison." Many women, she pointed out, continued to withhold the terrible knowledge even after they recalled it.

"Give Patty to us," Sister Traxler begged. "We will watch over her, help her, and most of all, love her."

Sister Traxler's uncommon, surprising request—the first time in her long and noteworthy career that she had offered sanctuary to anyone remotely like Patricia—naturally made the newspapers. The story started a war of words between Sister Traxler and a most formidable opponent—Illinois Appellate Court Justice R. Eugene Pincham.

As a Cook County Circuit Court judge in 1977, Pincham had presided over the trial of Patricia Columbo and Frank DeLuca. The case, he recalled now for the press, was the most cold-blooded ever heard in his courtroom. It was Judge Pincham who sentenced Patricia and DeLuca to two hundred to three hundred years in prison.

"I would have sentenced her to the electric chair if I could have," he said in an interview. Her, not them. At the time of the trial, the Illinois death penalty statute had been declared *unconstitutional; it was reinstated midway during the trial but, of course, was not retroactive.*

Of Patricia herself, Justice Pincham, a dignified, intellectual gentleman who reminded one of a black George C. Scott, said, "She was a vicious, cunning, coy, mean, disruptive person who had an exalted opinion of herself, her sexual ability, and her charm. You know, some people don't realize the advantage a judge has. From the bench, you can see the entire courtroom, see attitude and gestures, facial expressions. Here is a woman who maliciously contrived, planned, and executed the murder of her mother, father, and brother in the sanctity of their own home. My intent [when he sentenced her] was that she should never get out."

Sister Traxler rebutted, as kindly as she could, "Judge Pincham, I'm afraid, can't understand. He's a very closed man. Patricia is a different person today. People can change. God changes all of us in time."

Pincham demurred. "She should never be released even if she has learned to regret her deeds and reform her life. I could never say society has forgiven her for this crime. I don't think the issue is whether she's reformed. The magnitude [of the crime] is such that it would denigrate the value of motherhood, of fatherhood, and of life, to say she can now be freed."

Replied Sister Traxler, with noticeably less charity in her tone, "Men like Judge Pincham ride herd on these 'mean' women, yet it's men themselves that do it. They make them this way."

It was fun while it lasted, for the reporters anyway, but in the end nothing changed. The Prisoner Review Board turned down Sister Traxler's request.

For me, the time had come.

I had remained on the sidelines long enough, involving myself in other projects while my interest in this one continued to agitate. I finally decided that the case would probably never let go of me until I put some of the ill-fitting pieces into place and examined whatever murky picture they presented.

To learn about a criminal case, there are three places to start: a book about it, if one has been written; the trial *transcript, if a trial has been held; and, the least reliable, newspaper files.*

First, the book. I keep up with most of the true crime published, and I couldn't remember one about Patricia Columbo. But just to be on the safe side, I telephoned Patterson Smith, an antiquarian book dealer in Montclair, New Jersey, who deals exclusively in books related to crime. Pat said that he couldn't recollect any books that had been published on the case either. He would, however, research the matter to make certain we were correct.

Next, the transcript. I contacted the Cook County Court Clerk's office and learned that copies of trial transcripts could be purchased—for $1.25 per page. The person to whom I talked did not know offhand exactly how many pages were contained in State of Illinois v. Columbo-DeLuca, but one thing was known: it was the second-longest criminal trial in the state's history (the longest was the trial of John Wayne Gacy, the homosexual who murdered young boys and buried them under his house—in another Chicago suburb very close to where the Columbo murders occurred).

After doing some further checking, I eventually made contact with Ms. Margie Fuller, who was in charge of court records for the Cook County Clerk's office. Margie did know how long the transcript was: 12,080 pages. At $1.25 per page, a complete copy would cost $15,100. For half that much I could spend five or six weeks in Chicago, reading the transcript during the day, and making copies of the newspaper coverage of the case at night in the public library's microfilm room. I discussed the plan with Margie Fuller and she agreed to accommodate me by having the transcript—five file-drawer-size boxes—taken out of storage and sent to her office, where she would provide a place for me to read it and keep possession of it for as long as it took me. This is the kind of help true-crime researchers dream of, but seldom encounter.

Once again, as I had so often in the past, I headed back to Chicago.

The weather in October was typical for Chicago: beautiful one day, rotten the next. I rented a little kitchenette at the Lenox House down on Rush Street, just across the river from the Loop. It was one big room with a Pullman kitchen in the corner, a Murphy bed that folded into the wall, a TV on wheels that rolled wherever I wanted it, and a table large enough to spread out all the papers I knew I would accumulate and still leave a little room to eat. At a market a couple of blocks away, I stocked up on staples: gin, olives, doughnuts, frozen dinners, instant coffee. And I staked out a couple of delis for takeout food. I also found an independent taxi driver who agreed, for a flat fee, to pick me up every morning at eight and take me to the Criminal Courts Building, then come back for me at 4:30 in the afternoon and drive me back downtown.

On Monday morning at 8:30 I met Margie Fuller in her offices and got my first look at the trial transcript—all eighteen fat volumes of it.

"I hope you don't go blind," Margie Fuller said.

She gave me the first volume, about six hundred pages thick, and pointed me to a row of four partitioned cubicle desks along one wall. I shed my raincoat, hat, gloves—this was one of the rotten-weather days—got out my yellow lined pad for notes (the first of four I would fill), and went to work.

I had now begun serious research in my effort to learn what went wrong with that pretty little girl in ribbons and lace.

When my day of reading the transcript ended and George, my taxi driver, took me back downtown, I would heat a frozen dinner in my kitchenette or grab a bite out somewhere, then walk ten blocks to the Chicago Public Library at 400 North Franklin. There, on the third floor, I would find an available microfilm viewer that also reproduced pages—at a much more reasonable ten cents a copy—and begin my evening's work of reading the Chicago metropolitan newspaper coverage of the Columbo case—beginning with the discovery of the bodies.

I always selected one newspaper and followed it all the way from the first story that broke, to its most recent reportage, whatever it was. Then I would go on to another paper and follow the same procedure. Not only was that easier than trying to read each paper's coverage for each, which entailed constant changing of microfilm reels, but it also gave me an

*idea of the general feeling of each newspaper. They do have
their personal prejudices, despite loud avowals of neutrality.
Chicago newspapers, particularly regarding the Columbo
case, were, as I already knew from earlier reading, disturb-
ingly inaccurate—not to mention laced with implications,
suggestions, and inferences that left a reader annoyingly un-
informed.*

*Nevertheless, newspaper research was valuable. The chro-
nology of a case was generally correct in the papers, and
many reporters added some individuality to their stories with
descriptions of persons involved, clothing worn (DeLuca, for
instance, wore the same gray suit every day of the six-week
trial, while Patricia, who was borrowing clothing all over the
women's jail, never wore the same outfit twice), and other
personal touches that humanize a story.*

*While I was reading and copying those many newspaper
pages that October in Chicago, I probably turned past an
obituary in one of the editions that would have meant nothing
to me then, but would greatly affect the life of the person I
was researching, Patricia Columbo.*

*It was an obituary for Sister Margaret Burke, seventy-
seven, who had died at the University of Chicago Hospital.*

23
May 1976

Ten days after the discovery of the Columbo bodies, the sole
survivor of the immediate Frank Columbo family, his daughter Patricia, was locked up in the Cook County jail, formally
charged with murder and solicitation of murder. But Chief Investigator Ray Rose's work on the case was far from over; on
the contrary, it had barely begun.

There was no doubt in Rose's mind that Patricia had been
present when her parents and brother were murdered. That
conviction was further reinforced by a strange visit, later dis-
puted and left for the jury to evaluate, by two officers, Gene
Gargano and John Landers, with Patricia at the women's-
detention section of the jail. Gargano and Landers stated in an
official report which they both signed, and would later testify

to at Patricia's trial, that she had sent a message asking to talk to them. According to both officers, they met with her in a private office at the jail late one afternoon and again advised her of her constitutional right to have a lawyer present. They stated that Patricia replied that she understood her rights, fuck the lawyers, if she wanted to talk, she would talk.

Patricia Columbo allegedly then told the officers of a "vision" she had in which she saw her father lying on the floor in the living room of her parents' home. He was wearing dark pants and was on his back. She also saw her mother lying on the floor in the hallway, wearing nightclothes. And she saw her brother lying on the floor of his bedroom. She recalled that the hallway light was on and she saw scissors with blood on them.

Asked if she saw herself inside the house with the bodies, she said that she did. Asked if she saw herself involved in the killing of her mother, father, or brother, she became confused and said, "I might have, but I'm not sure; I can't be sure of anything."

Gargano asked if there was more she could tell them about the "vision," and she began to ramble, making the following statements, which the officers claim to quote verbatim in their report:

She saw her father, "who said Jesus would forgive her . . ."

And: "I am afraid I was there. I see myself there. I see them all at the same time in my mind."

Regarding a motive: "[I] felt fear and hate—fear that Frank [DeLuca] and I would be harmed—hate for my parents."

Regarding the scene of the crime, she vacillated: "I feel that I was there alone . . . or I was there with someone else that did it."

Regarding the night of the killings: "I see Michael answering the door for me. I don't think he wore pj's, I don't remember. I hear my father telling Michael to go upstairs to his bedroom."

Later: "I see my mother there lying on her stomach. I see my mother in a robe."

And apparently much later that night: "I remember that Frank [DeLuca] awoke when I was getting into bed. I startled him and he woke up. I was nude. I don't remember if I had been out or not. The [apartment] door was locked."

And: "I hated my mother mostly."

About the Cook County jail: "I can't stand being in this place—I can't take it. I might try to commit suicide."

And a final "vision" of the scene: "I see that someone else was with me. If Frank was with me, would you offer him immunity?"

Just prior to the visit by Gargano and Landers, unknown to them, Dr. Paul Cherian, a jail psychiatrist, had interviewed Patricia in a session that lasted about forty minutes. He found her to be in a confused, depressed condition, and a definite suicide risk.

"She had feelings of worthlessness, helplessness, hopelessness, generalized guilt feelings, psychomotor retardation, [and was suffering from] loss of sleep and loss of appetite," he reported.

There were, Cherian said, definite symptoms of mental illness.

It was in this condition that Patricia allegedly told Gargano and Landers about her "vision."

Following the Gargano-Landers visit, Patricia was removed from the detention section and put into the jail hospital.

Another member of Ray Rose's team, Investigator Russ Marinec, had turned up an interesting piece of information relating to Patricia Columbo's fear of her father. A boy named Jeff Jorgenson, age thirteen, who lived in apartment 909, next door to the apartment shared by Patricia and DeLuca, had become friendly with Patricia and often visited her when she was home alone; he sometimes even went shopping with her, and once had gone with her to the Columbo home and met Michael.

Just before Christmas, four to five months prior to the killings, young Jeff had been in the apartment when Patricia received a telephone call. Jeff recalled Patricia addressing the caller as "Dad." During the conversation, Patricia had motioned for Jeff to stand close enough to the receiver to be able to hear the caller say, "I'm going to get Frank."

Speculation was that Patricia was trying to get a witness to continued threats made by her father subsequent to his parking lot attack on DeLuca.

There is a written report of this information, signed by Investigator Marinec. Neither the report nor the information was revealed at the subsequent trial.

Because of information obtained from Lanny Mitchell that Roman Sobczynski had spoken to Frank DeLuca on the telephone regarding plans to murder Frank and Mary Columbo, and that DeLuca was under the impression that Roman was Patricia's "godfather," her *real* godfather, Phil Capone, the "Uncle Philly" from bygone days, was contacted by investigators and questioned about the crime. Capone denied any knowledge of the killings except what had been made public, and stated that he had not seen or spoken to Patricia Columbo in more than two years. He agreed to take a lie detector test.

Phil Capone's polygraph examination was administered at the Maywood sheriff's station by John Lenihan of the sheriff's department. Capone was asked numerous specific questions relative to any knowledge he might have of the Columbo murders, and whether at any time he had ever given a "weapon" (gun) to Patricia Columbo.

Capone candidly answered each question put to him. When the examination was over, polygraph examiner Lenihan expressed the opinion that Capone was telling the truth.

Following the test, Capone spoke with Sgt. Ron Iden of the Elk Grove Village Police Department, who had been present throughout the examination. Capone advised Iden that immediately upon hearing of the murders, he had suspected that Patricia might be involved. The reason, he said, was because he was aware of a great amount of friction between Patricia and her family.

Iden put the comments in his report of the polygraph examination and signed it.

Eleven days after the bodies were discovered, Ray Rose was contacted by a man named Edward Burnett, a truck driver in the nearby suburb of Addison. Burnett had in his possession a Johnson 23-channel CB radio, which he had purchased a week earlier on Maxwell Street, a large, outdoor, pedestrian, flea market-type area on Chicago's lower West Side. Subsequent to his purchase, Burnett had noticed what appeared to be the name Columbo and a series of numbers etched on the bottom of the set. Rose asked Burnett to bring the radio in.

When Ray Rose saw the CB radio, he felt his adrenaline surge. The numbers etched on the bottom of the set were 350–26–6560—Frank Columbo's Social Security number.

Rose questioned Burnett closely about the purchase of the radio, but all Burnett could tell him was that a black male had sold him the CB for fifty dollars. His description of the man contained nothing conspicuous. The radio was retained as evidence.

Rose now had still another loose end to tie up.

It was not, however, the principal loose end that concerned him. Despite the continual flow of miscellaneous potential evidence in the case, Rose himself was now focused on the second person he believed to be involved in the Columbo murders—Patty's lover, Frank DeLuca.

Rose had no hard evidence against the thirty-eight-year-old pharmacist. The closest thing he had was a smudged handprint found on Frank Columbo's abandoned Thunderbird, which could—*could*—have been made by DeLuca. But that, without anything else, was not enough for an arrest.

Rose kept looking.

The Columbo family cars, which had not presented a problem when a "gang" of some kind—home invaders, organized crime—had been suspected in the murders, now surfaced as a definite dilemma.

Frank Columbo's Thunderbird, found looted, vandalized, and abandoned in a Chicago ghetto, and Mary's Oldsmobile, located two days later on the parking lot of an apartment building in a nearby suburb, apparently had been taken from the residence by the killers in order, police believed, to delay discovery of the bodies by giving the appearance that the family was not at home. If a "gang" had been involved, it was easy to see how the vehicles could have been moved; but with only one person charged in the crime—Patricia—it was inexplicable, unless she had help.

Frank DeLuca, of course, was the obvious candidate—but Ray Rose, not having enough evidence yet to arrest him for the murders, could hardly implicate him in moving the cars from the murder scene. And that was not all that troubled

Rose. There was roughly forty-five to sixty minutes of driving time involved in taking the cars to the two locations where they were recovered. It was difficult for Rose to believe that whoever killed the family had driven around in the city and suburbs that long without being noticed—when they must have been covered with blood.

Shooting six bullets into three people, bashing in skulls, cutting throats, slicing young Michael's body so many times, saturating the carpet with blood, smearing the wall and spraying the ceiling with it—the killers had to have been drenched. It was almost inconceivable to Rose that *someone* had not seen them.

It was a problem that would never really be resolved to *everyone's* satisfaction; numerous theories would abound for fifteen years after the trial.

Even when Patricia Columbo herself finally related what she could recollect of that terrible night, the movement of only *one* car would be explained.

24
October 1990

Patricia was stunned.

She sat on the edge of a chair in the administration office, unable to believe the news.

Sister Burke was dead.

She had not shown up for her regular Thursday-afternoon visit the previous day, but Patricia had not known why. She had been taken to the University of Chicago Hospital and on the day she would have been at Dwight talking to Patricia, she had died.

"Did—they say what she died of?" Patricia asked the secretary who had passed on the message. The secretary shook her head.

"They only said it had to do with her age. She was seventy-seven."

Surprised for the second time, Patricia slowly shook her own head. "I had no idea she was that old. She was so—full of life, full of energy—"

"I'm sorry, Trish," the secretary said.

Patricia left the administration building as if in a daze. The early October air was cool as she walked back across the prison grounds toward her cottage; she instinctively pulled the hood of her sweatshirt over her head. All across the compound, grass was turning brown, yellowed leaves were dropping from the trees, potted flowers were withering. Everything was dying as winter approached. Tears came to Patricia's eyes as she hurried along; she kept her head down so no one would see them if they passed her.

In nearly fourteen years in Dwight prison, no one had ever seen Patricia Columbo cry—and no one was going to.

A short time later, Patricia's attorney and friend, Margaret Byrne, came to see her. Margaret, whom nearly everyone called Peggy, had been representing Patricia for several years. She had met her through another Dwight inmate whom Peggy was visiting. Herself an Irish neighborhood kid from Chicago, Peggy had gone to law school and come back to start a storefront practice in the same section of the Northwest Side where she had grown up. She didn't make a lot of money, because she represented clients, like Patricia Columbo, who had no money. She was intensely dedicated to women's legal rights.

Visiting Patricia this day, Peggy Byrne was very much worried about how the death of Sister Burke would affect her.

"How are you doing, Trish?" she asked with genuine concern.

"I'll get through it," Patricia assured her. She shook her head. "I can't get over how old she was. She didn't look or act anywhere near seventy-seven. If I'd known she was that old, maybe I wouldn't be so shocked by her dying—"

"I know." Peggy nodded. "Sister Burke was one of those people you kind of expect to go on forever." She paused a moment, then said, "This may be a bad time to ask, but do you have any plans to try and find a new therapist? I mean, you've been doing so well for the past year and a half, it would be a shame to stop your sessions now."

"I don't know," Patricia said, staring off at nothing as she had done so often with Sister Burke. The nun, being a psychologist, had given Patricia all the silent time she needed to let her accumulate and organize the thoughts she had to deal with. But Peggy Byrne was a lawyer, trained to keep the flow of conversation going.

"Do you think you *can* pick up with another psychologist?" the lawyer asked. "Or would you have to start all over?"

"I don't know," Patricia replied again, her voice weighed with uncertainty. "Sister Burke had a way of getting at so many things I wasn't even aware of till she pointed them out. Like, she felt I was too content in prison. Because I told her that I belonged here and should never get out. Institutionalized—that's what she called me. She kept insisting that I had to work on my self-esteem, which was practically nonexistent when we first started. She got upset with me for not going to my last parole hearing. I told her why I refused to be a part of that circus; you represented me, Peggy, you remember how it was: reporters, TV cameras, Ray Rose and those other Elk Grove police, the state's attorney, my aunts and uncles—all of them telling the board to keep me locked up. I told Sister Burke I didn't need that shit. I really was right where I belonged. I mean, what would have been the point in going? Sister Burke and I constantly argued over whether I even had a *moral* right to try to get out, let alone a legal right. I said I didn't think I had, but she disagreed. We went round and round over that." Patricia half smiled at the memory. "It was funny, in a way: me trying to convince her that I *didn't* deserve to get out, and her trying to convince me that I *did*. It wasn't what you'd call a textbook inmate-shrink relationship, which is usually the other way around." Patricia sighed wearily. "I just don't know, Peggy. I don't know whether I could start this all over again with somebody new or not."

Where she had slowly but steadily been gaining in self-knowledge during her months of therapy, Patricia was once again becoming mired in confusion about her ghastly past, her tenuous future.

With one of the three most important elements in her life abruptly removed, Patricia threw herself totally into the two remaining: tutoring other inmates, and her own studies.

A year before her arrest, Patricia had dropped out of her

senior year of high school in order to work full-time at Walgreen's for Frank DeLuca. During the years of her incarceration, she had completed the required studies to pass the GED examination for a high school equivalency diploma, and had gone on to earn a two-year associate of arts degree in general studies. She was currently working toward her four-year bachelor's degree.

Several women at Dwight before Patricia had continued studies for bachelor's degrees and earned them while still incarcerated, but no female convict in the history of Illinois prisons had gone all the way through college, from start to finish, while a prisoner. Patricia would be the first. When Sister Burke died, Patricia was in her last semester of work in the Illinois State University college program available to inmates. She was seven months away from graduation.

You *must* concentrate on this degree, Patricia lectured herself now. You *must* apply yourself. You must *not* let Sister Burke's death consume you.

But it did.

For the first few weeks, when Thursday came around, it was as if the day had been set aside for Patricia to become a zombie. Intense self-control was required even to get out of bed. She had to force herself to eat breakfast, compel herself to go to work. As a teacher's aide in the prison's department of education, she served as a tutor to a group of young prisoners known throughout the institution as "Columbo's Hoodlums." These were recalcitrant street kids, usually in prison for the first time, who as a matter of form felt they had to be insubordinate to authority and generally uncooperative. Basically, they were young women who could not, or would not, relate to the prison staff; they found it much easier to be taught by a convicted triple killer.

Patricia would mentally assign every new "Hoodlum" three *D*s, in an invisible tattoo across her forehead. DDD: Difficult, Disobedient, Defiant. She knew each new member would fall into at least one of those categories. Patricia's job was to erase those *D*s, to reach the *person*, to convince her she *could* learn. The gist of her job was to help them prepare for the GED test that would, she hoped, start them on the same educational path she herself had taken.

Patricia was personally committed to helping these young

women as the only way any part of her would ever be in the free world again. She felt, as she had argued with Sister Burke, that she did not deserve to leave prison, but spiritually she could send part of herself out every time one of her "Hoodlums" succeeded on the outside.

"Part of me goes out with you," she always included in her good-byes when they left the institution. Over the years, letters talking about school, jobs, family, children, were more gratifying to her than anything else in her life. And, as she moved into her mid-thirties, she realized something else: working with the kids, as she called them, satisfied two of her basic natural instincts: one was maternal, the other simply female. Acting almost as a surrogate mother to some of the students, Patricia was able to live a little easier with the haunting memory of Michael. And the occasional hug or smile of delight or sudden grasping of her hand fulfilled her need for personal affection.

Since coming to prison, Patricia had been involved in three intimate affairs, one with a male employee, two with fellow inmates. All had been for reasons in addition to sexual pleasure. With the male, a high-ranking officer, it had been to keep from being assigned to the kitchen, which was not only hard work but, at that time, had an entirely black crew she was fearful of joining. Her first lesbian affair had been for protection and favors; her second had been solely for protection—from her first female lover, who had been returned to Dwight and with whom Patricia did not wish to renew the previous relationship. All of the affairs had been short-lived, and for the last eight of her fourteen years locked up, she had been celibate. Feeling that she had experienced sex in most of its forms, even before being locked up, Patricia did not think she was missing much.

But not even the ongoing success with her "Hoodlums," or her own educational accomplishments as she neared her degree, could ease the pain of Sister Burke's absence.

She had felt a special sense of friendship, almost on a spiritual level, but it was not because Sister Burke had been a nun. The strong bond that had come with the exchange of words week after week, month after month, had nothing to do with religion; it had to do with trust. And truth.

There was so much still inside her that she and Sister

Burke had not yet reached. Her therapy with the nun had just begun to sort out the Patricia she had been at fifteen, about to meet Frank DeLuca, her first step on the path to murder.

Without Sister Burke, were the last eighteen years going to stay locked up inside her, just as she was locked up inside the prison?

In the honor cottage where Patricia lived, there was a telephone booth on the lower floor, from which residents of the cottage, all honor inmates, could place long-distance collect calls to family and friends. Patricia called Peggy Byrne several times a month just to chat. Before Sister Burke had been dead a month, she called Peggy one evening to hear the lawyer say, "A writer came to my office yesterday. He's going to write a book about you. He'd like to meet you."

"Not interested," Patricia told her. "I get contacted by writers a couple of times a year wanting to interview me, to get my help or permission or whatever, for some book or magazine. They all get the same answer: thanks but no thanks."

"This one is different," Peggy told her. "He's not asking permission; he's putting us on notice that he intends to write a book. And he's already had nineteen published, so he's for real. You might want to think about talking to this one. Most of what he writes is about prisons and people in them. He made an interesting point, too. If he writes the book without any input from you, you end up looking just like you did the day you were convicted. But *with* input from you, the reader will get a look at the person you are now. I think that's important, Trish."

"I don't know," Patricia said skeptically.

"There's something else to consider," Peggy continued. "This guy is an ex-street kid from right here on the West Side. His father did time in federal prison and his mother was a heroin addict. From the short time I spent with him, he seems like he understands how life can get out of hand, go wrong. Also, I got the impression he's very thorough; he just spent five weeks here reading your trial transcript."

"The *whole* transcript?" Patricia asked incredulously.

"The whole transcript," Peggy confirmed. "The man's serious, I'm telling you."

"Jesus, he must be. *I* haven't even read the whole transcript; I don't think anybody has."

"He's also been out to your old neighborhood on Ohio Street, and out to Elk Grove. He says he's been to the house where the crime took place, and to all the places mentioned in the testimony: the Where Else Lounge, the Ala Moana Restaurant, Walgreen's, the motels—"

"Christ!" Patricia said. It was neither a curse nor a prayer. More like an expression of astonishment. "Why now?" she asked, as much to herself as to Peggy. "After nearly fifteen years—"

"Maybe you should ask him that."

"I don't need this shit," Patricia bemoaned. "I've got enough goddamned things on my mind that I'm trying to deal with right now."

"I know," Peggy sympathized. "But if there's definitely going to be a book written anyway, don't you think you ought to show people that you aren't the same person you were fifteen years ago?"

Peggy heard her friend and client sigh wearily on the other end of the line. This time, as Sister Burke would have done, the lawyer gave her a moment of silence to gather her thoughts. It was the right thing to do; it moved the initiative to Patricia.

"Okay," Patricia said at last, "I'll meet him. I don't like the idea but I'll do it, just to see what he's like. But I want you there. And I want to wait until after the first of the year. I'd like to get through Thanksgiving and Christmas without a major goddamned trauma."

In her mind, Patricia was beginning to seethe. After *fifteen* fucking years! she thought angrily.

Goddamn son of a bitch!

C.H.
January 1991

Mid-January on the plank-flat plains of Illinois south of Chicago can sometimes seem like a frozen hell. Hard, cracked ground is covered with patches of treacherous ice; thin, biting

*air actually seems to attach itself to one's face; and overhead,
bleak, gray skies constantly threaten even worse punishment.
It is a perfect setting for a prison.*

*I parked my rented car on the rutted-dirt visitors' lot at
Dwight and trudged fifty yards over icy gravel toward the visiting office. At the counter, I told a male corrections sergeant,
"My name is Clark Howard. I'm here to meet Patricia Columbo's attorney, Margaret Byrne, and visit her client with
her."*

*The officer checked several notes attached to a clipboard,
then gave me a printed form.* "Fill this out, please."

"Sure. Is Miss Byrne here yet?"

"Not yet," *he replied.*

*There was a single table with half a dozen chairs around
it, and I sat down there to complete the form, piling my over-
coat, hat, and gloves on a vacant chair beside me. The form
was the usual prison visitor questionnaire:* Have you ever
been convicted of a felony? Are you currently on parole? Do
you use any other names? *I had filled out dozens just like it.*

*When I finished the form and returned it to the counter, the
sergeant was on the phone so the female officer took it and
asked me for identification. I gave her my California driver's
license and my membership card in the American Correctional Association, the national organization of wardens, corrections officers, and others in, or interested in, penology.
The officer had a name badge on her uniform, which read*
ESHELMAN.

"Are you related to Byron Eshelman?" *I asked.*

"Not that I know of," *she replied.* "Who's he?"

"He used to be the Protestant chaplain on Alcatraz," *I told
her, "then later at San Quentin."*

"It's my married name," *she said,* "but I don't think he's a
relative. I've never heard him mentioned."

*The sergeant, who was off the phone, listened to this ex-
change and then directed me into one of the inspection
rooms.*

"You can hang your coat up there." *He indicated a hook
on the wall.* "Remove everything from your pockets, please,
and take off your belt and shoes." *As I was complying, he
asked,* "You a clergyman?"

I was wearing a dark suit and a tie, but the question nev-

ertheless amused me. "No, I'm not a clergyman," I said. Nor had I ever been mistaken for one before.

After a thorough frisking, I was led to a bank of small metal lockers covering one wall, where I was given a key to one of them and told to leave all my personal belongings except twenty-five dollars, which I could take inside if I wished. None of the money could be given to an inmate, however; it could only be spent at the visiting room canteen counter.

The final step of my clearance was to have my hand stamped with ultraviolet ink and then to pass through a telephone-booth-size metal detector. On the other side of the detector, I sat on a bench to await admission to the big visiting room, which lay beyond a pair of windowed, electronically operated doors.

Back at the counter, the sergeant picked up the phone and asked, "Is Pat Columbo back there?" He paused a moment, then said, "Okay." Hanging up, he looked over at me and said, "She's in the visiting room but she won't see you until her lawyer gets here."

"No problem, Sergeant," I said.

I had waited a long time; a little while longer wouldn't bother me.

Peggy Byrne arrived a few minutes later, lugging a stuffed briefcase and complaining about the icy roads. She signed in to see Patricia and one other prisoner she had scheduled for that day, then went through the same search routine with Officer Eshelman. When she came through the metal detector, I said, "They search attorneys too, I see."

"Especially *attorneys*," Peggy cracked. The sergeant and Eshelman smiled.

Peggy Byrne was a smallish, attractive woman who was fair enough to have been Swedish or Norwegian instead of Irish. She had a straightforward manner and a voice that matched it. I got the impression the first time we met, in her office, that she had probably been a tomboy, as tough as any kid on her block. She was of indeterminate age, probably somewhere between thirty and forty.

After we'd passed through the electronic doors, Peggy led me to one of the private, glassed-in rooms where, I was to learn later, Sister Burke had held her therapy sessions with

Patricia. We settled down on two sides of a table and waited. It was only a moment before the door opened again and Patricia came in. I stood up and Peggy introduced us. We shook hands across the table.

"Patricia," I said.

"Hello."

We studied each other for a moment. "You're taller than I expected," I said.

"I could crouch down," she told me.

I wanted to smile but wouldn't let myself. "That's okay, I'll adjust."

We sat down, both of us wary, Patricia I'm sure far more than me.

A pretty little girl in ribbons and lace—

"Clark, why don't you tell Trish what you told me in my office, about your concept of her case," Peggy suggested. "Naturally, I've discussed it with her, but I think she should hear it directly from you too."

"Sure." I sat back in my chair for a moment, deciding how to start. A meeting like this can't be rehearsed, it has to be spontaneous. And it has to be completely on the level, without bullshit. When you're dealing with a person who's been locked up for nearly half her life, you are up against a convict mentality—whether or not that person realizes it. Years of confinement work subtle but eventually substantial changes in a long-term convict's thought processes. The most significant is the person's suspicion level. On a scale of one to ten, a person in the free world has a suspicion quotient that hovers around two or three, while the norm for a convict who has been inside for a long time is around eight. And that suspicion, conscious and subconscious, stays with a career convict every waking hour, an ever-present impediment to valid conversation. In addition, if the person is of superior intelligence, as Peggy Byrne had assured me Patricia Columbo was, the task of communicating can be transformed from an ordinary conversational challenge into a grueling psychological duel.

When Peggy asked me that day to tell Patricia my concept of her case, what the attorney did not realize was how much that concept had expanded in the two months since my visit to her office. In that time, I had researched and absorbed an enormous amount of information that went all the way back to the name of the doctor who had delivered little Patty Columbo. It was mostly virgin information, too: facts about Patricia Columbo that no one else had thought important enough to go after. I had found out from my New Jersey crime-book expert, Patterson Smith, that no one had written a book about her either.

What I had in mind now regarding Patricia Columbo was a book not merely about the murders, but a book about Patricia Columbo, the person. *The pretty little girl, dressed just so, in ribbons and lace, who now wore jeans and a sweatshirt, and lived behind a razor-wire fence. I wanted to know* why.

"Okay," I said to Patricia and Peggy. "Here's my concept, as of this moment. I see a triangle, with you in the middle of it, Patricia. At the top point of the triangle is your father, Frank Columbo. It's been reported that you remember him sexually molesting you as a child." Patricia and Peggy exchanged quick glances that registered and locked in my mind; of course, as I would learn, they already knew it was not her father. "If the sexual abuse story is true," I said, "I'll crucify your father in this book. But if it's not true, I'll tell the world it's not.

*"Second point of the triangle: Frank DeLuca. More than twice your age when you met him in the late spring of 1972. A man much like your father: almost as old, Italian-American, even the same first name. If you were looking for a substitute father, someone to have un*forbidden *sex with, this guy was perfect. When he came in the door as the new manager of Walgreen's the first time, he might as well have been riding a white horse. You fell for him like an adolescent falls for a rock star.*

"Then you're caught between two authority figures, between the two Franks: your father, who eventually finds out about DeLuca and vehemently opposes the relationship; and your lover, who is a sexual psychopath, as we all find out later, and is in the process of teaching you everything a teenage girl needs to know about sex—and a lot she doesn't *need to know.*

"Eventually Frank number one, your father, lets his Italian temper get the best of him; he smashes Frank number two,

your lover, in the face with a rifle butt on Walgreen's parking lot one night. You have your father put in jail; he swears he's going to kill you and your lover both. You probably don't really believe he would ever hurt you—you're his only daughter, you've been his little princess all your life; possibly you've been more than that. So apparently you're not afraid for yourself, but you truly believe that your father is sincere in his threat against your lover. And you believe your father has the connections to buy a contract on your lover's life. He works with the Teamsters' Union, with loading-dock labor, and he's involved in a couple of businesses that pay him in cash that he keeps in a wall safe at home. So he can probably arrange a hit if he really wants to.

"Third point of the triangle. Enter two hustlers named Lanny Mitchell and Roman Sobczynski. Again, two older men. They talk tough, they act tough, they carry guns. Lanny is a car salesman and a world-class liar; Roman is a former deputy sheriff, a married man with a family, who likes teen-age girls.

"Lanny offers to kill your parents so you'll be left as Michael's guardian and have control of your father's estate, even though you are now out of his will. There's a price for that kind of help, however, and since you don't have any front money, they accept a substitute: your lush young teenage body. So you start balling them as preliminary payment, with the cash to come after the estate is settled. You don't tell DeLuca about any of this because you don't want him to know you're sexually involved with these two; he thinks that you're trying to arrange through your godfather to somehow resolve the bad blood between you two and your father.

"Now, as time goes by, Lanny and Roman stall you with one excuse after another: they need a floor plan of the house, pictures of the occupants, their daily routine, later on cash up front, which they figure DeLuca can siphon off the drugstore receipts. Finally they tell you that one of the things really holding up the hit is your brother; it's too hard to kill your parents without killing him too. So you agree to that, in order to get the hit moving. You probably figure you can somehow get Michael out later.

"By now, DeLuca is a nervous wreck. He is so completely convinced that your father is going to get him first that he's

driving different routes to work every day, getting off the el-
evator on different floors in the building where you live, even
carrying a loaded derringer for protection. He's so shaky that
you finally persuade Roman, who he thinks is your godfather,
to talk to him twice on the telephone in an effort to calm him
down. In one of those conversations, DeLuca now tells Ro-
man to go ahead and kill your kid brother, Michael, too—but
not to tell you they're going to do it. Michael, according to
your lover, had been coming into Walgreen's and staring at
him, and he was convinced the kid was part of your father's
vendetta against him.

"All this convoluted business went on until it finally
dawned on your adolescent mind that these two would-be hit
men, Roman and Lanny, weren't going to do anything but
milk you dry for whatever they could get. It was at this point,
according to the prosecution's theory at your trial, that you
and your lover, Frank DeLuca, decided you'd have to do the
murders yourselves."

I sat back in my chair in the little visiting room. Patricia
Columbo's eyes were riveted on me, as were Peggy Byrne's.
This, of course, was only my initial, very early evaluation of
what had happened. There was much, much more that I
would uncover, later, that would erase the fuzzy edges of what
I knew then, and make some pieces of this complex story fit
snugly. Unfortunately, too, I was to learn that some of them
would never fit.

"You and Frank are ultimately arrested," I summed up,
"you first and him about six weeks later, and you are tried together for the killings. Roman and Lanny testify against you
in exchange for immunity from the state. You don't testify in
your own behalf, but DeLuca takes the stand and calls everybody but God a liar—even after a witness has come forward
to tell the jury how DeLuca tried from his county jail cell to
have two people killed so they couldn't testify against him.
Needless to say, he failed to charm the jury; it only took them
two hours to find you both guilty.

"Now," I said very evenly to Patricia, "here it is 1991 and
you've been confined for nearly fifteen years. You didn't testify at your trial, you refuse to talk to the press, you reject
writers who want to tell your story, you won't even make an
appearance at your own parole hearings. Some people call

*that an attitude problem; others say you're just stupid and
your own worst enemy. Whatever the reason, if you keep it
up, you'll stay in here until you're old and gray."*

*"Did it ever occur to you," Patricia asked in a tone just as
even as mine, "that maybe I should stay in here? Did it ever
occur to you that I might be exactly where I belong?"*

"That," I said, "is not for you to decide. It never will be."

*She shifted her eyes for a moment and allowed herself a
faint, controlled sigh. "Look," she said in a quieter voice, a
voice that had the hint of a tremor in it, "I've got a good life
in here. And I am accomplishing something. I don't even think
of this place as a prison, really; to me it's more like a rescue
center. It rescued me from a situation I was in that was totally
out of control: out of my control, out of everybody's control.
I should be dead by now—and you'll never know how many
times I've wished I was. But this place saved me and showed
me how to make a little something of my life by helping to
rescue other girls who come in here for the first time. I'm
doing something in here that I couldn't do on the outside. And
I'm safe in here; I'm protected from the Frank DeLucas of
the world, the Lanny Mitchells, the Roman Sobczynskis. I
don't want to be vulnerable to those kind of men ever again."*

*"You're not fifteen or seventeen or nineteen years old
now," I reminded her. "From everything about you I've heard
from Peggy, I'd feel sorry for any man who tried to take advantage of you now."*

*"I handle myself fine in here, in a controlled environment,"
Patricia pointed out. "I'm not sure I'd have the same ability
in the free world."*

*A single word reverberated in my mind: institutionalized.
She had been incorporated into this structured and highly
formalized system for so long that it had become part of her
character. It was the only home she had, the only life she now
knew; like a native in some aboriginal land, she was afraid
of the world outside.*

*"Clark, what is the focus of your book going to be, ex-
actly?" Peggy asked.*

*"Patricia Ann Columbo," I said. "From the day of her
birth until the present time."*

"So you intend to tell about her education here in prison,

and her work with the girls she tutors, her status as an honor prisoner, all that."

"Absolutely. I'll put in the book everything I find out about her—good and bad."

"Do you think the book will show her in a sympathetic light?"

I shrugged. "Only insofar as the facts are sympathetic toward her. I don't think the book will make anyone like her; it may make some people understand her." I looked at Patricia. "It may help you to understand yourself a little better too. That's happened before with books written about people in prison, even people on death row."

A silence came over our little room. I sensed that it would be a good time to let Patricia and Peggy have a few minutes of privacy. "Why don't I get us some coffee?" I suggested.

"Good idea," Peggy said.

I left the room and went to stand in a short line at the canteen window, from which I could see the entire visitors' room. The cross section of women in Dwight appeared to be a full range, ages from the teens to the mid-fifties; some women were having visits with grandchildren. Every color seemed to be represented: black, brown, tan, yellow, white. Most of the women were free to move about and play with their kids; a few were handcuffed and had to remain in one chair.

As I was waiting in line, an extremely pretty, petite Latino girl, probably still in her teens, rose from where she was sitting with a young man and came over to me. "Excuse me," she said with a radiant smile, "but are you with the parole board?"

"No, I'm not," I told her. "Just a visitor."

"Oh. Sorry," she said, and went back to her young man.

I had to wonder where the conversation would have gone if I had been a member of the parole board. But, neither a clergyman nor a parole board member, just a visitor in a suit and tie, I got the coffee and returned to the little private room.

"What would you want me to tell you if I agreed to help you with your book?" Patricia asked as soon as I sat down.

"Anything you wanted to tell me," I said.

"And whatever I tell you, you'll put in the book?"

"Yes."

"What if you don't believe what I tell you?"

"I'll still put it in," I said. *"The fact that I personally might not believe something doesn't mean that it isn't the truth. I put everything in, everything I find out; then I let the readers decide what* they *want to believe."*

"Are you going to talk to Frank DeLuca?" Peggy asked, probably to keep Patricia from having to.

"I will attempt *to talk to everybody who can tell me anything at all about Patricia,"* I replied.

"And what everybody tells you goes into the book too?"

"Yes. There's no other way to do it, unless I want to take one side against another. And that's not objective writing."

"Most of what you hear about me is not going to be very nice," Patricia warned.

"That's why it's important for you to finally tell your side of it," I pointed out. *"Telling your side of the story is something you've never done."*

"It's something I've never done publicly," she corrected. *"I had been telling my side of it to a friend, a nun. But she died recently."*

"I'm sorry. It's tough to lose a friend."

"Especially tough when you can fit all you've got into a broom closet. Free-world friends, that is." Abruptly she stood up. *"I've got to get out of here so I can have a cigarette. I presume I have some time to think this over?"*

"Sure. Peggy has my number; you can call me anytime. I'll be making another research trip to Chicago in a month or so, to interview people I've located and lined up. I expect to be working on this for at least another year."

"That long?" She seemed surprised.

"It's not like you're an easy subject," I said.

I got the faintest of smiles.

When I left Dwight Correctional Center that cold January day, I had no idea whether I'd ever hear from Patricia Columbo. I had been completely unable to read her. I knew I could write the book without her, but I feared readers would only know everything Patricia did; they wouldn't know Patricia.

And she was correct to assume that most of what I would hear about her would be negative; I had already discovered

*that in several conversations I'd had with lawyers and others
at the Criminal Courts Building while reading the transcript.
Patricia Columbo was not Chicago's favorite daughter. Without input from her, without knowing how she felt and reacted
at given points in her life, the book would definitely be heavily weighed against comprehending her.*

*I hoped for her sake, as well as my own, that she would
call.*

*At ten o'clock on Saturday night three weeks later, my private
line rang and an operator said, "I have a collect call from a
correctional facility. Will you accept charges?"*

It was Patricia.

We talked for five hours.

25
June to October 1972

Patricia worked full-time for Corky's that summer, and when
school began again and she entered her junior year of high
school, she resumed after-school and Saturday hours. Frank
Columbo was used to the idea by then and although he
voiced his disfavor on a more or less regular basis, he took
no serious steps to alter the situation. His disinclination to
act, some friends felt, was because Mary was more content
having Patricia gone from the house the extra twenty-three
hours a week, and because Patricia's attitude around the
house had markedly improved since going to work. Michael,
of course, thought it was super that his sister worked at
Corky's. He ate like a young hippo and ranged openly in and
out of the burger shop for fries and pop, which Patricia, as
Eunice said she could, gave to him gratis. Not only Patricia,
but Eunice herself when Patricia was not there.

"That Michael," Eunice would say. "If I had a kid, I'd
want him to be exactly like Michael. I swear to God, I never
saw a cuter kid in my life. And can he eat!"

If their supervisor happened to be around when Michael
came in, Patricia fed him anyway and simply paid his check
herself. Her father continued to give her an allowance every

week, and since she had begun working she had more money than she knew what to do with. She frequently gave Michael money without his even asking for it.

"Here's movie money," she would say, handing him a few dollars, or, "Here's money for the baseball cards you want." It meant that Michael was getting substantially more money than his parents had decided was suitable for *his* allowance, but neither of them criticized their daughter for the practice, nor asked her to stop. Where once it had been Patricia who was spoiled and indulged in the household, now it was Michael—with his sister's considerable help.

At school, the distributive-education counselor, as promised, offered to find Patricia a job with a little more glamour and appeal than counter girl at Corky's, but Patricia declined the offer.

"I really like it there," she told the teacher. "I like the lady I work with, and I've been given two raises already. It's lots of fun waiting on all the different people who come in. I think I'd be bored at a reception desk or doing office work."

Patricia was making tuna salad the first time the imposingly handsome man with the neatly combed thick black hair came into Corky's. He had dark, lively eyes, a straight, perfect nose, and slightly wide but finely formed lips. Eunice waited on him at a table in the farthest corner near the connecting door to Walgreen's. All he ordered was coffee.

"Who is *that*?" Patricia asked Eunice as soon as she could.

"He's the new manager at Walgreen's," said Eunice. "Works in the pharmacy and runs the store too, one of the cashiers said."

"My God, he's handsome," Patricia told her.

"Yeah, not bad," Eunice allowed, "if you like them real good-looking. Me, I like a man to be rugged, more outdoorsy looking. Take my husband Ed, now—"

Patricia appeared to be listening but she had completely tuned Eunice out, so riveted was her attention on the new drugstore manager. He was easily the most attractive man she had ever seen. The moment she saw him, there was a warm rush in her bosom and she actually felt her nipples harden. The man glanced over at her without smiling and she knew she must have blushed because then he did smile, just slightly, as if amused. He picked up a discarded newspaper from an adjoining table then and began reading it, paying no further attention to her. But Patricia was smitten.

Later that afternoon, when a Walgreen's clerk came in, Patricia asked about the new manager. "Yeah, Mr. DeLuca," the girl said. "He just transferred from the Schaumburg store. Cute, huh?"

"Cute's not the word for him," Patricia replied candidly. "The man's got dynamite good looks. Is he married, do you know?"

"I don't think so. He doesn't wear a ring. Not that *that* means anything anymore. I've got this girlfriend—"

Patricia paid little attention except to register the fact that the girl thought her new manager was unmarried. Patricia felt oddly pleased that with a name like DeLuca, he obviously was Italian like she. Or maybe more than she, since she was only half-Italian. The knowledge delighted her for some reason and gave her another warm rush in the chest.

The next day, DeLuca came in for a coffee break with one of the assistant managers who worked for him, and Patricia waited on them. DeLuca smiled pleasantly at her when he ordered, and Patricia gave him a definitely self-conscious smile in return. Their eyes met only fleetingly, but she thought she saw in them the same hint of amusement she had observed that morning. She hurried off quickly to get their coffee.

When Patricia served them, DeLuca was talking to the other man about college. "I played football for Purdue," he was saying, "the year Ohio State went to the Rose Bowl—"

Purdue, Patricia thought as she walked away. *Football. God, this got better and better!*

While DeLuca was still in Corky's that day, Patricia said to Eunice, "I cannot get *over* how handsome that guy is."

"Yeah, but he's too old for you, honey," Eunice said.

"How old do you think he is?" she asked.

Eunice gave DeLuca a brief, clinical look. "Around thirty-two or so. That's twice your age, honey."

"Listen," Patricia said seriously, "don't spread it around that I'm only fifteen, okay? If anyone should ask."

"Like him, you mean?" Eunice replied knowingly.

"Yeah. Pretend I'm eighteen. I *am* almost sixteen."

The older woman shook her head. "Oh, no. Not me, kiddo. I'm not getting involved in that kind of stuff, not with you being underage and all."

"Just say you don't know, then," Patricia pleaded. "Come on, Eunice, please."

"I'll say I don't know, but that's as far as I'll go," Eunice said. "I don't want your parents over here on my back if you get mixed up with this guy."

"I'm not going to get mixed up with him," Patricia declared. "I just don't want him thinking I'm some kind of teenybopper, that's all."

"Yeah, well, you better watch your step, young lady," Eunice warned. To Patricia she sounded incredibly like Mary Columbo.

For the next few days, Patricia took careful note of the approximate times DeLuca came into Corky's for his afternoon coffee break. She was careful to make sure the table he seemed to favor, the one nearest the Walgreen's door, was always cleaned off and waiting for him when he came in. A couple of times she even had other people move if they occupied the table at the wrong time.

"Excuse me, but that table's taken," she would say. "The manager of the drugstore is sitting there. He had to go answer a phone call." Then she would put a cup and saucer on the table, and bring DeLuca's coffee when he came in.

"What is this, special treatment?" he asked, the first time she did it.

"Could be," Patricia replied coyly. She surprised herself by not feeling like she was blushing.

One Friday afternoon he did not come in for coffee, and she went looking for him. "I'll be right back, Eunice. I have to run get a birthday card before I forget it."

In the big drugstore, she hurried to the greeting card section, randomly selected a birthday card, then strolled casually past the pharmacy. DeLuca was filling prescriptions.

"No break this afternoon?" she asked demurely.

"Oh, hello," he said. "No, too busy."

"I was afraid you might be tired of my coffee."

"Your coffee's fine," he said. Looking over the glass partition of the pharmacy, he smiled. "I'll make up for it by having lunch there tomorrow," he promised. By then he knew Patricia worked all day on Saturdays.

Beginning at noon sharp the next day, she was a nervous wreck. Every two minutes she looked at the clock, at the door, at "his" table, all the while trying to do her share of work during the busy lunch hour. She had primped her hair and freshened her makeup just before the noon rush, but by the time it was over, an hour later, she felt disheveled and sweaty. Hurrying into the employee bathroom, she quickly re-did herself. When she returned to the counter, DeLuca was walking in.

Patricia fixed him a sandwich and hung around his table while he ate. "Will you answer a question for me?" she asked at one point.

"What's the question?" he countered.

"How old are you?"

"Why do you want to know?"

"I want to settle an argument between a couple of the girls who work for you," she lied.

"Which ones?" he wanted to know.

"Come on," she hedged. "I don't want to embarrass them. They don't even know I'm asking."

"I'm twenty-eight," he said.

Eunice was off by four years, she thought.

"How old are you?" he asked. It was an unexpected question, but not so unexpected that it generated the truth.

"Eighteen," she lied.

"But you're still in high school." It was an inquiry without being a direct question.

"Yeah, I'll be in my senior year. I started a year late." How, she wondered, did he know she was still in high school? Had he asked about her as she had about him? She felt warm inside.

The next morning when Patricia brought him his coffee, he said, "Since we know each other's age don't you think we should know each other's name?"

Patricia shrugged. "Sure. Mine's Patricia." She didn't want to say "Patty"; it sounded so—immature.

"Mine's Frank," said DeLuca.

"No kidding?" she replied, surprised. "That's my dad's name too. So, Frank DeLuca, Italian, right?"

"Right."

"Me too." She gave her chest a quick pat as if he might not understand who she was talking about. "Columbo. I'm Italian too. On one side anyway."

Because she always looked at DeLuca's face, his eyes, his wavy black hair, Patricia did not notice the missing forefinger on his left hand until a few days later. The hand had always been in his pocket, or under the table, or holding a newspaper down at his side. When she did notice it, her lips parted slightly in surprise, but she was alert enough to check her words. DeLuca saw the look.

"I lost it in a skydiving accident," he said easily, as if it were inconsequential. "I used to skydive a lot. One day my primary chute didn't open. When I pulled the ring to open my safety chute, one of the cords wrapped around my finger and the pressure took it right off."

"My God, how terrible!" Patricia sympathized. DeLuca gave her a cavalier shrug.

"Could have been a lot more terrible," he said. "It was worth a finger to save the rest of me."

From that point on, after he told her about his accident, she felt as if they had known each other for years. She called him Frank, even though nearly everyone else addressed him as "Mr. DeLuca." He started calling her "Patrish," much to her delight. And he treated her not only like an equal, but as if she were a very close friend. This, she was thoroughly convinced, was a remarkably special man.

The age thing bothered Patricia. She was not worried about the number of years between them; only that DeLuca might find out that she had just barely turned sixteen. It mortified her to think that this handsome, educated, professional man, who had become so friendly, might then regard her as just a teenybopper like the ones who flocked into Corky's for Cokes and fries, sloppily dressed, loud, leaving a big mess behind them. Patricia could not have endured for Frank to consider her in the same category.

She was in love, Patricia now knew that. It had to be love, real love, for the first time, because never had she been so consumed, both physically and emotionally. Frank DeLuca was practically *all* she thought about anymore. She woke up in the morning thinking about him, he was constantly on her mind during the day, and she went to bed at night thinking about him. It was fascination, enchantment, and enormous physical attraction, all merged together to create a magnetic field that completely surrounded her.

She started closing her bedroom door at night, the old fear dying that her father would enter the room. Lying in bed in the darkness, she let adolescent fantasies take hold and completely captivate her. In her imagination, Frank DeLuca was *hers*; she visualized herself with him in dozens of situations: in a car together, her head on his shoulder, his arm around her; out to dine, the two of them at a small candlelit table in an elegant restaurant like the kind seen on television and in the movies; taking him home, introducing him to her smiling parents, sitting with him on the couch in the Columbo living room, holding hands while they all made wedding plans; the two of them taking Michael to a ball game. Grand flights of fancy.

Sometimes her reveries took her onto a more erotic plane. Frank, vitally handsome, his shirt off, black curly hair on his chest. Frank in a shower, with her. Frank in bed, with her— his naked body cleanly sculpted, that body that had played football and skydived; his hands loving and confident, not awkward like Jack's. Everything Frank did would be perfect. As perfect as her own hand when it found its way under her nightgown, when her fingers eased into the soft, warm folds of herself, already moist from thoughts of him, and found that wonderful, hidden kernel of her womanhood, the slightest touch of which would generate the beginning of rapture. Just thinking of it with Frank was almost too unbearable.

She was utterly in love.

Patricia found herself, in youthful eagerness, developing a keen possessiveness toward Frank DeLuca. She did not try to resist it; at times, she even relished it. Frank was making her feel like someone special in his life—just the intimate way he called her "Patrish" was proof of that—and it generated in her a desire, almost an obligation, to respond. She felt she had to let him know that he was someone special to her also. His table was always clean and waiting for him, cup and saucer there for her to pour when he sat down. All he had to do was walk in and she interrupted whatever she was doing to take care of him. If she was in the middle of taking an order, she simply excused herself and hurried for the coffee pot. Preparing an order, she just stopped, left it. It did not matter what she was doing; *nothing* mattered, except him.

There was no longer any question who would serve DeLuca when he entered Corky's. Eunice saw what was happening and had the good sense to back off; she wanted no part of a situation that she instantly perceived as, at best, inappropriate, and at worst, explosive. A couple of times she repeated her all-purpose, adult warning to Patricia: *You'd better watch your step, young lady*. To which Patricia only smiled, rejected the advice with a shrug of her young shoulders, and went blithely on with the game she was playing. Except to her it wasn't diversion or amusement; it was a persuasive urgency compelling her actions as surely as her lungs compelled her to breathe.

Physically mature beyond her sixteen years, Patricia was still leagues away from being emotionally developed. The complex arena of adult relationships had been experienced by her only in two extreme settings: the surroundings of people who loved and cared about her, and the submerged memory of the back of the candy van. The vast plain between was totally new territory. But she trooped onto it with wide-eyed confidence, as if she'd been there many times before. A pilgrim, oblivious to the predators.

Patricia sought to see Frank DeLuca at every juncture of her day. If she arrived at work and he was already in the drugstore, she would walk in near the pharmacy and wave to let him know she was there. If he did not open the store but came in later, she would watch for him and wave when he went by the connecting door. On his breaks she served his coffee; on hers she strolled around the big drugstore until she found him—filling prescriptions, setting up a display, checking receipts from a cash register: he was all over the place, but Patricia always located him. She would loiter wherever he was, engaging him in idle small talk just to be near him and hear the sound of his voice, which she thought had the most wonderful resonant tone she had ever heard; was there nothing, she found herself marveling, that was *not* wonderful about this man?

A day rarely passed in which "Patrish" did not have six, eight, even more encounters with "her" Frank, as she had begun to think of him. And when she was not actually meeting him to talk to, because he was behind the pharmacy partition or otherwise engaged, she was prowling the drugstore to spy on him. The least little sight of him with another woman made her jealous. If he chatted with a female customer and she observed it, she would later ask, "Who was the blonde you were so friendly with this morning?"

DeLuca was always composed. "What blonde?"

"You know what blonde," she would chide. "The one you were talking to in the liquor department. The one with the body."

"I don't remember." He would shrug off the query imperturbably. "Just a customer, I guess."

"Oh, sure." She would give him her best knowing look, then accuse, in as trivial a tone as she could muster, "I think you're a flirt, Frank."

"I think you are too, Patrish."

"Only with you," she would rightly claim. "I don't flirt with anybody else." And it was true. If Paul Newman had walked into Corky's, she wouldn't have given him a second look. Frank DeLuca was the *only* man in the world, period.

Once she saw him talking at length with an attractive, dark-haired woman whom he later walked all the way through the store to the front door and then kissed on the cheek when she left. Patricia seethed about it until his afternoon coffee break, then confronted him with her observation. "I suppose," she said coolly, "that the woman you kissed good-bye at the door was just a customer too?"

"No, she was a special customer," he teased. Her jealousy was obvious, as was her anger.

"Do you have many 'special' customers?" Patricia asked.

"No, just that one."

"What's so special about her?" It was clear that Patricia was approaching her boiling point.

"What's so special about her is that she's my baby sister," he said in a completely casual tone.

"Oh." Patricia wanted to disappear. Simply vanish. Never had she felt so totally stupid. It had not even *occurred* to her that the interplay between Frank and the woman could have been innocent. Never entered her mind. She had stepped into her first rut on the road of adult relationships.

DeLuca smiled. "Does that make it okay for me to kiss her?"

"Just barely," Patricia admitted grudgingly. She smiled back very self-consciously, and briefly touched his arm. "I'm sorry, Frank."

DeLuca winked at her. The wink spoke volumes to her: he understood, he cared, he forgave.

God, he was wonderful.

A month or so after she started back to school and returned to part-time work, DeLuca said to her on his coffee break one afternoon, "Do you like working at Corky's, Patrish?"

"Sure," she replied.

"Suppose I offered you a job, would you turn me down?"

"You know I wouldn't," she told him earnestly. She had reached the point where she wouldn't turn him down for *anything*. "Are you joking with me?" she asked.

"No. I've been thinking about asking you to transfer into the drugstore. You're already eighteen and this is your last year of high school. If you started working part-time for Walgreen's, when you graduate you could move right into a full-time job without looking for one. What do you think?"

What she thought was that she was *not* eighteen, *not* a senior, and had not the remotest notion how long she was going to be able to keep up her subterfuge. But at that moment it didn't matter. Frank wanted her to *work* for him! "I think it's a great idea," she said delightedly. She wondered if she was going to be a stock clerk, wearing one of those dingy gray smocks.

"I'd like to put you in cosmetics," DeLuca said. "Behind the counter where you can wear nice clothes and dress up. This job at Corky's is kid stuff. You're not a kid, you're a woman."

Patricia stared at him. *Cosmetics! God!* That was *the* best department in the whole drugstore. She could scarcely believe her ears.

"You can start as a part-time trainee," DeLuca said. "There are a couple of very knowledgeable ladies working alternating shifts there who can teach you all about the lines we carry, how to sell, how to order and restock. By the time you graduate next year, you'd be qualified for a full-time job. The next step after that is department manager."

"Do you really mean it?" It seemed too good to be true.

"Of course I mean it."

"Well, do you think Walgreen's would hire me?"

"Patrish," he reminded her, "I'm the boss. I do the hiring." He gave her a conspiratorial wink. "I don't think you'll have any trouble getting the job."

She stopped by the pharmacy later that day and DeLuca gave her an employment application. In her bedroom that night she carefully and neatly filled it out, altering her date of birth from June 1956 to June 1954. She was slightly apprehensive about doing it, because her original work application at Corky's showed the true date. If Frank for some reason compared the two, he was sure to challenge her about her age—and then her life would be ruined, forever.

The next day she gave DeLuca the application, and spent all morning waiting for something dreadful to happen. When he came in for coffee, she studied his expression for some sign that he had found her out. Frank, she feared, was such a straight person, that to catch her deliberately lying to him like that, in *writing*, would probably ruin her in his estimation forever. What did it matter how old she was anyway, for God's sake? She hated, absolutely *detested*, the fact that she was only sixteen!

But toward the end of the day, her young life was filled with sunshine again when DeLuca came in, had a few words with Eunice, then told her, "Well, it's all set, Patrish. I told Eunice to start looking for a replacement for you. As soon as she finds one, you can move over to the drugstore."

"God, I don't *believe* it!" Patricia shrieked. Her face flushed with joy. "I am so happy!" She wanted to throw her arms around Frank DeLuca and cover him with kisses. But she could not do that, not in front of the customers in Corky's, not in front of Eunice. So she just wrung her hands in gladness. DeLuca was smiling widely at her enjoyment, which enhanced the moment for her all the more. Patricia turned toward Eunice, to share her happiness with the older woman, but Eunice wasn't looking at Patricia; she had her eyes on DeLuca, in a cold, flat gaze that for a split instant provoked the pinch of a frown between Patricia's dark eyebrows. However, she was not about to let Eunice's disapproval dampen her own elation; Eunice had a beer-truck driver for a husband, the most positive thing she had ever said about him was that he could identify trees, and their goal in life was to live in a trailer home. How could Eunice understand the dream that Patricia was already cultivating: marriage to an accomplished, educated professional man; a nice home in the suburbs—in Patricia's mind it was nicer even than the Columbo home, in the farther suburbs, on a larger lot, with a white picket fence around it; a family, two kids: one little boy for Frank, whom they would name Frank DeLuca, Jr., and a little girl for her, whom she might name Mary after her mother.

As Patricia had done with Eunice's occasional advice, she did now with the older woman's look of censure: she shrugged it off. Patricia turned her eyes back onto her knight-champion-hero, her demigod of the drugstore, her rescuer from mediocrity, the pilot who would fly her on gossamer wing to the wonderful world of Cosmetics, Adulthood, and Happiness Ever After.

"Frank, I can never pay you back for this," she told him deliriously.

"Seeing you this happy is payment enough, Patrish," he replied.

She could not see far enough ahead to know that payment had not yet even begun.

DeLuca got off an hour before Patricia did one evening while she was still at Corky's, and waited for her. He knew that when she finished work, she customarily walked to the Arlington Heights Road side of the big parking lot, jaywalked across as soon as traffic permitted, and entered the residential neighborhood on the other side where she lived. DeLuca sat in his car, window rolled down, in the parking space nearest where she normally crossed, and was there, smoking a cigarette, when Patricia walked up.

"Hi," he said.

"Hi." She was not surprised, having expected him to make a move on her since the day her transfer to the drugstore was announced. She had even prepared for it, casually telling her parents that she had agreed to work a late shift to fill in for another girl who was getting married and expected a surprise bridal shower.

"It could be any night," Patricia had told her parents, "so when I don't come home, you'll know where I am." It was her first lie in the cause of Frank DeLuca.

"Do you have to go right home?" DeLuca asked when Patricia stopped at his car.

She shook her head. "No."

"Want to go for a ride?"

"All right." No hesitation, no apprehension. He was doing what she had been waiting for.

Patricia got into his car and DeLuca pulled onto the boulevard. When he made a U-turn to head north, she was swept by a feeling of déjà vu; it was exactly what Jack Formaski had done that first time he picked her up in front of the Cinema Two, which could be seen from where Frank had parked. And Frank, she suspected, was probably driving to the same place Jack had driven: the forest preserves. She couldn't help being just a shade disappointed; somehow it didn't seem right for Frank to be doing the same thing Jack had done. When DeLuca finally did turn into the main road that bisected the woods, she had to tell herself that she was probably being dumb. Maybe *all* guys took *all* girls here for the first time.

"Want to park for a while?" DeLuca asked, slowing the car even as he spoke.

"Okay." She began to feel nervous, even a little scared. This was no teenage kid she was with; it was unlikely that she would be able to check Frank DeLuca's passion, Frank DeLuca's advances, Frank DeLuca's physical intimidation, as she had done with Jack. She was not going to be in control here, and that prospect, while it was certainly what she desired, nevertheless raised the awareness of her own vulnerability.

"This looks okay," DeLuca said, pulling off the main road onto a short lane that ended at the base of a low grassy hill. As soon as he turned off the engine and headlights, DeLuca shifted in his seat and drew her toward him. She parted her lips as he leaned into her and they kissed for the first time. It was a long, slow, warm kiss, soft and dry despite the open mouths. He kept one arm around her shoulders, the other hand high on her turned right hip. There was no groping, no clutching, no sense of desperation in him. To Patricia, he seemed to know exactly how he wanted to proceed and was doing so with absolutely no sense of urgency. As she had anticipated, there was no question that he was in control.

They kissed a second time, a third, and then the kisses ceased being individual and became a long series of one coupled with another and another and another. Only as they continued to delicately press their lips together did Patricia first sense a rising of desire in him—not in their kisses but in the way his hands suddenly tightened on her body, as if he had to be sure that she could not extricate herself.

Finally they parted a few inches and DeLuca said, "Let's get in the backseat."

There, without the restriction of the steering wheel, he had her lie back on the length of the cushion as he unbuttoned her blouse and deftly, expertly, unfastened each strap of her bra to pull it down around her waist. He began sucking on her nipples, alternately kneading one breast while his mouth was on the other. Patricia lay her head back, closing her eyes, lips parting. She did not moan, but the slow, audible intakes of breath expressed the sensitivity of her nipples; Frank's presence, the sound of his voice, had made them harden numerous times under her clothes; now with his lips around them, tongue teasing them, her breasts felt so bloated, she thought they might burst.

"Does that feel good?" DeLuca asked in a whisper.

"Y—yes—"

"I know lots of ways to make you feel good," he told her. "Lift up—"

Under the guidance of his hands, Patricia arched her buttocks off the seat and felt DeLuca unzip her skirt and slide it and her panties down to her ankles and off. He laid them on the top of the passenger seat and then gently raised her right leg and put it over his shoulder. His head bent toward her and she felt his kisses in her abundant pubic hair. Her intake of breath began to sputter as her desire built. Presently the pubic kisses became slow, gentle licks from the bottom of her vulva to the top, wetting the hair, matting it aside, reaching the smooth lips of her pubes, sliding moistly up to the tiny teardrop of her clitoris. When his tongue found it, he had only a second to service it before Patricia's body stiffened and she peaked in an explosion of rapture.

"Oh—my—God—!"

She used both hands to force his head away. It was so euphoric she could not continue it, the ultrasensitivity of it too overwhelming to bear.

"Did you like that?" DeLuca asked. In the darkness, and the afterglow of her climax, his voice seemed very far away.

"Jesus, yes," she answered.

She became aware that his hands were moving in the darkness and she knew that he was probably undressing. Presently he was kneeling on the cushion between her legs and she could feel the head of his erection moving up and down the wet path made by his tongue. Then the stroking stopped and she felt the head being inserted between the tender lips. She let out an involuntary gasp and the inward movement stopped.

"Did that hurt?"

"Yes."

"You're so tight," he said. It wasn't a complaint. After a moment of stillness and silence, he asked, "Are you a *virgin*?" His tone, even in a whisper, was incredulous.

"Yes."

"Jesus Christ." This he muttered to himself. "It will probably hurt," he told her.

"Hurt me," Patricia said.

"You'll probably bleed."

"Make me bleed."

"Once I get started, I'll put it all the way in," he warned.

Sure, she thought. He'll go all the way. She gripped his shoulders under the shirt he still had on.

"Do it," she said.

The pain was excruciating.

26
June 1976

Ray Rose's investigators interviewed every employee of the Elk Grove Village Walgreen's store who had ever known

Patricia Columbo. The questions they asked were primarily about Patricia—but, because of Rose's suspicions about her lover, Frank DeLuca, queries were subtly interjected about the pharmacist as well. DeLuca, released after Patricia signed her statement, had transferred to another Walgreen's, so the employees in Elk Grove were able to speak freely. One of them, Grace Mason, related an incident in which DeLuca had apparently become very upset with her about a conversation regarding a gun. The story was so interesting that Rose asked Grace Mason to come to police headquarters for another interview. She arrived with her husband, Lloyd.

"I'm not even sure when the incident took place," Mrs. Mason told Rose, "except that I'm certain it was before Patty's family was murdered. There was a woman named Joy Heysek working in cosmetics with Patty. She had been with Walgreen's for several years and had worked with Frank DeLuca at another store. Apparently they had been pretty good friends. Joy was a blonde with a very voluptuous body and she was always attracting men.

"Apparently Joy told DeLuca that she was being bothered by someone—getting phone calls or being followed or something, I'm not sure exactly what the story was—but Joy wanted a gun, she said, for protection. DeLuca said he'd get her one. Well, Joy told me about it and I innocently mentioned to DeLuca that it was nice of him to try to help her. I mean, I didn't think it was supposed to be a secret; Joy had told me about it very openly. Well, DeLuca really blew his top. He let me know in no uncertain terms that I was not to mention that again—to anybody. He said—I remember his exact words: 'Something big is going down soon'—and he did not want the police to be able to put him with a gun. That was exactly how he said it: 'put him with a gun.' "

"Was that the extent of it?" Ray Rose asked. "Nothing further was said relating to the gun? And you never actually saw it?"

"Not *that* gun," Grace Mason said. "I mean, not the gun DeLuca was supposed to get for Joy. But one night when DeLuca and Patty and I were out eating, Patty opened her purse and I saw a little gun in it. One of those kind that fit in the palm of your hand."

The derringer, Rose thought. He knew about that. It was

the existence of *another* gun, possibly transferred between DeLuca and this Joy Heysek, that interested him—because the gun that shot and killed Frank, Mary, and Michael Columbo had not been found.

Grace Mason could not tell Rose anything else, however, and Joy Heysek, when later questioned by an investigator, denied ever being given a gun by DeLuca, although admitting the conversations about such a gun had taken place.

"After the murders," Rose asked Mrs. Mason, "did you have any suspicions that Patty might have been involved in the crime? Or DeLuca?"

"No," Grace Mason said. "Some people in the store did, but I wasn't one of them. I wasn't convinced at all that Patty and DeLuca had done it." She paused and looked Rose steadily in the eyes. "Then," she added, "Bert Green told my husband and me that DeLuca had admitted the killings to him."

Ray Rose managed to keep his expression inscrutable, even though the words were like a massive shot of adrenaline pumped directly into his system. *Then Bert Green told my husband and me that DeLuca had admitted the killings to him.*

Drumming his fingertips silently on the desktop, Rose considered Bert Green. He was a young assistant manager who had worked for DeLuca at the Elk Grove drugstore, and was still there. They were known to be close friends, went out drinking together, and about a month before the murders DeLuca had promoted Green to manager of the store's extensive liquor department. Green was one of the few Walgreen's employees who had not been altogether cooperative with the police. He had said he knew nothing about the murders or DeLuca or Patricia Columbo or anything else. His attitude had been very close to hostile. Now it was beginning to seem to Rose that Green knew quite a bit.

Ray Rose was aware that in this conversation with Grace Mason, he was getting well over the fence into the field of hearsay evidence that was not admissible in a court of law: DeLuca telling something to Bert Green, who in turn told Grace Mason, who was now telling Ray Rose—but every drop of information counted in a case like this, a case with no eyewitnesses, no murder weapon, a case overflowing with accomplished liars, schemers, and habitual lawbreakers. So Ray Rose pressed on.

"When did that conversation take place?" he asked Mrs. Mason. "When did Bert Green tell you and your husband that?"

"Sometime after the murders, I'm not sure how long," Grace Mason said. "Bert was over at our apartment. He and my husband and I had been watching television. I don't know what brought the subject up, but first thing Lloyd and I knew, Bert was telling us that the morning after the police say the Columbos were killed, but a couple of days *before* the bodies were found, that DeLuca told him he had killed them all. Bert said DeLuca told him exactly how he had done it and everything. It was then that I started believing for the first time that Patty and DeLuca had actually done it. And I still believe it." Grace Mason's eyes turned hard. "I hope they get exactly what's coming to them for doing what they did."

Grace Mason, thought Rose, had just joined a rapidly growing club.

Another person Ray Rose talked to about a gun that was possibly involved in the killings was Lanny Mitchell's good buddy, Roman Sobczynski. Unlike Rose's polite session with Grace Mason, this was not an interview, it was an interrogation. Sobczynski was an ex-cop, a cheap thief, a family man who fooled around with teenage girls, and, if not an accessory before the fact to murder, certainly a person who helped advance the *idea* of murder, and ultimately was part of the stimulation leading up to that act. Rose wasted no courtesy on him.

"Did you give Patricia Columbo a gun?" he asked bluntly.

"Yes, I did," Sobczynski admitted.

"When and where?"

"I gave her the gun last February, about three months before her family was killed. We were in a friend's apartment out in Wheaton."

Rose already knew the name of the woman whose apartment Sobczynski and Patty were using for their sexual trysts. She was employed by a friend of Sobczynski's and was generous with the use of her apartment, but otherwise had nothing to do with the Columbo case.

"What kind of gun did you give Patty Columbo?" Rose asked.

"It was a .32 caliber. I don't remember what make, but it was on a large frame. A seven-shot revolver."

The Columbos had all been killed by .32-caliber bullets.

"Did you give her bullets for it?"

"Yeah."

"How many?"

"Six. I left one chamber empty to, you know, prevent any accidents."

"So you gave her a gun and six bullets?"

"Yeah."

Rose's eyes were locked on Sobczynski. Six bullets. One for Mary, one for Michael, four for Frank. All present and accounted for.

"Why didn't you come forward when you first heard about the killings?" Rose asked.

Roman Sobczynski hung his head. "I couldn't face the idea that the gun I had given her was the gun used in the murders."

"Do you think it *was* the gun?"

Roman Sobczynski merely shrugged.

27
October 1972 to May 1973

For Patricia, the transfer from Corky's to Walgreen's was like moving from the tenements to Lake Shore Drive. The drugstore was a bright, shiny, marvelous place. She had seen it many times as a customer, or prowling the aisles to spy on DeLuca, but it was only now, working there, that she had a real overview of the store. What she saw delighted her.

It was a big store, one of those all-purpose establishments that had first originated in California in the late 1930s. Its development impeded by the scarcity of goods during World War II, the idea had mushroomed again in the 1950s. Based on the self-service concept that people would buy more if they could touch and pick up the merchandise, all those places shared with Walgreen's an emporium feel. There were eighteen long aisles from front to rear, with a crossover aisle bisecting them at store center. Between those aisles, islands of merchandise were arranged categorically by usage. Many items of similar classification were grouped in one area, which then became a "center," with a large sign above it: the Health Care Center, for over-the-counter medications and related stock; the Beauty Center, which was the cosmetics department with its seemingly endless variety of products for women; and even a Prescription Center, which was what the pharmacy was called.

The Beauty Center ran the depth of the store, front to rear, along aisles A and B, and also had the entire left-hand wall, which bordered aisle A. It was a fairyland of chrome, mirrors, and glass showcases filled with attractively packaged items guaranteed to make the plain beautiful, and the beautiful exquisite. Learning all there was to know about every line was tantamount to memorizing all the calculus formulae known to man. In lipsticks alone, there were more than a hundred different colors. Add to those the myriad brands and blends of face and body powder, the shampoos and color rinses, the fragrances, fingernail polishes, products for the eyelashes, cuticles, earlobes, toes, hands, neck—no part of the female anatomy was slighted.

Patricia worked primarily for a woman named Constance, who was tall, willowy, stylish, and had been buying, stocking, and selling women's cosmetic products for a decade. Patricia liked her at once, and Constance—or Connie, as she preferred—liked Patricia. There was a second woman, Abagail, who split the twelve-hour shift with Connie, but it was usually Connie with whom Patricia worked in her after-school hours; on Saturdays, Patricia's shift overlapped both of theirs. Abagail was as nice as Connie, but Connie seemed to have a special zest for teaching Patricia the ropes.

"Well," Connie said to Patricia when they met, "Mr. DeLuca tells me that you want to go into cosmetics full-time when you finish high school next spring. He said to teach you everything I could."

"I hope I can learn it all," Patricia replied self-consciously, looking around at the vast array of merchandise.

"It's not as bad as it looks," Connie said reassuringly. "Once you learn the basics, the rest of it will come pretty easily. And you'll find that as new products are introduced, you'll know about them from the beginning, so you'll just kind of absorb them. The secret is not to let the sheer number of products scare you. I'm sure you'll do just fine. And Mr. DeLuca seems to think you've got a lot of potential."

It was odd for Patricia to hear the two older women—Connie and Abagail were both in their thirties—refer to the store manager as "Mr. DeLuca," when she was so accustomed to calling him Frank. Following their example, she began using the more formal manner of address and adopted an earnest, businesslike attitude during work hours that was markedly different from her rather flip Corky's persona. DeLuca viewed it all with great amusement.

Patricia was profoundly serious about her new career. She suspected that the day would come when she would have to answer for her lie about her age—but by then she hoped to be so knowledgeable and so competent that Frank would excuse it. Frank was making a woman out of her, in every way possible. She was solemnly determined to succeed—at everything.

They parked in the forest preserves the first few times they had sex, and then DeLuca became dissatisfied with that scenario.

"I want you in a room, on a bed," he told her. "I want to be able to look at you naked. I want to do things with you in front of a mirror so we can watch ourselves." He said he was going to find a quiet, out-of-the-way motel for them.

"Why don't you just take me home with you, Frank?" She was *dying* to see where her dream man lived.

"I'm afraid my sister might object," he said. "She's kind of old-fashioned."

"Oh. I didn't know you lived with your sister."

"Yeah. We share a place."

He found a little motel on the edge of the suburbs called the Br'er Rabbit. The rooms were tacky but clean, small but large enough for their purposes, and reasonably inexpensive. Not that they noticed much about the room their first few times there. All they saw was each other, naked and lascivious. They wallowed in their mutual lust. DeLuca was almost beside himself with Patricia's voluptuous young body.

"Sweet Jesus," he said over and over as he feasted on every part of her. "Oh, sweet Jesus—"

He squeezed, licked, sucked, probed, using his lips, tongue, fingers, and throbbing erection. He couldn't make up his mind as to position and duration: he moved her from back to stomach to knees, from bed to floor to countertop in the tiny bathroom. He was like a small boy set free from some kind of restriction and now allowed to range freely. In the privacy of the room, he could have it any way he wanted—but he wanted it every way at once, which no one gets, and he could not make up his mind on the alternative.

For Patricia the orgy was not as ecstatic; she still hurt from the loss of her virginity, and her assaulted hymen still left traces of blood on his erection. But Patricia instinctively knew to conceal her pain, to affect the same lustful, lecherous attitude of wantonness that DeLuca displayed. She treated his body with the same lewd abandon with which he treated hers. The dialogue of their debauchery was crude and coarse.

"Suck it—suck it, baby—"

"Lick it all over—"

"Get on your hands and knees like a dog—"

"Rub it in my face—"

"Do it to yourself while I do it to myself—"

"Eat it, taste it, swallow it—"

After a while, Patricia wasn't sore anymore. After a while she was as impassioned and unrestrained as he was. They became kindred in what they wanted and what they did.

"God, we are so alike," DeLuca would marvel in the afterglow of their lovemaking.

At home, Patricia's promotion into the Beauty Center was received with mixed reactions. Michael, of course, was outraged; no more free food. His sister could have struck him blind, it almost seemed, with less fuss. Michael would not speak to her for two weeks.

Her father was actually proud of her, although his pride was necessarily tempered by his original disapproval of her going to work in the first place. That aside, Frank Columbo respected hard work and the theory of promotion as a reward for it—and he was genuinely gratified that his daughter had applied herself in the workplace and been elevated in position and pay.

It was Mary Columbo with whom Patricia had the most difficult time. She never said a word in opposition to the new job in front of her husband or son, nor did she really disapprove of the job itself. It was the way that Patricia began to dress for the new job—in shorter skirts, tighter, lower-cut blouses, higher heels—that Mary objected to. Patricia patiently explained that in the Beauty Center she was expected to dress the part of a mature salesperson, not a high school kid. It amazed Mary that Patricia's teachers had not said anything about the way she dressed. Actually, Patricia *had* been given some very long looks by several teachers, but nothing had come of it. Mainly it was the male students she was having trouble with; they followed her around the halls between classes like dogs in heat. For her part, she would never look at them; she considered herself far beyond that juvenile level.

On the whole, Patricia did not let her mother's attitude bother her. Nothing bothered her.

She had Frank DeLuca.

Lying naked, spent, in Frank DeLuca's arms at the motel, Patricia tried several times to work up the courage to tell him about the memory of her father the night she had the terrible dream. By now, all recollections of Gus Latini and the candy truck were buried somewhere deep in her subconscious, and it would be many years and much tragedy before a nun-psychologist would unlock the vault for her. Even the things she had done with Jack Formaski were now only a disgusting memory. Too immature at this point to know even vaguely about consequences such as psychological wounds, personality injury, ego wreckage, subconscious trauma, and all the other harm that a psychiatrist might then have diagnosed in her life, Patricia knew only that her feelings for her lover were so strong, so compelling, that she wanted to share with him every important moment she had ever experienced— good or bad. The memory of her father lying against her bare thigh was one of those moments, and she finally marshaled the nerve to tell DeLuca about it.

Frank was the personification of worldly understanding. He waxed philosophically about sex drives and outlets for them, about sexual gratification, sexual satisfaction, and the vast variety of desires that can ferment in a single person. Her father, he speculated, might have come into her room in all innocence the night she had the experience, and then been turned on by the sight of her nightgown pulled up. He might have subconsciously wanted to have sex with his daughter, but not actually *planned* it. If she had not awakened, DeLuca told her, her father might have had some kind of sex with her, short of actual intercourse, and she would never even have known it.

Patricia was aghast. She found it hard to believe such a thing could have happened—but if Frank said it could, it must be so. She was, as he often reminded her, very young and very inexperienced. There was so much she didn't know about sex, so many intricate ways for them to please each other. Each new scenario that Frank introduced was a delight for her; she loved being naughty with Frank. Earthy with Frank. Down and dirty with Frank. Anal intercourse was the latest routine she had learned, and with that it seemed to her that her sexual education must be almost complete.

She could not imagine anything more that two people could do together.

Several months after the affair began, Patricia was watching one of the cosmetics distributors, a handsome young black man named Andre, restocking his line behind the lipsticks counter, when Frank came out of the pharmacy and spoke to him.

"Andre, stop in and see me before you leave the store, will you?"

"Sure, Frank," the young black man said, smiling.

"Now you're going to get it," Patricia kidded him when DeLuca left. "That's the boss, you know."

"Frank and I are old friends," Andre said confidently. He now turned his smile on Patricia: it was a brilliant smile, the teeth even and white behind lips that were very thin and sensuous. Andre was light-skinned, with beautiful processed hair and manicured fingernails that looked like the inside of a conch shell. To Patricia, he was quite attractive.

When Andre completed his restocking, he went back to the pharmacy and Patricia saw Frank take him into a little room set aside as a coffee and lunch room for those employees who did not want to go to Corky's. They were in there for fifteen minutes or so, and when they came out Patricia saw Andre leave the store. Later that afternoon, when Connie was on her break, DeLuca came over to the Beauty Center.

"What'd you think of Andre?" he asked.

"Seems nice," Patricia replied.

"Do you think he's good-looking?"

"Yeah, I guess," Patricia equivocated. What was this? she wondered. Was her man jealous? God, how *great*!

"I'm glad you liked him," DeLuca said. "He's coming over to the motel tonight."

"What do you mean? What for?"

"We're going to party with him," DeLuca told her offhandedly. His tone was almost indifferent. Patricia was incredulous.

"Party with him? You mean you and me and—"

"Him," DeLuca finished the sentence for her. "I told you I was working on a surprise, didn't I? Well this is it. What do you think?"

"It's quite a surprise," Patricia allowed.

"You'll enjoy it. Trust me."

DeLuca usually had a pint of Canadian Club in his car, and over the weeks with Patricia in the motel had gradually introduced her to the pleasures of social drinking. On the night that Andre joined them in the room, there was a fifth instead of a pint, as well as extra glasses and ice. The evening began with them sitting around drinking, talking, getting comfortable with the situation. DeLuca was not *un*comfortable; he seemed to Patricia quite at ease, his conversation congenial, his manner calm, confident—as usual. It was Andre and Patricia who needed loosening up, and that was accomplished in less than an hour with the whiskey. When all of them were well relaxed, DeLuca got down to business.

"Patrish has never had a black man before, Andre," he said.

"That right?" Andre flashed his klieg-light smile at her.

"Never." She shook her head. Andre, she noticed, had shifted one hand down to where a bulge now appeared at the crotch of his tight pants.

"I told her on the way over that she was in for a treat,"

DeLuca said. He stood and started unbuttoning his shirt. "Let's get comfortable."

While Patricia merely watched, DeLuca and Andre stripped to their shorts. Both had erections that were straining for release.

"Come on, baby, don't you want to get comfortable?" DeLuca asked. It was a goad rather than a question.

Glancing in the mirror, Patricia saw that she had a lazy, almost silly smile on her face. "Sure, Frank," she said, "I want to get comfortable—"

By the time Patricia got down to her panty hose and bra, Andre was masturbating uninhibitedly and DeLuca was pulling back the bed covers. DeLuca steered Patricia to the bed and peeled off her panty hose.

"I'm going to get her good and wet for you, man," DeLuca said to Andre, and lowered his face between Patricia's legs.

As Patricia began to feel the spreading sensations created by her lover's tongue, she unhooked her bra and tossed it aside.

"Oh, yeah," Andre said, seeing her buoyant breasts laid free, their aureolas becoming gooseflesh, nipples stiffening like great bee stings.

DeLuca ministered to Patricia until he felt her body tense and her pelvis arch up to press desperately against his mouth as she reached a shuddering climax. Falling back limply, Patricia saw DeLuca unbend from her and wink conspiratorially at Andre. The black man, smile now gone, rose and moved on top of her.

At the dresser, Patricia saw DeLuca take a camera from the top drawer and put a flash attachment on it.

When DeLuca dropped her off that night, a couple of blocks from her house, Patricia waited until he had driven away and then sat down on the curb. She was by no means despondent over the ménage à trois in which she had just participated; in truth, she had enjoyed most of it—she was an intensely sensual young girl whose lines of carnal communication had now been effectively tapped by Frank DeLuca.

What troubled her this evening was not her own enjoyment, but DeLuca's. He had seemed to actually thrive on what they had done tonight. When Patricia looked at him while Andre was having intercourse with her, DeLuca's expression was the same one she saw when *he* was on top of her, when *he* was inside her. When he alternately took a picture of her and Andre, paused to masturbate for a moment as he watched them, took another picture, paused to masturbate and watch again, it appeared to her, at least as far as she could discern in her alcohol-addled mind, that he was relishing what they were doing. That she was enjoying it, and that DeLuca was also enjoying it, should, she guessed, make sense to her. But it did not. DeLuca was enjoying her with another man; if she saw DeLuca with another woman, it would infuriate her. She did not like for him to even talk to other women. So she could not equate the pleasurable feelings with the jealously repugnant act.

"I don't understand how you got such a charge out of watching," she said as he was driving her home. It was really a question.

"It's like I told you," DeLuca explained. "You're young and all this is new to you. I'm a man of the world; I've been around, I know how these things work, okay? Once you have a little more experience, you'll understand what I mean. You enjoyed it, didn't you? I mean, you got off with Andre, didn't you?"

"Yes," Patricia said, a little grudgingly. Turning her face away from him, she stared out at the night.

"Okay, then," DeLuca said. "You got off with Andre, he got off with you, and then you got me off with your mouth. Everybody got off. That's what it's all about, right?"

"Right," she replied. Her voice was quiet, its tone docile.

When DeLuca pulled over to let her out, she hesitated and said, "Most of the time it's just going to be the two of us, though, isn't it, Frank? Just you and me?"

"Sure, sweetheart," DeLuca assured. "But we've got to have a little variety once in a while, too. A little spice, as they say. Now don't worry about it. I know what's right. Hell, everybody does this kind of thing. Your own parents might be doing it, for all you know. I mean, you don't know what they do when they go out for the evening, right? When you get a little older and a little more experienced, you'll understand. Until then, just trust me, okay?"

Patricia felt she should have been reassured by his words,

but she was not. She attributed her lack of confidence in what he had said to her own immaturity, her deficiency in experience—just as DeLuca had indicated. Maybe, she reasoned, she was still doubtful about it all because she was *too* young to grasp it; perhaps if she had really been eighteen, she would have been better able to understand everything. Maybe the best thing to do *was* to trust Frank, until she became old enough to figure it all out for herself. God, she thought again, she absolutely, positively hated being so goddamned *young*.

With a weary sigh, the sixteen-year-old girl rose from the curb and started down the quiet, deserted suburban street toward home.

C.H.
March 1991

After a number of telephone conversations, Patricia invited me back to Dwight to visit her, without her attorney being present this time.

"I'm in an honor cottage, so if you come on a Saturday or Sunday," she told me, "you can come into the unit and we can visit in the community room. You can stay all day if you like, from ten to seven." She chuckled. "I'll even cook for you."

We decided on a Saturday and I planned another trip to Chicago.

Most of the long telephone talks Patricia and I had up to that time—they were never shorter than two hours, more often than not much longer—dealt with Patricia's early life on Ohio Street in Chicago. She usually called around midnight her time, when no one else in the cottage wanted to use the phone, and when she could reminisce at length without interruption. It was easier for her to tell me about the period of her life that involved Gus Latini, than it had been for her to tell Sister Burke, because through the nun she had been able to put it into perspective.

"My mind was really in a shambles before I began the therapy with Sister Burke," she said. "I don't mean I was crazy or anything; I just had a lot of stuff shoved away on

*different levels of my mind, and none of the levels were con-
nected. Or if they were connected, they weren't communicating. Sister Burke helped me to kind of rewire everything so
that it made sense. I can tell you now everything that happened back then, in chronological order. Two years ago, I
couldn't have begun to do that."*

"Sister Burke sounds like she was a wonderful person," I
said.

"She was a godsend," Patricia replied quietly.

On my second visit to Dwight, I had worn a sportshirt and
windbreaker so as not to be mistaken for anyone serious.
Patricia was waiting for me in the visiting room with a long
list in her hand.

"Hi," she said. "Did you bring twenty-five dollars in with
you?"

"Hi. Yes, I did."

"Want to spend it to help me play Easter Bunny?"

"Sure."

We got in the canteen line and Patricia spent twenty-three
dollars and change on miscellaneous candy and other snack
foods. "I'm making Easter baskets for my 'Hoodlums,' " she
explained, as the purchases were being packed in a box. "I've
been cutting out construction paper in my spare time for two
weeks and pasting it into the shape of baskets with little bun-
nies drawn on the sides. I'll fill them up with this candy and
deliver them on Easter Sunday morning. The kids will love
them."

Justice Pincham's description of Patricia to the press suddenly assaulted me: vicious, cunning, coy, mean, disruptive . . .

And Sister Traxler's reply: God changes all of us in time.

Carrying the canteen purchase, we were passed through a
duplicate set of electronic doors at the opposite end of the big
visiting room, and from there walked out onto the interior
grounds of Dwight prison. It wasn't a bad-looking place.

A long, meandering sidewalk snaked across grounds that
were still grassless from winter, past great old trees gnarled
with the years, leading to a series of scattered, low-profile
buildings, some with barred windows, some without. Patricia
observed me looking around.

"It looks like a run-down college campus, doesn't it?" she asked.

"In a way," I agreed. If you overlooked the prison fence with the slanted razor wire at the top.

"Actually, that's pretty much what it's like after you reach A-Grade status," she said. "When you're in an honor cottage, there are really very few restrictions. You're left pretty much to do your time without a lot of hassles." She pointed to an old but well-maintained two-story stone building that we were approaching. "The honor cottage is like a women's boardinghouse. We all have our own rooms or share a room on the second floor, and downstairs we have a recreation room, a kitchen, and a community room with a television. When the weather's nice, we can sit outside under the trees. I've got a favorite tree where I go to study, or read, or sometimes just to be alone."

"It must be difficult to find time alone in here," I suggested. Patricia shook her head.

"No, we all realize the importance of privacy and we respect it. For some of us, it's essential, and the others know that. Like me, for instance. I need a little private time every day in order to keep myself perfectly on track. I have to take time to remember where I am, why I'm here, and what I'm doing each day that is positive. Sister Burke taught me that. She called it getting a 'specific grip' on life."

At the entrance to the honor cottage, Patricia knocked on the window of the outer door and a female corrections officer admitted us through that and then an inner door. Then we were inside the unit itself. The rooms Patricia had talked about suddenly materialized for me. In the recreation room off to the right, two inmates in shorts and sweatshirts were painting the walls with rollers. A staircase in front of the doors led to living quarters on the second floor. Down a hallway to the left there was the duty guard's office on one side, a small kitchen on the other. At the end of the hall was the community room: a few tables for four, a couple of overstuffed couches, extra chairs, an older-model television. There was nothing cheerful about the room; everything was old, worn, scarred; the lighting was poor, the walls bare—and the razor wire could be seen from every window.

There were no other visitors in the community room when

we got there. Patricia led me to a table in the corner farthest from the door, and she lighted the first of many cigarettes she would smoke that day.

"The only vice I have left," she said wryly. "Make yourself at home; I'll get us some coffee. How do you take yours?"

"Just coffee," I said, "nothing in it."

While she was gone, several other inmates came to the door and looked in. Their eyes swept the room as if looking for someone, but always lingered curiously on me before they left. When Patricia came back with the coffee, she walked past a couple of them with a knowing look.

"They're not used to me having a male visitor," she said. "Nobody knows who you are except a couple of my close friends. I haven't decided yet how I'm going to handle it in here that a book is being written about me. It knocks the hell out of the low profile I've worked so many years to achieve. For the time being, I've decided to let word get around that you're my uncle. That okay with you?"

"As long as you don't say my name is Gus," I told her. During long hours on the phone, she had told me all about the candy truck.

She smiled and took a drag on her cigarette. "So," she said, "what do you want to talk about?"

"Frank DeLuca," I said.

"Why not."

We talked for nine hours that day, taking time out only for a midafternoon meal. Patricia made spaghetti.

One of the people I saw on that particular trip to Chicago was Andre. I had located him living in an apartment on the near North Side, and he agreed to meet me at a bar on State Street. He was, as Patricia had described, a smoothly handsome black man with perfect teeth and polished fingernails.

"How did you find me, man?" he asked when he sat down.

"It's not hard to find someone who isn't hiding," I said. "You're registered to vote. That's a public record."

"No, I mean who told you about me?"

"I'll give you a hint: it wasn't Frank."

"Shit," he said disgustedly. He ordered a vodka martini. I

was drinking one with gin. "Is this book going to fuck my life up?" he wanted to know. I shook my head.

"I won't even use your real name if you don't want me to. I just want information."

"About what?"

"DeLuca."

Andre's expression tightened. "That motherfucker. He could have got both our asses in a sling fucking with a sixteen-year-old girl." Andre leaned toward me with an urgency. "One thing you've got to understand, man: I did not know Patrish was underage, If I had, I wouldn't have fucked her with somebody else's dick."

"I believe you." There was no reason for me not to; at that point, even DeLuca hadn't known Patricia's true age. She had been playing grown-up. "How long had you known DeLuca when he became involved with Patricia?" I asked.

"About three years, I think. See, I stocked all the Walgreen stores in the western suburbs. And Frank had worked in quite a few of them: Oak Park, Elmhurst, Schaumburg, several others. I used to see him all the time."

"So you partied with him before he even met Patricia?"

"Oh, yeah. Frank was always setting something up. The man had a sex drive like one of those—what do you call them, those male nymphomaniacs?"

"A satyr," I said.

"Yeah, that was Frank. He had a hard-on most of the time—and he didn't believe in wasting one." Andre's drink came and he immediately took a long swallow of it. "Look," he worried, "there's no chance of me ever being charged with anything because of this, is there?"

"None at all," I assured him. "Patricia herself couldn't even press charges for statutory rape. Too many years have gone by."

Andre took another long swallow of his drink. "So what do you want from me?"

"I want you to tell me everything you know about Frank and Patricia. And about Frank before Patricia."

"And you won't use my real name in your book?"

"That's the deal. It's done all the time."

"Okay," Andre agreed. "Okay, man, I'll do it."

Andre had a great deal to tell.

28
June to September 1973

Somehow, Patricia reached her seventeenth birthday without having a nervous breakdown.

She was now in a constant state of tension. Nothing was easy; her entire existence had turned into a nightmare of lies. She was lying to her parents about her working hours so that she could be with Frank. She was lying to Frank about enjoying the sexual threesomes he arranged with Andre. The lie about her age continued to haunt her. She lied about where she was going, where she had been, who she'd been with, what she'd been doing, how she felt. She had to be constantly alert not to slip and tell the truth about something.

Oddly enough, it was also a period in which she did not have to endure much overt conflict with the various people in her life. Her father seemed to have so many other pressing matters on his mind that he had relegated to some lower priority the irritant of her being employed, and rarely mentioned it anymore. Plus, he had fallen off a loading dock at work—or *said* he had fallen—and broken his arm. Mary suspected he had been in a fight; Patricia overheard her questioning him about problems apparently arising out of his involvement in both a dock-laborers and trucking sideline. Frank, as usual, told her not to worry, it was his business, he would take care of it.

Mary did worry, of course; Mary worried about everything to do with her family. The fact that she was directing her current concerns toward her husband brought a period of relief to Patricia and Michael. Their mother was a focused worrier.

Michael, after the initial trauma of being severed from Corky's unofficial freebie list, bounced back with his usual resiliency and moved on to new challenges that did not involve how much he could eat. His participation with his father in the CB hobby was flourishing; he still refused to tell anybody what his handle "Blue Mule" meant—and, as things turned out, no one would *ever* know. Michael was also developing a serious interest in dirt bikes and other two-wheel motorized atrocities, which his mother probably already had scheduled to worry about in the future.

At school, Patricia had taken some initial flak over her new style of dressing. A couple of teachers spoke to her unofficially about the length—or lack of it—of her miniskirts; the boys continued to trail her like Indian scouts; and some of the girls ridiculed or criticized her behind her back. But after a while, everyone seemed to get used to the idea that she was simply going to be different. She had evolved into a figure of little more than mild curiosity.

With DeLuca, of course, there was never any strain, never any stress, as long as she did exactly what he wanted her to do. He was charming, gentle, loving, and considerate—as long as he got his own way. It was only when he felt that Patricia challenged him that he became moody and surly. And what he perceived as challenges were usually only Patricia's attempts to rationalize the things they were doing, or to indicate a preference for something else. Her complaints, when she drummed up the courage to voice them, were all of one theme: she wanted their relationship to be just *them*—Frank and Patrish—with no one else included.

Frank was inordinately patient with her. "It will be just you and me eventually," he promised. "But first I want you to experience all the different aspects of sex; I want you to know what everything's like, so when you say you just want to be with me, I'll know you really mean it. I'll know that *you* know what sex is all about, that you've tried everything, and that you still want me, see? Then I'll know that you really love me."

Patricia would shake her head. "I'm sorry, I don't understand that. I love you now. You *know* I love you."

"Sure, I know you love me," he would try to explain, "but you love me based on what you know *now*. Look, I'll give you an example, okay? You loved me before we partied with Andre, right? Then we partied with him, and you loved me when it was over, right? Now, let me tell you something you might not know: white women at some point in their lives always wonder what it would be like to get fucked by a black guy. All women wonder that; your own mother has probably wondered it. The reason is that black guys have this reputation for having huge cocks, see? And they're supposed to be able to fuck like baboons, just keep going and going until a woman is all worn out. So white women are naturally curious. They say they love a guy, but they still wonder how it would be with a big black stud. But, see, I've saved you from that. You *know* how it is. And *I* know that you still love me after you found out. There's no reservation on your love. You understand?"

"I guess." Another lie. But when she did not comprehend some of his gnarled theory and convoluted philosophy, and told him so, he invariably resorted to the same defense-offense: "You don't understand it because you're not *trying* to understand it."

That was bad enough. But when he occasionally added, "Grow up, okay?" it was like a vicious slap across her face.

She became very careful of saying she did not understand.

When summer came, Patricia finished her junior year of high school, very quietly celebrated her seventeenth birthday, and lost her best friend, next to Frank, at the drugstore.

"Well, I'm going to be leaving you, honey," Connie told her one day. "I finally got a transfer to a store closer to home."

Patricia was stunned. Connie lived in Tinley Park, one of the southern suburbs. She had often complained about the long drive, particularly during periods when Chicago area streets were icy or snowbound. And she always ended her grievance with a threat to quit unless Walgreen's personnel department would put her in a closer store. It was an old, familiar gripe to Patricia. Then, without warning, Connie was leaving.

On Connie's last day, a good-looking blonde came into the store and walked back to the pharmacy. Every male employee on the floor, stock boys to assistant manager, locked his eyes on her like radar. A thirtyish woman with large, pretty eyes, she had a breathtaking figure and a confident, almost smug bearing. At the pharmacy, while Patricia watched resentfully, DeLuca came out and escorted her into the employees' coffee room.

Patricia waited ten minutes, until she could not stand it any longer, then crossed the store and went in also, on the pretext of wanting a cup of coffee. DeLuca and the blonde were at one of the tables with foam cups of coffee between them. DeLuca glanced at Patricia when she came in, but did not speak. The expression on his face, which she knew so well by now, was sullen; something was not going his way. He and the woman stopped talking while Patricia got a cup of her own, drew coffee from the urn, and left. She wanted desperately to sit down at one of the other tables, but she was afraid it might make Frank angry. She knew from his expression that he was already unhappy.

Taking her coffee into the ladies' room, Patricia poured it out and returned to the Beauty Center. As she set up a new Revlon lipsticks display, she kept an eye on the "Employees Only" door leading back to the coffee room. A few minutes later, DeLuca and the woman emerged. Without much of a good-bye, the woman headed for the front door and DeLuca went back to the pharmacy. His face was set in a dark frown that told Patricia something definitely was wrong. Waiting until she could see him alone, she approached DeLuca.

"What's the matter?" she asked. "Who was the blonde?"

"Joy Heysek. Connie's replacement," DeLuca said bitterly. "She starts tomorrow."

Patricia felt piqued. Why hadn't he told her about this blonde? "When did you hire her?"

"I didn't. Regional personnel is transferring her in from another store."

"Oh." Patricia's annoyance vanished. "What are you so mad about?"

"Look, she's an old girlfriend of mine, okay? I just don't like the idea of her working here, that's all."

Patricia stared at him in astonishment. "I'm going to be working for an ex-girlfriend of yours? Can't you send her somewhere else? You're the store manager, I mean—"

"No, I can't," he told her emphatically. "She's been with Walgreen's for a number of years, so she has enough seniority to request a transfer if she's got an acceptable reason. She lives in Hoffman Estates and this store is closer to her home. The company tries to accommodate its employees that way."

"Did she pick this store because she knew you were here?" Patricia asked tightly.

"She says she didn't, but I think she did." DeLuca detected the rising irritation in Patricia's tone. "Look, this isn't my fault," he insisted. "I tried to talk her out of it just now; I told her I didn't think it was a good idea us working in the same store again. But"—he shrugged helplessly—"she's got her mind made up."

"Did you tell her about us?"

"No, of course not. That's got to be our secret, Patrish."

A cold shiver ran along Patricia's spine.

"There's a company policy about employees fraternizing," DeLuca continued.

"That doesn't seem to bother you much," Patricia interjected.

"Just listen to me, okay? I know what I'm doing. I don't want you even talking to Joy Heysek, except about matters pertaining to the job. I don't want you to have any personal conversations with her about anything. She's still very upset with me for dumping her, okay? Maybe she's looking to get even, I don't know. In any case, I don't want to give her any ammunition, okay? I don't want her to be able to go to my boss and say I'm fraternizing with one of my employees. You understand me?"

"Yes, I do. I understand," Patricia assured him. Her brief little peeve was over; she quickly regrouped to stand by her man. She touched DeLuca's arm. "Don't worry, I won't let her find out anything. She's not going to hurt you."

DeLuca patted her hand. "I knew I could count on you, honey. You know something, you're the only one in the world that I trust completely, one hundred percent."

"Really?" She felt herself glow with love.

"Really," DeLuca said.

Patricia walked on air back to the Beauty Center.

"I've been in cosmetics almost since I started with Walgreen's," Joy Heysek told Patricia. "Except for the first year. When I first started, I was a part-time cashier. My kids were still little, so I could only work until two-thirty every day, then I had to pick them up from school."

"How many kids do you have?" Patricia asked. Immediately she wanted to bite her tongue. No personal conversation, Frank had warned.

"I've got two," Joy said. "A boy and a girl."

"How old are they?" She had to ask, because she was trying to figure out how old Joy was.

"Nine and thirteen," Joy said.

If the oldest was thirteen, Patricia began to calculate, and Joy had married at eighteen, which was about the earliest one could reasonably assume, and if she had her first baby at nineteen, that would make her about thirty-two. At *least*. And more than likely she was a couple years older than that—say thirty-four or so. Twice my age, Patricia thought—not with any real gratification, because if there was one thing Patricia wanted to be, it was older.

In her early days working with Joy Heysek, Patricia found herself many times surreptitiously studying the older woman. Primarily she would like to have known what there was about Joy that had attracted Frank DeLuca. Joy was attractive enough as far as her face was concerned; she had large eyes that she accented to full advantage to compensate for somewhat ordinary other features. But in no way did she have Patricia's great overall beauty.

Comparing figures was really no contest either. Joy, as Patricia saw her, had a very nice body, but her breasts were too large, even top-heavy—although Patricia guessed most men would not agree. But Patricia was now, at seventeen, tall and supple bodied. Her shape, she felt, was by far better.

But Joy Heysek definitely had a bearing about her, an air of confidence that, despite Patricia's physical advantages, said clearly that Joy was the woman, Patricia the girl. Patricia recognized that and was nettled. She sensed that Joy felt she was just a kid, a "trainee," nobody important. Patricia dearly wished that she could tell Joy that Frank and she were lovers, that she was Frank's choice, and that she and Frank would marry someday, move into a house of their own, have children, and live happily ever afterward. And that she, Patricia, would never, ever, dream of being unfaithful to Frank the way Joy had been to her husband.

Of course, such a litany was impossible. Her affair with Frank had to be secret.

Patricia and Joy were working on a point-of-purchase eye makeup display when the same dark-haired woman entered the store whom Patricia had seen DeLuca kiss good-bye several months earlier. Joy, glancing at her now as she walked back toward the pharmacy, said, "Well, the reclusive Mrs. DeLuca finally makes an appearance."

Patricia stood stock-still. "I thought that was his sister," she said, exerting steel control over her voice to keep it even.

Joy turned to her with a half-knowing, half-suspicious look. "Oh? What made you think that?"

"I heard somebody say that the last time she was in."

"Well, whoever said it was mistaken," Joy told her emphatically. "That, my dear, is Mrs. Marilyn DeLuca, longtime wife of our esteemed store manager. And, I might add, mother of his five children."

Sudden death could have been no worse for Patricia. In fact, it might have been preferable. She was afraid to speak another word, or even let Joy look at her closely, for fear her voice or her expression would betray her utter shock. Turning away from the display she forced out the words, "Be right back," and walked briskly toward the ladies' room.

Her mind was a frenzy of confusion. *Mrs. Marilyn DeLuca? Five children?* Was that possible? Or was Joy trying to bait her? Was it conceivable that Joy had somehow found out about Frank and her, and was trying to spoil what they had? Break them up by getting Patricia so angry that she wouldn't even listen when Frank tried to tell her it was a lie? The bitch—!

Then, in the ladies' room, Patricia got control of herself and tried to rationalize what might and might not be true. First of all, she told herself, it would be stupid for Joy to say a thing like that unless it *was* true. If it was a lie, she must know that it would get back to Frank and infuriate him. So Joy had nothing to gain. It did not make sense. The only thing that made sense was—

Mrs. Marilyn DeLuca.

And five kids.

Jesus Christ, Patricia thought, Jesus Christ, no—it can't be—it just can't be—

She wet a paper towel and patted her cheeks and the back of her neck. Staring at her reflection in the mirror, she saw that she had gone sheet-white; even her lips, under their superficial gloss, were drained of color. She left the ladies' room and went into the coffee room. Only a couple of stock clerks were in there. Patricia got a glass of ice water, drank half of it, and dipped her fingers in the rest of it; she held them in turn to each wrist to try to compose herself.

When she felt she had control of herself, Patricia returned to the Beauty Center. Joy was still setting up the display.

"You okay, Patty?" Joy asked curiously.

"Yes, I'm fine. I think I might have a little bit of stomach flu. I get these really urgent calls of nature, you know?"

"Why don't you go back to the pharmacy and see Frank when his wife leaves," Joy suggested. "He can probably give you something for it."

"I might do that."

As Patricia resumed helping with the display, she positioned herself so that she could see Frank and the dark-haired woman talking behind the clear glass partition of the pharmacy section. It appeared to be a normal conversation; they seemed serious but not arguing. It did not look confrontational. Certainly nothing like what Patricia was planning for him.

In a little while, the dark-haired woman again received a kiss on the cheek and walked back through the store to leave. As Patricia's eyes followed her, she noticed that Joy was watching too. Patricia decided to see if she could extract a little more information from Joy, without making Joy suspicious.

"She sure doesn't look old enough to have five kids," Patricia said casually as they both watched the woman leave. "Neither does he. I heard one of the checkers say he was about twenty-eight or twenty-nine."

Joy shook her head emphatically. "Thirty-five."

"Really?" Patricia raised her eyebrows. "Are you sure?"

"Positive. I even know when his birthday is: June twenty-eighth. He's thirty-five." Joy tilted her head an inch. "You seem surprised."

"I am," Patricia admitted. "I guess I'm not very good at judging people's age." She put a hand on her stomach. "Listen, I'm going to go ask for something for these cramps. Be back in a minute."

Another pharmacist was working with DeLuca when Patricia walked over, so she kept up the pretense of stomach flu. "Sure," DeLuca said when she asked him for something to take. "Come on back here and I'll give you some Kaopectate with a little paregoric for the pain."

He led her into the pharmacy stockroom, where she immediately said, in a very quiet voice, "I don't really want anything. I haven't got a stomachache."

"What's going on?" DeLuca asked.

"I just wanted to ask how your sister was," Patricia said. "That was your sister, wasn't it?"

A knowing look instantly appeared on DeLuca's face. His dark, piercing eyes narrowed a fraction. "What's Joy been telling you?" he asked.

"What do you think she's been telling me?" Patricia challenged.

"I told you not to have any personal conversations with her, didn't I?"

"You sure did. Now I know why." Patricia's own eyes, just as dark and at the moment equally as piercing, locked onto his without blinking. "Is she your wife? Are you married, Frank?"

DeLuca sighed quietly. "Yes."

"And you have *five* children?" Please, God, this part of it couldn't be true.

But it was. "Yes."

She wanted to cry, she wanted to scream, she wanted to slap and kick and scratch. But she was suddenly and unexpectedly so weakened by his admissions that the strength to do any of that was not there—and she knew she probably would not have done it anyway. Frank DeLuca was not the kind of man you slapped; she suspected he would hit her with his fist if she did.

"I can explain everything, Patrish," he said.

Explain everything? Was he serious? Explain a wife? Explain five children—*five*, for Christ's sake! Explain the seven years he had pared off his age?

"Let's go out tonight," he said. "Let's go where we can have some privacy and can talk. I'll explain the whole thing."

"Will it just be the two of us, Frank?" she asked caustically. "Or do we need a third party there to make sure it's adult?"

DeLuca did not even address her acrimony. "I'll wait for you after work," he said.

* * *

By the time they got to the motel room that night, Patricia had become livid with anger. It had begun in the car on the way over.

"You must really have a low opinion of me," she accused. "You must really think I'm a very stupid, dumb cunt."

"I don't think that at all, Patrish," he defended himself. "I could never think that about you. I love you—"

"Bullshit. You love to fuck me, that's what you love. And to watch other guys fuck me. That's all you love, Frank."

"That's not true, Patrish. Just calm down until we get in the room. We'll have a drink and relax. Then we'll discuss this like two rational adults. It's not the end of the world, Patrish."

"It's the end of my world." She began to cry. "I thought we'd get married someday, Frank—"

"I never told you we'd get married," he disclaimed.

"You didn't have to *tell* me!" she snapped. "I thought that's what our relationship was all about. You were teaching me things, helping me to be a woman, showing me what life was like in the adult world. Why the hell were you doing all that if you didn't love me, Frank?"

"Patrish, I do love you—"

"Then why wouldn't you want to marry me, goddamn it? Isn't that how it works in the adult world? Two people meet, fall in love, get married, and have kids. That's how it is, right? You ought to know, you've sure as hell done it!"

When they finally got into the motel room, Frank gave her half of a little blue tablet and told her to take it.

"What is it?" she demanded.

"Five milligrams of Valium. It'll help you to calm down."

"Sure. It'll probably knock me out and then you can bring in the Bears football team to fuck me while you take pictures."

"I don't like that kind of talk, Patrish," he said sanctimoniously.

"Well, pardon me. I didn't mean to offend you. I must remember that you're a family man." She took the Valium, swallowing it with a shot of whiskey.

Taking off her shoes, Patricia fluffed two pillows and sat on the bed, knees drawn up in front of her. DeLuca pulled a

chair up next to the bed and sat facing her, holding a tumbler
half-filled with whiskey for himself.

"Look," he began, "I know I haven't been completely honest with you—"

"Jesus, is that an understatement!"

"I'm not going to try and talk to you if you're not going
to listen," he threatened. His eyes bore into her. "If you want
to call it quits right now, we'll do it."

That was his gauntlet. His way of saying he was unwilling
to pay for his deceit with recriminations from her. Either she
listened to, and accepted, his explanation—or they could
break up.

"Are you going to listen?" he asked.

"Go ahead." She said it grudgingly—but she said it. And
it told DeLuca that they would *not* break up over this.

His rationale, his justification, for all the duplicity on his
part, was a litany of every cliché, every platitude, every ba-
nality ever spoken by the cheater who gets caught. He had
married too young. He and his wife had too many kids, too
soon. Their life together had been reduced to the common-
place; there was no excitement, no fun between them anymore. His sex life with his wife had for several years been all
but extinct—and he had not—repeat, definitely *not*—had sex
with his wife or anyone else since the first time with Patricia.
It was very important to him that she believe that. He had begun falling in love with Patricia almost from the first time he
saw her working in Corky's. But she was so young; he had
been certain that she would have had nothing to do with him
if she had known the truth about his family. He hated, really
hated, lying to her, deceiving her, but there was no other way
that he could see to do it; after he had fallen completely in
love with her, he couldn't help himself, he had to have her no
matter what it took. It hurt him every time he had to leave her
and go home; he *did* want to marry her, he wanted to be with
her all the time, but there were obstacles; it would not look
good to Walgreen's management if he left his family, got a
divorce; it could affect his career. After all, Walgreen's had
subsidized his college education after he was injured and lost
his football scholarship; they had a lot invested in him, and
he in them, and he did not want to lose it. And he was an
honorable man, he had to take care of his children, and there

wasn't enough money to support two households if he should leave. There were so many, so *terribly* many, things that had to be taken into consideration in a situation like this. He would not regard himself as much of a man if he let himself think only about their love, as he so desperately wanted to do—

All right, all right! Patricia's mind began screaming at her. Enough! I forgive you, for Christ's sake! Just—please— shut—*up*!

She knew, of course, that she could not shut him up; he would go on and on, his voice droning through the minutes like an airplane propeller. Once he got on something, he didn't let go of it until he had worn it nearly to death. Patricia closed her eyes and tried to tune the sound out with her own thoughts. Did it really matter, she asked herself, that he was married and had a houseful of brats? Did it make any difference that he had been lying to her almost constantly from the moment they first spoke? Was it significant that he liked to share her with other men, photographing the acts so that he could look at them over and over again? Were these things of any consequence at all if they did not dim the glow of love she felt for the man?

She loved Frank DeLuca. He was *her* Frank—regardless of who else was in his life. Naturally she hated it that he had a wife, hated it that he had kids, hated it that with a few terrible words, Joy Heysek had burst her schoolgirl, white-picket-fence, rose-garden dream. She hated it, and she hurt—but it changed nothing insofar as her love was concerned.

"I don't know what else to say," DeLuca finally began winding down. "I love you, Patrish. I don't want to lose you. I can't make any promises about the future right now; all I can say is that I'll try to figure a way for us to be together. If you'll just trust me, give me time to sort things out, I promise not to lie to you anymore. I'll be straight with you all the way down the line."

When Patricia opened her eyes, DeLuca was leaning forward with his fingers entwined, elbows on his knees, his eyes, his whole expression, like a poor little whipped puppy. If he had not uttered a word, merely showed that countenance, she probably would have forgiven him just as quickly. Reaching out, Patricia put a palm on his coupled hands and said, "Frank, I couldn't stop loving you no matter what. I have to forgive you because there's nothing else I can do. But that doesn't mean you haven't hurt me, because you have—"

"I know, I know I have." He grasped her hand in both of his and clung to her fervidly. "I'll make it up to you, I promise I will. You'll see. You won't be sorry you forgave me. I love you, Patrish, I love you, I love you—"

Presently they were in each other's arms, embracing, kissing, undressing. They made love for more than two hours that night, and then fell exhausted side by side on the bed, spent, wasted, sated. But Patricia had saved the best for last. After all the nails that had been driven into her emotions that day, she was determined to put at least one tiny staple into Frank.

"Honey," she said, "you know that lie you told me about your age? Well, I told you one about my age. I'm only seventeen, Frank."

"What?" He was up on one elbow, looking down at her as if hit by a stun gun.

"That's right." She smiled. "I'm a minor, Frank. I was only fifteen when we met; only sixteen when we started having sex. You could go to jail for what we've been doing. Not only that," she added, tweaking his cheek, "if my father ever found out, he'd kill you. So you're lucky I do love you—because I won't tell."

DeLuca put his head back down and stared up at the ceiling. He was quiet for a long time.

29
June 1976

Ray Rose's head felt like little workmen were jackhammering a tunnel through both sides of his brain. Trying to correlate all the evidence against Patricia Columbo for the state's attorney's office was unsparing, mind-numbing work. Searching his desk, Rose found no aspirin. He went to the first aid locker; there were enough supplies to compress a gunshot wound, but nothing to stop a headache. What the hell, he thought, he needed some fresh air anyway. He got his coat and left the station.

Walgreen's was only a block away—*the* Walgreen's, where the Columbo nightmare had been predestined, Rose believed, from the day Patty Columbo and Frank DeLuca had met. A meeting decreed by blind fate, then ordained by the devil. What continued to amaze Rose was the sheer number of people who had seen it coming; people who, if they had given it a second thought, could have predicted murder—and possibly prevented it. All the people who, when they heard about the crime, immediately thought: *Patty did it.*

At the big drugstore, Rose bought a bottle of extra-strength aspirin and went into Corky's for something to drink. The teenage girl who served his coffee was cute, smiling, fresh looking, probably much like Patty had been four years earlier. *Please, young lady*, he thought, *go home to your family after work.* Then he wondered: would that have done Patty any good? Popping two aspirins into his mouth, he washed them down with a swallow of coffee.

It was while Ray Rose was sitting there that the blonde walked in, wearing a Walgreen's name badge. Rose stared at her; not at her exquisite figure, as most men would have, but at her face—because Rose was not looking at her merely as a man, but as a *policeman*. His lips had parted in astonishment. Was this possible?

Among the Columbo case evidence Ray Rose had in his possession, in addition to the sexually explicit photos of Patty, was a home movie that showed Frank DeLuca having sex with a blond woman with a spectacular body. Rose had viewed the film, but not all the men on his investigative team had. And the investigative team, as well as Rose himself, had interviewed all of the employees at Walgreen's—but Rose had not seen this particular employee, and obviously whichever men on his team *had* interviewed her, had *not* seen the home movie.

Because the blonde at the counter was the blonde in the movie.

Rose left his coffee and went over to her. The name badge read: JOY HEYSEK. Scattered pieces of information in Rose's mind began to come together.

Showing his identification, Rose said, "Excuse me, Miss Heysek, but I'd like you to come over to police headquarters with me."

"What for?" Joy Heysek asked.

"I have a home movie with Frank DeLuca in it that I'd like to talk to you about."

Joy Heysek turned bleach white.

In the headquarters interview room, Joy Heysek broke down. She admitted being sexually involved with Frank DeLuca for three years, while both had been working at other Walgreen's stores. Their relationship consisted primarily of the most bizarre sexual behavior, involving them in threesomes with other women, other men, a dog. They were all things Frank DeLuca wanted to do—and Joy Heysek, like Patricia Columbo after her, had done them, she said, not because she particularly liked that kind of activity, but because she was in love with Frank DeLuca and had wanted to please him. She was married, had two children, a nice home in the suburbs, a decent life; she could not explain what had happened to her good sense and judgment—except that it was what Frank DeLuca *wanted.*

"I just did it, I just did it," she said over and over. "Frank wanted to do it and I just did it."

Ray Rose was not interested in her sex life, except as a catalyst to generate further truth. "Tell me about the Columbo murders," he said quietly. It was not a harsh order—but it was an order nonetheless.

"He tried to make me a part of it," Joy Heysek said. "He wanted me to be his alibi."

"How?"

"He wanted me to go see a movie called *One Flew Over the Cuckoo's Nest* and tell him about it the next day so he could say he had seen it with me."

"When?" Short, precise questions, designed to keep the flow of words moving.

"On that—that Tuesday night," Joy Heysek said. "The night they were—" She couldn't get the word out.

"What else?" Rose asked. Keep it coming.

"The—the next morning—in the employee lunchroom at work—he said—'I took them all out last night.' He said—he had sh-shot Patty's father—in the back of the head—and that the bullet had come out his mouth—and that now Mr. Columbo's teeth were the same as his had been—after what happened on the parking lot."

"What else?"

"He—he was very high—elated about it. He had—cuts, scratches, on both hands. He said he had to—to—finish off the old man by hand."

"What about Mrs. Columbo?"

"He said she came around the corner from the hall and he shot—shot her between the eyes—"

"And Michael?"

"He said he shot Michael then."

Okay, Ray Rose thought. This was not hearsay; this was direct evidence that could be given in court.

He now had Frank DeLuca.

30
October 1973 to April 1974

With no more lies and no further deceptions encumbering their relationship—at least none that Patricia was aware of—she enjoyed some degree of relief from the pressures that had been weighing so heavily on her. The age problem was no longer a factor: Frank was thirty-five, she was seventeen—and that was that. The following June she would be eighteen, legally an adult, and Frank would be thirty-six, twice her age. Almost exactly twice, as a matter of fact, because both their birthdays were in the same month, which was kind of romantic in itself. But the conspicuous difference in their ages, now that it was known, bothered Patricia more than she cared to admit. Frank was almost as old as her own father; just three or four years separated them. And he had a daughter the same age as Michael. He had been married and fathering children when she was still in grammar school back on Ohio Street.

Putting their two lives in perspective like that—Frank's wife Marilyn giving birth to Frank's children while Patricia herself was still a child—was the catalyst for the most irksome thoughts in her. It was like turning on a neon sign in her head that alternately flashed: GROWN MAN-LITTLE GIRL. She was not a little girl, of course, except in the critical area of judgment, and she refused to acknowledge that. As with most seventeen-year-olds, she believed that she was smarter than most adults—certainly smarter than her parents and her teachers. They simply didn't "understand"; they were too "old-fashioned," and she intended to live her "own life" irrespective of their advice, guidance, or restrictions. No one was going to "live her life for her." Seventeen is, at best, a difficult age. Compounded by Patricia's experiences, it was emotionally unsparing.

Eventually, as a defense mechanism, Patricia simply stopped trying to rationalize her situation. She stopped dwelling on how old Frank DeLuca was and what he and his wife had been doing while she was admitting to her Talcott Elementary class that she had lied about getting a new baby sister. What the hell difference did it make? That was then— God, it seemed like *ages* ago—and this was now. She and Frank were in love, they were involved, their two lives were irrevocably braided like two strands of a rope; they could not be untwined, they could only be cut—and she was not about to let that happen.

Because she was still a minor, and due in part perhaps to her remark that Frank could go to jail for the escapades he had led her into, DeLuca curtailed the expansion of what was becoming a runaway sexual obsession with him. When he had explained to her how he wanted her to experience the entire gamut of sexual disciplines, in order to love him unequivocally, he had said that the threesome with Andre was only the first stage.

"Next," he had told her after that, "we'll have a different kind of party. With another woman."

DeLuca sensed Patricia's aversion at once, but persuaded her that she would come to like it fine. It would come out much later that the other woman he had in mind, and with whom he had already broached the subject, was Joy Heysek. But for now he had simply again said to Patricia, "Trust me." And she had told herself that she had no choice.

After the revelation that Patricia was a minor, DeLuca did not mention it again and abruptly geared down to a more temperate affair confined to the two of them. That, of course, was what Patricia wanted; it was really *all* she wanted. After a few weeks passed, she even entertained hope that DeLuca might have forgotten entirely the idea of the other woman, and that at last the love between them would be theirs exclusively.

It was not very long after the big Marilyn-and-the-Five-Little-Kids confrontation that Patricia had been hit with shock number two that year: Mary's cancer.

And during that, father-daughter trauma number two erupted, when Frank Columbo, apparently confused and consumed by fear of the unknown, momentarily lost control on the eve of his wife's surgery and kissed his daughter with a passion normally reserved for lovers.

There was no getting around it: this was a bad year for Patricia. And she *still* wasn't eighteen. At the rate she was going, she felt, she'd be an old goddamned woman before she ever achieved adulthood!

As quickly as the jolts of bad luck hit, however, just as quickly did they seem to be resolved. The Marilyn-and-the-Five-Little-Kids breach was closed very quickly, though the dull aftereffects of the discovery lingered in Patricia's mind for months.

Mary's cancer condition then took a turn for the better immediately following her operation. Dr. Laseman had come into the waiting room, still wearing his surgical scrubs, and said to Patricia and her father, "Good news, folks. No surprises, and the cancer hadn't spread much at all. We've removed a section of the large intestine and attached a colostomy bag, but only temporarily; she'll be able to get rid of that after a series of radiation treatments to eliminate any further diseased cells that might have been undetected. On the whole, she's doing extremely well. She's in recovery now."

As the doctor departed, Frank Columbo dropped into the nearest chair and expelled a great sigh of relief. Patricia walked over to the window and stared out at JFK Boulevard. Her eyes were dark circles, her expression strained. She was very tired. But through her weariness presently came a slight smile.

Michael, she thought. How happy he was going to be when he found out his mom was all right.

As Patricia was standing there, her father came up beside her.

"She's going to be okay, Patty," Frank Columbo said.

Patricia nodded without speaking.

"We're lucky," Frank said. "We're very, very lucky."

Patricia nodded again, but this time she also spoke. "Yeah, we're very lucky."

Frank put an arm around his daughter's shoulders. "Everything's gonna be okay now," he said, some of the old Frank Columbo confidence returning. It was as if the previous night, when he had kissed her, had never happened.

But for Patricia it *had* happened.

She twisted away from his arm.

"I've got to go to work," she said evenly.

She walked out of the waiting room without looking back.

It was then that Patricia made up her mind to leave home.

She would be eighteen in less than four months, legally old enough to leave and go out on her own. All she needed was enough money to do it.

"I'm quitting school," she told DeLuca when she got to the drugstore that day. "I want to start working full-time in the Beauty Center."

"Why?" he asked, putting aside a prescription he was filling. "What's the rush all of a sudden? I thought you were going to wait until this summer to start working full-time."

"I changed my mind. I want to work full-time now," she insisted. Without even realizing what she was doing, she seriously challenged him now for the first time. "If you won't let me work full-time here, I'll go find a job someplace else."

DeLuca studied her very intently, so intently that she felt the urge to turn away from him, to avoid his eyes. Abruptly she stepped over to the water cooler and drew a cup of cold water. She drank it with her back to him.

"All right," DeLuca quietly consented, "you can start full-time here. I'll work it out with Joy."

Joy again! Patricia was getting sick and tired of Joy Heysek being a part of everything that she said or did. It was almost like Frank had to have Joy's consent for anything he let Patricia do. Was he the goddamn store manager or was Joy?

"Why the hell does everything have to be worked out with her?" she demanded peevishly.

"Because she's the Beauty Center manager," DeLuca replied evenly. "I'm running a business here, Patrish; there are procedures to follow." His eyes were humorless. "If you want to act like a kid, maybe you'd better stay in high school."

Patricia walked away, mortified. How dare he talk to her that way? Who did the son of a bitch think he was anyway?

She walked out of the store, knowing her face was scarlet.

At home the climate for her was no better. Her mother was released from the hospital but semiconfined to bed rest for several weeks. Patricia's responsibilities multiplied. In addition to preparing meals for her father and Michael, serving her mother meals on a tray, keeping the house in order, and doing the family laundry, Patricia also had to take care of the colostomy bag. It was not pleasant. Besides emptying and washing the bag itself, she also had to make certain the stoma—the surgical bowel opening—was properly cleansed and sterilized. That was the most difficult part of the job, because Mary Columbo was never going to qualify for Patient of the Year. She was skittish, fidgety, and irrational about the real or imagined pain to which she was being subjected. Taking proper care of her was a daily battle for Patricia.

"Look, Mom," she finally said in exasperation, "if you don't like the way I take care of you, why don't you have Dad do it?"

"I couldn't ask your father to do a thing like this," Mary Columbo replied almost in revulsion, looking at her colostomy bag. "He's not the kind of man who can do things like this."

"Well, why doesn't he hire a nurse then?" Patricia demanded. "God knows he can afford it."

"Because he doesn't want an outsider taking care of me."

Swell, Patricia thought disgustedly.

Michael became a pain of another kind. Instead of complaining about Patricia's proficiency, or lack thereof, he simply decided that he wanted to be waited on hand and foot. He had finally learned what older sisters were for. For a while he got away with it. Patricia was so preoccupied with other problems that she acceded to Michael's requests without a lot of thought.

"Patty, can I have waffles for breakfast instead of cereal?"

"Yes, Michael. Sit down."

Michael got waffles.

"Patty, would you wash and iron this shirt for me every night so I can wear it every day? It's my favorite shirt."

"What? Oh, sure, Michael. Just leave it on top of the hamper."

Michael wore his favorite shirt every day.

"Patty, can I bring my friends in to have sundaes and watch TV?"

"Yes, but only if they're quiet so Mom can rest."

Michael led his friends in and Patricia served them ice cream sundaes, individually ordered.

Michael, as usual, went a step too far. One night when Patricia finally got everything done and fell exhausted across her bed, Michael meandered up to her door reading a comic book. Absently he said, "Patty, bring me a glass of milk," and sauntered on into his room.

Patricia sat bolt upright. "Michael! Get in here!"

Michael hurried back, the picture of innocent bewilderment.

"Since when are you a cripple, Michael Columbo?" she stormed. "You go get your own glass of milk, you little con artist!" Michael backed away, stunned. "And wear a different shirt tomorrow too—I'm tired of washing and ironing that dumb Evel Knievel shirt every night!" his sister lambasted him. As Michael shuffled dejectedly away, Patricia yelled after him, "Corn flakes in the morning, Michael!" Michael's shoulders slumped. He had worked his way up to hot cakes with strawberries and whipped cream—but now his bubble had burst.

A few minutes later, as Patricia was lying there feeling guilty, Michael walked contritely into her room and put a glass of milk on her nightstand. "In case you want one too," he said, and walked out, head hung.

Patricia *really* felt guilty after that. As she drank the milk, she decided that tomorrow she would buy him the new Jerry West signature basketball he wanted.

In the Beauty Center one day, Patricia saw Andre enter the store and proceed down an aisle where Joy was working.

Patricia stopped what she was doing and started over to introduce them. But she quickly saw it wasn't necessary.

"Hey, Joy!" Andre greeted her with delight. "Long time no see! I didn't know you were over here now."

They hugged like old friends and immediately went off to have coffee together.

Patricia's whole being started tightening up, but she instantly checked herself. *Don't jump to conclusions*, she warned herself silently. *Maybe it's perfectly innocent. Just two good friends in the wonderful world of cosmetics.*

Please God, don't let the lies start again, she silently prayed. Things had been fairly uncomplicated between DeLuca and herself since their night of confronting the truth. The tension and stress of their relationship had dissolved into a more or less comfortable familiarity, to the point where, because of the situation at home, the little room at the Br'er Rabbit Motel had come to be Patricia's refuge from the rest of the world. Erratic as the trysts were—only once or twice a week now, and usually rushed, a couple of hours at the most—they were still precious times to her.

Frank was very generous in his reassurances whenever she began anew to feel insecure about Joy Heysek. Time after time he comforted her—Patricia was special, different, unique, unsurpassed—he knew all the right words. The things he did with her, he had never dreamed of doing with anyone else. It should have been unthinkable to her, despite the intimacy of Andre's greeting of Joy, that more lies were about to surface—but it was not. She almost knew in her heart, no matter how vigorously she fought the premonition, that she was about to be emotionally razed again.

Patricia had to find out. So she waited patiently until Andre walked Joy back to where she had been working, then caught his eye and waved to him as he began restocking. He strolled over to where Patricia was cleaning a glass showcase.

"Hi, Patrish." He greeted her with his brilliant smile.

"Hi, Andre. I see you found an old friend."

"Joy? Oh yeah." He winked at Patricia. "We go back a ways, Joy and me."

"Joy and you and Frank, you mean," Patricia said, winking back.

"Oh, you know about that, huh? I wasn't sure Frank had
told you."

"Frank tells me everything, honey."

Sooner or later, that is. When he gets caught.

As Andre walked back to the pharmacy to see DeLuca,
Patricia threw down the cloth she had been using to clean the
showcase, went to the locker room for her purse, and walked
out of the store.

For the rest of that afternoon, Patricia sat in Morton Park
wondering what in hell to do about her life. Wherever she
turned, wherever she looked, whatever she did, there was
trouble, there was a problem. Was it her? she wondered. Was
there something about her that generated all this strife? Did
all these conflicts, all this goddamn discord and dissension,
come about because of some flaw, some defect, in her character, her personality, her *self*? There seemed to be absolutely
no harmony in her life—in any quarter. She seemed not to be
compatible with any other human being.

What's wrong with me? she silently asked herself, trying
hard to be very patient and rational about it. But she sensed
at once that calmness was not the answer, so she simply
turned loose her emotions and let her mind scream: *What—
the—fuck—is—wrong—with—me?* Without thinking, she used
the heels of her hands to pound herself on both temples, as
if the old cliché of knocking some sense into someone might
actually work. Suddenly realizing what she was doing, she
stopped as abruptly as she had begun and quickly looked
around to see if anyone had observed her brief frenzy.

The solitariness of the moment unexpectedly became important to her. In solitude there was no desperate desire to answer all the unanswerable questions. The problems were still
there—but in isolation they did not have to be dealt with this
instant. Remoteness from the people around whom her emotional troubles revolved seemed to lessen the immediacy of
those troubles. Maybe she simply needed to get away from
everyone for a while.

The prospect was tantalizing. Get away from Frank
DeLuca and his wife, Marilyn, and their five brats; and his
friend Joy Heysek; and his buddy Andre. Get away from her
house, from her father and his—*strangeness*; from her mother

and that goddamned colostomy bag; from that little prick Michael, who seemed to become more selfish every day. Get away from—

Everything. Everybody.

But how? Where could she go? She didn't even have enough money saved yet to move into her own apartment, let alone to run off to someplace—and where would she run to even if she had money? She didn't know *how* to run away; she didn't know how to do anything. She was just a dumb fucking seventeen-year-old who sometimes felt as old as the people around her: thirty-five, forty, forty-five. Except that they all seemed to know what they were doing, while she was stumbling like a blind, drunken spastic.

I'd just like to go to jail for a year, she thought fitfully.

And the thought seized her like a tentacle.

There were two part-time relief saleswomen in the Beauty Center, Helen Makin and Norma Ringel, who worked three or four hours several evenings a week when Patricia, Joy, and the other full-time employees were not scheduled for evening hours. Helen and Norma took whatever hours they could get, within the parameters of their personal schedules.

Patricia waited until a time when both part-time women were in the department, and she herself was off. DeLuca was on duty also, in the little glass-partitioned manager's office going over the previous day's register receipts with one of the cashiers. When he looked up from his work, he was surprised to see Patricia there.

"Hi. What are you doing here on your day off?"

"I forgot and left something in my locker," she said. "And I didn't bring my key either. Can I use the master key for a minute?"

"Sure." DeLuca unlocked a desk drawer and fingered through several tagged keys until he found the one with LOCKERS—MASTER on its tag.

"Thanks," Patricia said when he handed it to her. "I'll bring it back in a sec."

She went unobtrusively to the employee locker room, avoiding the Beauty Center where Helen and Norma were at that moment each waiting on customers. With the master key, Patricia first opened Helen's locker, removed her wallet from her purse, and locked it again. Several feet away, she opened Norma's locker and took two credit cards from her purse. She put the stolen items in her own purse and left the locker room. Back at the manager's office, she returned the master key to DeLuca, who was now alone.

"Thanks."

As DeLuca took the key, he said quietly, "Don't forget we're going to party tomorrow night."

"How could I forget that, Frank?" she replied in mock reverence. "It's in my thoughts every waking moment."

DeLuca gazed levelly at her. "You're getting to be a real smart-mouth, aren't you?"

"Am I, Frank?"

"Yeah, you are, Patrish."

"It must be because I've got such a good teacher," she said. She started to leave, but paused. Joy Heysek, she knew, was off tonight also. "What are you doing tonight, Frank?" she asked pointedly.

"Going home," he told her. "I have to spend *some* time with my kids, you know."

"Oh, yes. Your kids. Is number six on the way yet, Frank?"

The eyes behind DeLuca's level gaze became flat and cold. Patricia turned and left before she could become intimidated. But a thrum of fear rose in her nevertheless. *Don't get him mad at you*, her better judgment warned. *This is the kind of guy who will beat the shit out of you without thinking twice.* Her evaluation, she would learn much later, was dead-on; he had already done so to Joy Heysek.

Outside, in her father's car, which she had borrowed, Patricia examined the stolen wallet. It contained a little money, a driver's license, MasterCharge, checkbook with personalized checks in the names of George and Helen Makin, and a house key. The credit cards she had stolen from Norma were a MasterCharge and BankAmericard.

Okay, Patricia thought determinedly, let's go shopping.

She was more nervous walking into the Woodfield Mall than she had been stealing from the lockers. Glancing around, she expected every face she saw to be familiar. The huge indoor shopping center was actually in Schaumburg, the next suburb north of Elk Grove Village, but it was the one most residents

Above: Frank and Mary Columbo in the only available photograph of them. Relatives on both sides now zealously guard their photographs from publication. *(Chicago Tribune)*

Left: Michael Columbo in his school yearbook photograph, taken only weeks before his murder. He had just turned thirteen. (Lively Junior High School, Elk Grove Village, IL)

Police photos of Patricia Columbo and her lover, Frank DeLuca, taken for identification purposes only hours after the bodies of Patricia's family were found. (Elk Grove Village Police Department)

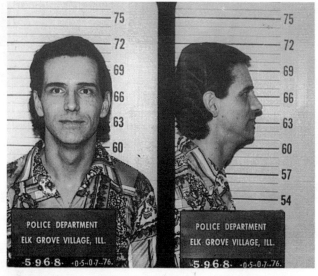

Patricia Columbo, age nineteen, returning to Cook County Jail after her indictment for the murder of her family. *(Chicago Tribune)*

Above: Artist's sketch of Marilyn DeLuca testifying at her ex-husband's murder trial. She claimed she didn't know that Frank DeLuca had involved her in a conspiracy to kill two of the state's witnesses against him. (*Daily Herald* graphic, Arlington Heights, IL)

Left: Roman Sobczynski, the unindicted co-conspirator who, in testifying for the prosecution, admitted agreeing to murder the Columbo family in exchange for sex with Patricia Columbo.

Patricia Columbo during her trial for triple homicide in June 1977. Even after being in jail for nearly a year, she still maintained some of her flash — note her fingernails, ring and earrings, and the pushed-up sunglasses. *(Chicago Tribune)*

Left: Al Baliunas, who led the team of prosecutors that convinced a jury to convict Patricia Columbo and Frank DeLuca of the triple murders. (*Daily Herald* photo, Arlington Heights, IL)

Below: William Murphy, half of Patricia Columbo's defense team, solemn after his client is found guilty on three counts of murder. (*Daily Herald* photo, Arlington Heights, IL)

Frank DeLuca just moments after being found guilty of murdering Frank, Mary, and Michael Columbo. DeLuca would continue to protest his innocence for fifteen years. (*Daily Herald* photo, Arlington Heights, IL)

Ray Rose, who led the investigation that solved the Columbo family murders, is now deputy chief of the Elk Grove Village Police Department. (Author's collection)

Patricia Columbo in May 1991, the night she received her bachelor's degree after fifteen years of incarceration. She was the first female convict in Illinois to complete her entire college education while imprisoned. (Author's photograph)

of Elk Grove went to for serious shopping. What the hell was she nervous for? she wondered. It wasn't like she was trying to get away with anything. She stopped a few steps into the mall and took a deep breath. Just calm down, *Patrish*, she told herself, sarcastically using Frank DeLuca's name for her, which had once so delighted her. Try to act grown-up, *Patrish*, she mocked DeLuca in her mind. You're a big girl now. If you can fuck Andre in a motel room while the man who says he loves you takes pictures of you doing it, you should be able to rip off a few stores in good form.

Several doors up was a Frederick's of Hollywood store. The enticing, scanty lingerie displayed in the shop's two entry windows could have been created with Patricia's figure in mind. Might as well get something nice for Frank to see, she thought, studying the merchandise, since it'll be one of the last few times he'll get to see his little protégée in bed. Marshaling her courage, she forced a stroll into the store.

The salesclerk who waited on Patricia that day was Theresa Gorey. She helped Patricia select a revealing red nightgown with numerous strategically placed eyelets and cutouts, and a slit on one side that went all the way up to *there*. It came to $56.18 with tax. Patricia wrote one of Helen Makin's checks to pay for it, and used Helen Makin's driver's license, which had no photo on it, and MasterCharge card for identification.

When she walked out of the store with her parcel, her mouth was dry and her palms were wet.

In the next three days, Patricia went on a buying spree of unrestrained indulgence. She bought blouses and skirts, sweaters and slacks, paying for them with Norma Ringel's MasterCharge. She bought leather boots with Norma's BankAmericard. She bought belts, bags, and scarves; costume jewelry; wigs; a large quantity of cosmetics—of all things. She bought merchandise she didn't need or even like, just to run up the bills. When she didn't use Norma Ringel's charge cards, she paid for things with one of Helen Makin's checks.

On the third day of her binge, she even took Michael with her and made a point of complaining to the salesclerk what a nuisance her younger brother was—just to make certain she was remembered.

This plan, she kept telling herself, *had* to work.

* * *

Walgreen's security department began an internal investigation of the thefts, and immediately suspended Patricia pending its outcome. There was no other choice; DeLuca could not conceal the fact that Patricia had borrowed the master key the day the thefts occurred; a cashier had witnessed him giving it to her. He himself could even expect a reprimand; he should have accompanied Patricia to her locker and opened it for her. After Patricia's suspension, the internal investigation was put on hold pending the report of any illegal use of the stolen checks or credit cards.

Patricia did not tell her parents that she had been suspended. Instead, the following day, she managed to obtain a new job, as a receptionist in the sales office of a small plastic pipings system company. It was an easy job; she was alone in the office most of the day, and spent a lot of time on the telephone with DeLuca.

Thinking she was going to be arrested at any time, and might not see or talk to him again—her original goal—she began to feel the loss already and was moved by a need to keep in close touch with him.

"Are you crazy?" DeLuca asked her the first time she called. "What the hell got into you? Didn't you think how this would look for me, how it might affect my future?"

"I didn't think about that, I'm sorry," she said. She really hadn't thought about it.

"Well, why the hell did you do it?" he wanted to know. He was upset, but did not sound actually angry.

"I don't know, Frank. I don't know why I did it." What else could she tell him? *I did it because I'm trying to get away from you, and from everybody else, and haven't got the guts or the strength to just walk away?* He would probably have said, "Oh, grow up!"

"Well, I'll try to help you if I can," DeLuca told her finally, "but I have to cover my own ass first. Credit slips and bum checks are starting to turn up all over Woodfield Mall. We've had cops in here from Elk Grove and Schaumburg talking to Helen and Norma. The cops have a picture of you and they're going to try and identify you with the clerks in the mall. If they do, you're going to be in deep shit."

Good, Patricia thought. *Let them come and get me.*

* * *

Patricia was at her receptionist desk at the little office of the plastic pipe company when the detectives arrived with their arrest warrant. It was a little after nine o'clock in the morning and she had just come to work. She knew when they walked in the door who they were and what they were there for. Girding herself, she thought: *Now, you don't have to worry about anybody anymore. You're going to jail.*

The detectives identified themselves and served the warrant. Patricia was handcuffed and led out to their car.

On the way to the police station to be processed, she was overwhelmed by the most dread fear she had ever experienced. It was followed by a complete shutdown of all the determination that had urged her forward in what suddenly was no longer a clever plan, but now a terrible, horrible mistake.

Suddenly it became totally insignificant to her that Frank DeLuca had partied with Joy Heysek and Andre before he knew her. And it became inconsequential that DeLuca had lied to her about it. She could not imagine now, in the back of the police car, why she'd become so upset over it; after all, didn't Frank lie about *everything*, just as she did? Their entire relationship had been an epidemic of lies from the very beginning. So what? Had it been all that terrible, really?

Now *this*—this was terrible. Being taken to jail in handcuffs was terrible.

Patricia began to bawl like a baby.

"I want to call my daddy!"

C.H.
May 1991

Helen Makin remembered Patricia Columbo well.

"Patty was one of the most troubled young girls I'd ever seen," the former teacher said. "After my baby was born and I gave up teaching for a while, I worked with her now and then on my part-time job at Walgreen's. I don't think Patty or any of my other co-workers even knew at that time that I'd been a teacher; I didn't go around broadcasting it. But I'd

*had some counseling experience with young people, and I
could recognize the signs in a kid who was in trouble and
who was crying out for help. Patty was crying out—and nobody was listening to her."*

"What," I asked, "were some of the signs you spotted in
her?"

"Well, for one thing, she worried a lot because she didn't
have many friends—didn't have any friends, I guess, is a
more apt way of putting it. She was lamenting about that one
time when she pulled an evening shift and I was on five-thirty
to nine-thirty. I don't know exactly what happened to bring it
on, but she was really down. 'There must be something wrong
with me,' she said. 'Nobody wants to be friends with me. The
kids at school go out of their way to avoid me. I can't understand it; I used to have lots of friends.' When she finished her
complaint, I said, 'Patty, do you think it might have anything
to do with the way you dress?' "

"How did she dress?" I asked, even though by then I already knew.

"She dressed very tackily," Helen Makin said. "Some of
her skirts were so short they weren't even minis, they were
micros. And she wore boots, wigs, outrageous colors, far too
much makeup; she fancied herself a cosmetician, but her
whole attitude seemed to be more is better—she really loaded
it on. I could certainly see why her peers at Elk Grove High
would have avoided her; she was an embarrassment."

"Frank DeLuca apparently found her very attractive," I reminded her.

"Apparently," Helen agreed wryly. "DeLuca was a real lo-
thario; he fancied himself a great, sexually liberated swinger.
He was always alluding to sex in one way or another; really
preoccupied with it." She sighed quietly. "I guess he and
Patty must have found something in each other to have gone
as far as they did—" There was sadness in her tone; she was
obviously thinking of the murders.

"Was there anything else about Patty that made you think
she needed help?" I asked.

"The lies," Helen Makin said. "The stupid, ridiculous, use-
less lies that she constantly told. She simply could not tell the
truth."

"What did she lie about?"

"Anything and everything. I remember one time we were working together, a month or so after we'd had the conversation about her choice of clothes. I had tried to talk to her about the way she dressed, particularly after I learned how it was affecting her peer relations; she never listened, of course. But this one time she came to work and she had on the nicest jumpsuit outfit—a really becoming style that looked great on her. I immediately saw an opportunity to impress upon her how much better she looked when she dressed more conservatively. 'Patty, honey,' I said to her, 'that is the cutest jumpsuit. You really look pretty in it.' Well, I'd never seen anyone so pleased in my life; you'd have thought I'd just told her she was the new Miss America. 'You really think so?' she asked me. 'You're not just saying it to be nice?' I assured her I was very sincere. 'Well, guess what?' she said. 'I made this jumpsuit myself.' Of course, I was amazed. Patty certainly didn't look like the type who could, or would, sew. She even asked if I wanted the pattern, and I said sure, because I did sew. Anyway, Patty got off before I did that night, and it was a couple of hours later that I went into the locker room and there was her jumpsuit, just tossed on a bench. I thought she'd accidentally forgotten to put it in her locker, so I went to hang it up for her. That's when I saw the label on the neck-band. It was a factory-made garment; she hadn't sewn it at all."

Helen Makin sighed her quiet sigh again.

"I've always thought she lied like that, and tried to get caught, because she wanted somebody's attention; the same reason she later stole the credit cards. She wanted someone to notice her and ask, 'What's the matter?' I guess nobody ever did."

"I guess not," I said.

Not until she made them.

Norma Ringel was the other part-time Beauty Center employee whose credit had been used by Patricia on her spree.

"I never understood it," Norma said. "I don't to this day. Patty would buy something with one of my charge cards—like those white boots or that awful wig—and then wear them to work, knowing I'd see them on her, and knowing that the charge slips would come back to me eventually and that I'd *probably put two and two together. I mean, I knew Patty was no rocket scientist, but she couldn't have been that dumb. Helen later said she thought it was Patty's way of asking for help, and I suppose Helen could have been right; I mean, she had been a teacher and all. But I'm still not sure that explains it. I'm not sure anyone will ever know what made Patty tick."*

"Prior to the credit card thefts, how had Patricia been to work with?" I asked.

"Oh, all right, I guess," Norma allowed. "Like Helen, I was only part-time, so I wasn't around her all that much. But she'd go along for a while, acting normal and all, and then something would happen that made her go into an act of some kind. Like, her father would come into the store. Well, she'd just go onstage immediately: she'd run over to him and throw her arms around his neck, be all lovey-dovey, and daddy darling this, daddy darling that—just made a complete fool of herself in front of customers, co-workers, everybody. It was like she had this compulsion to prove that somebody loved her."

"What was the feeling in the store about DeLuca?" I asked.

Norma all but dismissed him. "Oh, he just thought he was God's gift to women, you know. He used to look at himself a lot in different mirrors around the store; that kind of conceit. I think Patty was the only one who took him seriously. Patty and, I suppose, Joy Heysek."

"Did people who worked in the store know that he and Patty were having an affair?"

"Of course. It was so obvious; their little looks and touches and the way they'd talk when they were around each other, little double meanings that no one else was supposed to be smart enough to interpret. It was the store joke, the way they acted."

"How did people react," I asked, "when they learned that Patty and DeLuca had been charged with the murders?"

"Everyone was shocked by the murders, naturally, but I don't think anyone was shocked that Patty and DeLuca were involved. Surprised, maybe, but not really shocked. I guess that Walgreen's upper management was shocked. I don't

*know, it was all so terrible—that whole family—such a terri-
ble tragedy . . ."*

*Especially, I thought, to have come out of something that
was once just a store joke.*

31
May 1974

Frank Columbo got his daughter out of jail as fast as was hu-
manly possible. He sped to the jail with a fat roll of currency
and a list of lawyers' phone numbers. His little girl was not—
repeat *not*—going to be kept behind bars. Upon her arrest and
a review of the charges against her, Patricia's bond had been
increased to twelve thousand dollars. Her father counted out
twelve hundred dollars in cash, which was the 10 percent required to get the bond posted. Patricia was ordered to appear
in the Schaumburg court in four weeks, on May 22, 1974, at
1:30 P.M. The court date was one month before her eighteenth
birthday.

Frank Columbo was wholly supportive. "Don't worry,
honey," he assured her. "I'm gonna fix this up. I'm gonna
take care of this. We'll get this thing straightened out, don't
worry about it."

Mary was supportive too, though less unconditionally.
"Patty, for God's sake, cosmetics! You *work* in cosmetics!"

Michael, of course, was awed. "How does it feel to be a
jailbird, Patty?" he asked excitedly, though not in front of
their parents.

"Not funny, Michael," his sister said soberly. Patricia made
Michael promise solemnly never to steal. "It would really
hurt Mom and Dad if *you* ever did anything like that."

Somehow, she never thought of herself as hurting them,
only making them angry.

Frank Columbo telephoned Helen Makin at home.

"Mrs. Makin, this is Frank Columbo, Patty's father. I'm
trying to settle all this mess that Patty's got herself in and I
was wondering if you would consider withdrawing the complaint about your checks?"

"Well, I—I don't know, Mr. Columbo," Helen said. "I'm not at all sure that would be the right thing to do."

"Look, Mrs. Makin," he reasoned, "Patty's not a bad kid, I think you'll probably admit that; you've worked with her, you know she's not bad, not really. I'd like to straighten this mess out, you know? Now I realize that you've been put to a lot of inconvenience and I know you're probably mad and upset about the whole thing. But how about if I write you and your husband a nice check to kind of make up for all your trouble—"

"Mr. Columbo, I understand what you're trying to do for your daughter," Helen Makin said, "and I respect your feeling as a parent. But if you simply buy Patty's way out of this situation, you could be doing her a great deal more harm than good."

"What do you mean?" her caller said. "I don't understand."

"Look," Helen told him, "the job I have in that drugstore is only temporary. I am a teacher by profession, and I've had some training and experience counseling young people. Patty has some serious problems, Mr. Columbo."

"Problems? What kind of problems?" he asked.

"I don't know what kind of problems they are, not specifically," Helen Makin said. "But I sincerely believe she needs some professional help."

"Like what?" Frank Columbo's tone was bracing a bit.

"A psychologist," Helen said bluntly. "Maybe even a psychiatrist."

"A head doctor, you mean? A shrink?"

"Yes."

"My daughter's not crazy, Mrs. Makin," he said with an edge. "You're wrong if you think that."

"I don't think that," Helen disclaimed. "A person doesn't have to be crazy to have serious emotional problems—"

"Look, I called you up to try to pay you back for any trouble Patty caused you with this little spree of hers. Are you interested or aren't you?"

"Will you consider getting her some professional help?"

"Definitely not, because in my opinion she doesn't need it."

"Then I'm not interested in your check, Mr. Columbo."

* * *

The next day it was Mary who called Helen Makin.

"I don't think you and my husband got along too well yesterday," she said exploratively.

"Your husband doesn't seem to realize that Patty has some serious problems, Mrs. Columbo," Helen replied candidly. "Do you?"

"Of course I do," Mary declared. "My husband does too. We just think they should be kept in the family. Whatever the problems are, we'll solve them ourselves. I just wish you could be understanding enough to help us settle this little mess Patty is in—"

"Mrs. Columbo," Helen said firmly, "that is not simply a little mess that Patty is in; that is a cry for help. Can't you see that?"

"I don't know what you mean."

"All right, look. Patty steals credit cards and checks from two people she works with. She uses them in the same mall, the same stores, over and over. She uses my name one day at Ocso's cosmetics counter, Norma's name the next day, and even tells the woman there that she herself sells cosmetics at Walgreen's in Elk Grove. Mrs. Columbo, Patty was trying to get caught."

"Trying to get caught?" It must have seemed absurd to Mary. "Why would anyone try to get caught?"

"The usual reason is to call attention to oneself; it's a way of saying, 'Hey, look at me, I need help.' "

"Listen, if Patty needs help," Mary asserted, "all she's got to do is ask for it—"

"Some people can't ask for it," Helen said quietly. "They don't know how."

"You used to be a teacher, huh?"

"I still am a teacher; I'm simply not teaching at the moment. I took time off to have a baby."

"Oh. First one?"

"Second. I have a boy and a girl, just like you."

"Well, listen"—Mary cleverly sought common ground—"as one mother to another, can't you see your way clear to helping us straighten this thing out?"

"Yes, I can. And I will," Helen Makin said. "If you and your husband will agree to get some professional help for that girl—"

"I can see I'm wasting my time," Mary Columbo said. She hung up.

Frank Columbo also called Norma Ringel, with the same proposition: a blank check if she would withdraw the complaint against Patricia. Norma was understanding but not in a position to help. Unlike Helen, whose personal checks Patricia had forged, it had been Norma's credit cards that were used.

"I'm sorry, Mr. Columbo," she said, "but it's out of my hands. The credit card companies are the ones who have the complaint against Patty, not me."

"I don't understand," Frank Columbo said.

"All I did was sign affidavits stating that I hadn't made the charges. The credit card companies take over after that. I've been told I don't even have to go to court."

"Suppose you were to say you made a mistake?" Patricia's father suggested.

"I'm sorry, Mr. Columbo, but I couldn't do that," Norma said. "First of all, I'd probably get in trouble myself if I tried it, and besides that, it wouldn't be right. I'd like to help Patty, but I can't lie for her."

It grieved Frank Columbo that he apparently was so ineffective in his efforts to "save" Patty. Mary tried to console him, assuring him that he—and she—had done everything they could do as parents. But away from Frank, Mary would tell a friend that for once Patty was going to "have to take her medicine." She also frequently reminded her husband that their daughter was "almost grown"—nearly eighteen. But with philosophical sadness, Frank said to both wife and friends, "Eighteen don't make a person grown."

Mary couldn't argue with that. Patty *thought* she was grown with her outrageous clothes—white boots and black miniskirts, all the cheap junky jewelry, the heavy makeup; that purple mascara alone was enough to cause a mother to throw up—and the rest of it: the way she walked, the way she stood. But her father saw none of that. Frank went out of his way to shop at Walgreen's when she was on shift, knowing what a spectacle of daughterly love she would present in front of customers and co-workers alike, probably realizing that only in public did Patty pay any attention to him. The

nights of sitting by the radiator with his little girl and the
flashcards must have been an aching memory to him. Mary
told friends that Frank was hurting bad, and that she felt that
it was her responsibility to do something about it. Mary recognized her daughter for exactly what she was at that time:
a phony. She saw it in the faces of the people who watched
Patty perform in the drugstore. She was a phony and, the way
she dressed, she was a joke. And deep down, Mary must have
known that part of what the daughter was, was the fault of
the mother.

The friends in whom Mary confided her problems with
Patricia seemed to have recognized that Mary felt a nagging
sense of, if not guilt, at least unfulfilled responsibility. Everyone in Patty's life, Mary included, had been too busy spoiling
her to teach her anything. And in later years, with Mary, the
spoiling had been replaced by nagging. Still no direction in
life, no coaching toward maturity, no lessons in growing up.
No instilling of character, therefore no depth; the daughter
was superficial—and the mother had helped make her that
way. Mary was as distressed and miserable about Patricia's
problems as Frank. Except in a different way.

That great champion of women, Frank DeLuca, finally solved
everyone's immediate dilemma. Patricia walked up to Grove
Shopping Center and, as prearranged on the telephone,
DeLuca picked her up. It was their first meeting since her arrest.

"I've got a fantastic idea!" Frank told her enthusiastically.

His idea was for Patricia to move in with him. Not *just*
with him—but with him and Marilyn and the five little
DeLucas. Frank wanted her to become part of his family.

Patricia couldn't believe it. The plan was outrageous—
even for Frank.

But DeLuca had already laid his groundwork. He had told
Marilyn that Patrish's troubles with the law stemmed from
problems she was having with her "materialistic" parents,
who set high standards and then expected her to live up to
them. DeLuca told his wife that Patricia was almost eighteen
and planning to go out on her own soon anyway; that he felt
responsible for her since it was he who had brought her into
Walgreen's; and that it would be nice if he and Marilyn in-

vited Patrish to come stay with them until she got herself together and put all the trouble behind her. There was certainly enough room; five bedrooms, the master for Frank and Marilyn, a bedroom for the two oldest girls, one for the two youngest, Frank Junior's bedroom, and one for Patrish. It would be perfect, Frank told Patricia. It would mean they could be together all the time.

Together—not necessarily alone. As usual.

Patricia had grave doubts. The whole credit card and forgery scheme had originated as a strategy to get *away* from Frank DeLuca—as well as everyone else in her life. Of course, she had realized how preposterous the plan had been almost immediately upon her actual arrest. From the grimly determined, betrayed woman she thought she was, she reverted to the confused adolescent she really was. She had never stolen before, nor would she ever steal again. If she really was a thief, particularly a thief who wanted to be caught, she'd had all of Walgreen's to quietly plunder. Her motive, however, as Helen Makin believed, was probably desperation. Now the very person causing that desperation was asking her to move in with him and his family.

"Frank, I don't know about this," Patricia hedged. "I don't think I could, you know, feel comfortable around your wife and kids. And, I mean, in your own house, where your family lives, I don't think I could ever, you know, *do* anything with you—"

DeLuca went into his understanding mode. He realized, he assured her, what a sensitive situation it might at first glance appear to be. But he had talked to Marilyn about it, even promising that he would start spending more evenings at home with her and the kids if she would agree to do this. Marilyn *had* finally agreed, but only on condition that there be no fooling around between him and Patricia in the house. No sex.

Patricia recalled years later that this was the first time it had ever occurred to her that Marilyn DeLuca knew of her affair with Frank. The realization was so humiliating, she said, that it made her feel ill. Patricia knew that her affair with DeLuca was not as big a secret as she sometimes liked to think it was. Probably half the people in the store at least suspected it, and of course Andre knew, and Joy Heysek all but knew. But the thought that Frank's *wife* might know had never crossed her mind.

She had to ask. "Does Marilyn know we're having an affair?"

"She suspects it," DeLuca admitted.

"Did she know about you and Joy Heysek?"

"I think so."

"*Think* so? Aren't you sure?"

"Patrish," he said patiently, "you're still such a kid, you don't realize how things are. A husband never really *knows* how much his wife knows about what he does. Not unless she tells him. And Marilyn isn't the type to tell. You have to look at things from her point of view, okay? She's got a nice home, five kids, and a husband that supports her. A woman will put up with a lot not to lose that." He shrugged. "I'm not sure how much she knows—and I really don't care."

In retrospect, Patricia would recall, she did not know if there was any one reason that made her decide to move in with Frank DeLuca and his family. There *were* reasons, several of them—but no one of them seemed at the time to weigh more than the others. It was the overall effect that did it, like putting on one layer of clothing after another until you're finally warm enough.

The main reason she wanted to leave home now was no longer her father, but her mother. Frank Columbo had been a bedrock of support for her in the matter of the criminal charges. All thought of any sinister liberties she might have imagined in the past was relegated to some dark cranny of her mind, sent there by the natural fact that she had come running, figuratively, to him minutes after the handcuffs swiveled shut. Little Patty Ann had scraped her knee and needed her daddy, and Frank Columbo strode to her aid just as he always had. Nobody was going to fuck with *his* little girl—not even the law. At the jail, Patricia had flung herself into his arms like a frightened toddler. Any fear she felt vanished, certainly at least from her conscious mind.

Not so the problems with her mother. Mary Columbo, supporting her the first few days following her arrest and subsequent release, gradually, for some reason that Patricia did not remotely understand at the time, suddenly put herself *between* father and daughter—not to protect *her*, but clearly in defense of *him*. While she deferred to her husband when he was there, Mary became a radically different person when he was not. Left alone for five minutes with Patricia, Mary became her daughter's adversary.

"Patty Ann, you're going to kill your father if you keep on the way you're going," was a typical opener.

"Mom, it's over," Patricia would disclaim. "It'll never happen again, I promise."

And it *was* over—if what Mary was alluding to was simply the stolen credit cards. But at times Mary seemed to be insinuating that there was more on her mind. She made vague references to a friend of a friend who knew someone at Walgreen's, then stressed that as high-strung as Frank Columbo was, even a rumor might set him off. In other words, the implication of gossip. Perhaps even a warning of what could happen if that talk reached the volatile head of the household.

Patricia imagined with dread the trouble she would be in for if her father found out that Frank DeLuca, almost his own age, married with five children, had been intimate with Frank Columbo's teenage princess.

Aside from the provocation at home, there was a major new inducement offered by DeLuca.

"You know what I'd like to see you do?" he said one day. "I'd like to see you become a model. Like those Frederick's of Hollywood girls that model the lingerie for their catalogs. With your looks, I'll bet you could become a model easy."

Patricia was fascinated. Frank explained that he had it all figured out. First thing they would do was get some business cards printed up—with both names on them: hers as the model, his as her manager. Then they would take a lot of photographs of her—nude shots, underwear shots—and send the pictures along with one of the business cards to Frederick's and some other places that used models. Then all they had to do was sit back and wait for the phone to ring. They could, DeLuca was certain, have their own model agency in no time.

"And with you living at my house," he emphasized, "we'd have evenings together to plan everything, work out the details and all; it would be perfect."

From merely fascinated, Patricia became enthralled.

* * *

The sleeping arrangements proposed by DeLuca concerned her. She confessed to Frank that she was bothered by the fact that he would continue to share the master bedroom with Marilyn. Frank was ready with reassurance.

"Patrish," he attested, "Marilyn and I don't *do* anything anymore. We haven't for—hell, I don't know since when. Since before the baby was born, at least. It's been a good two years."

That was almost as long as the two of them had been involved. The thought brought a lump to Patricia's throat. "You haven't had sex with anyone but me in all that time?"

"Only you," he declared. "I haven't had anything left for anybody else. I love you, Patrish. You're all I want."

That did the trick.

She told her parents that she was leaving, that she had been invited by Mr. and Mrs. DeLuca to come live with them for an indeterminate time until she could put her life in order. Her parents could force her to remain with them for another few weeks until her eighteenth birthday if they wanted to, in which case when she left she would be gone for good and would not even come to see them. Or they could be reasonable about it, let her go at once, and they could all remain on at least cordial terms. It was up to them.

Frank Columbo had buried his face in his hands. "I don't know what to do anymore," he admitted helplessly.

"There's only one thing we can do, Frankie," his wife said. She put an arm around his bent shoulders and laid her face against his head. "We've got to let her go."

Frank Columbo began to cry.

Frank and Marilyn DeLuca came to get Patricia in their station wagon. The colossal gall of DeLuca at that moment must have been immeasurable, matched only by his wife's incredible complicity.

Patricia came out to the driveway with two suitcases and DeLuca opened the tailgate and put them in the back for her. There were no good-byes; her father was at work, and her mother was in the downstairs bedroom with the door closed. Patricia saw Michael looking around the corner of the house and started to go to him, but he turned and ran from her. She hated that, but knew in her heart that any breach between Michael and her would never be permanent.

After Patricia got in the car and they were driving away, she thought she saw her mother watching from the front window—but she wasn't sure. As the DeLuca station wagon took her away from Frank Columbo's suburban dream home at 55 Brantwood Avenue, Patricia felt as if she was leaving a nightmare behind.

Her real nightmare had not even begun.

32
June 1974 to May 1975

Marilyn DeLuca was shorter than Patricia, and thinner. Also Italian—her maiden name had been Marilyn Curcio—she had dark eyes and black hair like her husband. She and Frank actually made a nice-looking couple, Patricia grudgingly admitted to herself.

Patricia did not feel as awkward living in this unusual situation as she might have. One reason for her easy adjustment was the artful groundwork DeLuca had laid prior to her arrival.

Even the neighbors had been briefed.

"In case you ever talk to any of our neighbors," Marilyn advised her early on, "they think that Frank and I are being surrogate parents to you because you had a lot of problems at home. Frank's told everyone that you worked for him in the drugstore and that when you got into trouble, we volunteered to the court to take you into our home for a while. That story okay with you?"

"Sure, fine," Patricia agreed. It amazed her that no matter what lie DeLuca told, it always seemed to make him look good. The neighbors probably had him pegged as Mr. Nice Guy of 1974.

Marilyn DeLuca's relationship with Patricia was detached, almost impersonal. Neither friendly nor unfriendly, she seemed to be tolerating Patricia, with an attitude of: *This too shall pass.* Nor did she try, overtly anyway, to influence the way her children felt about the newcomer in the household.

There were indeed, as Patricia had finally, resentfully accepted, five young DeLucas. The oldest, Laurie, about Michael's age, on the edge of adolescence, treated Patricia almost the same way Marilyn did: with a kind of vague neutrality, perhaps following her mother's example.

The next oldest was the DeLucas' only son, also named Frank, and called "Frankie" by his parents and sister, just as Patricia's father was affectionately called by Mary Columbo. Frankie, as might have been predicted, developed an immediate crush on Patricia and shyly hung around her when and where he could.

Mary Beth, the second oldest daughter, was the most standoffish. She seemed to sense in Patricia something undesirable as far as her family was concerned. It was nothing she ever verbalized, perhaps only some kind of perception that her siblings lacked, perhaps no more than a child's intuition; whatever, Mary Beth instinctively liked Patricia Columbo least of everyone in the house.

Julie, the next-to-youngest DeLuca, was a preschooler, with her own little world that was quite behind her two school-age sisters, and very much ahead of her toddler younger sister, Chrissy, who was the baby of the family. Patricia's presence in the house did not seem to affect Julie's life at all, and she paid little attention to the "girl who worked for Daddy" who was going to be living with them for a while.

Chrissy, the youngest, was Mommy's little girl and that status could not have been upset by nuclear war, let alone Patricia Columbo.

Just one big happy family for Daddy Frank to come home to after another hard day at Walgreen's.

The criminal charges against Patricia were never prosecuted. The record officially states that the disposition entered in her case was "nolle pros" on May 22, 1974. She thought she had been put on probation for a year. That was what her parents told her when they all left court that day. Frank Columbo, of course, had by then paid for all the fraudulent purchases and made the necessary restitution involved in the forged checks. So Patricia, even though apparently believing that she was under some kind of conditional or restrictive obligation to the court, was actually free and clear.

DeLuca began working on his grandiose scheme to launch Patricia's skyrocket model career. His egotism, the monumental conceit that seemed to direct his every waking moment, evidently had him genuinely convinced that nothing more was required than some snapshots of Patricia in—and out—of her underwear, and a printed business card. Training never entered his mind. Forget posture, poise, presence; dismiss charm, carriage, charisma; never mind style or sophistication, fashion or form. Nude, or almost nude, photos of his Patrish would, he envisioned, bring immediate lucrative offers.

Frank DeLuca was, however, by no means a stupid man. Listening to Marilyn, Patricia soon learned a good deal more about his background. The DeLuca family, like the Columbos, had come from the lower West Side of Chicago. At one time, while Frank was in elementary school, his family lived at 608 South Albany, only about four miles from the 1803 West Ohio address of the Columbos. The father, also named Frank, was a truck driver. Like other inner-city families, they moved west in the path of encroaching ethnic groups with whom they did not care to integrate.

The DeLucas chose to go north and west to Kilbourne Avenue near Kelvyn Park. While living there Frank attended Austin High School, which at that time was considered one of the most desirable of the city's high schools. It was practically in the suburbs, situated only five blocks from where affluent Oak Park began. DeLuca, no more than an average student, cruised through his four years with mid-level grades, lackadaisically engaging in occasional sports, in the end leaving no memorable academic or athletic mark. He was graduated in June 1956, the same month Patricia was born.

The following school year, DeLuca went to Wright Junior College, taking a schedule of miscellaneous classes aimed at no particular discipline. Wright was a city college, so there was very little cost involved. During the summer he turned nineteen he worked construction as a laborer, earning what was then the going wage of $1.70 an hour. That fall he traveled to nearby Lafayette, Indiana, and tried out for the junior varsity football team at Purdue University. He was accepted

and allowed to enter Purdue as a sophomore with his Wright
Junior College credits.

The athletic scholarship lasted only two semesters before
being withdrawn. There was a difference of opinion as to
whether it was rescinded because, as DeLuca claimed, he had
been injured, or because he simply had been cut from the
team for not being good enough, not measuring up. Whatever
the case, his education at Purdue had ended until such time as
he could pay tuition.

It was then back to construction work for him. DeLuca
took off a full school year as well as the summers before and
after, and managed, because he was still living at home, to
save enough to pay for a second year at Purdue, returning
there in the fall of 1959. He had now learned of a pharmacy
scholarship-loan sponsored by Walgreen's, and decided to
pursue that career path. It was an appealing program because
if a recipient subsequently accepted employment with
Walgreen's, the loan was, after a certain period of time, forgiven.

In 1960, DeLuca married Marilyn Curcio and that summer
he worked for the 7-Up Bottling Company on its production
line, earning $2.10 an hour. In the fall, he returned to Purdue,
to its school of pharmacology. The following summer, he got
a job as a laborer once again, this time for Wilson Brothers
Construction in nearby Cicero. Back to Purdue in the fall of
1961, where he was now well on his way toward becoming
a pharmacist; so well, in fact, that when the end of that
school term arrived, Walgreen's, his scholarship mentor, put
him on as a stock clerk in their Melrose Park store. They paid
him $1.75 an hour but added a fifty-cent-an-hour subsidy to
that because he was one of "their" students. Later that same
summer, he was transferred to the Walgreen's in Elmhurst.

DeLuca had one final semester to go in order to complete
the requirements for a bachelor of science degree in pharmacology. He satisfied that in the fall of 1962 and was scheduled to graduate in January 1963. Walgreen's, meanwhile, put
him to work as a clerk in the same Elmhurst store two days
after Christmas; and the following month, when he became a
registered pharmacist, albeit in the state of Indiana, the company put him on the payroll as an assistant manager in the

Oak Park store. Nine months later, he received his certification, number 26155, as a pharmacist in Illinois.

Over the years, DeLuca climbed steadily up the ladder in the Walgreen's organization. He was considered hardworking, dependable, honest. They moved him around from store to store, community to community, manager to manager, to give him a wide range of experience. He worked in Walgreen's stores in the suburbs of Berwyn, Norridge, Glen Ellyn, Schaumburg, as well as returning to Oak Park and Elmhurst from time to time. In September 1969, six and a half years after his graduation, he was promoted to full manager status. Two and a half years later, Walgreen's put him in charge of their big Grove Shopping Center store in Elk Grove Village. By then his salary with the giant firm had increased from the original $2.25 an hour to eighteen thousand dollars a year—this in a time when the average wage earner in the United States made only seventy-five hundred a year.

Frank John DeLuca, son of a truck driver, was achieving the great American dream.

Patricia's suspension at Walgreen's had been amended to a termination for cause, and she was too embarrassed to go back to the place she had been working when she was arrested and led away in handcuffs. Since she was now living in Addison, she looked for work in that community and found a job at the Robert Hall Village, a warehouse-type department store, one of the forerunners of today's Wal-Mart and Kmart. She got an excellent reference from DeLuca. The job lasted only a few weeks, however, before someone from Elk Grove who knew her and knew about the Walgreen's thefts saw her behind the counter and spoke to the security guard on their way out.

"Don't you run a check on people you hire here?"

Patricia's background was rechecked, this time with Walgreen's personnel department.

She was fired.

It became fairly apparent to Patricia that DeLuca's haughty scheme to become a modeling mogul was not going to achieve overnight success; they had not received a single inquiry regarding Patricia's services. The whole idea began to take on a rather shabby character—sort of like the cheap little room at "their" motel.

Patricia began once again to make plans of her own—the same plans, in fact, that she had made back on Brantwood: she was going to leave home. The only difference was that it was DeLuca's home she would be leaving this time. And she made up her mind that she would *not* go back to her parents' house.

To avoid the public exposure and detailed background scrutiny that a salesclerk job would involve, she sought out the kind of low-profile job that she'd had at the plastic piping supplies office. It took her a few days but she found a perfect one: a one-girl secretary-receptionist at the small sales office of a cement resin company. DeLuca objected to it at once.

"I don't like the idea of you being the only woman in an office full of men," he complained. "A bunch of salesmen at that. There's no telling what kind of characters you're liable to run into."

I have to be real careful of that, *don't I?* she thought. "Look, Frank, it's a good job," she argued. "The guys are only there for an hour or so in the morning, and a little while at the end of the day. The rest of the time I'm by myself. Or with the sales manager."

"What do you do when you're with the sales manager?" he asked suspiciously.

"The same thing I do when I'm *not* with him," she asserted. "I type letters, answer the phone, mail out sales brochures—"

"Well, I don't like it," DeLuca said. He was almost pouting.

"Hire me back at Walgreen's then," she challenged.

That shut him up.

Mary Columbo could not let well enough alone. She telephoned Marilyn DeLuca.

"Patty is trying to steal your husband, do you know that?" she asked.

"I know she'd probably like to," Marilyn replied. "I don't think she can."

"You must be very sure of yourself," Mary said, "letting her come live in your own home like you have."

"I know my husband, Mrs. Columbo," Marilyn said confidently. "He'll get tired of Patty. One thing about Frank I can depend on: he always loses interest sooner or later. With Patty, I think it'll be sooner. When he gets tired of the sex, he'll drop her—because with Patty there *is* nothing else. Your daughter is a very shallow person, Mrs. Columbo. You didn't do a very good job raising her." Unable to strike out at DeLuca or Patricia, Marilyn found Mary Columbo a very opportune target.

"Never you mind how I raised Patty," Mary Columbo warned. "You just better watch out you don't lose your happy home."

"What makes you think my home is happy?"

It could have been a happy home; it *should* have been a happy home. Marilyn DeLuca had, she thought, the best kids in the world. If only Frank loved them like she did, if only he could *enjoy* them like she did—God, what a beautiful family they would have. But something inside Frank was not right; something was driving him toward—what? She didn't know. Maybe *he* didn't even know. But he *was* driven. And someday he would crash. Marilyn was determined to be there to pick up the pieces. For her kids. In the meantime, she would have to make do.

Making do was not easy. Frank had no intention of keeping his bargain not to have sex with Patricia in their home. The agreement he made with Marilyn, and subsequently used to help convince Patricia to make the move, was as worthless as most everything else he said when he was trying to get his own way.

Apparently Patricia tried to hold him to his word. "Not in the house, Frank, remember?" she said the first time he tried.

But Frank was persistent. He modified the agreement by saying that it only applied when someone else was at home. When the older kids were at school, Marilyn out with the younger ones grocery shopping, if Frank was on a late shift and Patricia ran home for lunch—what was the harm?

Patricia still balked, saying she didn't feel "right" about it, admitting years later that she was also terribly afraid of getting caught in the act. For all her considerable experience, she still bore the weight of adolescent anxieties; despite her superficial bravado, she would be recalled by many as having been quite easily embarrassed.

In vain, Patricia tried to persuade Frank to get a room; then he did the balking: "Why spend money for a motel when we've got a perfectly good living room couch right here?"

There was no way she could turn him down. He had too many moves for her; his arguments were like a shotgun shell exploding in all directions at once. And—she loved him.

Eventually they had sex in every room of the house.

Late one afternoon at work, the sales manager gave Patricia a small parcel of samples to take over to the Airport Hotel to a customer named Louis Osborne. She was to have him paged if he wasn't in his room, to make sure she gave the package to him personally.

Louis Osborne did not answer when the desk clerk rang his room, so Patricia did as instructed and had him paged. He did not answer the page either.

"I'm sure he's around here somewhere," the desk clerk said. "He just picked up some messages. I'll continue to page him, and you can look around for him if you like. He's a nice-looking young man, mid-twenties, has a mustache."

Prowling the lobby as she heard the page repeated, Patricia was about to go into the cocktail lounge when a nice-looking young man with a mustache walked out.

"Excuse me, are you Mr. Osborne?" she asked.

"No, I'm not," he replied. "Have you by any chance seen my mother?"

"What?"

"My mother. She's a slim, handsome woman with a very determined expression. Have you seen anyone like that?"

"Uh, no, I haven't." Patricia was slightly bewildered.

"What does your Mr. Osborne look like?" he asked.

"Like you, I think," she said.

His eyebrows shot up. "Really? That handsome? He shouldn't be too hard to find then."

Patricia couldn't resist smiling. He *was* handsome.

"How about having a drink with me?" he suggested. "We can plan our respective searches first, then talk about getting married."

"Are you crazy?" she asked. The question was serious; she was not smiling now.

"Possibly," he admitted. "I'm a medical student; most of us are crazy. What is it you object to discussing, our searches or our wedding? If it's the former, I'm perfectly willing to let Mother and Mr. Osborne wander around lost forever. Except I can't get home unless Mother drives me."

"Aren't you a little old for your mother to have to drive you around?" Patricia asked. This was the strangest person she had ever met. But curiously interesting.

"I'm not allowed to drive," he said. He had lost his license for driving while intoxicated. It had been after final exams the previous semester; a group of med students so relieved to be out from under all the pressure of school, going out to celebrate. He was the one who got caught driving. "It was really very stupid of me," he admitted, a little ashamed. He put a hand on her arm. "Have one drink with me. Please."

Patricia let him guide her into the cocktail lounge.

His name was Andrew Harper and Patricia was fascinated. He lived with his mother, a divorcée, in one of the moneyed sections of Wheaton. A lab technician for the summer at a clinic down the street, he had his mother pick him up at the hotel so his co-workers wouldn't see her; he was embarrassed at having lost his license to drive. Ahead of him stretched his last year of med school and then internship and residency.

"I haven't decided on my field yet," he said after their drinks came. "Mother says I should become a gynecologist because when I was little I was always trying to look up women's dresses."

Here we go, Patricia thought. Another weirdo. Finish your drink and go look for Osborne.

But then Andrew Harper turned serious. "What I'd really like to go into is pediatrics," he said. "I like working with kids. I think I'd make a good pediatrician. What do you do, Patricia?"

"Just office work," she told him. "Nothing special."

"Any ambitions?"

"I used to want to be a teacher," she said quietly. *Where the hell did* that *come from?* she asked herself. It had been years since she had thought of being a teacher.

Andrew was pleased. "We both like kids then, I guess."

"I guess."

Patricia studied him as he talked further about his medical career. There was a sort of little-boy quality about him; Patricia could picture him in animated conversation with Michael, talking about dirt bikes or something. He had such a baby face; had it not been for the mustache, he probably wouldn't have looked much older than Michael. There was nothing macho about him, not like other men in her life: her father, Jack Formaski, DeLuca. Yet he didn't give the impression of weakness either; there was self-confidence in his manner. He was an altogether interesting person.

"There's Mother," he said presently, indicating a tall woman entering the lobby. "Will you meet me here tomorrow? We can have dinner and then you can drive me home."

Tomorrow, Patricia knew, DeLuca worked from one until closing time at ten. "If you want me to," she said.

Patricia felt almost shy, as if being asked out for the first time. She couldn't believe what was happening.

Mrs. Harper, when Patricia met her briefly a week later, appeared to be every bit as unconventional and idiosyncratic as her son. She made one thing absolutely clear at once: she did not care who Andrew dated or to what extent he became involved with anyone, as long as he finished—repeat, *finished*—medical school and became a doctor. If not, she would disown him outright. That condition stated, she seemed genuinely to take to her son's new friend.

Patricia began to see Andrew regularly—at least, as regularly as possible. She could only see him in the evening when Frank worked the late shift, but she would meet him for lunch on days when she knew she couldn't get out that night. Refusing to give him a telephone number, she explained that her mother was recently home from the hospital and she didn't want the phone ringing and disturbing her. It was the same excuse she used for being able to see him so infrequently at night: she had to take care of her mother. Lies again—but what could she do?

Patricia and Andrew did not go to bed together; there was neither the time nor the opportunity. But they were definitely infatuated, so much so that when Andrew asked how old she was, Patricia automatically told him the truth; she was now going on nineteen.

"I thought you were older," he admitted. "Nearer to my age." He was twenty-four.

"Am I too young for you, Doctor?" she asked. She delighted in calling him that.

Andrew was obviously serious about her and pressed to meet her parents. Patricia was forced to realistically examine her feelings about him, and was surprised to find that she liked the idea of Andrew being in her future. Incredible as it was to her, she had developed an affection for this young man that began to chip particles off the solid block of love she had for Frank DeLuca. Astounding herself, she began to wonder if Andrew Harper—and not Frank DeLuca—was her first grown-up love.

Patricia tried to plot a course for herself that she was reasonably sure of being able to follow. She knew that her first priority, if she meant to include Andrew in her life, had to be getting out of the DeLuca home. She was old enough now to rent an apartment in her own name—if she had the money. On the salary she was earning, she couldn't pay deposits on rent and utilities, so she would need help there. Her father, she knew, would help her; he always had. Especially if she brought some decent young man home for him to meet.

This thing with Andrew *could* work out, she told herself excitedly. True, she wasn't wild about him the way she had been about DeLuca; he didn't produce the same blossom of passion that Frank had generated. But neither would he want to take pictures of her being fucked by another man, or want to fuck her in the same room his little girls slept in. Andrew had a few quirks; Frank had some very deep problems. If she could make it work with Andrew, there was no question that she would be far better off.

Mind made up, she began to make plans to take Andrew Harper home to meet her parents.

Patricia's relationship with her family since leaving home had been cordial but cool. Her father was friendly, just a little distant; he had been hurt and his wounds were still open. Mary Columbo tried to make up for it by being overly nice herself, while maintaining a vigil on the tenuous ground between father and daughter; she was determined that her husband would not suffer any *new* emotional trauma. Michael, as usual, went into a shell. Patricia was not his favorite person anymore; he could not understand why she had left home, and was angry at her for the grief she had left behind—particularly for the sadness he saw in his father's eyes now and again. He must have heard his mother comment about that sadness; it was something no one had ever seen before.

Patricia had no time to try to soothe Michael's feelings; he was a kid and would, she felt, eventually grow out of his animosity toward her. As far as her mother was concerned, Patricia knew that Mary would do whatever was best for Frank Columbo at that point. So Patricia's primary objective was to get back into the good graces of her father, to reestablish herself as a member in good standing of the family, if not the household. To do that, she had to convince Frank Columbo that she was repentant and ready to put her life in order. As evidence of that, she was ready to present Andrew Harper: young, nice looking, well mannered, unmarried, childless, and well on his way to becoming a doctor.

The perfect antithesis of Frank DeLuca.

It worked like a charm.

Mary helped smooth the way, her remarks as usual designed to start her husband thinking in a particular direction. She commented on the extensive work it took to earn a medical degree; Frank understood hard work. Andrew replied that anything worth having was worth working hard for. It was the perfect answer. Patricia had told Andrew to use a lot of clichés.

"My parents *love* clichés. My father has practically built his life around them. 'You can lead a horse to water'—that kind of thing."

Mary mentioned her operation, praising the wonderful doctors who had attended her. She asked if Andrew planned to become a surgeon. Frank would like that: a son-in-law who daily thwarted disease and death in the surgical arena. But Andrew told them he had decided to go into pediatrics; he wanted to work with children. Mary probably smiled; Frank would like that even *better*. Everyone knew he loved kids. And lately, Mary had told a friend, he had begun to pay at-

tention to toddlers in the shopping mall. Mary said his grand-
fatherly instincts were stirring.

Frank had a question of his own, much more basic. He had
noticed that Patricia drove Andrew over. "Don't you own a
car, Andrew?"

Patricia had already warned Andrew. "Don't you dare
mention losing your driver's license. My father thinks drunk
drivers should be hung by their balls."

"I'm not exactly a drunk driver," Andrew demurred. "One
incident hardly brands me for life."

"It would with Dad. *Don't* mention it."

In answer to Frank Columbo's query, Andrew smiled and
lied, "I let my mother have my car for a few days. Hers is in
the shop."

That seemed to satisfy Frank Columbo. Now, Patricia
thought, if Andrew will just remember that Dad is a Cubs
fan . . .

Later, Patricia caught her father alone in the kitchen and
told him she wanted to move out of DeLuca's house. She
wanted to get an apartment of her own. It was probably not
what her father had hoped for. Everything known about Frank
Columbo indicates that in all likelihood he had been thinking
wistfully that his daughter might come back home. But getting her away from the influence of that guy DeLuca had to
have been the most important thing in his mind.

After Patricia had left home, Mary had finally shared with
her husband some of the rumors about DeLuca and Patty; she
had no choice—it was only a matter of time until Frank
found out anyway; he had friends who talked to him too, just
as his wife did. Better to hear it from her than from someone
outside the house, Mary had decided; learning about it in a
calm, intimate fashion would help Frank keep his combusti-
ble temper in check. Mary had then gone about telephoning
Marilyn DeLuca to provoke her into driving Patty from her
home and back to the Columbos. That, of course, hadn't
worked. But now it looked as if things were going to turn out
just fine anyway. Frank was being very reasonable with his
errant daughter.

"You find an apartment for yourself, honey," he told her.
"Get out of that guy DeLuca's house. I'll pay the rent, don't
worry about it."

Father and daughter embraced that night for the first time in a long time.

DeLuca came into her bedroom when Patricia was packing to move out. Marilyn had just broken the news to him when he came home.

"This is crazy, Patrish," he said. "This is a big mistake."

"I don't think it's a mistake, Frank," she replied quietly. "I think it would be a mistake *not* to do it."

"But you've been happy here," he said, as if totally amazed that she would even consider leaving.

"Oh, Frank, please," she replied wearily.

As far as she was concerned, no one had been happy with their unorthodox living arrangement but him—and she felt he must have known it. His wife hadn't been happy, his kids hadn't been happy, and Patricia sure as hell hadn't been happy. Only Frank had been happy, because he got to have his proverbial cake and eat it too—so to speak. Patricia shook her head in utter rejection of his pleas.

"I'm leaving, Frank. I'm going to move into a motel room while I look for an apartment."

DeLuca tried every approach he could think of. How was she going to live on what she earned? That argument was squelched when she told him her dad was going to help her. Well, what about their plans for the modeling agency? The implication was that after all the work he had done, she was letting him down. Patricia simply told him to let her know when her first modeling assignment came in. DeLuca must have stiffened at that, as he always did when he felt someone, anyone, was not giving him the proper respect.

"You're going to find," he warned, "that it's not as easy out in the world as you might think it is. You've had me to give you advice for a long time, you know. What are you going to do if you get in trouble and I'm not there to help you?"

"I don't plan to get in any trouble, Frank," she told him. She was tired of trouble.

DeLuca sat dejectedly on the bed. "I can't believe you're doing this to me."

"I'm not doing this *to* you, Frank." She tried to make him understand. "If anything, I'm doing it *for* you. For both of us." She closed her suitcase. "We're not getting anywhere,

Frank. We haven't been getting anywhere for a long time. This is best, believe me."

She said good-bye to Marilyn and the kids and left.

For a couple of weeks, Patricia stayed at the Addison Motel and spent her evenings looking at apartments. It was a little scary being all alone, but she was determined to go through with it. More than once she considered asking her parents to help her look, or Andrew, or even somehow inducing Michael to go with her, and making up with him in the process. But in the end she rejected all of her options and forced herself to go it alone. Reverberating in her mind was DeLuca's warning about how difficult she might find life without him; it spurred her more resolutely toward independence. *You are going on nineteen, Patricia Ann Columbo,* she chastised and reassured herself at the same time. *You have got to take control of your life.*

She found the apartment she wanted in Lombard, the next suburb south. In a fairly new high-rise elevator building at 2015 South Finley Road, she rented number 911, a compact one-bedroom apartment on the ninth floor, with a storage locker on the same floor. It was perfect for her, and she moved in as soon as it was ready.

At long last it appeared that Patricia was heading in the right direction. She felt that she was a new woman. All the "old" Patty Columbos were being left behind. The spoiled, pampered little Patty. The little Patty who got whatever she wanted. The Patty who learned to lie so proficiently. The Patty who fell fast and hard for the new Walgreen's manager. The protégée Patty, learning about grown-up sex in a cheap motel room. The headstrong Patty, the spiteful Patty, the Patty who stole, cheated, forged. The Patty who walked out on her family and into the bizarre setting of the DeLuca home.

All of those Patty Columbos were now in the past.

She was watching television in her new apartment when DeLuca rang the bell. She had been expecting him. In fact, she had called him with her new address, determined not to hide from him, determined to go her own way with willpower and not secrecy. She had made her mind up not to have sex with DeLuca when he came over; that too she wanted left behind with her old self.

But what DeLuca did when he came over that night took her completely by surprise, totally stunned her, and shattered all of her wonderful plans for the future.

"I'm leaving my family, Patrish," he told her without preliminary. "I'm getting a divorce. I want us to get married."

Patricia could only stare at him, dumbstruck.

33
July 1976

It was twenty minutes past ten on a hot Saturday night in July when Ray Rose stood at the door of apartment A at 502 North Ardmore in Villa Park, the third suburb south of Elk Grove Village. The chief investigator rang the bell and presently Frank DeLuca opened the door. The two men looked at each other for a moment without speaking. Behind Rose, DeLuca could see the faces of several men with whom he had become familiar in the ten weeks since the Columbo bodies had been discovered. Elk Grove's deputy chief of police, William Kohnke, was there; also present were Frank Braun, Cook County sheriff's lieutenant, and Investigators Gene Gargano of the sheriff's office and John Landers of the Elk Grove police.

"I'm not surprised," DeLuca said quietly. "I've been expecting this." His lover, Patty, had been in jail for six weeks.

"Frank DeLuca," said Rose, "I have a warrant for your arrest for murder, conspiracy to commit murder, and solicitation of murder. You have the right to remain silent—"

As Rose recited for DeLuca his constitutional rights, the chief investigator turned him around and handcuffed his wrists behind his back.

At Elk Grove police headquarters, the officers took turns with the interrogation. Rose and Frank Braun went first.

"Do you want to tell us about your involvement in the Columbo murders?" Rose asked.

DeLuca shook his head. "I expect to go down for this thing, but I don't know anything about it."

Now Ray Rose shook *his* head. "Come on, Frank." Rose's tone was almost conversational. There was no reason to lean on DeLuca; Rose knew he had him. It was just a question of easing some information out of him. "If you aren't involved in any way, why would you expect to go down for it?"

"I just expect to be convicted for it, okay?" he replied with an edge. Then his voice softened a touch. "I expect to spend the rest of my life in prison."

"Innocent men don't talk like that, Frank," the chief investigator said. "Innocent people get mad and indignant when they're charged."

"I am mad," DeLuca told him. "Look, Patrish and I were in fear of our lives for months before this happened. Frank Columbo was constantly harassing us. His kid, Michael, came into my store and stared at me. Three different times, Patrish was followed when she left work by a car that had a CB antenna on the trunk. We were driving different routes to and from work, we were so scared of him; we were getting off the elevator on different floors in the building where we used to live, and walking up or down the stairs to our apartment. We even barricaded the door to the apartment every night, we were so scared."

"Did you ever actually observe Frank Columbo following you?" Rose asked. DeLuca looked away.

"No," he admitted. A slight frown appeared, almost as if the realization surprised him.

"You had two telephone conversations with a man named Roman," Rose said. "Tell us about those."

"He was Patrish's godfather," DeLuca said. "His real name was Phil/ Capone; Roman was just his street name. Patrish asked him to find out if her old man had put out a contract on me or on her. He found out there was one, but he got in touch with the hit men and bought it off. But later on, he told us that the old man was looking for somebody else to do the hit. Roman said it looked like there was only one way to stop him: that was to hit him first."

"What was your reply to that?" Rose asked.

DeLuca shrugged. "I said, well, if that's the way it has to be, then yes."

"How much did it cost to buy off the first hit men?" Frank Braun asked.

"I don't know. Patrish's godfather paid for it. See, he had raised her most of her early life; she said he was more like a father to her than a real father. Roman knew how Frank Columbo was, knew he had a crazy temper; he wanted to help Patrish and me."

"Did Patty ever tell you that she was having sex with this man Roman?" Rose asked.

"What?" DeLuca stared at the chief investigator. "Having sex with him? No. He was her godfather." DeLuca shook his head. "She would have told me if anything like that was going on. Look, we have a totally honest relationship, Patrish and me. If she wanted to go out with another guy, or I wanted to go out with another woman, there wouldn't be any problem as long as we each told the other one about it."

Gene Gargano and John Landers took over the questioning.

"You thought Patty's godfather was going to arrange Frank Columbo's death, is that correct?" Gargano asked.

"Yeah. Roman told me over the phone that he would take care of the whole problem. There were a couple of guys that were supposed to do the job."

"But they didn't do it?"

"No. A couple of months went by—longer than that, actually—and nothing happened. Patrish and I were getting more scared all the time. The hit men kept giving Patrish the runaround; they always seemed to have some excuse why it couldn't be done. Patrish finally said she thought the guys were just jacking us around and that we would have to do the job ourse—"

Realizing what he was saying, DeLuca abruptly cut off his words.

"Have to do the job ourselves, is that what you meant?" Gargano asked. DeLuca shook his head.

"You said that, not me."

"Look, Frank," said John Landers, "why don't you just tell us how the murders actually took place?"

"I don't want to say anything that will get Trish in any deeper." DeLuca's expression, except for his eyes, became very sincere; his eyes held back. "I'm the only person she has left," he said solemnly. "I can't let her down."

Gargano and Landers exchanged dubious looks and left the room.

Rose and Braun returned. Rose opened a large manila envelope and removed several glossy photographs, which he spread out on the table in front of DeLuca.

"These are blow-ups of latent prints taken off Frank Columbo's Thunderbird," the chief investigator said. "You see anything unusual about them."

"They look smudged," DeLuca offered.

"Anything else?"

DeLuca looked away and did not reply.

"Don't they look like they were made by a man with one finger and part of another missing?" Rose asked.

"Those prints don't have anything to do with me," DeLuca declared.

"Frank," Rose said evenly, gathering up the photos, "I'm going to give you one last chance to go over your involvement in this thing. One last chance to cooperate, for the record. One last chance to help yourself. Either take it or you're on your own."

DeLuca put both hands over his face and began to cry. "Can I—can I talk to Gargano again?" he asked brokenly.

Rose and Braun quickly got out and Gene Gargano hustled back in. Everyone felt that a confession might be imminent.

"Frank, we pretty well know how this thing went down," Gargano said, giving the sniffing man several Kleenex. "We'd just like to hear it in your own words. The smart thing would be to tell the truth."

"I want to ask a question," DeLuca said, wiping his eyes. "Hypothetically speaking, if this guy and this girl did commit these murders, what would be the penalty? There's no death penalty in Illinois, right?"

"No death penalty, right," Gargano confirmed. "When you say 'this guy and this girl,' do you mean yourself and Patty Columbo?"

"I don't want to say that," DeLuca replied. "I just want to speak hypothetically."

"I can't tell you what the penalty would be," Gargano said. "The judge and jury decide that."

"Well, if we did do it," DeLuca asked, "is there any way possible we could be sent to the same prison where we could

e together?" Gargano looked at him incredulously, but it did
ot deter DeLuca. "The only thing we ever wanted in life
vas to be together and be left alone," he said, beginning to
ry again. "I just want to know what the chances are, if
'atrish and I plead guilty to the murders, of us being sen-
enced to the same place. Or whether we might be sent to a
ospital instead of a prison because, you know, conditions
vould be better and our chances of seeing each other would
e better—"

"I can't answer those questions," Gargano told him hon-
stly. "But I can tell you this: we aren't getting anywhere
vith this hypothetical talk. I want you to tell me about *your*
nvolvement in these murders."

DeLuca shook his head. "I don't want to make any statement without talking to Patrish first. I just couldn't let her
hink I let her down."

Gargano opened the door and Ray Rose came back in.

"No statement," Gargano said.

"Look, I don't want Patty to know about this conversa-
ion," DeLuca said. "She doesn't have to, does she?"

"Before this is over, everybody is going to know every-
hing about everybody else," Rose told him. "Three people
ire dead, Frank, remember?"

34
July 1975

Everything had been all planned: leaving the DeLuca house,
finding her own place to live, being helped along financially
by her father, getting back into the good graces of her family,
going steady with Andrew Harper—in other words, straightening out the convoluted tangle that her life had become.

Then up jumped Frank DeLuca again with the one lure that
he must have felt confident would work. He knew it was
what she had dreamed of when she had first fallen in love
with him, before she learned about his wife and five children;
it was her adolescent reverie, her white-picket-fence fantasy:
she and Frank, married, having children, living happily ever
after.

When he announced that he was going to leave his family
and marry her, it had to have been, to her, the purest procla-
mation of true love that he could have made. If he had cut his
heart out and laid it on the table, the effect on her probably
would not have been any greater. This was "her" Frank, the
way she had always wanted him.

Finally getting what she had wanted most in the world for
such a long time effectively neutralized the precisely planned
new course she had designed for herself. She didn't immediately abandon all her latest plans, but she began pitting in her
mind, one against the other, the two persons around whom
the choices of her future revolved: Frank DeLuca and Andrew Harper.

It was the presence of Andrew in her life that had, if not
generated, at least bolstered her desire to make a new start.
But Andrew, she convinced herself now, was a strong factor
in her life *only* when she had negative feelings about Frank
DeLuca. With Frank suddenly back, bearing his fabulous pro-
posal, Andrew quickly became a problem. How, for instance,
would he react if he ever found out about her past indiscre-
tions? What would be the extent of his glib self-confidence if
he learned she had sucked Andre's black cock while being
photographed, been fucked in the ass in front of a mirror by
Frank, stolen and used credit cards, forged checks? If the
roles had been reversed, if she had done all those things with
Andrew and was now facing having to tell Frank about them,
there wouldn't have been a problem—of that she was completely confident. Frank would have understood, he would
have accepted it, not been critical or judgmental. But what
would Andrew's reaction be? No doubt horror and disbelief;
ultimately intolerance; finally condemnation. The Andrew
Harpers of the world liked things proper. He was ashamed of
his driver's license having been suspended, for Christ's sake.

Patricia convinced herself that she would not be able to
live a constant lie with Andrew; it would not be fair to him.
She would have to confess everything to him if they were going to continue becoming more seriously involved. And the
moment she revealed her sordid past, he would probably
blanch and vomit.

Frank, on the other hand, knew all, understood all, accepted all. And Frank was willing to give up *everything* for

her: his wife, his children, his nice home—perhaps even his very bright future in the Walgreen's organization; she recalled that he had once said it would not look too good on his record if he left his family for a co-worker. Of course, she wasn't a co-worker any longer, but it still amounted to the same thing—or was worse, really, because she was now a former co-worker who had been terminated for theft. Walgreen's would surely let him go, so he would be forfeiting his job for Patricia also. It would be like Frank was coming to her naked and alone in the world, and only her arms, her embrace, her warmth and love, would give him the courage and energy to begin anew.

Frank needed her. Andrew did not.

She told Andrew so.

Patricia agreed to let DeLuca move in with her. They changed the apartment lease from her name to "Mr. and Mrs. Frank DeLuca."

Now she was faced with once again having to ingratiate herself with her family—this time with a new and considerably more difficult scenario: she had to convince them to accept Frank.

She decided that the only way it could be done successfully was not by deceit or cleverness; it had to be approached directly and truthfully. It would be a novel way of dealing with her parents—and she had absolutely no idea what the results would be.

When she sat down with them and said she had something serious to talk about, Mary Columbo at once thought her daughter was pregnant—because that was probably the worst news she could imagine. Patricia assured them both she was *not*—then dropped it on them that she had broken up with Andrew Harper and would be seeing Frank DeLuca. DeLuca, she said, would be getting a divorce, after which he and Patricia would be married.

"Is he living with you at that apartment?" was the first thing her father asked. Frank Columbo was paying the rent.

"No, Daddy, he isn't." She had to lie about *that*. "He's still living at home for the time being while he and Marilyn work out the details of the divorce."

Mary Columbo began to lament at once about the poor innocent little kids, *five* of them, but Patricia wouldn't listen. Was having parents divorce, she asked, any worse than growing up in a house where they don't love each other anymore? Then Mary assailed the age difference. In ten years Patty would only be twenty-eight and DeLuca would be nearly fifty.

"The age difference doesn't matter," Patricia firmly declared. "We love each other, that's all that matters."

Frank Columbo alternately buried his face in his hands and looked up at his only daughter in anguish. She was planning to marry a man almost as old as he was. She would have five stepchildren, a couple of them as old as her own brother. She would have to help him support that family of his until all those kids were grown. She'd never have anything of her own—no house, no new cars, probably not even kids of her own. Frank Columbo must have felt that it was his worst nightmare come true.

Mary, disgusted, called DeLuca a "cradle robber," but Patricia refused to get into a name-calling argument with her. "I don't expect either one of you to like it," she said, having to blink back tears. "I know I've been a big disappointment to you; God, I've been a big disappointment to *myself*. I'm not out to hurt anybody: not either of you, not Marilyn, not Frank's kids. I just want to be happy." This man, she grimly pointed out, was willing to give up everything for her; give up all he had just to be with her and love her. She wasn't going to let her chance for that kind of happiness go by.

When Patricia was ready to leave, neither of her parents tried to stop her for further discussion; they both sat shaking their heads. At the stairs leading down to the front door, Patricia paused for one final comment.

"I hope someday you'll both understand."

As she walked out, she didn't believe that day would ever come.

When DeLuca moved in with her, Patricia found out within a month that it wasn't going to be the blissful arrangement she had imagined.

For the first couple of weeks it was almost like it had been when they first started going to the motel when she was sixteen. They could not seem to get enough of each other. To be

alone, naked, as much as they wanted to be; to go to sleep together and wake up together, to fondle, kiss, touch, say whatever they wanted to say without fear of being overheard; it
was like her original dream come true for Patricia: the dream
she had at sixteen, lost at seventeen, and never thought she
would get back.

Frank, it seemed to Patricia, felt the same way, but for different reasons. Getting away from his family—the scrutiny of
his wife, the constant activity of the five children—seemed to
take a weight from his shoulders that allowed him to relax
more than Patricia had ever seen him do before. "It's such a
pleasure to leave work and come here to the apartment," he
told her, "rather than having to go home to that zoo. I don't
know how I stood it all those years." He made arrangements
to have dinner with his wife and children on Wednesday and
Sunday evenings. Patricia encouraged him to visit his children as often as he liked, assuring him that he did not have
to adhere to any rigid schedule on her account. But he con-
formed to the routine anyway. "Two nights a week is plenty
of time to give them."

Marilyn DeLuca filed for divorce a week after Frank
moved out, and Patricia stopped by the Brantwood house to
give the news to her parents. They were not impressed. Her
father barely acknowledged her presence and her mother did
little more than shrug it off. Patricia had promised herself not
to become angry at them, no matter how insensitively they
reacted.

"I just wanted you to know," she said, "that Frank and I
are planning a June or July wedding for next year." That
would be around her twentieth birthday and Frank's thirty-
eighth.

Patricia got the impression that her parents didn't really believe a wedding would ever take place, and therefore saw no
reason to waste any enthusiasm on it. Patricia forced herself
not to show that she cared how they felt.

They'll see, she thought confidently.

Because she and Frank were now having intercourse as a
matter of regular routine, once or twice every day, DeLuca
began supplying Patricia with birth control pills. When he
kept track of her menstrual days and inquired whether she

had taken her pill each day, it did not strike her as being anything other than thoughtful and considerate. He was merely being cautious, she felt; it certainly wouldn't do for them to have their first baby before his divorce became final.

It soon became obvious to her, however, that the degree of regularity with which they were having intercourse was not Frank's sole reason for wanting to make sure that she routinely took her pill. She found out his other reason one night when they met after work and went to Oliver's Pub, a little bar not far from the apartment. They were in the habit of stopping in there two or three nights a week and relaxing over a couple of cold ducks before going home or out for dinner. On this particular night Frank didn't seem in any hurry to eat, so they stayed at Oliver's a while longer, had another drink, and started playing shuffleboard with a man named Neal whom they had seen in there from time to time. Eventually they had still another drink, Neal reciprocating for one they had bought him. After they had played shuffleboard for a while, Patricia went to the ladies' room. When she returned, the bar tab had been paid and Frank and Neal were waiting by the front door to leave.

"Neal's coming back to the apartment for a drink before we call it a night," Frank said casually.

"Oh?" Patricia did not have to scrutinize his expression to see that Frank had something planned. His eyes were shifting rapidly without meeting hers directly.

Once in the car, with Neal following them, Patricia asked, "Frank, what's going on?"

"Nothing. We're just going to have a little fun, that's all." Before she could object, he added, "Relax, okay? We'll have another drink or two, then maybe later we'll party if we feel like it."

At the apartment, DeLuca got out the Canadian Club and poured them all a drink. Patricia sipped at hers without any real enthusiasm; it had been a while since anything like this had happened, and she was uneasy. Presently, as the men sat drinking, she left them and went into the bathroom. With the door closed, she stared at herself in the mirror. *This is what you wanted*, she reminded herself. *You and Frank together.*

The bathroom door opened and DeLuca came in. "What's your problem, Patrish?" he asked.

"I don't know," she said, shaking her head helplessly. Her eyes pleaded with Frank in the mirror. "Who is this guy, Frank? Why is he here?"

"You know who he is, Patrish. And he's here because I asked him here." He opened the medicine cabinet and got out a bottle of Valium. "Here, take a couple of these. When you're relaxed, come on back out. You'll enjoy Neal. He's clean, not bad looking, seems healthy enough. We'll all have fun."

DeLuca made sure she took the Valium, then left her alone again. This time when she looked at herself in the mirror, the confusion was diminishing and a calmer voice was prevailing in her mind. It said simply: This is how he *is*.

Even before the Valium began its tranquilizing effect, Patricia had begun her own deliberate process of composing herself, pacifying the desperation that had seized her, allaying the creeping fear. Just the momentary presence of Frank had been enough to calm her. The Valium probably wouldn't have been necessary. The reassurance that he was there, the solace of his protection, the comfort of knowing that he was "her man"—now more than ever—worked better than any opiate.

That's the way he *is*, she told herself one more time, for fortification.

She returned to the living room with a smile.

After the night with Neal, picking up people at Oliver's Pub and other bars became more or less routine for Patricia. She no longer resisted either the concept or the performance. As long as she had enough cold ducks and Canadian Club and Valium, plus whatever other pills Frank kept on hand for her, she reached the point where she really didn't give a damn. Two thoughts dominated her mind, two thoughts *ruled*: Frank DeLuca was her man—and he was the way he was. If he liked to sit and jack off while he watched some half-drunk asshole put a barely hard cock in her, what the hell? If he wanted to take Polaroids of her sucking some strange dick, so what? If he wanted to fuck her in the mouth face-to-face with some guy fucking her in the ass, what was the big deal?

But even after all the tough talks to herself, she still tried to *justify* it. Was Frank like he was because he had been shackled so many years to Marilyn and those five kids?

Struggling so long for a decent education, laboring so hard to climb the Walgreen's ladder of success, had he missed out on so much fun when he was young that he was simply trying to make up for it? Or was he desperately searching for something sexually—better? He had recently brought home a magazine called *Swinger's Life*, which was filled with page after page of personal ads, with photos of people—all ages, sizes, colors, and orientations—who wanted to engage in some kind of sex with, it seemed, the world at large.

"Look at this," Frank had said excitedly, pulling her next to him on the couch to show her the magazine. "This is what I've been telling you all along. Look at all these people—hell, they're just like us, Patrish."

Nothing would do, of course, but for them to send in *their* photos and *their* ad, and become a part of this wonderful community of swingers. It was, for DeLuca, an opportunity for the definitive photo session. Creatively, Patricia could never remember him being better.

"Okay, just sit back on the couch—put your feet up on the coffee table—that's good—okay, spread your knees as far apart as you can—good—now spread your pussy open a little—good, good—hold it—"

DeLuca's preoccupation with sex was cosmic, totally without bounds. When and how it had begun, no one knows—but it was certainly long before Patricia Columbo happened into his life. Apparently he never tired of talking about sex, planning it, choreographing it, reading about it, referring to it, identifying with it, wanting it, doing it. He relished sex like a television evangelist relishes God—and wallowed in it. In Patricia he had found a perfect partner for his obsession. Tutored by Frank for more than three years now, she had not the least idea of what was standard sexual conduct. From elementary school with Gus Latini, a memory now buried, to high school with Frank DeLuca, this was the carnal education of Patricia Columbo. To her, aberrant behavior was typical; it was the norm—because, other than her adolescent diversion with Jack Formaski, she knew no other. Dementia, derangement, paranoia—she knew nothing of these conditions. Evaluating Andrew Harper vis-à-vis Frank DeLuca, she had concluded, as she tried to escape DeLuca in favor of Andrew, that the young med student had a few quirks, but that Frank

DeLuca had some serious problems. Now that she had become DeLuca's active partner in this peculiar and divergent life-style, her ongoing self-conditioning overrode her ability to manage that kind of rational assessment. What was normal for her now was DeLuca: whatever he wanted, whatever he liked, whatever he did. Allowable, acceptable, approved: they were *him*.

Go with the flow, Patrish, she told herself time and time again.

And the flow was Frank.

One afternoon Patricia stopped in to see her mother. She was determined to keep after her parents until they finally admitted to themselves that the love between her and Frank was real, and that a marriage, while not imminent, was most definitely impending. They simply *had* to accept Frank DeLuca. He was now a fact of their lives, just as she was.

"I was thinking of asking Auntie Janet and Uncle Bill to dinner," she said. "I want them to meet Frank. You don't have a problem with that, do you?"

"Why should I?" Mary shrugged. "You're living your own life. But you might have another visitor some night too—an unexpected one."

"What's that supposed to mean?"

"Your father. He thinks that DeLuca and you might be living together. He's been talking about dropping in unannounced to see for himself."

"He doesn't have to bother," Patricia said. "We *are* living together. Even if we didn't want to, we'd have to; there's barely enough money to support two households, much less three."

There, she thought, it was done. Now they knew for sure.

A few days after Patricia's visit to see her mother, her father called Frank DeLuca at the store. As DeLuca later related it to Patricia, Frank Columbo had said, "I think you and I ought to get together and have a talk about Patty. How about I meet you on the parking lot when you get off work?" DeLuca did not get off until ten-thirty that night, but that apparently was okay with Frank Columbo. "I'll see you outside the store, ten-thirty or so."

DeLuca immediately called Patricia at work. After telling her about the call, he asked, "What do you think?"

Patricia didn't know what to think. Was it possible that her parents were finally convinced that she and Frank were together for good? Had they decided to make the best of it?

"It's meeting on the parking lot that worries me," DeLuca admitted. "Why would he want to do that?"

"Maybe he's just going to pick you up," Patricia suggested. "Take you for a drink or something."

DeLuca worried about the meeting most of the day, calling Patricia several more times to express his concern. He had, of course, heard stories from Patricia about her father's warhead temper, and how even something done by the manager of a rival team to his beloved Chicago Cubs could infuriate him to violence. And he might even have recalled Patricia's comment to him the night in the motel when DeLuca admitted the truth about his family, and both of them confessed their real ages. Patricia had said: *If my father ever found out, he'd kill you.*

He finally called Patricia and said, "I'm not meeting him unless you're there too, Patrish."

Patricia could hear fear in his voice.

"All right, I'll be there with you."

At ten-thirty that night, Patricia was sitting in DeLuca's car on the parking lot. The lot was flooded with the hazy gray blue of vapor lights. There was no sign of her father or his car. She saw the late-shift employees leave the store, and watched Frank lock the door behind them. Then Frank started his final task of clearing the checkout registers. In less than ten minutes, he returned to the front door, set the night alarm, came out, and double-locked the doors. Patricia got out of the car and walked over to meet him. As she did, Frank Columbo's Thunderbird entered the parking lot off JFK Boulevard and drove slowly toward the store. Presently the Thunderbird caught them in its headlights and held them there as it drove slowly toward them. The light became too intense for them and the pair moved out of its glare.

Frank Columbo parked and turned off the headlights and engine. When he opened the car door, he was not ten feet from his daughter and her lover. As he stood up out of the

car, he pulled a .22-caliber rifle from the floorboard behind
the seat. Patricia and DeLuca were so surprised by the sight
of it, and Columbo was so close to them, that neither had
time to react. Columbo, probably remembering his army
training, advanced on them like an infantryman, holding the
rifle across his chest in port arms position. In several quick
steps, he was upon them.

Slashing out with the rifle, Columbo buttstroked DeLuca
across the mouth, splitting his bottom lip open, loosening
several teeth inside his mouth, and cutting open the middle of
his chin. DeLuca dropped to the sidewalk.

"Daddy—!" Patricia yelled.

"You motherfucker," Frank Columbo snarled down at the
fallen man, "you're gonna leave my daughter alone or you
are fucking dead!"

Patricia tried to grab her father's arm but he shook her off.
DeLuca, holding a hand to his mouth as if to catch the blood
that was streaming out, used his other hand to push himself
back onto his feet. As soon as he was upright, Columbo
swung the rifle again, this time driving its stock into
DeLuca's stomach. DeLuca pitched back to the ground.

"Stop it!" Patricia screamed. She advanced on her father
again, and again he slung her back as if she were weightless.

"I mean it!" Columbo warned hotly. "I'll kill you, you
motherfucker!"

Turning abruptly, he started back to his car. A passing car
had stopped nearby on the lot, and its driver was standing up
out of the car looking over its top at what was happening.
Columbo's eyes fell on his daughter and he paused to point
a menacing finger at her. There was a wild expression in his
eyes and on his face.

"I'll kill you too, Patty Ann!"

As Frank Columbo stalked on toward his Thunderbird, the
stranger who had stopped got quickly back behind the wheel
of his car and sped off toward Elk Grove's police headquarters, just two blocks away. Patricia rushed to DeLuca and was
helping him up when Columbo peeled off the lot on
squealing tires.

Patricia was furious. Here she was doing every goddamned
thing she possibly could to alleviate the animosity between

her parents, herself, and her fiancé—and her fucking father comes at them with a *gun*. Big shot Frank Columbo doesn't like the guy his little girl has chosen for herself, so he has to flex his dago muscles and kick ass. Well, fuck him! Patricia thought in silent rage. He wasn't going to get away with it!

She had driven DeLuca to Alexian Brothers Medical Center, just past police headquarters on the other side of JFK Boulevard. As Frank's mouth was being worked on by an oral surgeon, Patricia used a pay phone to call the Elk Grove police. When she began to explain what happened, the officer taking the report asked, "Is that the incident that took place in front of Walgreen's a little while ago?"

"Yes, it is."

It had already been reported by the passerby and two patrol cars were dispatched, but the officers had found no one at the scene. The officer taking Patricia's call got all the details from her and sent two investigators to the hospital to take her complaint. When the two detectives arrived and took down all the details, one of them asked, "Do you want to sign a complaint against your father, Miss Columbo?"

"You're goddamned right I do," she said angrily.

"You understand that he'll be arrested if you do?"

"Good! Arrest him! Throw his ass in jail! That's what he deserves!"

The officers left to return to headquarters and have an official complaint drawn up for Patricia to stop by and sign.

The oral surgeon straightened three of DeLuca's teeth that were displaced by the blow to his mouth, and a general surgeon stitched up his facial injuries. He had a large contusion from the body blow, but nothing was broken or ruptured. The doctor let Patricia in to see Frank before they bandaged his face, and when she looked at his grotesquely swollen lips, the bottom one stitched along its seam, and the skin on the middle of his chin split open and sewn back together again, she silently swore again that her father was not going to get away with this.

On the way home, Frank filled with painkillers and slumped in the passenger seat, Patricia stopped at Elk Grove police headquarters and signed the formal complaint.

Later that night, Frank Columbo was arrested at his home and taken to jail.

* * *

The following morning, when Frank Columbo made bail through a bondsman, he swore to his wife, "I'll never forgive her for this."

Mary and a friend tried to calm him down. But he was beyond reasoning.

"After all I did for her when *she* was in jail," he stormed, "and then she has me locked up over a son of a bitch like that! I should have killed him! I should have left the gun at home and just beat the bastard to death with my bare hands! Next time I'll know better!"

It was a short time later that Frank Columbo began telling everyone that he was taking Patty out of his will. Everything, he vowed, would go to Michael.

"Her own father," he continued to rant, "and she had me arrested like some street scum and put in jail."

He could not get over it.

DeLuca was terrified. He was certain that Frank Columbo really meant to kill him.

"He's going to get me, Patrish. The bastard is going to get me," the injured man said painstakingly through his freakishly puffed lips.

Patricia could not argue with him. What Frank said made sense. Never in her life had she seen her father that angry; he had looked like some kind of savage: fierce and brutish, bloodthirsty and merciless. His face had been contorted, the veins in his neck like blue rubber tubing, and there had even been a froth of saliva at the corners of his lips. Foaming at the mouth, she thought, like a mad dog. Maybe that CB handle of his was closer to the truth than anyone knew. Crazy Dago.

Could he hire someone to kill Frank? Probably, she guessed. He was involved with a lot of hard characters: dock workers, truck drivers, tough men. And he was Italian, from the lower West Side of Chicago, where if you didn't know at least one syndicate mobster you simply weren't paying attention. In all likelihood her father had, or knew someone who had, enough connections to buy a contract on Frank DeLuca's life. And he certainly had the money to do it. Frank DeLuca, she decided, had good reason to be fearful.

"He's going to get me, Patrish," her lover moaned through those appalling lips so often around the apartment for the next few weeks that Patricia thought she would go mad. She rationalized with him interminably to try to brace him up.

"Frank, even if he is planning something like that, he won't be stupid enough to do it while this assault-and-battery charge is pending against him. He'll have to wait until that's out of the way. We've got plenty of time to figure something out."

But DeLuca's fear was not assuaged. When he returned to work, he started traveling by different routes every day to try to determine if he was being followed.

One good thing came out of the parking lot incident, as far as Patricia was concerned. Their sex life decelerated from bizarre to ultraconventional. Not only was DeLuca temporarily impeded by his wounds, he was also in dread fear that Frank Columbo might, by virtue of having him followed, learn about some of their sexual habits and become even more determined to have him killed. DeLuca was so benumbed by the memory of what had already happened, those terrible, violent several minutes on the parking lot, and the foreboding of what he felt was *going* to happen, that he lacked even the desire to titillate himself with the new issue of *Swinger's Life.* Anxiety had, for the moment at least, curbed his hoggish sexual appetite.

Patricia, for a while, actually began to relax. Although giving credence to her father's murderous threats, she also sincerely believed, as she told DeLuca, that there was no *immediate* danger, and she was already framing in her mind the outline of still another plan to neutralize the animosity between her father and Frank DeLuca. Ever conniving, always scheming, she was instinctively cunning enough to quickly put behind her the blind anger she had felt toward her father, in favor of finding an overall solution.

Patricia knew her father, knew that after his sudden outbursts of anger he usually became contrite and conciliatory. And she knew that, as far as his only daughter was concerned, he was always quick to forgive—particularly if said only daughter made some concession, even a token one, that allowed him to save face as a father. Prior to the parking lot incident, the only concession acceptable to him was one that would have required some retreat in her relationship with DeLuca. Now, however, Frank Columbo himself had given Patricia a new card to play: the assault-and-battery complaint. With that new card, Patricia was already concocting a scenario in which she and DeLuca would magnanimously withdraw the complaint and be welcomed into the embrace of a grateful and all-forgiving Frank Columbo.

In formulating this latest strategy, there was one critical factor that she misevaluated: the depth of Frank Columbo's emotional pain.

35
October 1975

Several weeks after the parking lot incident in July, Patricia had resumed a sporadic friendship with Nancy Glenn, a former schoolmate from Elk Grove High. For a time, Nancy worked directly across JFK Boulevard at the big Jewel Market when Patricia had been at Corky's. They had been best friends for a while, then drifted apart when Patricia fell in love with Frank DeLuca and put the rest of the world on a back burner. But they ran into each other one Saturday in Grove Shopping Center and went to the Frontier Restaurant to have lunch.

"How's the big love affair?" Nancy asked. She was now a nurse's aide at Alexian Brothers. Patricia had been quite the topic of conversation when the rumor spread at Elk Grove High that, at seventeen, she was dating a thirty-five-year-old married man. "Are you and your pharmacist friend still seeing each other?"

"Every night." Patricia laid the news on her almost with glee. No one had expected it to last. "We're living together."

"Well," Nancy said, surprised and not unimpressed. She had seen Frank DeLuca in Walgreen's; he *was* a hunk. Nancy immediately asked Patricia what her folks thought about it. She knew the Columbos enough to surmise that they were probably not thrilled.

"Dad couldn't be happier," Patricia said sarcastically, then told Nancy all about her father smashing Frank in the face with a rifle butt. Nancy, aghast, listened in awe as Patricia brought her up-to-date on the continuing saga of her chaotic life: the credit card thefts, the ten months in the DeLuca household, the futile attempt to restructure her life with Andrew Harper. Nancy was spellbound; it was a *hell* of a story—even for Patty Columbo.

Nancy wasn't sure how much of it to believe; Patty by now had an unimpeachable reputation for playing fast and loose with the truth. But Nancy decided in this case to give her old friend the benefit of the doubt; the story was simply too incredible to be made up. She asked Patricia what she intended to do about the assault-and-battery complaint; surely Patricia wouldn't have her own father sent to jail.

"Why not?" Patricia asked indignantly. "He threatened to kill us, Nancy!"

Her friend scoffed at that. "Patty! You don't believe he'd do it."

"How do I know what he'd do? He's a crazy dago. Frank thinks he's going to buy a contract on him. I wouldn't put it past him."

Nancy shook her head. Same old Patty, she thought.

Before they parted that day, Patricia gave Nancy her phone number, which was in Frank DeLuca's name at the apartment. It was unlisted.

As Nancy Glenn would relate to Ray Rose after the murders, she had gone shopping for a car in September of 1975, and found a neat little '73 Camaro, dark blue, that she liked at Franklin-Weber Pontiac in Schaumburg. And there she met Lanny Mitchell, the car salesman who took care of her. She dated Lanny for several weeks, visiting his apartment and becoming intimate with him almost at once.

To Nancy, who was only five months older than Patricia, Lanny seemed very adult, very suave, such a *man* after the adolescent boys she had been going out with. He was cute and he was fun. She began to understand better how Patricia Columbo had become involved with Frank DeLuca. Older men *were* different.

When Lanny asked Nancy one day to fix up a pal of his

with a date, Nancy thought at once of Patty. Because of the problems Patty was having in her affair with DeLuca, Nancy imagined she could use a night out, just to have a little fun, no strings attached.

Nancy could not remember if she had ever mentioned Patty Columbo to Lanny or not. But when Lanny pressed her for a date for his friend, whose name was Roman, she told him that Patty was a possibility, and related a few details of Patty's situation—including Patty's statement to her that Frank Columbo was threatening to kill her and her boyfriend.

Lanny, who Nancy thought was a police officer waiting for reinstatement after a suspension, told her that his friend was a very "heavy" individual, with important political as well as underworld ties, who might be able to help Patricia with her problem.

Nancy telephoned Patricia and the blind date was arranged.

DeLuca was working late at the drugstore on the night Patricia was to go on the double date with Nancy, so Patricia was driving his car. Nancy had wanted to use her new Camaro, but Patricia would not agree to that.

"I want to be able to leave whenever I get ready to," she told Nancy. "I have to go get Frank when he closes the store."

Patricia picked Nancy up at home and they drove to the parking lot of the Elk Grove Village Bowl. Lanny and his friend Roman were already there, standing outside their own car. The girls pulled up and got out also. Nancy introduced Patricia to Lanny, and Lanny introduced both of them to Roman. No last names were exchanged.

The girls followed them to the Where Else Lounge, a modest little place set back on a postage-stamp lot with a lighted sign topped by the word *Where* and bottomed by the word *Else*, with neon tubing forming a large question mark between them. Inside, it was not much different from any other small, suburban cocktail lounge. There was the requisite bar with its line of vinyl-padded barstools, a few booths along the opposite wall, a miniature dance floor designed for no more than four couples, and a big lighted jukebox to provide the music. One bartender and one cocktail waitress could have handled the place even on New Year's Eve, it was that compact.

The four of them sat in one of the booths, Nancy with Lanny, Patricia with Roman. They ordered drinks and Lanny put money in the jukebox so they could dance. They drank a little, talked a little, danced a little, changing partners with each new record. Both men were wearing leisure suits, and at one point when Patricia was dancing with Lanny his coat was open and she could see that he had a holstered gun on his belt.

"What are you carrying a gun for?" she asked curiously.

"I always carry when I'm with Roman," he replied casually. "Didn't Nancy tell you that Roman is a very heavy man?"

"She mentioned something like that," Patricia said.

Lanny nodded. "You take good care of Roman," he assured, "and favors can very definitely be done for you if you need any."

Back in the booth, the conversation eventually got around to sex. Small adult theaters were currently in vogue, and X-rated film actress Linda Lovelace had become famous for her outstanding talent as a fellator in the movie *Deep Throat*. Roman and Lanny discussed the film—and Linda's talent—at length, speculating on how she was able to perform her unique routine.

Patricia became distinctly uncomfortable. She didn't like Roman at all; he was too fishy looking for her, with droopy eyelids and funny-shaped lips that reminded her of goldfish she once had. In addition, Nancy was drinking too much and Patricia was beginning to wonder how safe it was going to be to leave her with these two guys when she herself had to depart to go pick up DeLuca. This had not turned out to be such a good idea after all.

Before long, the men suggested they continue their party at a motel Roman knew. They would make the trip there the same way they had come to the lounge: the men leading the way in one car, the girls following in the other.

This was her chance, Patricia thought, to ditch these creeps and take Nancy home. Then she wouldn't have to worry about her.

When they got back into their respective cars and started

out, Patricia lagged behind a little as if she did not want to follow too closely. She kept up with them just enough for them to think, she hoped, that nothing was amiss; then when she felt the time was right, she made a quick turn and sped down a side street. The sudden jolt of movement stirred Nancy's stomach.

"Christ, I feel sick," she said thickly.

"Don't throw up in this car," Patricia warned. How the hell would she explain *that* to Frank?

Patricia took a circuitous route along residential streets, Nancy bitching all the way because she wanted to go to the motel, and finally pulled up in front of the Glenn home. A moment later, Lanny and Roman pulled up directly behind her. Patricia couldn't believe it. She thought about getting Nancy's brother, Norman, but there were no lights on in the house. Behind them, a car door slammed and one of the men approached. Patricia felt panicky.

"I want to go to the motel," Nancy said sullenly, recognizing her house.

Roman came up to Patricia's side of the car and tapped on the window. "I just want to talk to you," he said. Patricia rolled the window partway down. "How come you tried to ditch us after Lanny paid you money?" he asked.

"What are you talking about?" Patricia snapped. "Lanny hasn't paid me any money."

"You girls made a deal to go to the motel. What are you trying to run out for?"

"I'm going to the motel with Lanny," Nancy announced, and got out of the car before Patricia could stop her.

"Shit," Patricia said. Then to Roman, "Look, I've got to go pick up my boyfriend—"

Roman shook his head. "Not until we finish what was agreed on," he said flatly. "I thought you needed a favor done."

"Forget it, man," Patricia told him. "I don't want any favors. And I'm not fucking you, understand?"

"You made a deal," Roman said. "You're going to keep it."

Patricia caught a hint of menace in his voice. She recalled Lanny's words of an hour earlier: "Roman is a very heavy man." *Careful*, she warned herself. *Girls get the shit beat out of them for stuff like this.*

"Okay," she finally conceded, "I'll go to the motel. But I am not fucking you."

"So you can fuck Lanny," he said, shrugging. "I'll fuck your girlfriend. What's the difference? A fuck is a fuck. Wait here. And don't try nothing cute."

"Jack-off," Patricia muttered as he walked away.

Presently Lanny came up and got into the car with her. "Just follow them to the motel," he said, as Roman drove away with Nancy.

As Patricia drove, it occurred to her that she still might salvage something out of this botched evening. In the weeks since her father had attacked Frank DeLuca, Frank had been driving her crazy with his constant anxiety about her father's threat of murder. Patricia had not yet played her hole card—withdrawing the assault-and-battery complaint—and could not convince Frank that it would do them any good when she did.

"Your old man's going to get me, Patrish," her lover continued to lament incessantly. "He's going to hire someone to hit me."

Patricia had hoped that this guy Roman, who was supposed to be so "heavy," might, if Patricia was nice to him, find out for her if her father's threat was anything except dago mouth; find out if there was any *real* reason for Frank to feel threatened; find out if there *was* a contract on Frank.

But Roman was so repulsive that Patricia deep-sixed the idea minutes after meeting him. This other one, Lanny, wasn't nearly as objectionable to her, and driving along she came up with a new idea that might help her.

"Look, if I'm real nice to you at the motel," she said to Lanny, "could you get me a gun of some kind? My boyfriend is really freaking out because he thinks my dad has got a contract out on him. I mean, he can't sleep nights, he drives different routes to work, he's even started getting off the elevator at different floors in the building where we live, in case somebody has it staked out. He's got one of those little derringers, but if he had a bigger gun for protection, it would make him feel a lot better."

Lanny said sure, he could get her a gun, but it might take a little time. Patricia asked if, in the meantime, he could get her some bullets for the derringer, and he said he would.

They followed Roman to the Edgebrook Motel, where they waited while he left Nancy in the car and went in to register. Presently he returned with a key and led them all to one of the rooms. Nancy immediately slumped down in a chair and fell asleep. Roman left the room to get some hot coffee to wake her up. Outside, before walking away, he let the air out of the two front tires of Frank's car, which Patricia was driving. He was making sure Patricia did not try to run out on them again.

In the room, Patricia and Lanny were undressing. Patricia, as usual, had a dilemma. She had been a virgin the first time Frank DeLuca had intercourse with her, and since that time had been completely faithful to him except with other men that *he* selected for her—and in his presence. Even with Andrew Harper, she had not gone beyond passionate kissing. Now she was trying to justify in her own mind that she was doing *this* for Frank, to get Frank a gun, but she nevertheless felt guilty because it was her choice and not his. Seeking some way still to maintain a token of fidelity to her lover, she finally said to Lanny, "I want it in my ass, babe, okay?"

In the ass was perfectly all right with Lanny.

Patricia and Lanny were finished and dressed again by the time Roman returned with the coffee. Nancy was semiawake now and Roman drew a chair over next to her and started urging her to sip some coffee. He gestured for Lanny to take Patricia for a walk.

Outside, when she saw the two flat tires, Patricia's stomach jerked with a spasm of panic. She groaned aloud, knowing that now she would never get back to the drugstore in time to pick up Frank when he closed. Lanny saw that she was on the verge of tears.

"Relax," he said, "they probably just need air. We'll take care of it when Roman comes out."

Roman came out twenty minutes later. He and Lanny went with Patricia as she drove the car very slowly onto a service station lot next door. The place was closing, but Roman flashed a gun and had the attendant bring her tires up to proper pressure.

"I really have to go now," Patricia said to them. "I'm late picking up my man."

She did not particularly like leaving Nancy there, but Frank came first.

The next afternoon, Lanny was out on the lot looking at some used-car inventory when he was paged for a telephone call. He went into his cubbyhole office and picked up. It was Patty. She wanted to know when she could get the bullets he said he would get for her. Lanny said he could get them that day and asked what caliber Patricia needed. Patricia said her boyfriend had told her twenty-twos. Lanny said to drop around in a couple of hours. After hanging up, Lanny took off a few minutes and walked across to a sporting goods store in Golf Plaza and bought a box of bullets.

Patricia came by for the bullets several hours later. "I really appreciate this. My boyfriend will feel a whole lot better if he has at least some protection."

"Glad to help," Lanny said. "Listen, keep in touch. I want to help you out any way I can. Understand me?"

"Sure, I understand," Patricia said.

She thought she did.

DeLuca's fear of Patricia's father was getting completely out of hand. He bought and installed an extra lock for the apartment door, then insisted on bracing a chair under the doorknob as a further safeguard. It was as if he expected Frank Columbo, or—in his mind—whoever Frank Columbo *hired*, to attack the apartment with a battering ram. Patricia tried to reason with him, but he refused to listen; whenever they were at home, there was the kitchen chair stuck up under the doorknob like in some goddamn gangster movie.

As Frank's mouth and chin wounds healed, his mind seemed to deteriorate in the face of a constant pressure created by his all-consuming focus on the real or imagined peril he faced. His paranoia grew daily until he could see nothing except doom. Every stranger was now a spy, every unfamiliar face an assassin. Even poor Michael, whom he knew, enlarged to monster proportions.

"That kid brother of yours was in the store today," Frank complained a short time after the parking lot incident. "He was in the magazine section holding a magazine, but looking over it and glaring at me. He looked like he wanted to kill me."

Patricia summarily rejected the remark. "Michael wouldn't step on an ant."

But there was no way she could talk DeLuca out of this new obsession. He became convinced that Michael was part of the plot to kill him.

Patricia had planned to surprise Frank with the good news after she played her ace in the hole and negotiated a peace treaty with her father. But because of her lover's state of mind, she decided to tell him about her strategy ahead of time, hoping it would relieve some of his foreboding.

"I want to drop the complaint against Dad for hitting you," she told him. "I know him; I know he'll be grateful to both of us for letting him off the hook. I think we'll be able to put all this bad blood behind us."

DeLuca shook his head. "It won't work, okay? It just won't work. Your old man is crazy. He's going all the way with this thing."

But Patricia insisted her father was a forgiving man. She was his only daughter. If she offered him a reason to forgive her, she was confident that he would take it.

"Do it if you want to," DeLuca consented, "but it's a waste of time. This is a dago death feud to him, a fucking vendetta. Your old man won't be happy until I'm dead." DeLuca paused a beat, then added, "Or he is."

The assault-and-battery complaint against Frank Columbo was withdrawn, and he was notified by mail that his court date had been canceled and his bond remitted. Patricia waited a week, to allow her act of compassion and charity to be properly absorbed and digested by her father; then she paid a visit to the Brantwood house to measure its effect. When her father learned who was at the door, he went into his and Mary's bedroom, locked the door, and refused to have anything to do with her.

Patricia pleaded her case to her mother. She had dropped the charges against her father because she had wanted to put an end to all the fighting. Patricia realized, she told Mary, that they would probably never be one big happy family—they weren't exactly the Waltons, after all—but couldn't they at least try to be civil to each other? She and Frank would definitely be getting married next June or July, whenever his divorce from Marilyn became final. They would be starting over together, a new life for both of them. Frank knew what his responsibilities were toward his kids and intended to meet those obligations—but they'd also like to have a baby of their own. Couldn't everybody please just stop all the hostility, live and let live?

Patricia then girded herself to do the extraordinary. "I'm asking you to help me with this, Mother."

Mary Columbo shook her head, probably not in refusal or rejection—she was as tired of this business as anyone—but more than likely as a sign of the overwhelming skepticism that must have engulfed her.

"Your father, Patty Ann, will never get over the fact that you had him put in jail," she told her daughter. "They came to this house, the police did, and arrested your father like he was a common criminal! He will never forgive you for that."

But in spite of her deep misgivings, Mary nevertheless agreed to try. Her shortcomings as a mother aside—and all parents have them—she had to have wanted to see her only daughter happy. She would, she promised, approach her husband with the live-and-let-live concept.

Patricia departed the house without having spoken one word directly to her father, but with hopes that the Columbo-DeLuca conflict would soon be over.

It was simply not to be.

When Patricia returned a week later, optimistic about finally sitting down with her father and resolving the difficulties between them, he once again retreated to the bedroom, locked the door, turned on the small television set in there, and rejected any face-to-face discussion with his daughter. His compromise, the only one he would consider, was delivered by Mary.

"Your father says he is perfectly willing to start all over with you. But *only* with you. He says if you'll come back home, we can forget everything that's happened and start fresh."

Patricia was astounded. Their conflict had nothing to do with her coming back home. Her home was with Frank

DeLuca. He was the man she loved and the man she was going to be with. Why in hell wouldn't her father accept that?

Seeing the look of disbelief on Patricia's face, Mary, choosing neutrality, said, "I'm only telling you what your father told me to tell you. You leave DeLuca and move back home, that's what he wants."

"Never," Patricia said, shaking her head emphatically, collecting her purse and cigarettes and lighter. How dare he try to dictate her life like that?

As Patricia walked to the front door, Mary Columbo warned, "This may be your last chance to ever make up with your father."

Patricia didn't even bother to reply.

Some time later, Patricia called Lanny Mitchell at the car showroom.

"Can I pick you up for lunch?" she asked.

She went by for him and they drove to a nearby McDonald's to eat. At a little table in the corner, careful to keep her voice low, she said, "Look, my problems are getting worse and worse. I really need some help."

Lanny touched her hand across the table. "I told you I'd help you any way I could. I meant that, Patty."

Patricia told Lanny some of the background of the bad blood between her father and Frank DeLuca. Lanny listened attentively, nodding sympathetically from time to time. He was the kind of man who liked young girls with problems; the kind of man who knew they were easy to impress, easy to get next to. Lanny Mitchell must have thought that day that Patricia was one of the biggest pushovers he had seen in a long time. She had practically creamed when she saw the gun he was wearing that first night. Right now, he knew, she was working up to something. She probably wanted a favor. Whatever it was, Lanny was prepared to say yes.

When they finished eating, they returned to the car dealership. In Lanny's little office, with the door closed, Patricia finally got around to what was on her mind.

"My parents are giving me a harder time about my boyfriend than either one of us can handle anymore. Sometimes I really wish they were dead."

"That could be arranged, you know," Lanny Mitchell said quietly.

Patricia locked eyes with the little car salesman. "How?"

"I'll do it," Lanny said.

C.H.
June 1991

I stopped making notes and stared at Patricia across the little table.

"Is that when it started?" I asked.

"Is that when what started?"

"Murder."

Swallowing nervously, she nodded. "It must have been. Yes."

The community room had been filled with visitors this particular Sunday, so Patricia and I were out on an enclosed porch behind it. It was not comfortable, but it was private.

"You took Lanny seriously?" I asked. "From the beginning?"

"I thought the guy was a cop," she said by way of answer. "Nancy had told me he was a cop; he was supposedly selling cars as a sideline or something until Roman could get his suspension lifted. And he acted like a cop; he carried a gun, talked about Roman being 'heavy,' being 'connected.' " She shrugged resignedly. "I was nineteen; I fell for it. I was getting desperate. On a subsequent visit to the house, after Dad started speaking to me again, he said that he didn't want to hear any more talk about me marrying Frank. He said there wasn't going to be any wedding because there wasn't going to be any DeLuca. And he started calling me at the apartment, saying that he was going to get Frank."

She told me about the young boy named Jeff something— she couldn't remember his last name—who lived in the next apartment, and how one day she'd had him listen in on one of her father's threatening calls. I let her talk, not telling her that I already knew about it from the report written by the officer who had interviewed Jeff, the report never presented at the trial.

"You really believed your father was going to kill DeLuca?" I asked.

"Yes, I did. Wouldn't you have?" she challenged. "He smashes Frank in the face with a rifle; he threatens to kill us both that night; he says there won't be a wedding because there won't be a Frank; he calls me on the phone saying he's going to get Frank; and when he got out of jail after I had him arrested, he told everybody we knew that he should have killed Frank and that next time he would know better." She took a deep drag on her cigarette. "Yes, I believed Dad was going to do something violent again. I'd have been a goddamned fool not to."

She was getting edgy. I moved the conversation away from her father.

"Did your friend Nancy know you'd seen her boyfriend again?" I asked. Patricia shook her head.

"I don't think so. We really didn't stay friends after that fiasco at the motel. She called a couple of days later and really got on my case. She was pissed because Lanny was supposed to have been her date that night, and she ended up in bed with old fish-eye Roman. I told her I didn't see what the big deal was; she'd been so looped she wouldn't have known it if the hunchback of Notre Dame had fucked her. Anyway, to answer your question, I think if she'd known I had called Lanny, she would have raised hell about that too."

"Did you see or talk to Nancy at all after that call?"

"No. The next time I even thought about her was when I found out she'd turned me in for the murders."

I was making notes, using Patricia's pen and her personal pink-and-violet stationery, because I wasn't allowed to bring my own pen and notepad into the prison. Apparently they didn't care what a visitor took out. Before a visit, I would dictate a list of subjects to Patricia over the telephone and she would bring it with her to the visit. That kept me from having to memorize so much for each visit, and gave her time to reflect on what I wanted to talk about, in case she wanted to veto anything. Our arrangement was that she would talk only about what she wanted to—without pressure from me. I asked what I wanted to ask; she answered what she wanted to answer.

It had worked fine up until now. Patricia had brought me

all the way across the same ground she had covered with Sister Burke, from her earliest childhood through the sexual abuse period with Gus Latini, then on past that time to new terrain with Frank DeLuca. At times she had seemed eager to talk; her words rose like bubbles under a waterfall as she seemed to purge herself of one unpleasant memory after another. But as we got closer and closer to the murders and what led up to them, I sensed a gradual downturn in her desire to talk, a subtle but definite reticence in her side of the dialogue.

At one point, when I questioned a conclusion she had drawn about something, she became hostile. "Look, I didn't send for you," she snapped. "I didn't ask you to come along after fifteen years and fuck up my life with your goddamn book."

"I'm not fucking up your life, Patricia," I said. "You already did that a long time ago."

"When I started out with you, I didn't mean for it to go this far," she complained. "I hadn't intended to tell you as much as I have. I don't really need this shit, you know; I don't need you or your book."

"Look," I told her evenly, "you're goddamned lucky you've got me, you just don't realize it yet. Sooner or later, somebody was bound to write a book about you. A few minutes ago, you mentioned being desperate. How would you like it if I was some Ivy League asshole from Princeton whose only personal experience with desperation is when his zipper gets stuck? I know you, Columbo, and I know DeLuca. I came from the same Chicago streets that both of you did—only they were a lot meaner to me than they were to either of you; my old man never moved me to the suburbs. I stayed on those streets for a long, long time; I learned about desperation just like you did—the hard way. I know what it means to be pushed so far back into a corner that you'll do anything—anything—to get out of it so you can breathe again. A lot of writers can't relate to that kind of emotional weight; a lot of writers wouldn't even try: they'd look at you like you were some kind of evil spore, some kind of monster. They'd say you were born bad, and let it go at that. Is that what you want the final word on you to be: Patty Columbo, the bad seed?"

Her silence told me that she did not.

That kind of confrontation is bound to erupt when one human being gets too close to the core of another. It had happened to me before with others. But Patricia and I always got past it and got back to what we were doing—because both of us knew it was meant to be done.

"Okay," Patricia would say, lighting her tenth or fifteenth or twentieth cigarette of the visit. "What do you want to talk about now?"

"Let's talk about Lanny Mitchell some more. After Lanny offered to kill your parents, what happened in the days that followed?"

Patricia looked down at the tabletop and her eyes narrowed as once again she reached back into the nightmare of her memory.

36
November 1975

The most incongruous element of the Patricia Columbo—Lanny Mitchell association, and the most ironic, was the fact that it was the first adult relationship Patricia had ever entered into on a completely truthful basis. She was totally and unreservedly up-front with Lanny, something that in the past few years she had not been with anyone: not her parents, friends, teachers, co-workers, not even her lover, for whom she professed to care more than life itself. Now, in a life-and-death situation, she decided that truth must rule—and she pledged that fealty to a confirmed, habitual, and zealous liar, as he would later admit himself under oath.

The truth simply was not in Lanny Mitchell when he was dealing with a woman whom he was intent upon seducing, swindling, or otherwise taking advantage of. It is doubtful that he ever once made an honest statement to Patricia. When she asked him what he "did" for Roman, he said, "Well, I used to be a Cook County sheriff's deputy but I got fired. Roman's got connections and I'm waiting for him to get me back on." That was the first time Patricia realized that he was not an active policeman.

When she asked how much a "hit" usually cost, he immediately came up with a figure. "The going price is ten thousand per person," he said. Whatever the question, Lanny had an answer.

Their initial discussion of murder, in Lanny's office, following lunch at McDonald's had been interrupted by the arrival of a customer Lanny was waiting for.

"This is going to take a while," he told her. "Let's talk tomorrow. Call me."

Patricia left the car showroom that day fully believing she had found a hit man to get her father before he got Frank DeLuca.

Patricia called Lanny again and they agreed to meet at a Dunkin' Donuts shop at a time when they knew it would not be crowded. They met and took their coffee and pastry to a rear booth.

"Did you mean what you said the other day?" she asked.

"Sure, I meant it. I said I'd help you, didn't I?"

"All right then, I want you to do it," Patricia told him.

"You're sure?"

"I'm sure."

"Okay." Lanny must have put his scheming mind into high gear at once. "First thing I want you to do is get me a run-down on the house they live in: floor plan, types of locks, who sleeps where, schedule and habits of all occupants, descriptions of everybody." He said it all with a straight face. Lanny the hit man.

"I'll get you whatever you need," Patricia assured him.

"Now what about the money?" he asked. In addition to getting some sex, Lanny was looking to make a few bucks too.

Patricia assured him that there would be plenty of money when it was over. She and her brother would be the only heirs. Patricia had been told by both her parents that she had been taken out of their will. But with them gone, she would be Michael's guardian anyway, so she would still control the estate. Let her father do whatever he wanted to with his fucking will, she thought. He was the one causing all the trouble.

Lanny agreed to wait for payment until after the hit.

"It's arranged then?" Patricia asked. "It'll be done?"

"Definitely," Lanny guaranteed. "After you get me the stuff I asked for."

When they parted in the Dunkin' Donuts parking lot and Lanny drove off, Patricia sat in her car for several minutes staring into space. She could scarcely believe it had been so simple. She wondered why more people didn't do it.

It would come out at the trial that after each meeting with Patricia Columbo, Lanny had telephoned his friend Roman.

When he called after the first meeting at McDonald's, Roman wanted to know all the details. He was easily as cunning and devious as Lanny. Despite his past employment as a Cook County deputy sheriff, and the fact that he held a somewhat coveted position in that same government as a civil service recruiter, he was also a cheap thief. His criminal record went back at least as far as 1960, and he had been arrested in no fewer than four Chicago suburbs for larceny and shoplifting. That he was ever badged as a deputy sheriff speaks reams about the Cook County personnel selection process for peace officers; that the county employed him for years as one of its recruiters defies all concepts of civil service principles.

At the time Roman Sobczynski met Patricia Columbo, he was still employed as a recruiter, but the county, in its employee evaluation procedures, seemed to be slowly catching on to him. His numerical appraisal in five job factors—work habits, quantity and quality of work, and so on—averaged 84 in August 1973, only two points shy of being considered an excellent performer who had gone beyond satisfactory in the fulfillment of his job requirements. Scarcely two years later, in September 1975, he had dropped to a 79, only four points above a rating that indicated he did not fully meet the requirements of his present job. The quantity of his work, in particular, had dropped from 85 to 76, and his work habits from 80 to 75. Roman was going downhill, slowly but surely.

As a scheming opportunist, however, he still ranked somewhere in the 90s.

Roman was intrigued by what Lanny Mitchell told him. He saw unlimited potential for a scam in this naive, shallow nineteen-year-old. There was no telling what they could get out of her. Good pussy, for sure, and who knew what else?

"Didn't you say her boyfriend manages a big Walgreen's?" he asked Lanny.

Roman might have been licking his lips here, a hungry predator smelling fresh carrion. And Lanny was only too pleased to keep fanning the scent into his nostrils. Lanny hoped Roman understood that he himself wanted more out of this deal than some teenage pussy. Unlike Roman, Lanny got all the gash he wanted. He could get fucked every day of the week and twice on Sundays just on charm alone. But Roman, he must have sensed, was different. Roman was uptight, putting on some weight, and had a kind of fishy look to begin with. To get laid, Lanny probably suspected that Roman had to have a hook of some kind, a carrot on a stick. Lanny had no doubt seen his type before: the kind of guy a woman would only fuck *for* something—a job, a favor, money. But women fucked Lanny Mitchell because they enjoyed it.

Lanny wanted a cushy Cook County job out of all this. He was tired of being a used car hustler. He wanted to be respectable.

Like his friend Roman.

Meanwhile, Frank DeLuca was going over the edge.

Apparently doing a complete turnaround from tempering his and Patty's sex life out of fear of her father, he now bought a big German shepherd dog named Duke and brought him home to the apartment.

"We're going to take some far-out pictures," he announced.

"What—kind of pictures?" Patricia asked.

"Pictures of you and the dog."

"Frank, are you crazy?" she asked. "You want me to have sex with a *dog*?"

"You don't actually have to have sex with him if you don't want to," he said.

Patricia stared at him. If she didn't *want* to?

"No," he explained, "all you have to do is pose like you're getting ready to. You know, suggestively." He started loading the camera. "Come on, get undressed."

"I'm not going to do this, Frank," she said evenly, shaking her head. "This is not—normal."

DeLuca gazed levelly at her. "Normal? What the fuck is normal?" he asked. "Are you normal, Patrish? Am I? If I was normal, would I have left my wife and kids for you? If you were normal, would you have a father who's trying to have me killed? Normal, Patrish, is what people call themselves when they don't do anything out of the ordinary. If we were normal, honey, we wouldn't be together. If you never understand anything else, try to understand that. Now get undressed."

When she still hesitated, DeLuca put down the camera and walked over to her. It was not a threatening move, but it was calculated nevertheless. Frank DeLuca always knew what he was doing when it came to sexual intimidation.

"Joy did it for me," he said quietly.

Patricia did not react.

"Joy Heysek never refused me anything, Patrish. She did it with black men, white men, women, dogs—whatever I wanted. Maybe she loved me more than you do, Patrish."

"Nobody's ever loved you more than I do, Frank," Patricia said. She wanted to add: *I'm arranging the murder of my parents for you. Is there a greater love than that?*

"The woman who loves me the most is the woman who does the most for me," DeLuca told her quietly. "That's how I measure love."

No matter how much her mind rebuked her, Patricia's heart and emotions overruled her reason. DeLuca stood before her a fear-crazed, unreasonable, unreachable hollow shell of the man she had first known. He was trying to salvage some of his sanity with the only resource still at his command: his obsession with bizarre sex of every ilk.

And Patricia felt she had no option but to help him as he tried to help himself. The structure of their relationship was ever so slowly changing. It had begun as man teaching girl, and appeared now to have evolved into woman helping boy. That was how far it seemed to Patricia that DeLuca had regressed. He was like a helpless kid, stricken with the terror of the unknown, begging someone to put a comforting arm around him.

"All right, Frank," she said, and began taking off her clothes.

Patricia prepared the material that Lanny Mitchell had requested as quickly as she could. She felt she *had* to get the pressure off DeLuca with the utmost urgency, or he might go to pieces entirely. Somehow she had imagined that a man who once played football at Purdue, a man who had engaged in skydiving as a sport, would somehow have more courage in the face of adversity than DeLuca had displayed. He had feared her father from the very first sound of Frank Columbo's voice when he called to arrange the parking lot meeting. Experiencing the violence of that incident itself seemed to have cemented the fear into a dread that cast its shadow into every part of his brain. He was like a man standing at the bottom of an elevator shaft, waiting for the car to descend all the way . . . and crush him dead.

Patricia's first priority was to stop that elevator.

She called Lanny at the dealership and they agreed to meet at the Elk Grove Village Bowl parking lot. Lanny was already there when she drove up. He left his car to get into hers, and noticed that she had a large German shepherd in the backseat.

"Big dog," he commented. "Friendly, I hope."

"You wouldn't believe how friendly," she said. "I've got the things you wanted."

Lanny took the sheets of paper she gave him. The top one was a floor plan of the house at 55 Brantwood. Patricia leaned over to point out significant locations: the stairs going up to the main level of the house and down to the lower bedrooms and rec room; her brother's bedroom; her parents' bedroom, which, since Patricia had left home, was back upstairs; doors leading into the house from the porch, the garage, the backyard.

Lanny let Patricia finish her excursion through the house plan, then began asking questions he imagined a professional hit man would ask. "The garage door, is it electric?"

"Yes."

"I can probably find out what frequency it operates on and get in that way," he said smoothly.

"If you can't," Patricia offered, "I could always stop by the house pretending to want to leave a present or something for Michael; while I'm there I could unlock a sliding glass door for you. They'd probably never even notice."

Patricia gave him another sheet from under the floor plan: her parents' normal schedule. She suggested Lanny go in just before daylight and hide somewhere in the house until Michael went to school.

"I could take care of your brother too if you want," Lanny said.

"No!" Patricia was momentarily horrified. "No, not Michael. He's not to be hurt in any way."

The meeting ended that afternoon with Lanny telling Patricia he would get in touch with her if he needed anything else.

As Patricia drove back to the apartment, she was still slightly dismayed that Lanny had offered to kill Michael too. *Fucking asshole*, she thought. Have her own brother killed?

What kind of person did he think she was?

During the next several weeks, Patricia did what she could to keep a lid on Frank's paranoia, while waiting for some word from Lanny Mitchell as to when the hit would be carried out. She might have had an easier job of it except that twice Frank came home infuriated by the fact that Michael had been in the drugstore again, pulling his same staring act.

"I swear to God," DeLuca threatened, "I'm going to come out of the pharmacy and grab that kid by the throat if he doesn't knock it off! Your old man is putting him up to it, I know he is!"

Patricia begged him to calm down. Michael, she pleaded, was just a kid. He'd probably heard their father bad-mouthing DeLuca and was trying to act like a tough guy. She finally got DeLuca to promise not to hurt Michael.

When Patricia didn't hear from Lanny during the next ten days, she called him. He gave her a vague hit-man excuse.

"The people who have to approve this kind of contract are still thinking about it."

Another week went by. She called Lanny again. He did not seem to be in any particular hurry to accommodate her.

"These things take time, Patty," he said casually.

Wonderful, she thought. She was caught between a rifle-swinging hothead father and a delusional, irrational boyfriend, with a smartass little brother and his evil-eye trick thrown in for good measure—and fucking asshole hit-man Lanny tells her these things take time. She was just about *out*

of time. And, she thought, would soon be out of her fucking
mind as well.

But she had no option except to continue waiting.

Another ten days went by. It was November, getting colder.
Daylight Savings Time had ended and it now got dark just after four o'clock in the afternoon. That meant Frank had to
come home after dark every day instead of just the days when
he worked the closing shift. He now became afraid of shadows as well as strangers. Once he got into the apartment and
put the chair under the doorknob, an earthquake could not
have made him go out again. Naturally it was left to Patricia
to walk the goddamn German shepherd every night.

When she finally broke down and called Lanny a third
time, it was almost beseechingly.

"Look, I've got to talk to you, I've got to get this thing settled. Can we meet somewhere?"

Lanny agreed to meet her at the Where Else Lounge. As
Patricia was getting dressed to go there, she was determined
to make Lanny understand the seriousness of the time element involved in this situation. She had to make him see that
each day was torment and torture for her and the man she
loved.

Somehow, she had to make Lanny Mitchell act.

When Patricia walked into the Where Else Lounge, she
was surprised to see Roman Sobczynski with Lanny. But
she played it cool.

"Hi, guys. How's it going?"

Lanny greeted her in the same way, affably, but Roman
merely nodded and kept his expression inscrutable. This was
the first time he and Patricia had been together since the night
she was supposed to be his date and had refused to have sex
with him. Had even called him a jack-off. He in turn had let
the air out of her tires, ostensibly to keep her from running
out on the party, but probably also with some degree of mal-
ice, of spite, to repay her for the ultimate insult to the male
ego: the denial of sex.

Patricia knew she was on shaky ground with Roman
Sobczynski. She had refused to fuck him and called him a
disparaging name—*after* Lanny had emphasized how
"heavy" Roman was, how Roman was in a position to do

"favors" for her. She decided now to take a contrite approach, and began with Lanny.

"Look, I'm sorry I've been bugging you with all the calls. It's just that I'm up against it, you know, time wise. My boyfriend Frank is going off his rocker thinking my father is going to get to him first. I really do need something done as soon as possible."

Lanny said nothing, merely looked across the table at Roman. Patricia followed his gaze and found that Roman was staring intently at her with his fishy lips pursed. Patricia got the message loud and clear. Roman was the one she was going to have to talk to. Son of a bitch.

"I guess Lanny has told you what I want done." She addressed Roman directly.

"Yeah," Roman said quietly. "You want your parents hit."

Patricia waited for Roman to pick up the conversation from there, but he just sat drumming his stubby fingers on the tabletop. Occasionally he would glance over at Lanny as if they were silently communicating around her. It was a little unnerving, which was probably what the two schemers had in mind.

"Let's talk about it over dinner," Roman finally said.

They went to the Ala Moana Restaurant, two blocks away. The sign outside said CANTONESE-AMERICAN-POLYNESIAN in Oriental-type lettering with two palm trees on each side. It was like something out of a B movie. Inside it was not much better: dusty fishing nets and fake coconuts; ersatz South Pacific à la Chicago suburban.

After they sat down at a secluded table and ordered dinner, Patricia brought up the subject of the hit again. "Is it going to be done or isn't it?"

"It can definitely be done," Roman allowed.

It was not until after dinner that Roman finally deigned to discuss the matter at length.

"Patty," he said quietly, "I'm going to have to give you a few facts of life. First of all, we haven't seen any money upfront from you for this contract."

Patricia told him that she didn't have any money, but again reiterated, as she had told Lanny Mitchell, that when it was over she would have plenty. Michael and she were the only heirs. She knew her father had about fifty thousand dollars in the bank, and about a hundred thousand in life insurance. She would be able to pay whatever they wanted when it was over.

Roman seemed to ponder that possibility. He glanced at Lanny a few times, then said that he supposed the front money could wait. After the contract had been carried out, he said, they could set up a dummy corporation and Patricia could pay their money into that, as if she were investing. Patricia said that would be fine, however they wanted to do it.

But Roman was still hesitant. So was Lanny. Roman toyed with a book of matches while Lanny stirred an after-dinner drink. They glanced at each other, at her, at each other again. Patricia had no idea what was coming next.

"It's not good business to go into a deal like this without something up-front," Roman said at last.

"Some token of good faith," Lanny added.

Patricia shook her head. She had already told them that she didn't have any money, and that she couldn't get any. What did they expect from her?

"You could put your ass on the table," Roman suggested quietly.

The eyes of both men were riveted on her, Lanny from the side next to her, Roman from across the table. Patricia sat back and nodded in slow understanding. So that was it. The old story. If a woman can't pay with money, she was expected to pay with sex. And men always seemed to know just when to make the proposition; always seemed to sense when a woman had reached the end of her string, when she was backed into a corner, when desperation had set in. Then it was usually, "Well, look, maybe we can work something out." Subtle, in a way, but with a meaning that was always obvious.

With these two, there wasn't even any subtlety. *You could put your ass on the table.*

You're grown up now, Patty Ann, she told herself. This is the adult world.

"Okay," she said after a long silence, "if that's what it takes, my ass is on the table."

Patricia was to meet them later that night at a small house in Glendale Heights, one of the suburbs south of Elk Grove Village. The house belonged to Ron Tross, a co-worker of Lanny's at the car dealership. Lanny told Roman that Tross frequently loaned the place to other car salesmen for sex.

When they left the Ala Moana Restaurant that evening, Lanny had boosted Patricia's spirits a little by asking her to bring photographs of everyone who lived in the Brantwood house. The request was, to her, as good as if he had said, "It's all set now, I'm really going to make it happen."

But then she realized what she had gotten herself into this time. Going to a strange house to have sex with two guys she hardly knew—one of them already pissed at her for refusing him sex the first time. *You are so fucking stupid, Patty Ann*, she silently chastised herself, even using her "old" name, which she now detested. *You could walk into that goddamned house and never be seen again.* This could even have been a setup for a gang bang, with every scuzzy used-car salesman in the greater Chicago suburbs lined up to get a piece of her. Maybe, she thought, she should call Frank and have him bring his camera.

But she knew no one was forcing her to do this. It had been her own idea, her own solution to a problem she and Frank could not handle.

When she got to the Ron Tross house, Roman and Lanny were already there—alone, thankfully. Patricia sat down in the living room with them, and for some reason felt compelled to try to defend why she was there.

"I want you guys to understand that I'm doing this for my man, Frank. I love this guy more than anything in the world, and there's nothing I wouldn't do for him."

Roman and Lanny assured her that they not only understood but respected her for it as well.

Patricia gave Lanny the photographs she had brought: one of her father, one of her mother, and one of Michael holding the family dog. "Now," she said, as Lanny looked at the pictures, "you have everything you need to kill my parents, right?"

"Yeah, right," Lanny replied casually.

Patricia asked how soon it could be done; Roman replied emphatically not before the first of the year. Patricia's heart sank. It wasn't even Thanksgiving yet. She dreaded having to go through the holidays with this thing hanging over them all. And she couldn't be sure how long it would be before her father acted. She was afraid she could not put up with the tension and pressure for another six weeks or longer.

"No way you could, like, do it before Thanksgiving, as a kind of holiday present for me?" she asked, trying to be coquettish.

Roman shook his head. There was no way. No way at all.

"Ready to get down to business?" he finally asked Patricia.

Patricia and Roman went into the bedroom and undressed. With his clothes on, Roman looked big, formidable; with them off, he looked soft and flabby. He had been drinking too much and had trouble maintaining an erection; Patricia had to help him get it hard enough to enter her, then she had to pump her hips like a pneumatic drill to bring him to a climax before he lost the poor thing again.

When he was finished, Roman opened the door and called to Lanny, "Hey, your turn!"

Patricia felt like a piece of meat. She got up and strode naked past him. "I need a cigarette first," she said.

In the living room, Patricia sat down, crossed her legs, and lighted one of the brown More cigarettes she had recently begun smoking. Lanny was sitting opposite her, looking at the picture of her mother.

"Your mother is very attractive," he said.

Patricia could feel her eyelids narrow and had to force herself not to look at Lanny with a cold stare. "You wouldn't like her, Lanny," she managed to say. "A guy as good in bed as you are would probably think she was a dead fuck."

"Think I'm pretty good in bed, huh?" Lanny asked.

"Better than some guys I know," Patricia said, rolling her eyes toward the bedroom where Roman still was.

"Okay, baby, come on." Lanny rose from the chair. "I don't want you to go home unsatisfied."

Patricia put out her cigarette and followed him. Thank God, she thought mindlessly, her man Frank wasn't like these two animals.

When Patricia left the Tross house that first time, Roman said, "Lanny, you drive Patty's car and follow us. I want her to ride with me."

On the ride to the Elk Grove Village Bowl parking lot, where Patricia was to be dropped off, Roman asked a lot of questions about why she wanted her parents killed. From the tone of the questions, it seemed obvious to Patricia that Lanny had already gone over the entire matter with him. She wondered if Roman was testing her in some way, or even trying to corroborate what Lanny had told him. Since she had started out being scrupulously honest with Lanny, vowing to be straight with him all the way, she maintained the same position with Roman.

Patricia told him her story, just as she had Lanyon Mitchell, without embellishment, but with the full measure of fear included. She wanted Roman *and* Lanny to understand the urgency involved in this matter. And although Roman had stated without equivocation that the hit would not be carried out until after the first of the year, Patricia still harbored hopes of getting it done sooner. It was the last thing she brought up before leaving his car that night.

"Do you think there's *any* possibility of getting this done sooner than after the first of the year?"

It was a definite entreaty; Patricia was close to begging. Roman said he'd see what he could do, and told her to give Lanny a call in a few days. It was only a scrap, but it was better than nothing. If she had to go through all the holidays—Thanksgiving, Christmas, New Year's Eve—with Frank in his present state of mind, Patricia was certain she would lose her own mind completely.

She decided to wait just five days and then call Lanny. Maybe if she kept on these two, they'd get so sick of putting up with her that they'd go ahead and get the job done just to get her off their backs.

Arranging murder, she now decided, was not nearly as easy as it had seemed in the beginning.

37

December 1975

Patricia waited the five days she had promised herself to wait, then called Lanny.

"Hi. What's happening?"

"Not too much," Lanny replied. "What's happening with you?"

Patricia asked him to meet her after work; she said she had an idea to tell him about. Lanny agreed. Patricia parked at the usual spot and Lanny showed up shortly after six and got in the car with her. Patricia dredged up as much charm as she could.

"I thought we could go over and take a look at the house. Just drive by, you know, so you'd be sure which house it was."

Lanny looked at her like she was retarded. "We haven't had enough up-front yet, Patty."

Patricia sighed almost inaudibly. It was clear what he meant. More sex.

"Come on," Lanny suggested, "let's go meet Roman at the Where Else."

Patricia followed behind Lanny as they drove down Higgins Road. Lanny must have called Roman after she called Lanny, Patricia guessed. She wondered how long she would have to put out before they would feel they'd had enough up-front. As she parked at the Where Else, she was shaking her head. *You just go deeper and deeper, don't you? Everything you do, or try to do, turns to shit.*

In the lounge, Roman was already a couple of drinks ahead of them; they sat down and had a couple more with him. After a while, when Roman had enough to drink, he decided it was time to go.

"Come on, Lanny, let's get out of here. You ready, Patty?"

"Sure." Patricia mustered a smile.

Had it not been for her constant apprehension, Patricia would have to have felt totally ludicrous. *Come on, guys, let's go somewhere so I can make you feel like great big macho*

*men, and then maybe you'll get on with killing Dad and Mom
for me, after which I can live happily ever after with Frank—
and men he picks up in bars—and other women—and the
goddamned German shepherd . . .*

For the first time, Patricia seriously felt she might be going
crazy.

Early in December, Patricia finally got Lanny Mitchell
to agree to case, or at least reconnoiter, the house at 55 Brantwood.

"I still have a key to the house," she told him. "My parents
will be bowling and my brother goes over to a friend's house.
I can take you inside and you can look the whole place over."

Lanny had decided to do it and get it out of the way. He
did not particularly like the idea, but Roman had said to
string Patricia along so they could keep getting free pussy;
Lanny, if he wanted to continue cultivating Roman's friendship, had no option but to comply. He had thought it all out
ahead of time anyway, and figured he was on pretty safe
ground. It wasn't as if he was breaking into the place; Patty
had a key and he was going in at her invitation.

Patricia picked him up at the Elk Grove Village Bowl lot
and they drove south on Arlington Heights Road. Lanny noticed something white between the two front seats. Pulling it
out, he found that it was a twelve-inch hunting knife with a
pearl handle.

"What the hell is this?" he asked.

"For protection against my father," she told him. "Frank
carries the derringer in his pocket. We keep the knife in the
car."

Lanny, ever the performer where there was a female to impress, pulled a gun from a shoulder holster he was wearing.
Dropping open the cylinder, he showed Patricia the gleaming
bullets it held.

"Wouldn't this be better protection, Patty?"

"Yeah," she said, glancing wide-eyed at the weapon. "Can
you get me one?"

"I'll try," Lanny said, snapping the cylinder back in place
and reholstering the gun.

When they drove past JFK Boulevard, Patricia pointed to

the big Walgreen's and said, "That's where Frank works, my man."

At the house, Patricia parked on the street. Lanny looked around nervously. All of a sudden this didn't seem like such a great idea. String her along, Roman had said, but where the fuck was he?

Patricia went up to the front door. She was digging in her purse for the now little-used door key, when to her surprise the door opened and her mother was standing there.

"Mom—?" Patricia did not know what to say.

Mary Columbo stuck her head out and looked past her daughter at the parked car. Lanny saw the woman looking at him and quickly turned his face away.

Patricia disappeared inside the house and Lanny was left sitting outside. She had even taken the goddamn car keys with her, or he would probably have started the car and gotten the hell out of there right then. The woman in the house—Patricia's mother, probably—must have gotten a good look at him. He began to fret.

By the time Patricia came back to the car, Lanny was definitely on edge. "What the fuck took you so long in there?" he demanded.

Patricia was not in the jolliest of moods herself; she had just been in another verbal brawl with Mary. "I had a fight with my fucking mother," she snapped. Starting the engine, she peeled rubber away from the house.

"You said nobody was going to be home!" Lanny accused.

"Hey, I didn't think there would be!" Patricia lashed back. "I was hoping we could hide inside and get them when they came home!"

"What?" Lanny stared at her in disbelief. "You meant for me to kill them tonight?"

"Yes!"

"And you wanted to be there?" There was repugnance in his tone. As if Lanny Mitchell had finally found something that disgusted him.

"Yes, I did!" Patricia stormed. "I wanted to see them get what they deserve for all the fucking grief they've caused me! I wanted to put an end to all this shit!"

In moments they were again at the busy intersection where

Walgreen's was located. Lanny recalled Patricia's words of a little while earlier: *That's where Frank works, my man.*

Lanny jerked the gun from his shoulder holster again. "You ever try to trick me like that again, you little cunt, and you can kiss your boyfriend Frank good-bye, understand me?"

His threat was like a bolt of lightning striking her. All the while she had been associating with Lanny and Roman, since the very first night at the Edgebrook Motel with Nancy, Patricia had realized the possibility existed that she could be in jeopardy of some kind. She accepted that, telling herself that, like everything else, it was part of the price she had to pay for all the trouble she was in. She did not dwell on the uncertain menace; risk to herself had never bothered her. But now, for the first time, there had materialized a threat to Frank.

It had never occurred to Patricia that what she was doing might create a hazard for Frank. She had been careful to keep Frank out of her negotiations with Lanny and Roman—but she had not been discerning enough to conceal who he was or where he worked. Because she naively perceived Lanny and Roman as people who were going to help her, people on her side, it never crossed her mind that whatever she told them might at a later time be used by them *against* her in some way. The realization of how gullible she had been sent a chill along her spine.

"Lanny, please don't ever hurt Frank," she said now in a voice that was almost prayerful. "He's all I've got to live for, all I care about. Without him I don't have anyone. Please don't hurt him."

"Just don't ever try to trick me into anything again," Lanny warned her.

I've got to be more careful next time, Patricia thought.

It was just before Christmas when Patricia telephoned Lanny at the car dealership again. There was an urgency in her voice.

"Look, this is an emergency. I've got to see you right away. Something serious has come up."

What the fuck is it now? Lanny must have wondered irritably. He had to have felt that this whole goddamned scam was getting out of hand. If it was still a scam, that is. He per-

sonally wanted to drop the whole show; it was simply too
much trouble for a little sex, which was all they were getting.
But Roman for some reason would not let go. It was hard for
Lanny to believe that Roman was still stringing Patty along
just to get fucked a few times. Lanny had to have begun to
wonder by now whether Roman was thinking *beyond* their
simple deception.

Whatever the exigencies, Lanny had no alternative at the
moment but to continue playing the game with Patty Columbo, as Roman had instructed. After her urgent call, he met
her on the usual parking lot when he got off work; it was
their ninth meeting. Patricia appeared as nervous in person as
she had sounded on the telephone. In the car with her, Lanny
had to help her light a cigarette, her hands were trembling so.

"What the hell's wrong?" he asked, getting a little nervous
himself.

"I got a call from my godfather last night," she said in a
shaky voice. "He says unless we get my father first, Frank is
dead." It was a story she made up, hoping to make Lanny act.

"Your godfather?" Lanny said, frowning. "Who's your
godfather?"

Patricia said his name was Phil Capone and he was in the
restaurant-supply business. Supposedly he knew a lot of mob
guys who had interests in restaurants and clubs that he serviced. A mob guy had heard about the contract on Frank
DeLuca and told him.

"And he told you about it?" Lanny said. This was incredible to him.

"Yes." Patricia explained that her godfather, whom she
called "Uncle Phil," and her father had been on the outs for
a long time. They no longer even spoke. But her Uncle Phil,
she said, had always loved her like she was his own daughter.
He wanted her to be happy.

"Why doesn't your godfather do something to help you?"
Lanny asked. "If he knows so many mob guys, couldn't he
stop the contract?"

Patricia shook her head. Uncle Phil did not know them except as customers. He was strictly straight, not involved with
them or anything. And he was too honest to get involved,
beyond warning her for her own safety.

"We've got to do it first," Patricia said evenly. Her nervousness seemed to have been replaced by grim determination.

"I'll see what I can arrange," Lanny replied vaguely.

"Can't you just go ahead and do it?" she pressed.

"I can't do anything without approval from Roman," he reminded her.

"You've got to talk to him, then," Patricia insisted. "It's *got* to be done before Christmas." So desperate had she become now that she might have been ordering bread at the bakery. A loaf of white, sliced. Two murders in time for the holidays, please. "It'll be a present from me to them," she added.

Lanny must have felt that her words were as cold as the December wind outside the car.

"I'll talk to Roman and start things on the way," Lanny promised.

Lanny got out of the car without another word. As they parted, neither wished the other a merry Christmas.

The holiday season that year was the worst of Patricia's life.

Despite her urgent plea to Lanny Mitchell, despite her elaborately concocted story that her godfather had warned her of a contract on the life of her lover, and despite Lanny's promise to "talk to Roman and start things on the way," nothing at all happened.

Roman Sobczynski spent a happy holiday season with his wife and three children in their Glenbrook Drive home in suburban Mount Prospect, where all of them enjoyed the delights of a gift-laden Christmas tree and the joyful fellowship and love of friends and family.

Two days after Christmas, Lanny Mitchell got married to a lovely young woman who believed her groom to be an honest, upright automobile salesman with aspirations and, indeed, very good prospects of a solid, respectable job in Cook County government. The newlyweds prepared to move into a new home they had made arrangements to purchase in the upwardly mobile suburban community of Lake Villa.

Frank, Mary, and Michael Columbo spent Christmas Eve at the home of Frank's sister Gloria in Elk Grove Village, and on Christmas Day visited Mary's sister Carolyn in Cary, Illinois. They spent what turned out to be for them a terribly melancholy Christmas holiday. It was the first Christmas since Patricia was born that she had not at least seen her family. The previous year she had been living with the DeLucas, but she had come over to the Brantwood house to visit and exchange gifts. This year, she made no appearance at all.

It was difficult to gauge who was hurt most by her absence, Frank or Michael. The father was brooding about more than just her nonappearance, of course; *where* she was, and who she was with, played far greater roles in his despair. Michael moped around because he did *not* know where his sister was. He knew that the guy who ran Walgreen's, DeLuca, had something to do with her not being with them anymore, but he couldn't have known how all the pieces of the emotional puzzle fit. ·

The DeLuca family endured an equally dismal holiday. For the four older DeLuca children, the *fact* that their father was not with them had to have been less disturbing than the *reason* for his absence: he had left them to go live with Patty Columbo. He obviously loved Patty Columbo more than he loved them, individually as well as collectively, and more than he loved their mother, their baby sister, their home, and being part of their family. He still visited and had dinner with them on Wednesdays and Sundays, but Christmas that year was on Thursday, and it was strange for the children who still believed in Santa Claus to go to sleep knowing that tonight was the wondrous night when Santa came—but that Daddy would not be there with them when they woke up.

For them, it would be the first of many tarnished holidays.

Frank and Patty. Together at last, alone at last, with all the privacy they could want at last, free to romp in their love and wallow in their lust. But elysian fields it wasn't, and even when they squinted they couldn't see nirvana.

What had gone wrong? they wondered. How had their lives become such a hell?

The two lovers strung a few colored lights around their little apartment, and hung tinsel here and there, but for the most part they depended for their holiday spirit on cold duck, Canadian Club, Valium, and whatever else Frank was able to misappropriate from the pharmacy by shortchanging a pill

here, a pill there, in the prescriptions he filled. Patricia had no
idea what he brought home. Frank used terms like *hypnotic,
psychotropic, anticholinergic, parasympathetic*; who knew
what the hell they meant? She took what he gave her and
most of the time it made her feel better—or at least made her
feel *less*.

When Patricia got drunk enough, and high enough, she
went around the apartment singing "Love Will Keep Us Together," a swingy, catchy tune that was high on the charts for
a good part of the year. It had been recorded as a single by
a duo billing itself as the Captain and Tennille. Patricia liked
the song; it could have been written for her and Frank. Love
had to be strong, it said. Love would keep us together.

"Will it, Frank?" she asked. "Will love keep us together,
baby?"

"How the fuck should I know?" DeLuca replied. He
poured himself another slug of whiskey. It was the one thing
that *never* let him down. "You know what I'd like to do?" he
said.

"I couldn't even guess, baby." *You want me to fuck a don-
key, right?*

"I'd like to buy a sailboat. One of those big oceangoing
jobs that you can do some serious sailing on. But not so big
that a guy and a couple of women couldn't handle it."

Patricia smiled knowingly. Yeah, right. A guy and a *couple*
of women.

Either Frank did not realize what he said, or he didn't give
a damn. "Yeah, I'd like to just *live* on it, you know. Go wherever the warm waters are and sail from place to place, but
spend most of the time out on the water in peace and solitude. Jesus, I wish I had the money to do that!"

"I wish you did too, Frank." Patricia was sincere. She
loved him so much that she wished he could have whatever
he wanted that would make him happy. She remembered a
childhood game: if you had one wish, what would you wish
for? The answer was, you'd wish for *two* wishes, and with
one of them you'd always wish for two more. That way, you
would never run out of wishes. If Patricia had all the wishes
in the world, she would have given them to Frank.

Somehow they managed to get through the cheerless, dismal holidays, with the help of liquor, pills, and a little half-

hearted sexual activity. Patricia kept telling herself that 1976 would be better. It could not, she reasoned, be any worse.

As usual, she was wrong.

In January, she missed her period for the first time.

C.H.
August 1991

Fifteen years after the murders, in a small city as far away from Chicago as you can get without wading into an ocean, a place where it never snows in the winter, I met Nancy Glenn on a street corner and we walked two blocks to a little seafood restaurant she knew about.

"How does Patty look?" she asked curiously when we were seated at a postage-stamp table next to the rear wall.

"She looks fine," I said, "considering how long she's been locked up."

"What do you mean?"

"Prison," I explained, "is not the best place in the world to mature gracefully. Your diet is a choice of starchy institutional meals or junk food from the canteen. You don't get enough exercise or fresh air. You smoke too much; Patricia smokes a couple packs a day. Your sex life is covert, homosexual, or both. There's a constant underlying threat of physical violence that can be brought on by the most trivial matter: an accidental bump, eye contact a second too long, forgetting to repay a can of Pepsi. And worst of all, there's the certainty of knowing that's where you'll be for years and years to come—maybe until you die. Taking all that into consideration, Patricia looks pretty good."

"Does she know you're talking to me?" Nancy asked.

"She knows I was trying to find you. I'll tell her about our meeting when I speak to her again."

"You promised not to use my real name," she reminded me of our initial telephone conversation.

"Your real name won't be used," I assured her.

"Did Patty know you were going to promise me that?"

"Yes."

"How did she feel about it?"

"When I told her I was going to offer to conceal your identity in exchange for an interview, she said she thought I ought to do it even if you wouldn't agree to talk to me. She said if you had your life together, she saw no reason for me to possibly upset it by using your real name in the book. She said what she had done had hurt enough people over the years and she hoped no one else would ever again be hurt by it."

"I'm surprised she feels like that," Nancy said. "After all, I'm basically the one who turned her in. My brother and I got the reward money from Western Auto. I thought Patty would hate me."

"It's my impression," I told her, "that Patricia Columbo doesn't hate anyone anymore—except perhaps herself from time to time."

"Well, I hate her," Nancy said. "Not particularly for what she did to her parents, but for what she did to poor little Michael." She shook her head sorrowfully. "He was such a great kid. I think I'll always hate Patty for Michael."

There was a decided absence of conviction in Nancy Glenn's voice. I got the feeling that she might be trying to hate Patricia, or trying to convince me that she did; perhaps even trying to convince herself.

Nancy was now going on thirty-six, half a year older than Patricia, who had recently turned thirty-five. She was shorter than Patricia, with her hair stylishly coiffed, and wearing a suit, blouse, and tasteful necklace and earrings. Married, she had a nine-year-old daughter. She would tell me later that she and her husband very much wanted another child, but they were small-business owners, both of them working in their store, and the annual net profits simply did not provide enough income for them to consider a larger family just then.

We talked the entire afternoon at that little table, about things both incidental and important. Nancy recalled the Patty Columbo she had once been best friends with—before Frank DeLuca; recalled the Columbo family, especially Michael; how Patty changed after going to work at Walgreen's, how nothing seemed to matter to her any longer except the man she had fallen in love with; how Nancy had met Lanny Mitchell and found herself, if not as smitten as Patty was, certainly attracted to the older, seemingly more worldly, pol-

*ished car salesman-*cum-*suspended-policeman, who carried a gun and associated with "heavy" people.*

"I don't actually remember telling Lanny about Patty's problems with her father, how he beat up DeLuca on the parking lot and all," Nancy thought back, "but I don't see how he could have known it if I hadn't told him. We'd been seeing each other pretty regularly for about six weeks when I called Patty to arrange the date with us and Lanny's friend Roman. I let Lanny talk to Patty. He said later that Patty asked him for a hundred bucks to go out with his friend—in other words, to have sex with the guy—and that he agreed to pay her."

"Did you believe him?" I asked.

"I wasn't sure," Nancy admitted.

I nodded—because I wasn't either. Years later, Patricia would deny that there was any mention at all of money; she was in it strictly for favors to be gained. And Lanny Mitchell would admit under oath that he never actually gave her any money, not even after having sex with her that night.

"Roman apparently believed that Lanny had given Patty money," I suggested.

"Yeah," Nancy agreed. "I think Lanny must have told Roman that he paid Patty something, because one of the reasons Roman got so hot when Patty tried to ditch them that night was because he thought she was paid for."

"So Patricia did try to get you and her away from Lanny and Roman that night?"

"Oh, yeah. She got us all the way to my house before they caught up with us."

"Did they force you to go to the motel with them?"

"They didn't force me," Nancy replied candidly. "I wanted to go, to be with Lanny. But Patty, I don't know; she was in the other car, so I'm not sure. I don't think she wanted to go; she was in a hurry to pick up DeLuca at the store."

Nancy had not seen Patricia again after that night, and had not seen Lanny Mitchell for several months, until early in 1976, after Lanny had gotten married. Nancy did not know Lanny and Roman were continuing to see Patricia until about a month before the murders, when Lanny called and asked her out to dinner. He had taken her into Chicago and they had met Roman. It was then that Lanny and Roman told her *that Patricia was trying to hire them to kill her parents. Nancy did not know if they were serious or not; and having known Patricia for so long, known her well, did not even know if Patricia was serious. It had all sounded so farfetched.*

But on that ghastly Friday night a month or so later, farfetched had suddenly become appalling reality. Word of the murders had raced through the neighborhood; Nancy had hurried to the Columbo home like scores of others, in disbelief, until she had seen the police cars, the officers, television cameras, the "POLICE LINE—DO NOT CROSS" yellow tape being strung all around the house. Stunned, Nancy Glenn had turned away and started back home, a single racking thought agonizing her.

Patty did it.

"*It was the first thing that came to my mind,*" *she said.* "*I never doubted it for a minute.*"

"*Were you so certain because of what Lanny and Roman had recently told you,*" *I asked,* "*or because of your own conversations with Patricia?*"

"*What conversations with Patricia?*"

I felt my brow pull into a frown. "*The search warrant served on Patricia and DeLuca at the apartment on the day Patricia was arrested was issued on a complaint that stated that you'd had conversations—plural—in which Patricia had repeatedly—*repeatedly—*told you that she wanted to have her parents killed.*"

Nancy Glenn shook her head. "*That's not true. Patty only said something like that to me* one *time. I remember it perfectly; we were in my bedroom at home and she was very upset with her parents about something, and she said, 'I'd like to get somebody to kill them, then it would be just Michael and me, and I could raise Michael myself.' That was the only time Patty ever mentioned the murder of her parents to me.*"

"*That couldn't have been around the time of the murders, then,*" *I said,* "*because you hadn't seen her since the night at the motel, which was about six months earlier.*"

"*Oh, no, it was* long *before that; back when we were best friends. Otherwise she wouldn't have been in my bedroom. It was probably even before she met DeLuca.*"

There had, I knew from reading the trial transcript, been a pretrial hearing at which Judge Pincham had considered a

*motion to disallow any evidence seized from apartment 911
under the authority of the search warrant. That evidence included the pornographic photographs of Patricia taken by
DeLuca. The judge eventually allowed the evidence—and the
jury got to see the photos. To assume that those photos did
anything but intensify the jury's enmity toward Patricia would
be nonsense.*

*Nancy Glenn's story fifteen years later opened up an in-
triguing question: Was the search warrant complaint still
valid in spite of a possible error regarding her original statement? If not, the inflammatory photographs should have been
kept from the jury; they were not pertinent to the murder
charge anyway.*

*It was a moot point. Even Patricia said she should have
been convicted.*

*It's always neater, of course, if the evidence relates to the
crime and not merely the accused.*

38
January 1976

January 1976 was divided into two distinct parts for Patricia.
The separation point was the fifteenth, the day her period was
due.

In the early part of the month, Patricia was gearing herself
up for a confrontation with Lanny Mitchell and Roman
Sobczynski. The two men, she had finally begun to suspect,
were not the hardasses she had originally thought. So far all
she had netted in her relationship with them was a lot of
tough talk. She was determined to see if that was all there
was going to be.

Shortly after New Year's, she called Lanny. "Hi. What's
happening?"

"Hello, Patty," he said cordially. "Not much. How's everything with you?" He might have been talking to a customer.
How's the car running, Mrs. Jones? His tone, his whole attitude, offended her.

Everything, she told him, was the same with her. She was
still in the same mess she had been in the last time they

talked, the mess he and Roman were supposed to help her out of.

After some preliminary haggling, Lanny finally agreed to get in touch with Roman and arrange for the two of them to meet Patricia for dinner at the Ala Moana.

When Patricia arrived, she was as finely tuned as a boxer on the last day of training camp, a coil, ready to spring. As soon as their drinks had been served, she threw down the gauntlet.

"I want to find out what's coming off here," she said firmly. "I've been putting out sex for you guys and neither one of you does anything in return for me. What's the deal?"

Smooth-talking Lanny jumped right in; double-talk and charm were his terrain. Once again he began explaining how matters like this took time, how certain arrangements had to be made—

Patricia didn't even let him finish. "You're full of shit, Lanny," she said.

Lanny looked at her incredulously; she couldn't have surprised him more if she'd thrown her drink in his face.

"Look, you started this whole thing by telling me you'd do it," Patricia reminded him. "But all I've got from you since then is bullshit!"

Trembling with anger, Patricia took a cigarette from her pack. Across the table, Lanny's expression was stricken; no doubt he did not get talked to like that very often.

"I don't think you ever *intended* to do it, Lanny," Patricia accused. "I don't think you've got the balls to do it. You're chicken. You've got no balls, Lanny—"

Patricia had just put the cigarette between her lips to light it when she saw Lanny's hand arcing over the table toward her. She was faster than he, but not by much. As she drew her head back, she felt the displacement of air against her face, and the cigarette was slapped from her lips and went flying away.

"You fucking little bitch—" Half rising, he was preparing for a second swing when Roman grabbed his arm and held it.

Roman glanced around. A couple of people had turned to look from other tables, but they quickly went back to their own business. Roman rose and pulled Lanny to his feet.

"Go over to the bar and have a drink," he told the little car salesman. Red-faced, Lanny rose and walked away.

When they were alone, Roman chastised Patricia for the way she had talked to Lanny. But they were all, he pacified, a little tense over the plans they were making. He told Patricia to stay at the table and calm down, while he went over to the bar and cooled off Lanny.

The men returned to the table a few minutes later. Lanny and Patricia looked at each other uneasily, almost embarrassed instead of angry about what had occurred.

"Okay, no more fighting in the ranks," said Roman the peacemaker. "We're all in this thing together, so let's try to be friends." He leaned toward Patricia. "One of the problems we have, Patty, is that there are three people in the house and you only want two of them killed. That's a condition that worries us."

"You're talking about my brother," Patricia said. Her eyes flicked from one to the other. This apparently was going to be their out, the way they would renege on the agreement, the way they would leave Patricia alone in a battle zone between a crazy dago father and a boyfriend who was practically climbing the walls in fear. Patricia would not have it. This thing had gone too far to end like that. "Okay," she said evenly, "do my brother too."

"Include your brother in the hit?" Roman asked, surprised.

"If that's all that's holding it up, yeah."

"You know what you're saying?" Lanny asked in disbelief.

Patricia knew she had to convince them. "Look, it's probably the best way, anyhow. I mean, when he got older he might put two and two together and come after me, right?"

"So you want a contract for three now instead of two?" Roman said.

"Right."

"We're talking about ten thousand per, you know," Lanny clarified.

"Right."

Everyone fell silent. Patricia was determined not to let them off the hook. When the thing was ready to go down, she would see that Michael was not around. In the meantime, Lanny and Roman would have no further excuse to keep putting it off.

The two men finally agreed at dinner that night that including Michael would make the whole situation a lot easier.

Everything was on again.

That was early in January.

Then Patricia missed her period the first time.

It blew her mind. She was so regular that farmers could have planned crops around her menstrual cycle. When classmates at school had complained of being "late," Patricia had thought for a long time that they meant for class; she assumed everyone was as precise and routine as she was.

"My period didn't start today," she told DeLuca.

"It'll probably start tomorrow," he replied with disinterest.

That was Thursday. It didn't start on Friday either. Or Saturday.

"Frank, are you sure those are birth control pills you gave me?" she asked. The little pills were loose in an unlabeled vial.

He was sure, he replied testily. He *was* a pharmacist. Was she sure she'd been taking them as he instructed?

To be certain, Patricia went into the bathroom and counted the remaining pills. There were exactly enough left from her two-month supply for the next cycle. She immediately had an anxiety attack. DeLuca tried to calm her down.

"Look, it doesn't necessarily mean you're pregnant, okay? It could be a lot of things: stress, hormone changes, a side effect to other pills you took recently. There's nothing to be worried about unless you're late by at least two weeks."

Patricia got control of herself—but she continued to worry.

While Patricia was sweating out the two weeks DeLuca had set as a cooling-off interval, Roman called her to meet him for lunch. It was the first time he had ever called; the first time a meeting had not been arranged by Lanny. It made Patricia feel that something was up.

Roman picked her up at the bowling alley parking lot and they drove into Chicago to the Coach and Six, a restaurant done in dark paneling to give it an Old English atmosphere.

"We're meeting a friend of mine for lunch," Roman said as they walked in.

The friend was Nick Carbucci. He was a short, nice-looking man, well dressed, softspoken; a Lanny Mitchell with a little class. Patricia was certain he was a hit man.

The lunch, however, turned out to be disconcerting. Patricia had convinced herself that this was a meeting to make final plans for the hit, and she kept waiting for some discussion in that regard to begin. But, distressingly, the subject of the contract never came up.

After lunch, Roman and Nick left the table for a brief private discussion at the bar, then Roman returned to the table alone.

"Come on, we're going for a little party," he said.

What the hell was happening here? she wondered. Was she supposed to put out to this guy Nick now? These guys never *told* her anything—and she didn't feel she could ask without somehow antagonizing them, making herself look more like a nag than she already did, and jeopardizing whatever tenuous status she had with them.

Patricia left the restaurant with Roman and he drove out to Wheeling, the last Chicago suburb still inside Cook County. While Patricia waited in the car, Roman registered at the Flamingo Motel. She kept looking around, waiting for this Nick Carbucci to show, but as it turned out he never did. She ended up spending a couple of hours in the sack with Roman. It was her third time with him; she was getting used to the fact that after he had a couple of drinks, as he had at lunch, it was difficult for him to perform. She had to use every trick she knew that afternoon or they would have been there until breakfast.

When Roman dropped her off back at the bowling alley parking lot, there had still been no mention at all of the hit.

"I'll call you in a few days," was all Roman said.

A week later, Roman called the second time. He was at the Where Else having a drink with a friend and wanted her to join them. She said she couldn't; she had no car. Roman said he'd come by and get her. He picked her up in a big, expensive Cadillac and drove back to the Where Else Lounge. There he introduced her to a man named Jim Leary. Maybe, Patricia thought, *this* will be the guy. Perhaps *now* this thing would take off and fly.

They had a couple of drinks, then drove to the Navarone

Restaurant to eat. Afterward, they went to Spinnaker's Lounge and drank some more. Before long, Roman was too looped to unzip his trousers.

Patricia helped Jim Leary get him into the backseat of the Cadillac, which was Leary's car, and then Leary drove her home.

It was Lanny who called her next, toward the end of January.

"Let's meet for lunch," he said.

DeLuca was at home. Patricia did not want to turn Lanny down; she felt she had to hang right in with this thing if she wanted to get it done. At the same time, she had to have an explanation for DeLuca.

After agreeing to meet Lanny, she hung up and said to DeLuca, "That was my godfather, honey. He wants me to come have lunch with him."

"I'll come with you," DeLuca said. "Maybe I can get him to help square this mess with your old man."

"Frank, my godfather is already trying to help us. I didn't tell you before because I didn't want you to have anything else to worry about. But my godfather has checked into it and found out that Dad does have a contract on you—"

DeLuca turned white. His worst fear was now confirmed.

"Frank, my godfather is going to take care of it," Patricia assured him. "He's not going to let anything happen to you. If necessary, he'll have Dad taken care of first. That's why he wants to talk to me today: to get the whole story."

DeLuca didn't understand. He thought Patricia's godfather and her father were close friends. They had been, Patricia explained, but they had a falling-out. She was like a daughter to her godfather, however, and he was going to help them.

"Shouldn't I meet him then?" DeLuca asked, confused.

No, Patricia told him emphatically. He was a stranger right now; her godfather wouldn't discuss the matter in front of him. Patricia could see that DeLuca was on the verge of not believing any of it.

"Look," she promised, "I'll have him call you after he and I talk, all right? I don't think he'd mind talking to you on the phone. Will you wait here and talk to him on the phone?"

"Yeah, okay, I guess," DeLuca reluctantly agreed. "Your godfather's name is Phil Capone, right?"

"Yeah, but he uses the name Roman," Patricia said quickly. "That's his street name."

Patricia met Lanny and he drove to the Navarone Restaurant. Roman and another man were already there. The man was introduced as Chuck Novak. *Now what?* Patricia wondered. Every meeting brought a new face, but nothing ever got said or done.

Everyone had a drink and then ordered lunch. As they were eating, with the conversation as usual going nowhere for Patricia, she made up her mind to put some pressure on Roman and Lanny again. She had to; she was in a bind now that she had divulged to DeLuca a modified version of what was going on. If he didn't get a call from her "godfather," as she had promised, she might as well not even go back to the apartment because he would be so wild with fear by then that there was no telling what he would do.

As soon as Roman had taken the last bite of his lunch, Patricia leaned close to him and said, "I really need to talk to you in private for a minute."

Roman gestured for Lanny to come with them, and they went out to the foyer of the restaurant. Patricia, realizing more and more the position she had put herself in, was almost trembling from shot nerves.

"Look, I've got a real problem with Frank, my man," she told them. "Now I realize you guys need time to set this thing up, like you've been telling me, and I understand that. But could you"—she directed her words to Roman now—"just talk to him on the phone for a sec and, like, reassure him that the contract my father has on him isn't going to come down before, you know, you guys do your thing? Just kind of take some of the pressure off him?"

Lanny was reluctant, but to his surprise Roman agreed at once. "Get him on the line," Roman said, guiding her toward a pay telephone on the wall.

Patricia quickly dialed the apartment. Frank answered on the first ring; she imagined he had been sitting staring at the telephone since she left.

"Hi, honey," Patricia said. "Listen, I'm here with Roman and he's going to talk to you—"

She held the receiver out to Roman, who took it and said, "Hello, Frank."

"Hello, Roman."

"Patty tells me you're a little shook up by this business."

"Yeah, I guess I am. I'm not used to this kind of thing—"

"Nobody ever gets used to it," Roman said expertly, as if he lived with hit contracts every day. "But I wanted to let you know that I've taken care of the contract that was on you. I bought it off."

"Bought it off?"

"Yeah, so you can stop worrying, for the time being anyway."

"Jesus, thanks, Roman—"

"Don't mention it. I'm going to stay on top of this matter with Patty, and if anything comes up, I'll let her know—"

"Christ, thanks, Roman."

"Okay. Here's Patty."

Patricia got back on the phone. "See, I told you everything would be taken care of, honey," she purred. "Listen, I'll be home in a little while, okay?"

"Okay, yeah."

Patricia hung up and they went back to the table where Chuck Novak waited. Patricia fully expected to have to fuck Roman and Lanny and maybe even this Chuck guy before the afternoon was over; she would have to pay in *some* way for Roman's magnanimity on the telephone.

But she was pleasantly surprised for a change. The three men started drinking after lunch and an hour later Chuck Novak pleaded some kind of business and left. Roman and Lanny continued drinking. Another hour passed and the two men got pretty well sloshed. When Patricia thought the time was right, she casually got up from the table and said, "Well, I've got to run, guys. I'll talk to you soon."

She couldn't believe how lucky she was until she was actually in a taxi on her way back to where she'd left her car.

Early in February, Roman called her around seven o'clock one evening. He was at Spinnaker's Lounge, drinking with his friend Jim Leary again.

"Jim's going over to his secretary's house for a little

party," Roman said. "I'm going too and I'd like you to join us."

DeLuca was again at home. Patricia turned her back to him and said quietly into the receiver, "It's really not convenient right now, Roman."

"I want you to join us," Roman said evenly. Clearly it was not a request.

When she hung up, DeLuca asked, "Was that your godfather?"

"Yeah. He wants to talk to me. I'm going to meet him."

"Does he want me to come too?"

"No, just me. I won't be long."

As Patricia got ready to go, she realized that DeLuca was studying her suspiciously. That would be all she needed, Frank not trusting her anymore. He'd probably get it into his head that she was trying to help her father kill *him*.

As she was about to go out the door, DeLuca said, "Have Roman give me a call again, Patrish."

As with Roman, it was not a request. *Christ!* she thought, and started sweating again.

At Spinnaker's, Patricia sat down and had a drink with Roman and Jim Leary. They were going to Jim's secretary's apartment, Roman told her. Barb Abbott was her name.

They left the lounge after only one drink together and drove to an apartment complex in Wheaton. Barb Abbott greeted them at the door of her apartment and Jim Leary introduced Patricia to her. Inside, they all sat down and Barb fixed drinks for everyone. Roman and Jim Leary seemed to know their way around the apartment enough for Patricia to assume they had been there before.

Patricia watched closely and the instant Roman took the last swallow of his drink, she said, "Roman, could I speak to you in private for a minute?"

Roman led Patricia to the bedroom and closed the door.

"Would you mind talking to Frank on the phone again?" Patricia asked. "He needs to be told again that he's all right, that he's safe."

"No problem," Roman granted.

Patricia used Barb Abbott's bedroom extension to call DeLuca. "Hi," she said when he answered, on the first ring again. "Here's Roman."

"Hello, Frank," said Roman when he got the receiver.

"Hello, Roman. Have you heard anything new?"

"As a matter of fact, I have, yeah. Our friend is shopping around for a new contract."

Patricia's mouth dropped open. What the fuck was he telling him *that* for?

"Jesus," DeLuca said to Roman. "What are we gonna do now?"

"There's only one thing we can do," Roman told him. "We have to get him before he gets you."

"Will you help me?" DeLuca asked.

"I'll work something out with Patty," Roman assured him.

"Okay." DeLuca paused a beat, then said, "Listen, junior's got to go too."

"What?" Roman frowned.

"Michael. He's got to go too, Roman. He keeps coming into my store and staring at me. I think he knows everything that's going on. He may even be in on this with the old man. So junior's definitely got to go too. Only, I don't want Patricia to know about it in advance, okay?"

"I understand," Roman said. Patty obviously had not told her boyfriend that she had already given them the go-ahead to hit the kid.

"Patrish told me she gave you some diagrams and pictures and stuff for the hit men," DeLuca said. "Is the stuff sufficient or do you need more?"

"It's fine," Roman said. "We've got everything we need."

"Okay, so it's all set then, Roman?"

Roman promised him it was all arranged.

Roman called her again the following week and asked her to meet him and Jim Leary later that day at Spinnaker's.

"I'm not in the mood to meet you anywhere," Patricia replied curtly. "You've got me in very deep shit again."

Telling DeLuca that her father was shopping for another contract on him had Frank going completely bananas, she told Roman irascibly. DeLuca was expecting some Mafia hit man to show up at the drugstore with a fucking machine gun, and complaining that all he had to protect himself with was a little derringer. Lanny, she complained bitterly, had promised weeks ago to get her a gun for Frank and he'd never

come through. Neither of them ever came through with anything.

"Okay, okay, calm down," Roman placated. "Is that what
you're pissed about, that Lanny didn't get you a gun? Why
didn't you say something to me? You want a gun for Frank,
I'll get you one."

Patricia was skeptical. She'd heard enough empty promises
from them. But Roman surprised her.

"I'll get you one today," he said. "Meet me at Spinnaker's
at four. I'll have it for you then."

At Spinnaker's, Roman met her when she came in the
door.

"Have you got it?" Patricia asked without preliminary.

"Yeah, I've got it. I said I'd have it, didn't I? I'll give it
to you at Barb's; we're going over there."

Along with Jim Leary, they again went to Barb Abbott's
apartment and drank and talked for a while. Later, she and
Roman had sex in Barb's bedroom, as they had done the previous time. When it was over, Patricia said, "Okay, can I
have the gun now?"

Roman got a .32-caliber revolver from the inside pocket of
his coat. Dropping the cylinder, he removed one of the weapon's seven bullets, leaving an empty chamber next to the
hammer. In case Patricia dropped the gun, it could not accidentally discharge.

"See, just like I said," Roman boasted, handing it to her.
"Now your boy Frank will have something to protect himself
with until we can arrange the hits."

"When do you think that will be?" Patricia asked.

"Soon," Roman assured her.

Driving home that night, Patricia hoped desperately that
giving Frank the gun would relieve some of the pressure on
him—and on her. She didn't know how much longer she
could take the stress of this thing between DeLuca and her father. Especially now that she had a new problem on her mind.

Her period was now more than three weeks past due and
another one was supposed to be coming up. She was worried
sick about it.

Please, God, she thought, no.

No, no, no.

February and March 1976

Several days after he had given Patricia the gun, Roman telephoned her at the apartment. There was something in his voice that she had never heard before: anxiety, fear, she wasn't sure what.

"Listen, doll," he said, "I've got a little problem with that piece I gave you. I found out it's dirty. I want you to get rid of it right away, see. Toss it in the lake or something. I'll get you another one later."

"Okay, no problem," Patricia said.

She didn't even have the gun anymore; Frank had taken it from her as soon as she brought it home, and she hadn't seen it since. Frank had given her the derringer to carry, now that he did not need it anymore.

A couple of days later, Roman called again, just to make sure Patricia had disposed of the gun.

"It's at the bottom of the lake," she lied.

Later in the week, Roman called from the Ala Moana. "Lanny and I are having a drink. Come on over and join us."

DeLuca was at home, but at that point, what with the prospect of missing a second period now dangerously close, Patricia really didn't give a damn. "That was one of the hit men," she told DeLuca when she hung up. "He wants me to meet him and his partner at a restaurant."

"I'll drive you," DeLuca said.

Patricia didn't have the energy to argue.

DeLuca drove her to the Ala Moana. When they pulled up in front of the place, DeLuca saw two men standing at one of the restaurant's front windows, looking out. They exchanged glances when they saw someone in the car with Patricia, and seemed to be studying DeLuca curiously. Patricia leaned over and kissed DeLuca good-bye, then got out and he drove away.

Both Roman and Lanny could probably tell from the expression on her face that Patricia had been handled just about enough; she looked very perturbed, very agitated.

"Hi, doll," Roman said pleasantly, leading her to a table.

"What's happening, Patty?" Lanny asked with his customary smoothness as they sat down.

"Nothing is happening," Patricia replied evenly. "Ab-so-lute-ly nothing," she said, accentuating each syllable, shifting her eyes from one to the other with each beat. Then she drilled Roman with a cold, steady stare. "I want to know once and for all if you're going to do this job or not."

"Sure we are, Patty—"

"You put me off over and over again," she said, tapping a long red fingernail on the tablecloth. "I don't believe you're going to do it."

Both men began to reassure her again, the same reassurances they had been using for months, founded on the same excuses. These things took time; certain arrangements had to be made; there had to be approval from some shadowy authority that was never identified. And, that old standby, she had not given them "enough up-front" yet.

"Bullshit," she spat in scorn for the last excuse. "I've been fucking your eyes out every time you wanted it. This could go on forever."

"It won't," they promised. "It's almost set," they swore. "It won't be much longer now," they pledged. "It will definitely be done," they guaranteed.

"Come on," Roman said, "Lanny's got the key to Ron's house. Let's go over there and we'll talk about it some more."

Because she clung to a modicum of hope that they still might come through, Patricia agreed to go with them. If there was even the remotest chance that she could still get it done—

They drove to Ron Tross's house. In the living room, warming up from the bitter winter cold outside, as Patricia dug in her purse for a cigarette, she came across the derringer she was now carrying. She hadn't the foggiest notion whether it was even loaded or not; all she'd done was toss it into her purse when Frank gave it to her. Now, sitting across a coffee table from Lanny Mitchell, she was presented with a temptation she couldn't resist. Taking the little gun out of her purse, she pointed it at Lanny.

"Look how easy it is, Lanny," she said. "All you have to do is squeeze the trigger."

Lanny Mitchell turned white. "That's not funny, Patty—"

"Come on," said Roman, "put that thing away. We're all friends here. Patty, let's go in the bedroom and have a talk. Come on."

Patricia preceded him into the bedroom, taking her purse and the gun with her.

Patricia had sex with Roman, participating mechanically, thoughts elsewhere, mind trying to shoot down one worry after another as it took flight. Roman, sensing that he was practically fornicating alone, did not try to prolong the act; he came quickly and rolled over.

"Come on now, how about a little for Lanny?" he asked. "Let's keep on his good side. We need him."

Patricia stared coldly at him and lighted another cigarette.

"I don't want us to part today with any unfriendly feelings," Roman stressed. "We're all in this together. Come on now."

With a quiet sigh, she finally nodded. Roman went to the door.

"Come on in, buddy," he called to Lanny with a smile. "Get it while it's hot."

The next time Roman called, Patricia put DeLuca on the phone. She sat and listened as DeLuca recited for Roman a long litany of the fears and frustrations he was enduring.

"You don't know what it's like, Roman," the threatened man lamented. "I mean, I'm constantly worrying, constantly afraid; I dread getting up in the morning, I'm scared to go to work, scared to come home. Jesus, this apartment looks like a fucking fortress; we've got great big bolt locks on the door, and I bought this German shepherd to wake us up if anyone tries to get in after we go to bed, and we keep a loaded gun handy—"

The bemoaning went on and on. Roman couldn't get a word in edgewise, not even to ask about the gun DeLuca had mentioned. He probably hoped to God it wasn't the piece he had given to Patricia; she had assured him that *that* gun was at the bottom of the lake.

"Look, Frank, I'm sorry about your problems," Roman finally got to say. "All I can tell you is that we'll take care of

this matter as soon as we can. These things take time. Just try
to stay calm. Let me talk to Patty now, will you?"

DeLuca held the receiver out to her but Patricia refused to
take it. Lips compressed, she shook her head emphatically.
Not this time. She'd had it with both Roman *and* Lanny.

DeLuca put the receiver back to his own ear. "Uh, Roman,
she must have stepped down the hall to see a neighbor."

After he hung up, he said to Patricia, "Why the hell
wouldn't you talk to him?"

"I'm tired of talking to the son of a bitch!" she snapped.
"You deal with him for a change."

"Shit, he's *your* godfather, Patrish!"

For a moment she had forgotten who Roman was supposed
to be; actually forgotten—and the mountain of lies she had
been building for so long almost caved in on her. DeLuca
was staring at her with obvious suspicion. She took a deep
breath and began nodding her head.

"Okay, all right, I'll talk to him the next time he calls. I'm
sorry, okay? I'm sorry, sorry, sorry!"

She stalked into the bathroom for the Valium bottle.

When she missed her second period, Patricia sat DeLuca
down at the table and insisted that they discuss it.

"I'm pregnant, Frank. I must be."

"Yeah, probably," he reluctantly agreed.

"I've got to get an abortion, right away."

"You're not going to abort my kid," he said. "This might
be the last baby I ever father."

Patricia stared thoughtfully at him. For the first time in
weeks his expression was not one of fear or anger or desperation. He looked mellow, almost serene. He had the look of
a man discussing his unborn child. Frank DeLuca had many
bizarre and debauched habits, but aborting children was not
one of them.

"Frank, be reasonable," Patricia said. "I smoke, I drink, I
take pills—"

"You can stop all of that right now," he said, "and the baby
will be all right." Reaching over, he took the cigarette out of
her hand and crushed it out in an ashtray.

Patricia cautioned herself to go easy. Frank was *serious*.
She decided to try being practical.

"Frank, honey, we can't afford a kid. You're supporting five already—"

"When your old man is out of the way, there'll be plenty of money."

"I thought you wanted to buy a boat," she reminded him. "Sail around where the weather's always warm—"

"Listen"—he snapped his fingers in sudden inspiration—"maybe we don't have to have your old man hit! Maybe if we tell him about the baby, tell him we're going to get married as soon as Marilyn's divorce is final, he'll let bygones be bygones—"

"That's wishful thinking, Frank. You said yourself he'd made this a blood feud."

"Yeah, but that was when there was just the three of us involved: you, me, and him. Now there's an unborn baby to consider. His first grandchild, Patrish. That's going to *mean* something to him—"

"Salt in his wounds is what it's going to mean."

"No, you're wrong." DeLuca shook his head emphatically. "I'll be the father of his first grandchild, Patrish. He'll have to call off the contract. We'll all have to find some way to reconcile, for the baby's sake." He rose and began pacing. "Your old man will make peace, I know he will. He'll probably even help us financially, maybe even help us get a house to raise the kid in. For Christ's sake, this is his *grandchild* we're talking about!"

Yeah, right, Patricia thought. *But what if the kid comes out looking like Lanny Mitchell? Or Roman Sobczynski? What then?*

Curbing the urge to reach for her pack of cigarettes, Patricia did some quick, silent calculating. She'd had sex a total of four times with Lanny, six with Roman. The first time with Lanny didn't count, it had been up the ass. The second and third time with Lanny had been in November, and she'd had a period in December. The last time with Lanny had been early in February, after she had missed her period in January.

Patricia's hopes rose. The baby could not have been Lanny Mitchell's.

Heartened, she applied the same formula to Roman. The first and second time with him had been in November, and she'd had a period in December. But the third time with Ro-

man had been in January; it had been the day he called her
to meet him at the Coach and Six restaurant, and they'd had
lunch with that guy Nick Carbucci. Afterward, Roman had
taken her to the Flamingo Motel in Wheeling. As usual, he'd
had a few drinks and she'd had to really work it out of him.
A spectacular orgasm it wasn't.

Then, the next three times with Roman had all been in
February—after she had already missed.

The only single possibility, out of ten, was that one time
with Roman at the Flamingo Motel in January. Had that been
before or after she missed her first period? She couldn't remember for certain. Had she talked to Frank yet about being
late? She couldn't remember that either. She didn't think she
had really begun to worry yet about being pregnant, so that
afternoon session at the Flamingo might have been right after
she missed the first time.

Or right before.

Son of a bitch. She shook her head at the irony of it. That
would be perfect, righteous punishment for everything she
had ever done in life that was wrong; every sin she had ever
committed; every unspeakable act. To have a baby fathered
by Roman Sobczynski.

On reflection, she chose to think it was *not* Roman's baby.
One instance with him, a few alcoholic dribbles from his pathetic, barely upright organ, could not outweigh the numerous
times with Frank. As racked with worry as he was, Frank
DeLuca *performed*.

It was DeLuca's baby, she was sure of it.

But did it really matter?

Late in March, Lanny called.

"Hi, Patty, how's it going?" he said when she answered.

"Just like it always goes, Lanny," she said. "Sour."

"That's what I was calling about," he said. "I'd like to get
our little arrangement back on track. I'd still like to help you,
Patty."

You gutless little cocksucker, she thought. *All you want to
help me do is get undressed.*

When Patricia did not respond to his overture, Lanny said,
"I think I can get it back on track if you can come up with
some front money. Think you can?"

"No," she said flatly, without hesitation. Then a thought struck her. "You wouldn't be out of work, by any chance, would you, Lanny?"

It took him a few beats to contrive an answer, but he regrouped as smoothly as he always did. "Yeah," he said with a slight chuckle, "as a matter of fact I am. And because of that I'll have a lot more time to devote exclusively to this problem of yours—"

"No money, Lanny. I haven't got any."

"Well—what about your boyfriend?" Lanny suggested. "He's in charge of that big Walgreen's; he could probably lay his hands on some money and then pay it back a little at a time—"

"No. I don't want Frank to get in any trouble at Walgreen's." Frank's job was just about all he had left.

"Look," Lanny tried to reason with her, "all you'd need is a little to put up in good faith—"

"No."

"I'm not talking about much. A couple thousand—"

"No."

Patricia hung up.

DeLuca became livid when she continued to talk about an abortion.

"This is *my* kid!" he bellowed. "I do not kill my own kids! We're going to have this baby no matter what! I don't want to hear any more talk about a fucking abortion!"

When he got like that, all Patricia could do was back down. There was simply no reasoning with a macho dago who was pounding his chest about fatherhood. She dared not even light a cigarette in front of him when he was expressing his manliness and virility so tenaciously. When he calmed down, he usually became more flexible as far as reasonable discussion was concerned—but he still stood adamantly by his decision.

"Look, Patrish," he said almost humbly, "this is just something I can't do. This kid might be the last baby I produce. To just—flush it down a toilet at some abortion clinic—I don't think I could live with myself if I did that. It—it's against the church, against the sanctity of human life. It's against everything I believe in."

Everything he *believed* in? As far back as Patricia could remember, Frank DeLuca had to her knowledge not believed in anything except what he *wanted*. Satisfying himself had been his cardinal priority since the day she met him. Now all of a sudden he believed in something? Patricia did accept that he was sincere in not wanting her to abort; it was *why* he was sincere that was suspect—and she did not think for a moment that it had anything to do with the sanctity of human life. If Frank had thought for a second that the baby wasn't his, the sanctity of human life would have gone out the window. He would have used the knitting needle himself.

Patricia went to the Women's Clinic in Lombard and had her pregnancy medically confirmed. She inquired about an abortion and was referred to the Albany Clinic on Irving Park Road in Chicago.

On March 6, Patricia went to the Albany Clinic. In the waiting room she filled out the customary patient questionnaire. On it she listed her true age of nineteen, noted that her family medical history included cancer of the intestine, indicated that at the time of getting pregnant she had been using a birth control pill, and stated that she was not using any medications at the present time. A nurse measured her height at five feet seven and one-half inches, and weighed Patricia at 132 pounds.

In a small examination room, wearing a wrinkled white gown that was open all the way down the back and smelled of bleach, Patricia was examined by Dr. John Taparia. He approved her for an abortion procedure and she was required then to sign a statement that she was seeking the abortion of her own free will. After she had signed the form, Dr. Taparia gave her an injection of Carbocaine and removed thirty cubic centimeters of blood and tissue from her uterus.

The whole affair took less than two hours. With all the turmoil of the past six months weighing on her perplexed young mind, it almost seems incredible that she went through the entire medical procedure and got all the way back to her car before she started crying.

40

August 1976

Ray Rose had an imaginary hammer in one hand, imaginary nails in the other. He was getting ready to nail a lid on the Columbo murder case.

Across the table from him sat Hubert Francis Green, Jr., better known as Bert. A department manager at Walgreen's, he was the same Bert Green who was known to be a close friend of Frank DeLuca's; the same Bert Green who refused to talk to police investigating the Columbo killings; who claimed he didn't know "anything about anything"; who became closemouthed every time an Elk Grove police officer walked into the store; who had been lying for weeks to every official working on the case, right up to and including the assistant state's attorney who would be prosecuting the case. The same Bert Green who then blithely told Grace Mason and her husband, Lloyd, that DeLuca had *admitted*, before the bodies were found, committing the crime.

Ray Rose finally had enough of Bert Green's stonewalling attitude and lack of cooperation. This was not a divorce suit, it was a *murder* case. If Ray Rose had his way, *nobody* was going to withhold information that would help solve it.

Rose had Bert Green at Elk Grove police headquarters. It was Green's last chance: either he told what he knew about the murders, or Ray Rose was going to have him locked up for obstruction of justice and anything else he could think of that would stick.

"Okay, Bert, how about it?" Rose said now. "You ready to make a formal statement?"

Perhaps Bert Green sensed the chief investigator's ire, because he nodded and said, "Y—yes."

Rose gestured through the open door for a witness and a stenographer to join them.

It was the most shocking statement of the entire case.

Bert Green was twenty-eight, the son of a physician from Sioux Falls, South Dakota. He was a rather collegiate-looking

man—some would have said "square"—who wore his hair
neatly trimmed and wore old-fashioned wire-rimmed eye-
glasses. Bert and his wife, Peggy, had one child, an infant
daughter a year old. They lived in an apartment at 122 Board-
walk, barely a block from the Elk Grove Village Walgreen's
store. Bert had gone to work there as a manager trainee in
February 1975. He soon became good friends with his boss,
Frank DeLuca; they frequently went out for drinks after work
and socialized at informal parties in people's apartments. Bert
knew DeLuca's girlfriend, Patty Columbo, a former employee, and had visited their apartment on occasion. He also
knew Joy Heysek, the Beauty Center manager, and was aware
that she was an ex-girlfriend of DeLuca's.

DeLuca had told Bert Green that Patty Columbo's crazy father was trying to kill him. Bert commiserated with his boss
and was always ready with a sympathetic ear. DeLuca appre-
ciated that; he eventually promoted Bert, making him manager of the liquor department.

Early in April 1976, DeLuca called Bert into the stockroom
and asked, "Bert, can I trust you? *Really* trust you?"

"You know you can, Frank," the younger man assured his
boss.

DeLuca then gave him a brown paper-wrapped package
and said, "I want you to keep this for me for a while. Hide
it somewhere in your house. Don't even tell your wife about
it."

Bert Green took the package home and hid it in a closet
behind some winter boots. About a week later, DeLuca asked
him to bring the package back. When Bert returned it,
DeLuca unwrapped it in front of him and Green saw that it
was a .32-caliber revolver.

On the afternoon of Monday, April 19, DeLuca came into
the liquor department and said, "I need a favor, Bert. I've got
the late shift and Patrish needs a ride someplace tonight. Can
you run down to the apartment for me and drive her back up
to Elk Grove?"

Green said he was sorry, he couldn't do it. "Tonight's my
little girl's first birthday, Frank; we're having a party for her."

DeLuca was insistent. "It's really important, okay? Look, if
you'll do it, I'll give you the whole day off tomorrow."

Green finally agreed. When his shift was over, he walked

home to have supper with his wife and daughter, then drove his car back to the drugstore and stopped in to let DeLuca know he was on his way to get Patty, so that DeLuca could call her.

At the apartment building where Patricia and DeLuca lived, Green drove to the rear entrance, as he had been instructed, and Patricia quickly got into the passenger seat. Green noticed at once that Patricia was not wearing one of her usual flashy outfits; instead, she had on jeans, a long, dark brown coat, and her jungle of hair was contained under a scarf tied around her head.

"Where do you want me to take you?" Green asked her.

"Just drive back toward Elk Grove," Patricia said. "I'll tell you where to go."

Patricia eventually had Bert Green drive to the parking lot of a Lutheran church on Arlington Heights Road, not far from the intersection of JFK Boulevard, where Walgreen's was located.

When Patricia got out on the dark and deserted parking lot, Green asked, "Do you want me to wait?"

"No," she replied, and walked off into the darkness.

Bert drove to the store and told Frank what had transpired. DeLuca thanked him. Bert took the next day off and DeLuca falsified Green's time sheet to make it appear that he had worked.

When Bert Green returned to work on Wednesday, his boss called him into the stockroom where they could talk privately.

"I've got a major problem, Bert," Frank began, "and I'm telling you about it because I know I can trust you. Patrish's old man and old lady have got a contract on me, okay? They want me dead. But I've hired two hit men to do them first, okay? That was what it was all about Monday night; the hit men were supposed to meet Patrish at that church parking lot and she was going to get them into the house—but they didn't show. Anyway, I might need your help again next Monday, okay?"

The following Monday, April 26, DeLuca asked Green to do the same favor again: pick up Patricia at the apartment and drop her off at the Lutheran church lot, which Bert had now learned was very close to Frank Columbo's home. Not wanting to alienate DeLuca and possibly jeopardize his recent promotion, Bert agreed. That night he again picked Patricia up at the rear of the apartment building and drove her to the same place. She was once more dressed in jeans, long coat, and scarf. This time, on the ride there, she herself spoke for the first time of what was taking place.

"The hit is going down tonight," Bert Green claimed she said.

After dropping Patricia off, Green drove directly home without stopping at the store to report to DeLuca.

On Tuesday morning, DeLuca told an anxious Bert Green for the second time, "The hits didn't go down again."

DeLuca stated further that Patricia had been in her parents' house, apparently prepared to let the hit men in, when the telephone rang and she answered it. There was no explanation for this—whether she thought it was the hit men calling to verify that she was in fact there, or whether she simply picked up the ringing phone out of habit—but she did answer it. The caller was a relative. DeLuca told Green the hit had to be called off because Patricia could be placed in the house. The subject of what happened to the hit men was not broached.

It was some time after this conversation, perhaps a day or two later, when they were discussing the plan again, that DeLuca said, "If the hits don't go down next time, maybe I'll have to do it myself."

When another Monday rolled around, this one May 3, and DeLuca again asked Bert Green to chauffeur Patricia, the new liquor department manager balked.

"Frank, I can't do it, no way. My wife is starting to get really upset about this."

"You've got to do this for me, Bert," DeLuca insisted. "It's all set for sure tonight."

"I can't," Green pleaded. "I just can't get out of the house again. My wife—"

"Look, get out of the house any way you can," DeLuca all but ordered him. "Put the blame on me, whatever it takes, okay? But you've *got* to do this for me, Bert."

As before, Bert Green capitulated and agreed to take part.

This time, while Bert was parked behind the building waiting for Patricia, he became very nervous. A lot, he said, was going through his head: the gun he had held for DeLuca; hit men supposedly after everybody; clandestine meetings with people who never seemed to show up. And he, Bert Green, was beginning to feel that he was in it up to his throat. This was the last time, he promised himself, that he would have any part of it.

When Patricia finally came out, Bert Green had worked himself up to such a state of nerves, and was so anxious to be done with this matter, that he was exceeding the speed limit in his efforts to get his passenger quickly back to the church parking lot. Patty Columbo, he said, had to tell him to slow down. By the time Bert Green got home that night, he was practically in a state of collapse.

Green was not scheduled to work the following day, Tuesday, May 4, but dropped in at the store that morning anyway because DeLuca had told him to "come in and check with me." Green recalled DeLuca as being "very uptight" as he told Bert for the third time that the planned hits "didn't go down again." But this time, DeLuca had a new excuse for the failure: it might not be going down, DeLuca said, because Frank Columbo had "bought off" DeLuca's hit men. And again, according to Bert Green, DeLuca said, "I'll have to do it myself."

Bert Green left the store after that and claimed he did not see Frank DeLuca again that day.

The day of the murders.

The most critical part of Bert Green's statement began when he told of arriving to open the drugstore the next morning, Wednesday, May 5. He arrived about eight-thirty, prepared to perform his first two duties: go to the fuse box and turn on all the store lights, then open the safe and remove money for the cash registers. He claimed that he was in the store and halfway to the fuse box before he realized that the lights were *already on*. And so was the soft piped-in music that continually played during business hours.

Seeing no one in the public area of the store, Bert walked through a door marked EMPLOYEES ONLY and headed down the hall toward the employee lunchroom. The lights in there, which should have been off too, were also on. At that point, Green heard the familiar low, rumbling roar of the store incinerator burning. And then he encountered Frank DeLuca coming out of the incinerator room, and saw behind DeLuca the red glow of a burning fire. The two men momentarily stared at each other. Then DeLuca spoke.

"It went down last night. I took the whole family out. That's the reason for the fire; I'm burning my clothes. I was a fucking bloody mess; I was covered head to toe with fucking blood." DeLuca shook his head. "I haven't had any sleep; I didn't get home until four o'clock this morning." He drew in a deep breath. "Come on in the coffee room and sit down with me. Punch in first."

When Bert Green entered the lunchroom, he saw that the coffee, which took a few minutes to prepare, was already made. DeLuca, he recalled, was very nervous, agitated, talking very fast. He showed Bert Green his hands, which had a number of small cuts on them.

"I got these when I smashed a lamp over the old man's head. I shot him twice. The first shot was in the back of his head; it blew his teeth out. Then I shot him again. Then I went up and shot the old lady. Michael was easy; all I had to do was stand him up and shoot him——"

Bert Green listened, mesmerized, as Frank DeLuca continued his rambling litany of cold-blooded murder.

"The old man was a tough old bird——I had to take a lamp and smash it over his head. He said to me, 'Who are you? Why are you doing this to me?' I told him, 'Fuck you,' and I shot him. There was no lights on in the house——I hunted around for a flashlight to clean up the glass——couldn't find one——finally I used a candle to clean up the mess. I had a stocking cap and I put it in a bag; it's being burned up with the rest of the bloody clothes——"

Bert Green recalled telling DeLuca something to the effect that DeLuca was "going to get picked up" for the crime, to which DeLuca replied, "No. No, I won't. I did some really smart things to cover my tracks."

DeLuca said he had cleaned up the pieces of glass from the lamp he had touched and put them, along with the murder gun, in a big bag, which he had then dumped in the river.

Fortunately for Bert Green, he was scheduled to work only until noon that day. He was, he said, very relieved to get out of the store and away from Frank DeLuca.

* * *

On Thursday, May 6, the second day after the murders, Bert Green stated that he was working in the stockroom when DeLuca came in to talk to him. DeLuca was perplexed.

"I can't believe it, Bert. Nobody's found the bodies yet. Since Tuesday night, and this is Thursday, and nobody's found the fucking bodies yet."

Bert Green could only agree with DeLuca that it seemed odd.

On Friday, May 7, DeLuca was nervous and visibly upset. "Jesus Christ, I can't fucking *believe* this! Those fucking people have been lying dead over there for three fucking days now and nobody's *found* them!"

It did seem impossible, Bert agreed with his boss. "Michael's been missing from school for three days; Mr. Columbo hasn't been to work in three days. It doesn't make sense, Frank."

Late that afternoon, of course, DeLuca was relieved of the nagging worry. The bodies of the murdered Columbo family were found.

Part Two

The Trial

41
April and May 1977

On Monday, April 4, 1977, exactly eleven months to the day after Frank, Mary, and Michael Columbo were murdered, formal legal proceedings began in the case of *The People of the State of Illinois* v. *Patricia Ann Columbo and Frank John DeLuca*. The actual hearing of evidence against the defendants was not to begin until Wednesday, May 18, seven weeks and two days later. During the interim, the judge assigned to the trial, R. Eugene Pincham, would hear numerous pretrial motions from both prosecution and defense, would preside over the selection of a jury, and would conduct a minitrial on whether to allow into evidence certain items obtained from Lanny Mitchell, other items seized by police when Ray Rose and his men served the search warrant on Patricia and Frank the day Patricia was arrested, and the statement Patricia made to police before an attorney was appointed for her.

Representing the state during this period and subsequently throughout the trial were Algis Baliunas—Al for short—one of the most capable prosecutors then on the state's attorney's staff, who would remind some involved in the case, when they looked back, of an older, rounder Michael J. Fox as Alex Keaton in the television series "Family Ties." Others said he would have made a perfect Kennedy brother to Jack, Bobby, and Ted.

Baliunas would be supported by two other assistant state's attorneys: Terry Sullivan, a somewhat cherubic-looking Irishman who would go on to prosecute serial killer John Wayne Gacy; and another Patricia, this one spelling the shortened version of her name *Patti*—Patricia Bobb, a tall blonde, on the thin side, very precise in manner.

Opposing them, representing Patricia, were William Swano and William Murphy, two young, dedicated public defenders; and representing DeLuca, Michael Toomin, a court-appointed private attorney brought in, presumably, so as not to present a conflict of interest by having the public defender represent both accused parties.

The pretrial hearing began with the defense's motion to suppress certain evidence that the prosecution intended to present.

Bill Murphy, one of Patricia's counsel, began direct examination with Elk Grove chief investigator Ray Rose. After establishing that Rose had been with the Elk Grove department for nine years—five as a uniformed officer, four as an investigator—Murphy asked Rose if he had an *arrest* warrant at the time the search warrant was served and Patricia arrested. Rose admitted that he had not had one.

Al Baliunas, examining Rose for the state, and obviously more concerned with the Lanny Mitchell evidence than with the lack of an arrest warrant, asked if Rose had been present when Lanny Mitchell made his statement accusing Patricia of soliciting Roman Sobczynski and himself to murder her parents. Rose had indeed been present. Did Lanny Mitchell have in his possession at that time certain items relevant to that accusation? Yes: photographs of the Columbo family, a timetable of their usual routine, and a diagram of the house at 55 Brantwood. In apartment 911—Patricia and Frank's apartment—Rose had found, lying on a table, a notepad of paper matching the paper on which the diagram was drawn; he had taken the pad as evidence. Apparently satisfied, Baliunas then turned to the matter of the arrest warrant: had one eventually been obtained? Yes, at 11:00 P.M. at night bond court, after Patricia Columbo had been in custody for sixteen hours.

Lt. Frank Braun testified that he had been a Cook County sheriff's deputy for fifteen years, nine of them in his present rank. In apartment 911 he had collected samples of cigarettes identical to the brand found in Mary Columbo's recovered Oldsmobile, and also the sexually explicit photographs of Patricia, which he said he found on the kitchen counter.

Frank DeLuca took the stand to contradict and discredit Rose and Braun. The notepad, he said, had been on a shelf in the closet; the photos on a top shelf in a kitchen cabinet. Neither item had been covered by the search warrant; if they were not lying out in plain sight, the defense maintained they could not be seized and used as evidence.

Ray Rose returned to the stand. He testified that Patricia Columbo had waived her right to have an attorney present, had at first denied knowing Lanny Mitchell, and denied ever seeing the family photos and diagram before. Subsequently, when Lanny Mitchell was brought to the door of the juvenile-detention cell to identify her, she admitted, "All right, all right, I wrote it," with reference to the family timetable. Regarding the cutthroat sign Lanny had made, Patricia told Rose that she thought Mitchell was making a threat on her life.

Glenn Gable and Roy Fiske, both sheriff's deputies with six years of service, denied that, while transporting Patricia to Elk Grove police headquarters, either had made comments to her, as she had alleged to her lawyers, that she was going to "fry" in the electric chair for "killing your family." There was no capital punishment in Illinois at that time, but Patricia had been unaware of that.

John Landers, who had since left the Elk Grove police to work as an administrative assistant for the director of law enforcement for the state, testified that he had been present when Patricia Columbo made a nine-page statement regarding her relationship with Lanny Mitchell and Roman Sobczynski. He also testified that Patricia had related to him her "vision" regarding the night of the murders. That interview had taken place, he said, in the office of Mrs. Claudia McCormick, the superintendent of the women's jail, who had ordered Patricia brought down.

Claudia McCormick then took the stand. She testified that no such meeting as John Landers described had ever taken place. Her secretary, Thelma Hawkins, corroborated the superintendent's testimony: there was no meeting between Patricia Columbo and John Landers in Mrs. McCormick's office.

Dr. Paul Cherian, the Cook County Jail psychiatrist, took the stand and described his forty-minute evaluation examination of Patricia, in which he found her to be severely overcome by feelings of helplessness and hopelessness, which he described as an acute situational reaction, depressive type, resulting in psychomotor retardation. In layman's terms,

Patricia's mind had slowed nearly to a crawl, and her body was doing likewise.

Patricia's godmother, Janet Morgan, testified that Patricia had called her from Elk Grove police headquarters to say that she was going to make a statement so that Frank DeLuca would be released. Janet asked her if she would be telling the truth, to which Patricia replied, "No, but that's the way it has to be. They told me that if I gave them a signed statement, they would release Frank."

Rita Matsukes, secretary to the Elk Grove chief of police for ten years, testified that she heard Patricia say to one of the officers, possibly John Landers, that "my first concern is taking care of Frank. He didn't know anything I did."

Patricia herself then gave testimony that Deputy Chief Kohnke had intimidated her by asking, "Do you have a preference who goes to the electric chair, you or Frank?" This was the same ploy sheriff's officers Gable and Fiske allegedly had tried: threatening a punishment that could not be carried out. The electric chair, gas chamber, hangman's noose, firing-squad bullet—and now the lethal needle—can all be strong coercives if one is unaware of their disuse. It is unlikely, however, that Patricia felt threatened by Kohnke; her primary concern was, as always, "poor Frank."

Patricia also testified that Ray Rose had, in her presence, referred to DeLuca as a "perverted jack-off," and that, because Rose was looking at the pornographic photos at the time, Patricia had retorted, "Look who's a perverted jack-off." Rose, she said, then threw the pictures at her, called *her* a pervert, and angrily kicked a chair at her.

It was all for nothing. Judge Pincham ruled to permit everything to be entered as evidence.

The voir dire began on Friday, April 29. This was the jury selection process, *voir dire* being an Anglo-French term meaning, literally, *to speak the truth*. For more than three hundred years it had been used in the legal community to designate a preliminary examination to determine the competency of a juror.

In *People* v. *Columbo and DeLuca*, it took nineteen days to select twelve jurors and two alternates. The chosen came from all over the city and suburbs of Cook County. The final panel was pretty much what a criminal jury should be: a mixed lot from the mainstream of the population. They ranged in age from twenty-two to sixty-one, the former being a black female science major in college, the latter a white housewife. The average age was just over forty-three. Eight were women, ages twenty-two to sixty-one; six were men, ages thirty to fifty-eight. The average age of the men was just over forty-four; the women, just over forty-two. Six were black, seven white, one Filipino-American. Occupationally, they ranged in all directions: refinery worker, telephone company account representative, toolmaker, coronary care nurse, cook, immigration inspector, carpenter, part-time cashier, retail salesperson, piano store owner, radio repairman, student. Eight of them came from the city, six resided in various suburbs. Most of them were married, in unions that ranged from five to twenty-seven years. Their hobbies were fairly mundane: golfing, bowling, fishing, dancing, bicycling; only one was particularly interesting: the immigration inspector collected and played various reed instruments.

All of them, these almost stereotypically "average" people, felt that they could impartially and fairly judge whether Patricia Columbo and/or Frank DeLuca were guilty of the murders with which they had been charged.

Justice—for Frank, Mary, and Michael Columbo, as well as for society—was in their hands.

On the afternoon of Wednesday, May 18, Judge R. Eugene Pincham formally welcomed the jurors to his courtroom, addressing each of them by name, and People's Indictment 76-4046 was ready to be tried. After opening statements from all the lawyers involved, testimony began. Prior to that, however, defense counsel Michael Toomin requested that, due to the complexity of the case, an additional attorney be appointed by the court to assist him in defending DeLuca. He asked for a lawyer named Stanton Bloom. Judge Pincham granted the request.

The first witness to be called in regular order was Chicago police officer Joseph Giuliano, who with his partner made the initial report on Frank Columbo's Thunderbird, parked on the lower West Side of the city. Two significant points were made by Giuliano: first, he had tried "several times" to call

Frank Columbo at home on the afternoon of Friday, May 7, and got no answer; second, he saw no markings or smudges on the trunk lid of the recovered car; nothing, in other words, that would have obliterated latent finger- or handprints. DeLuca's attorney asked if he recalled that Chicago had two inches of rain in the two days prior to his finding the car—but the officer did not remember the weather conditions.

Officer Kenneth Kvidera of Elk Grove took the stand next to tell of discovering the bodies when he was sent to 55 Brantwood to make a routine notification call. The prosecution entered eleven photographs of the house and bodies into evidence at this point.

Chief Investigator Ray Rose was called. It was his third trip to the witness stand; he had testified twice in the pretrial hearing on the admission of evidence. He now related on direct examination how he and John Landers had entered the house and what they had found. During the course of his testimony, it was explained why, in all probability, Mary Columbo's panties were down to her knees: in the toilet, in the bathroom outside which her body lay, was human excrement, indicating that Mary had likely been having a bowel movement when her husband was shot twice in the back of the head. It was believed that she heard the shots, jumped up, and rushed out the bathroom door—to be shot once between the eyes herself.

During Rose's testimony, sixteen additional photographs of the interior of 55 Brantwood were introduced as evidence and shown to Rose to clarify various areas of the house to which he referred.

Ray Rose finished out the day on the stand and resumed testifying on Friday, May 20. Patricia's attorney asked if he saw a number of beer cans on the premises at 55 Brantwood; Rose recalled none. Were cigarette butts found in the bathroom near Mary Columbo's body? Yes, Pall Mall brand. Detectives at the scene also found a leather key case with an ignition key to the Thunderbird—but no ignition key to the Oldsmobile was ever recovered.

Elk Grove evidence technician Christopher Markussen testified to recovering the bowling trophy that had been used as a bludgeon. Markussen explained the difference between a patent finger or other print, and a latent print; the former could be seen with the naked eye, the latter could not. Approximately twenty latents were recovered from the murder house. Pieces of physical evidence inventoried numbered approximately one hundred.

Robert Salvatore, Markussen's partner, testified to recovering the gold-handled scissors apparently used to inflict the numerous incised, or slight, cuts on Michael's body, as well as the puncture wounds. The scissors, he said, were "deformed": the looped rings on the handle overlapped from too much pressure, causing the two points to spread past each other by about one-quarter of an inch. Salvatore also testified to recovering the single strand of hair embedded in the blood on the front of Michael's T-shirt. The brown paper bag into which Salvatore later put the hair at the morgue was introduced and marked as evidence.

Bill Murphy, on cross-examination, asked Salvatore if he had witnessed the autopsies; Salvatore answered yes. Was he present for the *entire* procedure? Yes. Were blood samples taken from the deceaseds? Yes. Swab specimens? Yes. Hair samples? *Yes.*

One wonders if Robert Salvatore was really unaware at this point, nearly thirteen months later, that no hair sample had been requested or taken from Michael's body. It does not seem possible that the three prosecutors failed to realize this incredible oversight—but if they did, why was not their witness briefed and prepared for this line of questioning from the defense? It would be nearly three weeks before the coroner, Dr. Robert Stein, testified; perhaps the prosecuting attorneys hoped that this lapse in building the foundation of evidence would, in that time, slip by judge, jurors, defense counsel, accuseds, press, the world—but that is unlikely. Whatever everyone was thinking, it *did* get by without incident on this particular day early in the testimony.

The next witness to testify was Patricia's uncle, Frank Columbo's brother, Mario Columbo. Under direct examination by Patti Bobb, he said that he was the younger brother of Frank Columbo and lived with their sister, Gloria Rezzuto, in Elk Grove Village not far from the 55 Brantwood address. Prior to the Columbo wake on Monday after the bodies were found on Friday, he had not seen his niece Patty since March

1974, three months before her eighteenth birthday, just prior to her leaving home to move into the Frank DeLuca household. He saw the rest of the family regularly, and had been taking tennis lessons with Frank twice a week.

On Sunday, May 9, two days after the bodies were found, Mario Columbo had gone to the morgue to make formal identification of the bodies. That same day, early in the evening, "Patty Ann called me. She said, 'Uncle Mario, I've made all the arrangements. The bodies will be laid out at Galewood Funeral Home and the wake will be Monday. Then they'll be cremated on Tuesday.' I said, 'But we don't believe in cremation, Patty.' She said, 'It will be all right. Mom and Dad and Michael will all be together.' I said, 'Patty, you can't do that. We're Catholic. We don't believe in cremation.' Then she said, 'Listen, you fucking asshole, who the fuck do you think you are? I'm the heir. I'll do it my way.'"

After the conversation, Mario Columbo had called the funeral home, the coroner, and his lawyer, attempting to prevent the cremation—but there was nothing he could do about it. Patricia *was* the heir.

Patricia came to the wake with Frank DeLuca. "Was that the first time you had ever seen Mr. DeLuca?" Patti Bobb asked.

"First time I seen him," the uncle confirmed.

"Did you, during the time you were at the wake, see Miss Columbo cry or show any visible signs of emotion?"

"Objection!" Both Swano and Murphy came to their feet.

"He may answer," said Judge Pincham.

"No, I did not," said Mario Columbo.

Swano asked on cross-examination, "Had you ever, prior to that date, heard your niece use vulgar language of that type?"

"Never," replied the witness.

"Mrs. Mary Columbo was not a Catholic, was she? As a matter of fact, she was a Baptist?"

"Correct."

"Did Frank Columbo go to church on a regular basis?"

"Not to my knowledge," Mario Columbo admitted.

Toomin took over for DeLuca. "Are you presently being represented by an attorney in a matter involving the heirship in this case?"

"Correct," Patricia's uncle replied.

"Is the sister of Mary Columbo, Carolyn Tygrett, also being represented by an attorney in that matter?"

"That is correct."

"You are a potential heir in the Columbo estate, are you not?"

"Objection!" said Patti Bobb.

Judge Pincham called a sidebar—a brief private discussion among counsel, out of hearing of the jury but taken down for the record. "What's this got to do with the case?" the judge asked Toomin.

"I'm attempting to bring out a reason for this man having a feeling of animosity toward Patty Columbo."

Pincham shook his head. "You can't go into that; you don't represent Patty Columbo." Turning to the jury, he said, "Objection sustained. Jury will disregard that question."

Bill Swano had not gotten to the bench quickly enough to hear Toomin's argument. "Judge, I missed the first part of that sidebar," he complained.

"Learn to move faster, son," Pincham told him paternally.

Mario Columbo was excused.

Geraldine Strainis had been Frank Columbo's senior clerk at Western Auto and had worked there twenty years. She testified that Columbo had not reported to work on Wednesday, Thursday, or Friday, May 5, 6, and 7, of the previous year, 1976. This was not unusual, however, since Columbo was in charge of the entire warehouse-consolidation operation and pretty much came and went as he pleased.

On cross, Stanton Bloom asked Ms. Strainis if she knew of a company called Dock Help. She did; it furnished dock labor for the warehouse. Was it a separate company? Yes. Did Frank Columbo work for Dock Help? No. Did he have contact with Dock Help regarding employing dock labor? Yes. Did she know if Frank Columbo had any interest in a trucking company called Chicago Cartage Company? Answer: I don't know. Did she know how much Frank Columbo earned? No.

At this point, at the prosecution's table, Al Baliunas and Patti Bobb apparently chuckled at this line of questioning, and Bloom, evidently high-strung, at least at the moment, heard them. Throwing them a scathing look, he turned to the judge and vehemently complained. Sighing wearily, Pincham said, "Let's go into chambers."

In the privacy of the judge's office, Bloom said that he felt maligned by the prosecution; he felt that their chuckling had sullied his courtroom strategy and tactics. Judge Pincham replied that from his position on the bench, he had not heard the exchange of chuckles, although he did not question Bloom's veracity. However, because a judge sometimes has to assume the role of a playground monitor when it comes to the lawyers practicing before him, and because he was as astute as he was, Pincham used the opportunity to pleasantly deliver a lecture of sorts. Personality conflicts between counsel were improper, he reminded them, and surely they knew that a scene such as had just transpired was not the way to try a lawsuit. Artfully, the judge suggested that such behavior was beneath counsel. Let's be professional out there, he said, however indirectly. Pincham disliked having to slap a lawyer's hand, but he was not above doing it if necessary. This was their warning.

Back in the courtroom, Bloom seemed to have lost his momentum. Through Geraldine Strainis he established that Frank Columbo had business transactions with a firm named Mulvihill Motor Service, but she had no knowledge of whether or not he had a personal interest in that firm.

Frank Columbo's longtime senior clerk was then excused and court adjourned for the day.

On Friday, May 27, a thirteen-year-old boy named Glenn Miller took the stand. Residing at 53 Brantwood, next door to the murder house, he had been Michael Columbo's best friend.

At one of the two defense tables, the color drained from Patricia Columbo's face as she stared at the boy. Her hands began to tremble. At one point, she turned her head to look at Frank DeLuca, sitting with his counsel at the other defense table. DeLuca did not return her look. He did not look at the young witness either.

Patti Bobb gently established through the nervous boy that on the afternoon of Tuesday, May 4, 1976, at about four-thirty, he and Michael Columbo had been riding skateboards back and forth across the Columbo garage. That was the last time he and Michael had played together.

The next witness was Judy DiMartino, a waitress at the Around the Clock restaurant in Arlington Heights. The Columbos, she said, were regular customers and she knew them well. They ate dinner there between seven-thirty and nine o'clock the night of Tuesday, May 4. All of them had stuffed bell peppers; Frank and Michael had baked potatoes, Mary did not. As the coroner's autopsy would later prove, it was the family's last meal.

Martin McCauley, age twenty, lived on the other side of the Columbos, at 57 Brantwood, with his parents. At home in his upstairs bedroom, he testified, he was trying to watch television about eleven-thirty that night, and was experiencing reception interference off and on. He knew that the Columbos operated CB radio equipment in their home, and telephoned them to complain. The line, he said, was busy, and he did not call back. He heard no unusual noise from the Columbo house.

Testimony regarding the Columbo automobiles was now forthcoming. First up was Investigator Russell Sonneveld, who described how he and his partner, Investigator Richard Cribben, had met a tow truck from the Village Standard station and removed Frank Columbo's Thunderbird from the area of 140 South Whipple Street in Chicago, towing it to the Elk Grove Village police garage where it was put in a "sealed-off" area.

Sheriff's Deputy Gene Gargano testified that the Columbo Oldsmobile was recovered from 121 South Spruce in Wooddale, the next suburb south of Elk Grove Village. Gargano had processed the car at the Columbo home, dusting it for latent prints, vacuuming material from its cushions and carpeting, collecting everything in the car and packaging and marking it as evidence. How many prints had he recovered? Five. From where? Inner-right-front window, inner-rear-door window, front passenger door near lock, driver's door near rearview mirror, and rear-door window on the left side.

Patti Bobb was doing the questioning. This was technical evidence; her questions were methodical, matter-of-fact;

Gargano's answers straightforward, also matter-of-fact. Then Ms. Bobb slipped in a hand grenade.

"Were the contents of the ashtray identified?"

"Yes," Gargano replied. "It contained More cigarettes."

"What is it about the More cigarette that allows you to distinguish it from others?"

"It's the brand Patty Columbo smokes."

"Is there anything about the appearance of the cigarette—" Bill Murphy leaped to his feet. "Object, Judge!"

"—that allows you to distinguish it?" Patti Bobb finished her question.

"We have an objection!" Murphy yelled.

"Overruled," Judge Pincham said.

"Yes, there is," Gargano answered the question.

"What is that?" Patti Bobb asked.

"Judge, I would like to be heard!" Murphy insisted.

Pincham called counsel forward for a sidebar. Murphy was incensed. "This is some sort of setup! It's a hearsay response!"

"You waited too long to make your objection, didn't you?" the judge asked him.

"Because the question snuck out!" Murphy contended.

"You had a standing to object," Pincham pointed out, "and move that it be stricken, which you did not do. You waited until such time as another question was put and the answer given."

"But, Judge—!" This was Bill Swano, Murphy's co-counsel.

"Wait," Pincham told Swano. "I heard what went on. You"—indicating Swano—"told him"—indicating Murphy—"to object, and during the second question he caught on and objected. You"—to Swano—"had the authority to object yourself—am I correct about that?"

He was, of course. Why Swano told Murphy to object instead of doing so himself was never made clear. Not that it would have made much difference: the jury still *heard* Gene Gargano's answer; striking it from the record would not strike it from anyone's mind. But Swano and Murphy argued so relentlessly on the point—it was hearsay, it was answered too late, it was not responsive—that the judge finally agreed to instruct the jury to disregard the last answer. He was tossing the defense a bone with absolutely no meat on it. When testimony resumed, Patti Bobb merely restructured the question.

"Can you describe for the jury the difference between the More cigarette and other cigarettes with regard to its appearance?"

"A More cigarette is very thin," Gargano replied, "much thinner than an average cigarette, and is rolled in brown paper. It looks like a small cigar."

And what types of cigarettes had Gargano observed Patty Columbo smoking? More, of course.

In spite of defense's vehement protest, one fact had to be cemented in the jury's collective mind: Patty Columbo's cigarette butts were found in her murdered mother's car.

At this point in the trial, prosecutor Patti Bobb complained to Judge Pincham that Stanton Bloom, at his defense table, was laughing. Bloom denied it.

"I didn't. I think it's just a game they're playing because I caught them the last time—"

"You are now even," Judge Pincham said patiently from the bench.

"No, we are not even," Bloom contradicted. "I did not do it. It's just a little game because I caught them and they can't catch me. They want to make it one apiece, but it's just not true. I did not laugh. In fact, I'm not in the mood to laugh this morning. I have other problems, physical problems. I don't feel like laughing."

"Whoever laughed," Judge Pincham ordered firmly, "cut it out."

Bill Swano cross-examined Gene Gargano. How many cigarette butts were found in the Oldsmobile ashtray? Fifteen. Some had lipstick on them? Yes. But some did not? Yes.

At noon, court recessed for lunch.

When the trial reconvened at two o'clock, defense attorney Toomin complained that his client, Frank DeLuca, had not received any lunch.

"Is he asking for lunch now?" Judge Pincham patiently inquired.

"He's hungry," Toomin stated. DeLuca appeared to be pouting.

"We'll see that he gets something during the first break,"

Pincham said. This trial, he must have been thinking, should be presided over by Job, the Old Testament character renowned for his limitless patience in the face of adversity.

The first witness of the afternoon was Robert Gonsowski, who had, until two weeks earlier, been a serologist for the state of Illinois. A serologist, he explained, was an individual who examined blood and other fluids to determine their species of origin. During his tenure with the state, he had examined between three and four thousand specimens—among them those taken from the three Columbo bodies. His testimony to Patti Bobb was that he had tested the hair samples of Frank and Mary Columbo and determined that they showed the presence of group A human blood. The vaginal swab specimen from Mary was negative: no seminal material present. He had also received for examination Michael's T-shirt, the one so carefully rolled up by evidence technician Robert Salvatore after he noticed the single hair on it. Serologist Gonsowski had examined it for trace material: anything that could be removed from the material of the item. He found *two* hairs: one in a bloodstain on the front—this was the one Salvatore had seen; and one in a bloodstain on the back. The two hairs had been mounted on slides and put in the laboratory's security vault. Gonsowski had also tested the gold scissors and the bowling trophy, finding them both to be blood positive.

When Bill Swano got the witness for cross-examination, he posed a couple of preliminary questions about blood, then—whether innocently or by design—asked, "Did you do a comparison of the two hairs from Michael's T-shirt?"

"No," the serologist said.

Indeed, what could he have compared them *to*—besides each other? They could not be compared to Michael's own hair, because no sample had been taken from Michael. In other words, there was absolutely no way to determine unequivocally whether the two hairs had come from Michael's own head—or were possibly the killer's hair.

And at this point, there was no way of knowing yet exactly who realized that fact.

The prosecution next called Bruce Radke, a Goodyear Tire store manager who a year earlier had run the Goodyear store in Grove Shopping Center, near the Walgreen's that Frank DeLuca managed. Radke identified DeLuca as the man who, on Monday, May 3, one day before the murders, had brought a 1968 Buick Skylark in to have a radiator hose replaced. He left the car at 1:00 P.M., returned for it at 4:00 P.M., and paid cash for the work.

This Buick was a rented car; DeLuca's own vehicle supposedly was in a repair shop. The real reason he had the Buick, however, was probably that he needed a car that would not be recognized by anyone in the Elk Grove neighborhood between Walgreen's and 55 Brantwood. He could not take a chance of its stalling, either, so when it began overheating, he decided to quickly have the radiator hose replaced.

John Norton, a Walgreen's employee, was called. Bobb questioned him about May 4, the day of the murders, and Norton, an assistant manager to DeLuca, stated that he worked from 2:15 until closing time at 10:45 that night. It was customary, he said, for him—or whichever assistant manager closed up—to telephone Frank DeLuca at home to let him know that the store was secure and that there were no problems. On that particular night, however, Norton hadn't made the call by 10:50 P.M.—and DeLuca called him. DeLuca inquired why Norton was late in reporting; Norton explained that he had experienced a couple of cash-register checkout problems but had cleared them up. DeLuca then said he was going to bed.

Susan Summers, age fourteen, was the carrier who delivered the *Elk Grove Herald* to the Columbo residence. When she delivered on Wednesday, May 5, she noticed nothing unusual. On Thursday, May 6, however, she noticed the previous day's paper still on the porch. Then, on Friday, May 7, she noticed the previous *two* days' papers there when she dropped the third. Asked if there were usually cars in the Columbo drive, she said yes. Asked if there were cars in the drive on those days, she said no.

Connie Larocco, an employment counselor for Advance Personnel in Lombard, testified that for a week prior to the murders she had been attempting to help Patricia Columbo find a job. She had scheduled Patricia for a job interview at 1:30 P.M. on the day of the murders, and called her at 10:30

that morning to remind her. Patricia never showed up for the interview. That evening, Ms. Larocco attempted several times to call Patricia at the apartment to find out what happened. The last call she made was at 11:35 that night. She got no answer.

Susan Twardosz, a criminalist for the Illinois Bureau of Identification in its Maywood laboratory, was a specialist in firearms and tool marks. She had examined the slugs taken from the Columbo bodies and crime scene, and determined them to be .32 caliber in size. She could not tell whether they had been fired from a revolver or automatic pistol.

Henry E. Thomka, a Wooddale police sergeant, was the watch sergeant on duty when a patrol officer found the Columbo Oldsmobile parked in their jurisdiction. Thomka had ordered the vehicle kept under surveillance until Elk Grove authorities towed it away.

Evidence technician Chris Markussen was recalled. He testified this time to processing the Thunderbird that had been towed to the police garage from Chicago. Quantities of broken glass were found on the seats and floor. Two partial fingerprints had been found on the left rear fender, palm prints on the trunk lid.

Al Baliunas asked Markussen if he had, at another time, taken palm prints of Frank DeLuca, and Markussen said he had.

"Did you notice any unusual characteristics of Mr. DeLuca's prints?"

"Yes, he had had two amputations on his left hand. The index finger is missing, and the tip of the next finger is gone."

Murphy, representing Patricia, then asked a question that DeLuca's lawyer, Toomin, might have asked. "When you printed DeLuca, did you notice any scabs or cuts on his hands?" Markussen had not. Eight days had passed between the night of the murders and the time DeLuca was printed. One wonders, if he had sustained cuts on his hands during the murders, whether they would have been completely healed by then. And why not a magnification examination to see if he had a number of small, recent scars on them? With the plethora of scientists available to the state, that certainly could have been done.

Jack Lilly, owner of Jack's Top and Trim, a shop that performed body and fender work as well as other automobile renovation, testified that he had rented Patricia Columbo one of his loaner cars, a 1968 Buick Skylark, which had been in overall filthy condition when she took it on April 30, four days before the murders. When he got it back on May 7, three days after the murders, it was in exceptionally clean condition. This was the same car that Frank DeLuca had a new radiator hose put on—one day before the murders.

On Thursday, June 2, the first of the prosecution's stars appeared. Lanny Mitchell was sworn in at 10:00 A.M. and examined by Terry Sullivan. Preliminary questions took Lanny from his first meeting with Nancy Glenn, through their relationship, and up to the phone call he made to Patricia Columbo to arrange a date with her and Lanny's friend Roman Sobczynski.

"I asked her if she'd go out with a friend of mine who was heavy in politics—for a party, for pay, a hundred dollars. She said yeah, she needed the money."

After the four of them met, and while Lanny and Patricia were dancing at the Where Else Lounge, Lanny said the coat of his leisure suit had come open and Patricia had seen a .38-caliber Colt Diamond pistol he was carrying.

"Patty looked impressed. She asked what I was carrying the gun for. I told her I always carried when I was with Roman because he was heavy. I told her if she took care of Roman, that favors could be done for her."

"Did she make any response to that, sir?" Terry Sullivan asked rather formally.

"She was impressed," Lanny Mitchell replied. "She said she'd fuck his eyes out."

Lanny then described how Patricia had subsequently tried to get herself and Nancy away from him and Roman, but the men had caught up with them in front of Nancy's home. It was there that Patricia had called Roman Sobczynski a "jack-off" and told him unequivocally that she would not have sex with him. Lanny had finally gotten into the car with Patricia and she drove to the motel with him. Lanny admitted that Patricia had repeated to him her dislike of Roman.

"She said she would not fuck him because he was a jack-off. She said she would fuck me. I told her to keep cool, that Roman was very heavy and could get things done for us."

During the ride, Patricia had asked Lanny to get an "unmarked" gun for her. He said he would, but that it took time. In the interim he agreed to get her some bullets for her boyfriend's derringer.

At the Edgebrook Motel, Lanny said he and Patricia had sex. Terry Sullivan asked, "Prior to engaging in sex with Patricia Columbo, did you have any conversation in the motel?"

"The only conversation I had with Patty was that she wanted it in her ass."

That question and answer, like the earlier one about Patricia allegedly saying she would "fuck [Roman's] eyes out," had no bearing on the charges against Patricia, and appeared to have been worked into the testimony of this unindicted co-conspirator to make Patricia out to be a slut. The tactic would continue to be employed, presumably because the prosecution felt it would be easier to convict a slut of murder.

Lanny next testified to the days, weeks, and months following that first meeting. He admitted offering to kill Patricia's parents for her, requesting a diagram of the house, a timetable of her parents' routine, and photographs. Recalling the meeting just before she had begun having sex with him and Roman as payment "up-front" for the hits, Lanny testified that it had been Patricia who offered the sex. "You want me to put my ass on the table too?" she allegedly asked them. Roman had said yes. "Okay, it's on the table," Patricia, according to Lanny, had agreed.

Lanny's buddy Roman, however, would contradict that testimony when he took the stand.

From the alleged sex offer, Terry Sullivan took Lanny through all the meetings that he had with Patricia, either alone or with Roman Sobczynski. In all, from the first meeting on November 17, 1975, to their last on February 17, 1976—a three-month period, ninety-two days to be exact—Lanny met Patricia alone six times, and in the company of Roman six times. He had sex with her a total of four times, including the first meeting when Nancy Glenn was also present.

After the final meeting on February 17, Lanny admitted calling Patricia in March from Roman Sobczynski's home, a toll call, which he made collect so that it would not reflect on the Sobczynski family telephone bill. Lanny, out of work by then, attempted to reopen negotiations for the murders, suggesting that Frank DeLuca could get the front money from Walgreen's to put up in "good faith." Patricia flatly declined. (At that point she was having nothing further to do with the two men, having realized that she had merely been used by them.)

Sullivan asked if after the February 17 meeting, and the phone call in March, Lanny had ever seen or spoken to Patricia Columbo again. Lanny said he had not. That, of course, was another lie. He had seen her at the Elk Grove Village Police Department two months later when Deputy Chief Bill Kohnke brought him in to identify Patricia—when, charmer that he was, he had made the cutthroat sign to her. Surprisingly, none of the defense counsel caught the flagrant misstatement—or if they did, they failed to challenge it.

Bill Murphy was the first to cross-examine Lanny. "Everything you told Patricia Columbo during your meetings was a lie, wasn't it?"

"Yes," Lanny admitted.

"You lied for sexual gratification?"

"Yes."

He had also lied to Nancy Glenn when he told her he was a police officer, that he had been involved in an armed robbery, that he was on a two-year period of probation with the mob, that he was also a burglar and burglarized factories for the mob.

Back to Patricia. "Everything you told her was a lie . . . for your own gain, wasn't it?"

"Yes."

"For sex?"

"Yes." Lanny's voice was emotionless, bland; he appeared not to be bothered at all by this.

"You've been given immunity by the prosecution, haven't you?"

"Yes."

"In return for testifying against Patricia Columbo?"

"Yes."

"In return for this testimony, you won't go to jail?"

"Yes."

On a roll with "yes" answers, Murphy apparently tried to slip one past the witness. "Are you Roman Sobczynski's pimp?"

But Lanny was far too sharp for the young public defender. "No, sir."

Still, Murphy pressed the point. "You know he's married?"

"Yes."

"You know his wife?"

"Yes."

"But you say you offered a girl a hundred dollars to go out with him?"

"Yes."

"Did Roman pay you to fix him up?"

"No."

"You were going to pay out of your own generosity?"

"Yes."

"Did you ever give Patty Columbo that hundred dollars?"

"No, sir."

The court day ended. Lanny Mitchell had been on the witness stand all day. He would have to return the following day.

Friday, June 3. Lanny testified that he told Roman Sobczynski that Patty wanted her parents killed. Roman had said, "Good."

"Meaning"—Bill Murphy was still cross-examining—"that you and Roman could use her?"

"Yes."

"Did you decide how to use her?"

"Yes."

The structure of Murphy's questions was not the best. They allowed Lanny Mitchell to simply answer yes, rather than forcing him to extemporaneously relate how he and Roman planned to proceed. The latter method at least might have shown the jury more clearly what kind of individual he was—this man whom the state of Illinois had decided it would let go free in order to get Patricia and DeLuca.

Murphy forged on with his elementary style, however. "Did you wear a gun to impress Patricia Columbo?"

"Yes."

"Did all the lies you told Patricia Columbo come spontaneously?"

Lanny frowned. "Can you tell me what *spontaneously*
means?"

Murphy did not bother.

After Lanny and Roman had sex with Patricia together the
first time, what had Roman said to Lanny when he drove
Lanny home? "He told me we were going to keep her on the
string."

"Did you ever threaten Patricia Columbo by saying, 'You
bitch, I'll put a bullet in your head'?"

"No, sir."

Murphy referred to the sworn statement Lanny had given
Terry Sullivan prior to the trial. In it, Lanny stated that after
he and Patricia failed in an attempt to case the Columbo
house, because Mary Columbo was unexpectedly at home,
Lanny "took her to the Ron Tross house and balled her . . .
then I grabbed her and told her if she ever tried to fuck me
again like that, I would put a bullet in her head."

"Did you give that answer?" Murphy asked.

"Yes."

"Were you lying to Mr. Sullivan then?"

"Yes."

"You think you're a pretty convincing liar, don't you?"

Patti Bobb objected and Judge Pincham sustained it.

"You'd lie for sex, wouldn't you?" Murphy drilled.

"Yes."

"You'd lie for money?"

"Yes."

"You'd lie to get a job?"

"Yes."

"You'd lie to keep yourself out of jail?"

Again Lanny was quicker than Murphy. "No, sir."

Court adjourned at one o'clock that Friday, to reconvene at
one o'clock Saturday. Lanny had been on the stand a day and
a half. He was to return yet again.

On Saturday, Bill Murphy kept Lanny only a little while be-
fore turning him over to DeLuca's attorney, Michael Toomin.
The main point Murphy made in that final session with
Lanny was summed up in one question.

"Was Patricia Columbo afraid of you?"

"Yes, sir."

Toomin began by immediately establishing Lanny's status in the trial. "Despite your immunity, you are named as a co-conspirator in this case, isn't that correct?"

"Yes."

"Why did you carry a gun?"

Lanny shrugged. "To act tough. To pretend I was something I wasn't."

"How old is your friend Roman Sobczynski?"

"In his mid-thirties."

"He's married and has a family?"

"Yes."

"Both of you carried guns to impress young girls, right?"

"Yes."

Lanny had gotten married on December 27, 1975, during the three-month period he and Roman were manipulating Patricia. "When you got married, you took an oath, didn't you?" Toomin asked.

"Yes."

"After you took that oath, did you cheat on your wife?"

"Yes."

"When you cheated on your wife, did you disregard the oath you had taken?"

"Yes."

"When you came into this courtroom to testify, you also took an oath, didn't you?"

Lanny swallowed dryly. "Yes."

Toomin shook his head in disgust and walked away from the witness.

Lanny Mitchell was finally excused. He had done his job for the state and was now free from the threat of prosecution.

Monday, June 6. Ray Rose, previously sworn and on the witness stand three other times, was called still again. Patti Bobb solicited more "slut" testimony.

"Calling your attention to May fifteenth, 1976, approximately eleven A.M., at the Elk Grove Village Police Department, did you have a conversation with Miss Columbo at that time with reference to certain photographs that were recovered in her apartment?"

"Yes, ma'am, I did."

Rose was allowed to elaborate. When he first asked Patty about the photos, she acted as if she did not know what Rose was talking about. He became specific, referring to a photo of her and her dog in a lewd position. Patty then said, according to Rose, that her morals were probably different than his. Rose said she did not feel there was anything wrong with it— meaning the photograph. (It was not clear in Rose's testimony whether Patricia Columbo *said* the latter, or whether it was Rose's own conclusion—and it was not challenged by the defense.)

Swano cross-examined. Did Patty Columbo tell Rose that she was afraid that Lanny Mitchell and Roman Sobczynski would kill her? Yes. Did she say that more than one time? Yes. Was she also afraid for someone else? Yes.

All of this had transpired during the fourteen hours Ray Rose had Patricia in custody before charging her with the murders. It was part of the nine-page statement she had made—at someone's suggestion—John Landers's, perhaps—in order to get DeLuca released. At one point, before she realized what frauds they were, Patricia probably *had* been afraid of Roman and Lanny—particularly the latter, who seemed to take great delight in drawing his gun in front of her, and who in fact had threatened to harm DeLuca. At any rate, much of this was trial strategy designed to mitigate Patricia's actions.

And when she said she had indeed been afraid for someone else, it had to have been clear to everyone listening who that someone was.

John Landers was called for the second time. He testified to a conversation he had with Patricia on the day she was arrested, in which Patricia reminded Landers of the problems she had been having with her father. Landers had been involved in the aftermath of the incident when Frank Columbo attacked DeLuca. Patty went on to say that the problems had never been resolved; neither of her parents, she said, had been able to accept her boyfriend, and the difficulties "just kept growing." Landers said that Patricia told him she felt the problems were being caused by her *mother*, who persistently encouraged her husband's dislike of Frank DeLuca. (A later witness would substantiate that there was at least *some* truth to that.)

It was just after her conversation with Landers that Patricia agreed to give a formal statement—and it was *between* that conversation and the giving of the statement that Patricia telephoned her godmother and said she was going to give the statement because "They've got Frank down here and the only way they'll release him is if I sign a statement." Obviously *someone* had made that arrangement with Patricia. It could have been John Landers; he was the only police officer besides Gene Gargano with whom Patricia felt comfortable, and Gargano had already left. Certainly, Patricia would not have made a deal with Bill Kohnke, who she said was threatening her with the electric chair, or Ray Rose, for whom she was developing a rapidly increasing animosity. At any rate, whatever subtle persuasion was used, the defense did not subsequently challenge John Landers to spell out exactly *how* he got Patricia Columbo to agree to make the statement. Obviously, some enticement was used; releasing Frank would have been the ideal inducement.

Since Judge Pincham had already ruled, in the pretrial hearing, that the statement was admissible, Patti Bobb now read it to the court. Landers, who was still on the stand, had done most of the questioning—but an assistant state's attorney had also been present, and in fact participated in the dialogue toward the end. That assistant state's attorney was Terry Sullivan.

Patricia Columbo's statement began with a recounting of her father's attack on DeLuca the previous summer, and Patricia's having Frank Columbo jailed for it, then subsequently dropping the charges against him. (Her intent had been to earn Frank Columbo's gratitude, she maintained, and thereby reconcile their differences, but it had not worked out.) Several months later she agreed to go out with her girlfriend Nancy on the double date, which had turned out to be such a disaster—and which apparently led to murder. Patricia's story was that after she had tried to get Nancy and herself away from Lanny and Roman (an undisputed fact by now), and the men had caught up with them, that she was, if not actually forced, at least intimidated into going to the motel. She said she knew she had to "put out" if she wanted to get away from Lanny and Roman. She admitted to asking Lanny Mitchell for anal intercourse so as, in her mind, to justify it as not cheating on Frank DeLuca. She corroborated Lanny Mitchell's version that Roman Sobczynski had let the air out of her tires to prevent her attempting to flee a second time.

Patricia's claim was that after the first evening, both Lanny and Roman threatened to tell DeLuca about her indiscretion, and also threatened to "harm" DeLuca unless she continued to "put out." At the same time, her father was "ranting and raving" with threats to kill DeLuca. Patricia swore that Lanny and Roman asked *her* if she wanted her father "taken care of." Because she had just had a vicious argument with her father, in which he allegedly said, "There'll be no marriage, Patty Ann, because there'll be no Frank DeLuca," she took advantage of the opportunity Lanny and Roman presented and "told them to go ahead and do it."

Subsequently, Patricia was supposed to help Lanny Mitchell "case"—or reconnoiter—the Columbo house. When they failed, Lanny insisted Patricia tell Roman they had been successful or Lanny "would get in trouble with Roman." Various police officers have speculated that, at this point, Lanny believed that Roman may have been *seriously* considering the hits. If true, Lanny probably would have been terrified that *he* might have to help in some way. He had certainly shown himself as a cravenly faint-hearted person since the night Ray Rose picked him up.

Landers asked in the statement if, during discussions with the two men, Patty had ever indicated that all three members of her family should be killed. She replied emphatically, "No, all I wanted was my father. They said that if my father went, that my mother had to go too. But not my brother."

Did Frank DeLuca have any knowledge of her plans to have her parents killed? "No, I never told him about it. I was afraid for him . . ."

Eventually, Patricia claimed, "Dad's attitude changed," and she wanted to "call off the contract." She felt that Lanny Mitchell was "sick" and would rape her mother. She said she telephoned the men repeatedly to call it all off. (There is subsequent testimony to support Patricia's position that her father's attitude had indeed softened—but that Mary Columbo's had not.)

John Landers testified that after Patricia's statement was typed, she signed it.

Patti Bobb then asked Landers about the meeting he said he had with Patricia Columbo at the Women's Detention Center; this was the "vision" conversation that supposedly took place in Superintendent Claudia McCormick's office, but which she and her secretary denied—at the pretrial hearing, *not* before the jury—ever occurred. Under oath here, however, Landers maintained it had occurred. His recollection was that Patricia had related to him that in her vision she had seen her father on the living room floor, seen her mother in the hallway wearing nightclothes, and that her brother "was in his bedroom but it was dark" and she "couldn't tell if he had on any clothes or not." She also said, according to Landers, that she saw the scissors with blood on them.

Assuming here that *no* one was lying, that Superintendent Claudia McCormick and her secretary were somehow simply mistaken, and that the superintendent did have Patricia Columbo brought to her office, and that Landers did indeed have this conversation with her there—what can be made of it? Jail psychiatrist Dr. Cherian has already stated what kind of mental condition Patricia was in: "acute situational reaction . . . with psychomotor retardation." If, through her oppressive condition, any truth surfaced, what was it? That she had been in the house? Yes. Seen her father dead? Yes. Seen her mother dead? Yes. Seen her brother dead? *No.*

If it was so dark in the bedroom that she could not tell whether Michael was clothed or not, how could she have seen the bloody scissors across the room on his desk? And if it was *not* too dark to see the scissors, then she would have been able to see that Michael was dressed in blue sweat pants and a white T-shirt. The other strong possibility: Patricia saw the bloody scissors someplace *other* than in Michael's room.

If John Landers is to be believed, and is correctly quoting what Patricia Columbo told him, then the question must be asked, why would Patricia's so-called vision accurately show her father and mother, but *not* Michael? She was too wasted at the time Landers says he talked to her to lie; even as accomplished as she was at braiding truth with lies, her mind was simply not energized enough at that point to do so. If the sworn testimony of John Landers is to be unequivocally accepted, then it must also be accepted that the *possibility exists that Patricia Columbo did not see her brother's body that night.* This despite enormous popular belief to the contrary.

During their "vision" conversation, Landers asked Patricia several leading questions.

"Do you see yourself in the house that night?"

Patricia: "Yes."

"Do you see yourself involved in the killing of your father, your mother, or your brother?"

Patricia: "I'm not certain . . . I'm confused . . ."

The last thing Patricia apparently told John Landers, according to him, was that in the vision, Frank Columbo told his daughter that "Jesus would forgive" her.

When Bill Murphy cross-examined Landers, the young defense attorney concentrated on Patricia's "vision," but his questions seemed to focus only on the position of her mother's body in the vision as opposed to its position at the murder scene itself. In her "vision," Patricia was alleged by Landers to have said she "saw" Mary's body in the hallway near her parents' *bedroom.* Ray Rose's testimony had been that Mary was shot and fell in the hallway directly outside the *bathroom.* Perhaps Murphy was trying to show that Patricia's "vision," even if real, was inaccurate, therefore not an indication that Patricia had been in the house. A careful study by Murphy of the crime scene photographs and a floor plan of the house—or even a personal visit to 55 Brantwood, which would have been permitted to the defense if requested—would have shown Murphy that *both* references to Mary's body were correct. Frank Columbo had at some point closed off the door to the master bedroom, so that the only entry was now from the hall, through the bathroom, and through a second door into the bedroom. Patricia probably considered the bathroom door to be the bedroom door.

It was a pointless line of questioning. The defense would have been far better off getting Superintendent Claudia McCormick and her secretary, Thelma Hawkins, back on the stand, *in front of the jury*, to challenge whether the meeting between Landers and Patricia even took place. Or, when sheriff's deputy Gene Gargano subsequently returned to the stand, the defense might have questioned *him* regarding the "vision" story, since he was supposed to have been there. The prosecution, although it had Gargano on the stand twice, did *not* ask him to corroborate the testimony of John Landers—which in itself is curious, to say the least. These are the kinds of irregularities in prosecutions that defense lawyers can sometimes make great capital of. It may, of course, simply have been an oversight by the state. Then again, there may have been a *reason* Gargano did not testify to that very important element of the case, such as the possibility that his recollection conflicted with the Landers version.

Star number two now took the witness stand.

Roman Iganatius Sobczynski.

Al Baliunas handled the direct examination. He first established that Roman was thirty-four years old, married, had three children, resided on Glenbrook Drive in the suburb of Mount Prospect, and had been a recruiting officer for the Cook County Department of Personnel for eleven years. Had the jury not already heard Lanny Mitchell's testimony, it probably would have thought at this point that Roman was Mr. Average Middle-Class America.

Roman testified that his understanding of the purpose of the first meeting among his friend Lanny, himself, Nancy Glenn, and Patty Columbo had been for a sex party. He denied knowing anything of the hundred-dollar fee Lanny alleged he had arranged with Patricia, but later in his testimony admitted that, after he and Lanny chased the girls when Patricia tried to run out on them, he had asked her, "Why'd you try to ditch us after Lanny paid you?" (These two conflicting statements came only a minute apart; they were never challenged by the defense.)

Roman also admitted telling Patricia that she was not free to leave until they "finished what was agreed on." Patricia got angry at that point, Roman claimed, saying, "Okay, I'll go to the motel, but I won't fuck you, you jack-off." (This is the man of whom, according to Lanny's testimony, Patricia had only an hour earlier said she would "fuck his eyes out" for favors he could do for her.) Roman had simply responded, "Okay, you can fuck Lanny," apparently not caring *who* he had sex with, as long as he had it.

Roman was wearing a gun that night "to impress the girls,"

and did not deny letting the air out of Patricia's tires so that she could not try to "ditch" them again.

Testimony from Sobczynski that directly contradicted Lanny Mitchell's testimony had to do with the meeting the two men had with Patricia at the Ala Moana Restaurant. Roman had not seen Patricia since the motel fiasco, so this was only his second meeting with her, but Lanny had seen Patricia four additional times in the interim; this was Lanny's sixth meeting with her. It was now mid-November 1975, Lanny Mitchell had already offered to kill Frank and Mary Columbo, and Roman, ostensibly Lanny's "heavy" friend, was being consulted about the hit.

Roman admitted telling Patricia that the hit "could definitely be done." But there was the question of money up-front, and Patricia had none. Roman testified, "We mentioned that she could put her ass on the table." Lanny, of course, had testified that it was Patricia who suggested sex instead of money up-front. (Patricia's recollection fifteen years later was that it was Roman. But at the trial, Roman said it was "we"—Lanny and he.)

Roman admitted under further direct examination that at subsequent meetings with Patricia, both with and without Lanny Mitchell present, Roman assured Patricia that "the hits were being arranged," that they were "working on doing the hits." Roman met with Patricia Columbo a total of ten times, four of them without Lanny being there, and had sex with her six times. (Some policemen speculated, because Roman was inviting Patricia to lunch where other men besides Lanny Mitchell were present, that he might have had an ambition to establish Patricia as a call girl, with himself as her pimp. There was no more substantiation of that theory, however, than there was that Roman may have been seriously considering actually committing the murders. This kind of conjecture probably arose because of the feeling that Roman, like Lanny, would do *anything* for money, sex, or whatever else was in it for him. There was more conjecture about Roman than Lanny, presumably, because Roman had nerve enough to do things the mere thought of which might have sent Lanny running to the bathroom.)

After the first of the year 1976, Roman admitted that Patricia began to get impatient with him and Lanny, but they

gave her "more assurances" that the plan was still moving
along.

Roman admitted giving Patricia a .32-caliber revolver with
six bullets. Later, worried that the gun might somehow be
traced back to him, he telephoned Patricia and told her to get
rid of it because it was "dirty." Two days later he called her
again and she told him the gun was "at the bottom of the
lake."

Finally, on February 17, the three had their last meeting. It
was at the Ron Tross house; each of the men had sex with
Patricia, Roman first as usual, Lanny taking leftovers. It was
a Tuesday night, exactly eleven weeks before the murders.

(Patricia apparently had nothing to do with either man after
that, although Lanny did telephone her once when, out of
work, he made an attempt to reopen the "hit" discussions if
Frank DeLuca could get some money up-front from Walgreen's. Patricia refused. It was during this period that she
claimed she began going to see her family again; she was at
home for Michael's thirteenth birthday on April 10; she began borrowing her mother's car again from time to time; and,
she claimed, her father's attitude, as it invariably did toward
his only daughter, was moving away from anger in the direction of reason. This is the time in which Patricia, in her original statement to police, said she telephoned Roman and
Lanny a number. of times to call off the hits, because her
problems looked as though they might be starting to work
out.)

Patricia aside, there *is* evidence that Frank DeLuca had
contact with Roman Sobczynski, on the telephone at least.
Roman admits *returning* a call to DeLuca on March 10, after
DeLuca left an "emergency message" for him. This was more
than three weeks *after* Patricia's last personal contact with the
men. During that call, DeLuca told Roman that he was living
in constant fear of Frank Columbo and could not wait much
longer for the hits to be made. Roman now assured DeLuca
that it would soon be done. (No one bothered to ask Roman
Sobczynski on the witness stand whether he had any *subsequent* conversations with Frank DeLuca after that date. It
hardly seems reasonable that a frightened, vulnerable individual like DeLuca, with easy access not only to cash but a
plethora of marketable commodities—liquor and drugs, for

instance—would have been let off the hook by the likes of Roman and Lanny—especially when DeLuca was calling *them*. Patricia's well might have run dry by then, but Frank's was virtually untapped. It is extremely difficult to visualize Roman and Lanny simply walking away from that well without lowering the bucket a few times first. Particularly with Lanny being out of work.)

Before Al Baliunas turned Roman over for cross-examination, he deprived the defense of one pleasure by asking, "You have received immunity in this matter in exchange for your testimony, is that correct?"

It was.

Baliunas tried one last quickie. "As you sit here today, do you feel morally responsible for the murders of Michael, Mary, and Frank Columbo?"

In other words, do you think Patty and/or DeLuca killed them with the gun *you* gave Patty?

Swano, Bloom, and Toomin bolted to their feet with objections, which Judge Pincham sustained.

No one would find out here whether Roman Sobczynski—or Lanny Mitchell, for that matter—felt any moral responsibility for the tragedy. Most people thought they did not.

Bill Swano was the first defense counsel to cross-examine. His entire line of questioning established absolutely nothing to help Patricia's case. True, he put another coat of paint on Roman to show the jury how despicable and contemptible a character Sobczynski was—but it was simply overkill: everyone involved in the trial knew by then that both Roman and Lanny were predators without conscience.

Swano questioned Roman about his movements on the day of the murders—which did nothing but establish that Roman had not committed the killings. There was no lengthy probing of just how much Roman had encouraged the crime, advanced it, approved it, supported it; he, like Lanny Mitchell, was guilty of conspiracy to murder the Columbo family—but "conspiracy" was a word that the members of this jury probably never used in their lives; someone at the trial should have brought alive for them, made real for them, given some impact to the fact for them, that without the fuel that Roman

Sobczynski and Lanny Mitchell added to the burning desperation in Patricia Columbo, the murders might never have been committed. There is a strong likelihood that the jury never understood that.

Stanton Bloom cross-examined Roman Sobczynski for DeLuca. He brought out Roman's shoplifting and petty-theft record; emphasized that Roman had let the air out of Patricia's tires at the motel probably out of a bruised ego because Patricia would not have sex with him—so that the only sex he got that night was from her drunken friend; made him admit that a lot of his "tough guy" pose had been learned from watching television; also made him admit that he had taken at least five other women to the Edgebrook Motel for sex; that he sometimes used the alias of "Sobin" or "Soben"; that he portrayed several different roles in his life: thief, big shot, hit man, great lover—but that in reality he was a colossal fraud who lied to everyone, including his own wife, but now wanted the jury to believe he was telling the truth.

Again, a very good attack on Roman Sobczynski, without impressing the jury of the *effect* Roman had on Patricia. Making Roman look worse and worse only made Patricia look worse and worse, because she was having sex with him. Emphasizing what his manipulation did to her might have served Patricia Columbo better.

Bloom did make one good point, however; he made Roman admit that he *had* to tell the story he had related on the stand, by asking him if it was not true that, if he changed that story at all—the story he had agreed to tell in exchange for immunity—the prosecution would indict him for perjury.

Roman's answer: Yes.

Sheriff's deputy Gene Gargano was recalled to testify about Frank DeLuca's remarks when Gargano interviewed him the day Patricia was arrested. DeLuca had not made a formal statement that day, but he might as well have. All of his clever "hypothetical" questions had told Gargano exactly what was on DeLuca's mind. "Suppose" a hypothetical "guy and gal" did it, what would the penalty be? What were the chances of the "hypothetical guy and gal" being sent to a hospital instead of a prison? Questions like that don't occur to *innocent* people even before they are arrested. DeLuca probably would have fully confessed that day if Gene Gargano had been empowered by the state to offer him an appealing deal. If Gargano could have promised adjoining rooms for Patty and him at a comfortable mental institution, Cook County could have saved the cost of a trial—and sent Roman Sobczynski and Lanny Mitchell to prison as well.

Robert A. Cabanne, a questioned documents examiner for the state Bureau of Identification, had been a handwriting expert for twenty-five years. He had examined People's Exhibit 166, a drawing of a floor plan of a split-level home on which the word *downstairs* was written; People's Exhibit 169, which was a list of routine daily activities beginning with the name "Frank Peter Columbo"; and People's Exhibit 176, handwriting specimens from the defendant Patricia Columbo. Mr. Cabanne identified the handwriting on the first two exhibits as being identical to the third. He also testified that the paper on which the first two were written had come from the same notebook as the one seized in apartment 911.

Michael Podlecki, a criminalist for the state Bureau of Identification, had examined during his career more than five thousand body hairs and other fibers, and was declared an expert witness after some preliminary questions regarding his background. On direct, Patti Bobb asked whether he had examined hair standards from the Columbo homicides. He had: samples of hair taken from Frank and Mary Columbo, and samples taken from defendants Patricia Columbo and Frank DeLuca.

The prosecution was about to begin to try compensating for someone's failure to take a hair sample from Michael.

Podlecki testified that he had compared the two hairs taken from Michael's T-shirt with the sample from Frank DeLuca, and found no positive similarities. Comparing them to samples taken from Patricia Columbo, he found that the hair from the front of Michael's T-shirt was *similar* to hers. Since the state could not prove that the hair *wasn't* Michael's, they would insinuate that it *was* Patricia's.

Bill Murphy cross-examined. "Can you state that they are similar beyond a reasonable degree of scientific certainty?" he asked.

"They are similar," the state witness replied smoothly, "to the degree that I could not find any *dis*similarities."

Murphy turned to the bench. "Judge, instruct the witness to please respond to the question. I ask that the last answer be stricken."

Pincham shook his head. "An expert witness is entitled to answer questions in his own terminology."

Perhaps this was Pincham's way of telling Murphy that he was on the wrong path anyway. The jurors weren't scientists. A "reasonable degree of scientific certainty" was a lot like "conspiracy" in that it needed to be illustrated rather than merely spoken. There would have been no harm in asking, "Could the hair have come from someone *other* than Patricia Columbo?" The answer would have been yes.

But Murphy pressed doggedly on. "What courses have you taken in heredity or genetics?" Answer: basic undergraduate courses. But what difference did it make? The witness had been qualified by the court as an expert. It was too late to cast doubt on his credentials. Now was the time to cast doubt on the *hair*.

"Are you familiar with the DNA molecule?" Murphy asked.

"To a certain degree."

"It carries and establishes the genes from parents to children?" Yes.

Then, almost as if he suddenly remembered that it was one strand of *hair* that was at issue, Murphy asked, "You didn't have a hair standard from Michael Columbo?"

"No."

At last. Accidental or not.

"You don't know whether that hair came from Michael Columbo, correct?"

"Correct."

"You can't say whether that hair came from Patricia Columbo, can you?"

"Correct."

A point for the defense, finally.

Blair Schultz was another criminalist for the Illinois Bureau of Identification, employed in the Trace Section. His duties, he explained, included analyzing glass, paint, metals, residue from explosives, and all manner of other "trace" materials. He had a bachelor's degree in chemistry, a master's in forensic science.

Al Baliunas showed Schultz a number of exhibits that the criminalist had previously examined: People's Exhibit 30, glass from the living room floor at 55 Brantwood; 32, sweepings from the living room rug; 35, miscellaneous material from the floor of the top landing; 40, glass from the hallway; 50, miscellaneous material from the stairs; 70, contents of the glove box of Mary Columbo's Oldsmobile; 74, contents from the interior of the Oldsmobile; 77, sweepings from the floor of a 1968 Buick Skylark; 78, material from Frank Columbo's Thunderbird.

"Did you intercompare these items?" Baliunas asked.

"Yes."

"Did you find any comparison?"

"Only one."

"Designate them by item number."

"Numbers thirty and seventy-seven."

"Where did number thirty come from?"

"The scene of the crime, Fifty-five Brantwood."

"Where did number seventy-seven come from?"

"There was one piece of glass that came from the floor of the 1968 Buick Skylark," the car that had been loaned to Patricia Columbo by Jack Lilly of Jack's Top and Trim.

Toomin cross-examined. The floor sweepings from the 1968 Buick included twenty-five pieces of miscellaneous glass. All but two were very small. Only one was similar to glass from the Columbo home. It could have come from some other broken glass having similar optical properties. In fact, it could have come from, literally, hundreds of thousands of other pieces of broken glass in other places.

The jury, of course, was probably not thinking of those hundreds of thousands of other places. It was almost certainly thinking of 55 Brantwood.

When Mr. Schultz was excused, court adjourned, ending the fourth week of the trial.

On Monday, June 13, the first witness in the morning was Eugene Giles, PhD, a professor of anthropology at the University of Illinois. Under questioning by Patti Bobb, he testi-

fied that he had examined the fender and trunk lid of Frank
Columbo's Thunderbird and discovered a marking, which he
determined had been made by a gloved human hand. A left
hand. With the second digit of the index finger missing. The
marking was compatible with the handprint of Frank DeLuca.

It was while Dr. Giles was testifying that some spectators
in the courtroom began to suspect that Patricia Columbo was
being heavily medicated every day. She seemed at times to be
totally uninterested in what was going on around her, and frequently appeared to be staring off into space. She was not
medicated at all, of course, but in fact was doing something
her counsel advised her to do: staring at the bronze eagle on
top of the staff holding the United States flag next to Judge
Pincham's bench. This advice had been given after Patricia's
sudden rush of emotion when young Glenn Miller, Michael's
best friend, testified. Patricia's lawyers might not have
wanted her hands trembling again, and certainly would not
have wanted her glaring at DeLuca as she had while Michael's friend was on the stand. So someone on the defense
team started looking for some fixed object for her to concentrate on, and came up with the bronze eagle. After that,
whenever Patricia felt nervous, depressed, or simply weary of
it all, she would fixate on that eagle and tune the proceedings
out. When she had done it often enough, the rumor spread
that she was "doped up."

Following Dr. Giles was another of the prosecution's
"stars"—Hubert Francis Green, known as Bert.

Green identified Frank DeLuca as the store manager for
whom he previously worked, and Patricia Columbo as
DeLuca's girlfriend who came into the store about "three
times a week to see DeLuca." Bert related how DeLuca had
given him a package to hold for him, and subsequently
opened the package in Green's presence to reveal that it was
a gun. Then he told of being asked by DeLuca to pick up
Patty at their apartment building on three consecutive Monday nights and drive her to a church parking lot near the Columbo home. He recounted remarks that DeLuca had made
about Patty going to meet hit men whom she would then let
into the Columbo home. Patty had also spoken of "the hits
going down tonight," Green said, on the second trip. After the

first two Monday night trips, DeLuca subsequently told Green that something had gone wrong each time and that the "hits didn't go down." After the second trip, DeLuca allegedly said that if "they didn't go down next time, *he and Patty* would do it" themselves. (In his original statement to the police, Green had stated that DeLuca said, "*I'll* have to do it *myself*.") After the third failure, Green said, DeLuca was "very upset, very nervous," and told Bert that "the old man and old lady" had bought off his and Patty's hit men.

Court adjourned for the day with Bert Green still on the stand.

When court reconvened at 10:00 A.M. on Tuesday, June 14, Judge Pincham was advised, before the jury was brought in, that Bert Green was ill. He was just out of the hospital, the prosecution said, was under a doctor's care, and needed to take "medicine" every half hour. The "medicine" was Maalox, a popular over-the-counter antacid suspension liquid that helps neutralize stomach acid. Bert Green apparently was hyperapprehensive, perhaps even on the verge of a nervous breakdown. Had the cold glare of Frank DeLuca from the defense table something to do with it?

Judge Pincham decided to tell the jury that court would be recessing every thirty minutes or so, but not why. While Green was on the stand, the court clerk would give him his Maalox in a paper cup as if giving him a drink of water. The reason for concealing Green's condition from the jury was never made clear. Perhaps Judge Pincham simply wanted to prevent the jury from reading anything into Bert Green's nervousness—such as a fear of DeLuca—to protect DeLuca's presumption-of-innocence status. It was a good call as far as the prosecution was concerned, because the state definitely would not have wanted the jury to suspect that Bert Green might have had a guilty conscience of his own.

On this second day of Green's testimony, Al Baliunas took Bert to the morning of May 5, 1976, when Green had arrived to open the store and found DeLuca already there. Here Green covered essentially the same ground he had in his statement to Ray Rose: the incinerator burning; DeLuca's statement that "it went down last night"; that he had been "a fucking mess . . . covered head to toe with blood"; that he

had shown Bert the cuts on his hands and said he got them
when he smashed a lamp over the old man's head—the whole
story Frank DeLuca had told him about killing Frank, Mary,
and Michael Columbo. Green repeated, as he had told Ray
Rose, that DeLuca had said Frank Columbo had asked him,
"Who are you? Why are you doing this to me?" and DeLuca
had said, "Fuck you!" and shot him again—presumably for
the third or fourth time. DeLuca said he had been wearing a
"stocking hat" and that it was in a bag being burned up with
the rest of the bloody clothes.

Baliunas then asked Green, "Did he at any time indicate
whether he shot the old lady?"

Green answered, incredibly, "No, sir."

Only moments earlier, Green had said DeLuca told him
that after shooting Frank Columbo twice, he had "gone up
and shot the old lady." Meaning, apparently, that he had shot
Frank Columbo twice on the stairs leading from the foyer up
to the living room, then continued up the stairs and shot Mary
when she rushed out of the bathroom.

But now, only moments later, Green contradicted himself
and said DeLuca had *not* in fact indicated he had shot the
"old lady."

This is curious. Had the prosecution rehearsed Bert Green
to say DeLuca had not indicated shooting Mary Columbo,
perhaps to insinuate that Patricia had done it? And then had
Bert Green simply forgotten to leave that part out earlier—in
other words, slipped and told the truth—and Baliunas tried to
get it in anyway? The state's case against Patricia at this point
was very strong in proving *conspiracy* to commit murder—
and in establishing that she was a world-class slut—but so far
the only evidence directly linked to the actual murders was
against DeLuca. The state was definitely reaching now to put
Patricia in the house—and to show some overt violence on
her part.

Even more extraordinary than Bert Green's contradicting
himself is the fact that the defense did not challenge it later
on. It remains on the record today that Bert Green said
DeLuca *did* and *did not* admit shooting Mary Columbo.

While Green was relating how DeLuca had told him about
the "really smart things" he did to "cover my tracks," Bert
became visibly nervous and began trembling. Judge Pincham

immediately had the jury removed and allowed Green to take some Maalox.

After Bert calmed down, Baliunas took him quickly through the next few days: DeLuca growing increasingly incredulous about the bodies not being found, then being "arrested" with Patricia Columbo a week later but being released (after Patricia signed a formal statement), and Bert going to the Elk Grove police department to drive DeLuca to his former home in Addison where Marilyn DeLuca and the five children still lived.

Bill Swano was the first to cross-examine. He established that Bert had left the employment of Walgreen's two months earlier, but did not ask why (an oversight Michael Toomin would correct). Swano then had Bert admit that, even though DeLuca had told him about committing the murders, Green had not gone to the police, in fact had not cooperated with officers investigating the crime, had not even cooperated when subpoenaed by the grand jury; had, in fact, concealed everything he knew about the case until July 28, *thirteen weeks* after DeLuca allegedly had told him he did the killings. And Swano asked bluntly, "The reason you did not tell the police . . . any of this information until three months after the incidents was because it took you that long to contract these lies, isn't that correct?"

"That's false," Bert Green insisted.

Swano let him go with surprisingly few bruises. Michael Toomin would not be so inclined.

"Do you know Joy Heysek?" Toomin asked.

"Yes."

"Was she an old girlfriend of Frank DeLuca's?"

"Yes."

"Did you subsequently develop a relationship with her yourself?"

"Uh, not the same kind of relationship."

"After Mr. DeLuca was arrested, you transferred to the Walgreen's store in Oak Brook, and Joy Heysek remained at the Elk Grove store?"

"Yes."

"She called you almost daily, did she not, at the Oak Brook store?"

"Yes."

"What did you talk about?"

That she was "extremely fearful about DeLuca."

"Did she ever tell you of any photos taken of her by DeLuca?"

"Yes."

"Did she tell you that in those photos she was depicted in various sexual acts with men, women, and dogs?"

"Objection." It was Baliunas. Sustained.

Under further questioning, Bert Green admitted that Joy Heysek desperately wanted the photos back but that DeLuca had refused to give them to her. Joy, Bert said, had told him she "would do anything" to get the photos back.

Between the murders and the trial, eleven months, had Bert Green ever met with Joy Heysek? Yes. How often? Almost daily.

Toomin abruptly changed the subject, apparently hoping to leave the jurors with the impression that Bert Green and Joy Heysek might have conspired to get DeLuca out of the way. Moving on to the third ride Bert said he gave Patty from the apartment building to meet the hit men, had not Green told police that he came to work the next morning, May 4, the day of the murders—when DeLuca had allegedly said, "I'll have to do it myself"—but that actually Green had been *off* that day? And had not police determined that by Walgreen's time sheets? And had not Al Baliunas discussed that discrepancy with him, told him that the discrepancy had to be cleared up, and hadn't Green then changed his story and said DeLuca told him that he would have to do it himself when Bert "just happened to come in to pick up some things for home"?

Yes—to all of it.

Toomin asked whether or not Bert, when DeLuca said he would "do it himself," had tried to dissuade his friend. "Did you say, 'Don't do it, Frank, it's wrong,' or anything like that?"

Bert shrugged. "No. I figured he was old enough to know what he was doing."

"And on May fifth, he told you about three murders he had committed the night before?"

"That's right."

"And you made no outcry to anybody?" Toomin asked incredulously. "It was just business as usual at Walgreen's?"

"Far from it," Green stated in his defense.

Before Toomin could continue, court adjourned for lunch.

"Was your relationship with Joy Heysek platonic?" Toomin asked when they reconvened.

"Yes."

But wasn't it true that Joy Heysek had written a love poem to him, that his wife had found it in the house, and that she left him?

"She never left me," Bert said. "She just went on a vacation."

Well, were there problems between him and his wife over Joy Heysek? Yes.

When did he transfer to the Oak Brook store? June 1976, a month following the murders. Was he transferred following an incident in which he had been caught in a stockroom with an employee named Barbara Cooper? "It wasn't because of that." That occurred, did it not? Yes. Was his relationship with Barbara Cooper just a platonic one? No. Had his wife left him because of *that*? Yes.

While Bert Green was vulnerable, Toomin nailed him. "Did DeLuca say he entered the Columbo house with anyone but himself?"

"No, sir."

It was a question one might think *Patricia's* counsel would have asked.

"You knew about this so-called hit while it was being planned, didn't you?"

"Correct."

"You knew about it and could have stopped it?"

"Correct."

Toomin turned away, disgusted again. "No further questions."

His last two questions had been strange indeed. By establishing that Bert Green could have stopped the murders, Toomin as much as said that his client had *committed* them.

Baliunas asked on redirect why Bert Green had not gone to the police. Bert said he thought DeLuca "was in the Mafia and could get hit men to do the same thing" to him, his wife, and child, that was done to the Columbos.

And after DeLuca's arrest, why not then? Bert shrugged. "I was afraid he would get out."

When Bert Green was excused that day, many close to the case felt that there was much more to his involvement than they had heard.

Joy Heysek took the stand.

Terry Sullivan established that she had known Frank DeLuca for seven years and had a sexual relationship with him from 1970 through 1973. In July 1975 she was head cosmetician at Walgreen's in Elk Grove Village. That was at the time Frank Columbo had attacked DeLuca on the parking lot. DeLuca told Joy Heysek that Columbo had "knocked my teeth out" and that DeLuca would "get even" for it.

In November 1975 Joy said DeLuca told her that Frank Columbo had a contract on him, but that he had "stopped the contract and arranged one on Frank Columbo and his family." DeLuca had asked her during this period to tell him every time she saw Michael Columbo come into the store.

Early in 1976, Heysek said, DeLuca told her that the hit men had deserted him and he "would have to do it himself"—a statement identical to the one Bert Green originally gave to the police but changed when he testified. Joy had asked DeLuca how he would do it, and he told her he would make it look like a robbery.

One week before the murders, in the Walgreen's stockroom, DeLuca warned her that if she went to the police and repeated anything he had told her, he would have her son run over by a car when he was riding his bike, have her daughter, Kim, "picked up and raped," and have Joy herself "beaten up so badly that nobody would ever recognize" her again.

On May 4, the day of the murders, DeLuca was leaving work at 4:00 P.M. and stopped to ask Joy to go see the film One Flew Over the Cuckoo's Nest and give him the details of it the next day. Joy told him she couldn't, she had to attend a class she was taking at Harper College.

On the morning of May 5, Joy had come to work at nine o'clock and found DeLuca in the lunchroom having coffee. He was "elated, very high," and showed her cuts and scratches on both hands. "What happened?" she asked.

"It went down last night," she testified that he replied—

again the same statement he had made to Bert Green. "I took them all out last night," he elaborated. "Old man Columbo gave me a rough time. I had to shoot him twice and finish him off by hand. I shot him in the back of the head ... the bullet came out through his mouth ... took his teeth with it ... now his teeth are the same as mine. The son of a bitch never knew what hit him."

"What about Mrs. Columbo?" Joy had asked.

"No problem. She came around the corner and I shot her between the eyes. Then I shot Michael."

Joy Heysek said that although "very upset," she went to the cosmetics department to begin work. Twenty minutes later, DeLuca called her back to the pharmacy and warned her for the second time to forget everything he said.

On Thursday, May 6, Joy testified, DeLuca was "anxious" because the bodies had not been discovered. Then, on Friday, May 7, at about 5:30 P.M., she had gone into the lunchroom and found him crying. One of the assistant managers was with him. DeLuca looked up at her and said, "They've found Mr. and Mrs. Columbo but can't find Michael." Apparently the employee who called to tell him of the tragedy only knew that Frank and Mary had been killed. When the assistant manager left, DeLuca stopped crying and began laughing. Joy Heysek said, "You ought to get an Emmy for that performance."

Sometime during the second week after the murders, DeLuca telephoned her at the store and asked her to meet him. She refused. DeLuca, by then transferred to another store, said he had heard that the police were questioning employees in the Elk Grove store about him, and warned her to remember what he said.

"I mean business," he told her.

Stanton Bloom cross-examined Joy Heysek for DeLuca. He established that she lived in Hoffman Estates, her husband's name was Ralph, and she now worked for the J. C. Penney Company, having left Walgreen's the previous September, four months after the murders. She had two children, ages thirteen and seventeen.

Joy had begun working at Walgreen's at Parkway Plaza in Schaumburg in 1970, as a part-time cashier. She had been hired by the store manager, Frank DeLuca. A year later, he transferred her into cosmetics. Her relationship with DeLuca began, she related in court, as one of friendship only; her marriage had "turned bad," and DeLuca was someone to "tell my troubles to." He asked her out "a couple of times," but she declined; she knew he was married and had, at that time, three children. Before she began her intimacy with DeLuca, she had been involved, she admitted, in one other "brief" affair.

When Joy Heysek finally agreed to go out with Frank DeLuca, she admitted that she "suspected" it would lead to a sexual relationship, and it had. The first time had been at a motel in Villa Park and had lasted three and a half hours. Joy said she fell in love with DeLuca "a few months" after the affair began.

Did Frank DeLuca "jilt" her for Patty Columbo? Stanton Bloom asked. "No," Joy Heysek replied calmly. "He was still seeing me while he was seeing her, still asking me to go out. He even wanted me to go out with both him and Patty."

"Did you have a falling-out with him?"

"Yes, when he asked me to do certain things I didn't want to do."

"What kind of things?"

"Sexual," Joy said simply.

Bloom now began a relentless personal attack on Joy Heysek. "Did you have a conversation with prosecutor Bobb about certain pictures?"

"Yes."

"Do you know what's in those pictures?"

"Yes. Sexual acts I didn't want to do."

"Were you forced?"

"Forced may be bad terminology," she allowed.

"Nobody put a gun to your head, did they?" Bloom asked dryly.

"No."

"Were you forced to take off your clothes?"

"I was beaten up once for not taking them off."

"How many times were photos taken of you?"

"I don't know."

"Twenty times? Thirty?"

"Not that many."

"But you took your clothes off each time you were photographed?"

"Yes."

"On one occasion was another woman there?"

"Yes."

"Did you perform oral acts on her?"

"No, she did on me but I didn't on her."

"The time they brought the dog in, did they force you to take off your clothes then?"

"No."

There was an odd absence of interference from the prosecution during this vitriolic questioning. Bloom had not established, for instance, who he meant by "they"—yet there was no objection. One had to wonder *who* brought the dog in.

"Did you ever have intercourse with a dog on any occasion?" Bloom asked scathingly.

"No."

Bloom would not be held off. "Well, did a dog ever mount you when you were in the nude?"

"Yes," Joy Heysek admitted.

"Did you ever allow a dog to perform an act of oral sex upon your vaginal area?"

"Yes."

Numerous people in the courtroom began to resent Stanton Bloom. He was going too far. But he would not desist—and Judge Pincham did not stop him because the prosecution didn't object.

"Did you ever perform an act of oral copulation upon a male dog?" the defense attorney for DeLuca demanded to know.

"No."

"You never put your mouth to a dog's penis?" he asked skeptically.

"Not that I recall," Joy Heysek answered rather lamely. She was becoming visibly distressed.

"There have been sexual pictures taken of you with various men, in various ways, various positions," Bloom said. "Were you forced on each occasion?"

"There are different forms of force," Joy said wearily.

How did she explain that she was smiling in the pictures?

She had "tried to make it look good," as if she were "enjoying it."

Testimony was now going into the evening hours. At some point earlier, Stanton Bloom had asked the court for a continuance due to some unspecified "health problems" he was experiencing, but Judge Pincham had not allowed it. Bloom obviously wanted to call it a day—but he wanted Joy Heysek back the next morning. Apparently there was a strong feeling at the prosecution table that if the court let Joy go, it would never see her again. It was fairly clear to everyone by then that she was almost totally thrashed by Bloom's punishing line of personal questions. Whether Judge Pincham independently realized that, or the prosecution somehow conveyed its concern to the bench, court was kept in session until 9:00 P.M., at which time there was only a short recess; the witness was not let go, and the trial resumed, much to Stanton Bloom's displeasure, a few minutes later.

"When did Frank DeLuca beat you up?" Bloom asked as the session moved toward 10:00 P.M.

"One time when he wanted me to pick up a black man and I refused," Joy Heysek said. "He slapped me in bed and beat me up."

But, she admitted, there were photos of her with a black man *before* DeLuca beat her up, so Bloom made the point that DeLuca had beaten her up because she did not want to do it *anymore*. Perhaps she had known the previous black man—DeLuca's friend Andre—but simply balked at performing with a stranger.

Had DeLuca hit her with his fists? Yes—twenty or thirty times, inflicting bruises on her face and breasts. She had explained them to her husband by telling him she had fallen down.

Did she like being beaten up? Bloom asked. No.

Would she come into court and make up stories about Frank DeLuca? No.

But didn't she hate him for jilting her for Patty Columbo?

"He didn't jilt me," Joy maintained firmly.

It seemed to be her one straw of self-esteem.

When Stanton Bloom finally excused Joy Heysek, it was 10:50 P.M. The unhappy attorney immediately moved for a mistrial. He reminded Judge Pincham that earlier he had asked for a continuance due to his health problems; the judge had denied his request and let the trial go into the evening, forcing Bloom to continue his examination of Joy Heysek. Bloom felt that the denial was "unduly unfair" to defendant DeLuca. In addition, Bloom stated that he "happened to know that one of the jurors was sleeping" during his cross-examination.

Al Baliunas advised Judge Pincham that the prosecution had observed no jurors sleeping.

Judge Pincham ruled, "I certainly don't feel that Mr. DeLuca has been prejudiced by working until this hour. The motion for a mistrial is denied."

The next witness was Dr. Robert Stein, chief medical officer for Cook County, who had performed the autopsies on Frank, Mary, and Michael Columbo.

Under Patti Bobb's direct examination, Dr. Stein testified that Frank Columbo had been shot four times: once in the back of the head, once on the right side of the face, once on the left side of the face, and once in the mouth. In addition, he had been beaten on the top, sides, and front of his head by a blunt instrument. And he had suffered a number of incised wounds on the left side of his neck.

Mary Columbo had been shot once at the bridge of the nose between the eyes. She had also been struck in the head by a blunt instrument, and suffered incised wounds of the neck compatible with the use of a sharp instrument.

Michael had been shot once at the outer aspect of the left eye, had suffered forty-eight incised wounds to the right side of the chest, and thirty-six wounds on the back, of which twenty-eight were incised and eight were deep puncture wounds.

During the testimony regarding Michael, Patricia began to cry softly at her defense table.

All three victims, Dr. Stein continued, had in their stomachs meat particles and green vegetable particles consistent with the meal served to them by waitress Judy DiMartino on the evening of May 4, 1976.

Dr. Stein had determined the time of death at between 11:00 P.M. on Tuesday, May 4, and 1:00 A.M. on Wednesday, May 5.

Producing People's Exhibit 113, the scissors found in Michael's bedroom, Patti Bobb asked whether they could have imposed the puncture wounds on Michael's *chest*. Yes. Whether the jury was confused by this question or simply let it pass is not known. Michael's puncture wounds were, of course, in the *back*, but anatomically speaking, the back *is* the posterior chest wall, so the question was technically correct. But it serves as still another example of the failure of counsel on both sides to spell out for the jury exactly *what* various testimony meant. How many people really consider one's back as the back of one's chest? Who ever complains of a pain in the back of their chest instead of simply a back pain? The important point, however, was that the scissors *could* have caused the puncture wounds, wherever they were. And by this time, the jury had probably forgotten that in the testimony of state serologist Robert Gonsowski, *eighteen days earlier*, there was not enough blood on those scissors to even distinguish whether it was A-positive or A-negative in type. Since the scissors were being presented as having made the eight deep puncture wounds, it is curious that at least one of the four defense attorneys did not wonder why there wasn't a *considerable* amount of blood on them. When something is stuck deeply into the human body, it comes back out with more than simply a trace of blood on it.

On cross-examination, Bill Murphy had Dr. Stein admit that no hair sample had been taken from Michael Columbo because none had been requested by the Elk Grove police department.

Toomin, cross-examining for DeLuca, asked Dr. Stein about the angle of the bullet that probably caused Frank Columbo's death. The pathologist replied that it was a bullet entering the front of the head, or face, angulating downward to destroy brain tissue in its path.

Was it fired by a man taller, shorter, or the same height as the victim? "I have no opinion on that," Dr. Stein replied.

Was the victim standing or sitting when he was shot? "I cannot answer that," the doctor said.

Was the person firing the gun holding it in his right or left hand? "I have no idea at all."

Dr. Stein did admit that in his estimate of the time of death, it could have been a little earlier, between 10:30 P.M.

and 12:30 A.M. It might even, he conceded further, have been as early as 10:15 P.M., as late as 1:15 A.M.

Murphy, recross-examining, asked whether the bullet that killed Michael struck his head "with great force?" Yes. Did it have a "jarring effect?" Yes. Was there hair at the entrance wound? No. At the exit wound? Yes.

On redirect by Patti Bobb, she asked again how many wounds Michael had on his body. Approximately ninety. (There were actually eighty-four.)

Would those wounds have caused a certain amount of pain? Answer: "Very much pain." (There was no objection from the defense, even though the cause of death had been positively established as a gunshot wound, and the prosecution had laid no foundation for its question by asking this witness whether in his *expert* opinion Michael might still have been alive and conscious after the bullet went through his brain, or even, again in Dr. Stein's professional opinion, whether the numerous wounds were inflicted before or after Michael was shot. Here Patti Bobb was clearly insinuating to the jury that Michael was still conscious enough to suffer.)

Without objection, she pressed on. Would there have been a reaction from a person still alive in terms of struggle? Answer: "Very definitely."

If Ms. Bobb had stopped at that point, she would have left the jury with the impression that Michael *might* have suffered. But, incredibly, she asked, "Were there any defense wounds on Michael Columbo?" Answer: "None."

So Michael had *not* struggled, even when "very much pain" was being inflicted. The obvious conclusion was because he was already dead. But how many jurors figured that out?

Dr. Stein was excused.

At this point, the clerk announced, "The state calls Clifford Lee Childs!"

At his defense table, Frank DeLuca looked down and sighed wearily.

At her own table, Patricia looked over at DeLuca and frowned. She had no idea who Clifford Lee Childs was.

She was about to get the surprise of her young life.

42

March 1977

On March 1, 1977, one month before the trial of Patricia Columbo and Frank DeLuca began, the Illinois state's attorney's office received a letter from an inmate of the Cook County Jail named Walter Bush. The letter stated that Bush had information concerning a murder case. Investigator Ralph Willer was sent to interview the man.

Bush, being held in jail on a burglary charge, related that another inmate, Clifford Lee Childs, said he had been hired by Frank DeLuca to kill a witness he expected to testify against him in his upcoming murder trial. Childs, who had been in jail twenty-one months awaiting trial on three counts of armed robbery, allegedly agreed to do the job for $15,000 if DeLuca would arrange to get him out of jail. Childs was being held in lieu of $42,500 bail, 10 percent of which would secure a bond for his release.

Because the information from Walter Bush was relevant to a murder case then being prepared for trial, prosecutor Al Baliunas, chief investigator Ray Rose, and sheriff's investigator Gene Gargano were all notified. A quick check of jail records gave frightening corroboration to Walter Bush's story. Clifford Childs had not only resided in cell 16 of tier C-1, with Frank DeLuca as his cellmate, but had been bailed out on February 24—nine days earlier.

A copy of the bond slip releasing Childs was pulled. It listed as his address 1521 Holtz in suburban Addison—the residence of DeLuca's ex-wife and five children.

Rose and Gargano immediately located the circuit court clerk who had issued the bond. He recalled that Childs, a black man, had been bailed out by two white people: a short man in his forties with graying hair, and a taller woman in her thirties, dark-haired, attractive, wearing a light-colored trench coat. From the latter description, together with the address on the bond slip, Ray Rose and Gene Gargano were convinced that the woman was Marilyn DeLuca.

A conference held in the state's attorney's office resulted in the decision that the two primary prosecution witnesses against DeLuca—Bert Green and Joy Heysek—should be put under twenty-four-hour protection, and that the two main witnesses against Patricia—Lanny Mitchell and Roman Sobczynski—should be informed of the situation. Photos of Clifford Lee Childs and copies of his criminal record were distributed to everyone concerned.

Childs, twenty-nine years old, six feet four, 210 pounds, was due to appear in court in five days. Meanwhile, his whereabouts were unknown.

Ray Rose and Gene Gargano interrogated Walter Bush and learned that he had known Clifford Lee Childs casually for several years. When Bush came into Cook County Jail, he was assigned to cell 21 on tier C-1, just five cells down from Childs and Frank DeLuca. Renewing his acquaintance with Childs, Bush said Childs told him DeLuca would soon be bailing him out. Childs said that DeLuca had been looking for someone to kill a witness and had first approached an alleged contract murderer, Michael Brooks, but Brooks was being held without bail and supposedly referred DeLuca to Childs. DeLuca asked one of the jail officers to transfer him to cell 16, where Childs was quartered. The reason DeLuca gave for the request was that his present cellmate was a "hillbilly" with whom he was having trouble. The cell change, not uncommon, was granted.

Subsequent to DeLuca's moving in with Clifford Lee Childs, Bush, during a visit with his own wife, had observed DeLuca, being visited by a dark-haired, attractive woman, calling Childs over from another part of the visiting room and holding a conversation with him and the woman.

Childs, according to Bush, was a jail trustee, and regularly handled the passing of "kites"—illegal correspondence—between DeLuca and Patricia, over in the women's section of the jail.

On March 8, 1977, Clifford Lee Childs, with an attorney, Clinton O. Sims, appeared as scheduled in the courtroom of Judge Joseph Machala. He was immediately taken into custody by sheriff's officers and the proceedings against him in the three armed robbery charges were continued until a later

date. Childs was then taken to the state's attorney's office to
be interrogated by Ray Rose and Gene Gargano.

During his conversations with Rose, Gargano, and later Al
Baliunas, Clifford Childs admitted that he had been solicited
by Frank DeLuca to kill not only Bert Green but Joy Heysek
as well. He was to receive ten thousand dollars "up-front,"
another ten thousand dollars upon completion of the murders,
and a twenty-thousand-dollar bonus "later on." Childs had
been bailed out of jail by Marilyn DeLuca and Frank's
brother, William DeLuca. In order to cover Frank DeLuca in
case anything went wrong with the plan—such as Childs getting caught—DeLuca had drawn up a promissory note for a
"loan" to Childs of his bail money. That would be DeLuca's
excuse for giving Childs the money: not to buy a hit, merely
a loan. Childs had signed the document and DeLuca, he said,
had it under the mattress of his jail bunk.

There was other physical evidence, as well. Rose and
Gargano learned that Patricia Columbo was not the only one
naive enough to draw diagrams and write out descriptions of
victims; DeLuca had also done it. He gave handwritten descriptions of Bert Green and Joy Heysek to Childs, drew a diagram of Grove Shopping Center, and drew a map showing
Childs how to get to Joy Heysek's home. He even wrote a list
of things for Childs to do when he was released—which included buying small cans of liquid chloroform and renting a
van in which to transport the unconscious victims. On top of
everything else, DeLuca had described for Childs, in even
greater detail than he did for Bert Green and Joy Heysek,
how he murdered the victims.

At this point, Rose and Gargano must have thought Frank
DeLuca the stupidest, most bungling, incompetent murderer
in history. The blunders he made were monumental.

Only Frank, Mary, and Michael kept it from being funny.

On March 9, Gene Gargano appeared before Judge James M.
Bailey and obtained a search warrant to enter cell 16 on tier
C-1 of the Cook County Jail in order to seize, if it was still
there, the promissory note Childs allegedly signed for
DeLuca. Childs had also told Ray Rose and Gargano about
being allowed by DeLuca to read numerous pieces of correspondence Frank had received, many of them illegally trans-

mitted through unauthorized channels, from Patricia Columbo. In one of those letters or notes, Childs recalled, Patricia had written that if it were not for her "conduct," DeLuca would not be in his present situation. Childs took that to be an admission of her involvement in the murders. The search warrant obtained by Gargano also authorized the seizure of all DeLuca's correspondence in order to obtain what was believed to be further incriminating evidence. Additionally, the warrant listed one other item to be seized: four single-edge razor blades—personal weapons which, when not being carried, DeLuca kept secreted under the bottom cardboard flap of a cereal box.

With the search warrant approved, Gargano contacted the security section of the jail and requested that DeLuca and his new cellmate be removed from cell 16 and that the cell be secured. Shortly thereafter, accompanied by jail officers, Gargano entered the cell and took possession of the following items: one stack of folders containing letters; two boxes of letters; five photographs; two paintings; four books; one additional folder containing letters; and miscellaneous papers.

He also found the four razor blades, which were turned over to jail officers as contraband.

The promissory note was not found.

It appeared from the quantity of correspondence Gargano found that DeLuca had saved every note and letter Patricia had written to him during the eight months they had by then both been incarcerated. Now, all of that material was removed to the state's attorney's office where Rose, Gargano, and other investigators would go over every word Patricia had written to her lover.

Later the same day that DeLuca's cell was searched, Ray Rose and Gene Gargano waited outside Cook County Jail until they saw Marilyn DeLuca and Frank's brother, William DeLuca, emerge from having visited Frank. The two investigators approached and advised them that a representative of the state's attorney's office wished to speak to them, and requested their cooperation in accompanying the officers.

Upon arrival at the state's attorney's offices, Mrs. DeLuca and her brother-in-law were shown into the office of Al

Baliunas, who at that time was preparing the prosecution's case against Patricia and Frank.

Baliunas asked Marilyn DeLuca if she knew an individual named Clifford Childs. She replied that she did. Baliunas asked if she had posted bond to have Childs released from jail. She replied no, she had not. Baliunas pointed out that her home address was on the bond release slip of Clifford Childs. In addition, there were copies of two Western Union telegraphic money orders, numbers 60969 and 60970, in amounts of $2,000 and $1,420, respectively, sent to Clifford Childs at Cook County Jail from Marilyn DeLuca. And there was a witness, the circuit court clerk who accepted in cash the balance of the $4,250 bond from a "dark-haired, attractive woman in her thirties."

Marilyn DeLuca was asked again if she had posted bond to have Clifford Childs released from jail. She then admitted that she had.

Asked if she had been present when Childs was released, Marilyn admitted she had been. She had driven Clifford Childs from jail to her residence in Addison, where she gave him Frank DeLuca's 1973 Javelin automobile.

Asked why she had done that, Marilyn DeLuca replied lamely that she was "carrying out the instructions" of her "ex-husband."

At that point, Marilyn DeLuca asked Baliunas why he was asking her "all these questions." Baliunas replied that they were investigating an allegation that Frank DeLuca had solicited Clifford Childs to kill two of the state's witnesses in the murder case presently pending against him.

Marilyn DeLuca said she did not believe that accusation. Al Baliunas told her that Clifford Childs was in the next office and asked if she wished to hear him relate that allegation himself. Marilyn said yes.

Clifford Childs was brought in. He stated in Marilyn DeLuca's presence that Frank had hired him to kill Bert Green and Joy Heysek for a fee of ten thousand dollars each. Childs had no personal knowledge of whether Marilyn DeLuca did or did not know of the murder plot. He was of the opinion, he said, that she did not.

After Childs was taken away, Al Baliunas asked Marilyn if she had a reasonable explanation for her actions in getting

Clifford Childs released from jail, taking him to her home, and furnishing him with a car. Marilyn stated that she had a reason but did not wish to disclose it. She then asked Baliunas if she was under arrest. Baliunas said, "Not at this time."

Marilyn then stated that she did not wish to answer any further questions until she could speak to public defender Bill Murphy. (At that point in the trial preparation, Murphy represented both Patricia and DeLuca. It was not until after this incident that Murphy asked to be relieved of Frank DeLuca's defense, and the court appointed outside counsel for DeLuca to avoid a conflict of interest within the public defender's office. There were also reports at the time of a growing animosity between Bill Murphy and Frank DeLuca, and DeLuca in fact bitterly criticized Patricia for being "too friendly" with Murphy.)

When Bill Murphy arrived at the state's attorney's office, Al Baliunas brought him up-to-date on everything that had transpired to that point. Murphy then asked Baliunas the same thing Marilyn had asked: Was she under arrest? And got the same reply: "Not at this time."

Murphy then left with Marilyn DeLuca and her brother-in-law, William. There is no record of William DeLuca having been asked any questions at all during the interview.

After the Murphy group departed, no one was left but Clifford Childs, who no doubt was waiting patiently in the other office to see what kind of deal he could cut for his testimony.

43
June 1977

Clifford Lee Childs was tall, well built, with a long, narrow face topped by naturally curly hair that needed no processing. He was handsome and sported a neatly trimmed mustache. As his testimony progressed, he became one of the most enigmatic personalities of this serpentine trial.

Terry Sullivan began by asking Clifford Childs where he

resided. "Twenty-six hundred South California," Childs replied. "Cook County Jail. Witness quarters."

"Are there any criminal indictments pending against you?"

"Yes. Three charges of armed robbery."

"Are you guilty of those charges?"

"Yes."

That answer was all anyone needed to know that a deal had been made. Childs was admitting his guilt only because he already knew what his sentence was going to be. By being on the witness stand right then, he was guaranteeing that sentence.

Sullivan carefully guided Childs through his friendship with Frank DeLuca while they celled together in number 16. He brought Childs up to the time when DeLuca first broached the subject of having Bert Green and Joy Heysek killed. It was after lockup one night. DeLuca asked Childs if he could get two hits "taken care of," and how much it would cost? Childs told him ten thousand dollars each. DeLuca then said he wanted two people killed who could "put him in the pen for a long time." Could Childs do it? Sure, he could. Shades of Lanny Mitchell and Roman Sobczynski.

Childs testified that DeLuca outlined a murder plan for him. Childs was to get DeLuca's 1973 Javelin from Marilyn after she bailed him out and have it painted black. He was to steal different license plates and put them on it. Then he was to use the car to watch the movements of both Joy Heysek and Bert Green until he had established their daily routines. When he was ready, he was to rent a van, use chloroform to put the victims to sleep, drive them across the state line into Indiana, dig a hole somewhere, put them in it, pour lime over them, and bury them.

Sullivan asked Childs if DeLuca had ever discussed Frank Columbo. He had. "Frank told me he shot the whole family."

DeLuca had told Childs that earlier on the day of the murders, DeLuca had called Frank Columbo and asked if he could come to the Columbo house at eight o'clock that evening for a reconciliatory meeting. Columbo agreed, but DeLuca said he never intended to keep the appointment; apparently he only wanted to make sure Columbo stayed home that evening.

Later that night, DeLuca allegedly told Childs, he put a

change of clothes into the "borrowed" car, but he himself
drove the "other" car. (This had to have been inordinately
confusing to the poor jury. There were two "borrowed" cars
that day: the 1968 Buick, which Patricia had borrowed or
rented from Jack's Top and Trim; and the Columbo
Oldsmobile, which Patricia had borrowed from her mother
two days earlier and still had.)

Unknown to DeLuca, Patricia had been seeing her family
for more than a month, beginning with an impulse visit on
Michael's birthday, April 10. It was, according to her, an effort to pave the way for her to leave DeLuca and return
home. She was borrowing Mary Columbo's Oldsmobile to
look for work. It angered DeLuca when he found out, but
Patricia placated him by assuring him that it was only her
mother she was seeing, not her father or Michael.

At the trial now, it was a question of *which* "borrowed" car
DeLuca had been referring to, and which he had been calling
the "other" car. No one on either side of this case bothered
to inquire or, if they already knew, to tell the jury. As with so
much else in the trial, the jurors were simply left to guess,
and try to figure it out for themselves.

DeLuca told Childs that he parked the "other" car a block
away and got into the "borrowed" car where he had put his
change of clothes. He then proceeded to 55 Brantwood and
parked behind the "other" car (presumably a second "other"
car, probably Frank Columbo's Thunderbird) in the driveway.
No lights could be seen from the outside of the house.

The doorbell was rung. Frank Columbo answered and let
him in. Columbo turned and started up the several steps leading from the entrance foyer to the living room. DeLuca said
he shot him in the back of the head when he got to the top
step.

DeLuca went on to tell Clifford Childs that after shooting
all members of the household, he "messed up the house to
look like a home invasion." DeLuca said he took $150 in
cash, some jewelry, and other items, and put them "in the
first car, nearest the garage" (presumably the Thunderbird).
Then DeLuca got in the car "near the street" (this was one of
the "borrowed" cars, either the '68 Buick or the Columbo
Olds).

DeLuca said he drove to an open field and changed

clothes. Then the "other" car (here he had to have been talking about the Thunderbird) was driven into Chicago, to the
lower West Side, and left in a black neighborhood in the
hopes that some "dumb niggers" would break into it, steal
the items he had taken from the house, go joyriding, then
"get busted and take the weight for home invasion."

Then, DeLuca said, he *rode* back, picked up his own car,
"dropped off the Olds," and returned to his apartment.

The murder weapon, DeLuca assured Childs, would never
be found.

After DeLuca had written out descriptions of Joy Heysek
and Bert Green for Childs, written out their possible schedules, drawn Childs a map to get to Heysek's home, and a diagram of Grove Shopping Center and the Walgreen's store,
all of it was put into a sealed envelope marked "DO NOT
OPEN," then into a larger envelope and mailed by Clifford
Childs to his mother in New Jersey.

The stage was apparently set for the second pair of murders for hire. All that remained was to get Clifford Childs out
on bail.

As Terry Sullivan continued questioning Childs, he paved
the way for his witness to avoid a murder conspiracy charge.

"Did you intend to carry out the killings?"

"No."

What, then, had been his purpose in becoming involved in
the plan? He saw it, Childs said, as a way out of Cook
County Jail, where, unable to post bond, he had been lan-
guishing for twenty-one months awaiting trial.

At this point, Terry Sullivan had Childs identify the
handwritten descriptions and diagrams DeLuca had drawn for
him, which Childs had retrieved from his mother in New Jersey. Then Sullivan asked, "Was Frank DeLuca communicating with Marilyn DeLuca at this time?"

"Yeah, he was sending her all over the place trying to get
a loan."

On November 18, 1976, DeLuca received a visit from
Marilyn and his brother Bill. Following the visit, DeLuca told
Childs that the money had been obtained and "the plan was
go."

One week later, on November 25, Childs received two
Western Union money orders, one for $2,000 and the other

for $1,420. With that money in his jail account, Childs attempted to get a bail reduction. (His bail was then $42,500, the bond for which was 10 percent. He was still $830 short.) When his bail reduction was denied, Childs told DeLuca that "he had to come up with the rest of the money." At this time, DeLuca was "real shaky, paranoid." He wanted Clifford Childs out and "the business taken care of." Eventually, Marilyn DeLuca and brother Bill paid the balance of the bond and Childs was released.

Marilyn DeLuca was waiting for Childs when he walked out of the county jail. She drove him in her station wagon to her home in Addison, and there, in the kitchen, gave him the keys to Frank DeLuca's Javelin and an envelope containing $1,300.

Childs drove DeLuca's car to O'Hare Airport, parked it, and flew east to New Jersey to visit his parents and son, whom he had not seen in three years. After a ten-day stay, he returned to Chicago, checked into the YMCA, and with an attorney appeared in court on March 8 as scheduled. Arrested there, he subsequently entered into an agreement with the state to testify against DeLuca in exchange for a reduced charge from armed robbery to simple robbery. With a plea of guilty, he would receive a sentence of one-to-twenty years (the armed robbery charge carried a much higher minimum sentence).

When Michael Toomin cross-examined, he immediately assailed the witness's background. Childs had a rape arrest in 1967, was charged with possession and sale of narcotics in 1970; possession of stolen property and forgery in 1971; possession of a knife, a blackjack, and a controlled and dangerous substance in 1971; distribution of heroin in 1974; grand theft in 1975; and possession and sale of heroin in 1976.

Stanton Bloom took over cross-examination from Toomin. "Did Frank DeLuca say he had one of the Columbo cars?" he asked.

"He said he *rode* in it," Childs replied. Which car, the Olds or the Thunderbird? "He didn't say."

"At the Columbo house, did DeLuca say whether or not he rang the doorbell?"

"Didn't say *he* rang."

"Did DeLuca tell you how long he was in the Columbo house?"

"Twenty minutes, no longer."

"Did he say he was wearing gloves?"

"Yes."

Establishing that DeLuca's left index finger and the tip of the next finger were missing, Childs said DeLuca told him he "stuffed" the fingers of the gloves he wore, but Childs did not know with what. Childs went on to say that DeLuca told him he burned his bloody clothes in a field rather than the Walgreen's incinerator. And DeLuca had said the clothes were *not* very bloody.

"Did DeLuca mention the slashings?"

"He told me throats were cut.'

"Whose?"

"The old man and old lady."

"How about the kid?"

"No, he didn't say nothing about it."

"Did he tell you the kid was cut at all?"

"He mentioned it."

"You would lie to get out of jail, wouldn't you?" Bloom challenged.

"Yes."

"Would you lie to get out from under armed robbery charges?"

"No."

"You have three and a half years of college, don't you?"

"Yes."

"Have you taken any courses in acting or drama?"

"No."

"You would lie to get your freedom, wouldn't you?"

"I would lie to get my freedom," Clifford Childs admitted.

On redirect, Terry Sullivan established that Childs had indeed signed a promissory note to Frank DeLuca for the money Marilyn DeLuca had sent Childs, but only as "Frank's alibi in case the state came down on him after the hits."

There was not much the defense could do about Clifford Childs, at least not as far as his direct testimony was concerned. He maintained his story throughout—and he knew far too much for it not to be believable.

* * *

The prosecution now sought to nail down what Clifford Childs had said. It called Julia Jallits, a Western Union employee, who testified that Marilyn DeLuca had purchased the two money orders for Childs, paying for them with a cashier's check drawn on the Elmhurst National Bank. Gertrude Charavot, an employee of the bank, testified that Marilyn DeLuca had paid cash for the cashier's check and that it was made out to Western Union. Mary Little of the Cook County Department of Corrections' trust department verified that the funds had been received and credited to the inmate account of Childs.

Joseph Mortimer, a latent fingerprint expert for the state of Illinois with thirty years' experience, testified that the white envelope and the manila envelope mailed to the mother of Clifford Childs, as well as the yellow paper on which were written the descriptions of Joy Heysek and Bert Green, all carried the fingerprints of both Clifford Childs and Frank DeLuca.

There was no doubt that everything Clifford Childs said happened, *happened*. The only salvation for the defense would be to prove that it happened for some reason other than planned murder.

Tuesday, June 21, was a day of legal arguing before Judge Pincham. An attorney named Charles Whalen had been called by the prosecution to testify to the contents of the Columbo will, presumably to imply motivation for Patricia's participation in the crime. After hearing all the pros and cons of it, Pincham ruled in favor of the defense, not to allow Whalen's testimony, since there was no proof that Patricia *knew* the contents of the will.

Next, the attorneys argued over a crime scene photo of Mary Columbo, showing her robe open, gown pulled up, panties down. The defense did not want it shown to the jury because, even though it was not, it *looked* like a sex crime photo, and could possibly influence the jury by its offensive nature. Pincham again ruled for the defense, excluding that particular photograph.

Other state exhibits were allowed, however: People's Exhibit 113, the gold scissors; People's 116, Michael's bloody T-shirt; People's 131, 132, and 133, the photos of her family that Patricia gave Lanny Mitchell; 169, the daily routine of her parents written by Patricia; 148, the trunk lid with DeLuca's handprint on it; 117 through 130, crime scene photos; 143, the bullets taken out of Frank Columbo; 144, the bullet taken out of Mary Columbo; and dozens of other pieces of physical evidence: fingerprints, blood samples, charts, reports, records, documents. In all, 219 state exhibits were admitted into evidence.

Then the prosecution rested its case in chief.

It was Patricia Ann Columbo's twenty-first birthday. In the attorneys' conference room, she shared a birthday cake with her counsel and court employees. The cake had white icing, but inside it was devil's food.

That, someone in the courtroom commented, seemed appropriate.

On the morning of June 22, the defense began its case.

Clifford Jackson-Bey was called by Toomin. He was thirty-one, married, had two children, and was a Cook County Jail inmate on tier C-1. At that time, he was under sentence in Illinois of fifteen to eighteen years for armed robbery, and under federal sentence of fifteen years for bank robbery.

Jackson-Bey had known Clifford Childs since mid-1975. He testified that Childs had told him in the Cook County Jail, "I got some irons in the fire. I put together a master plan . . . and don't anticipate being in jail much longer."

Childs, Jackson-Bey said, had been "stroking" DeLuca. He had been looking through DeLuca's papers when DeLuca was out of the cell. DeLuca, Childs told Jackson-Bey, was "gullible. Thinks he's smart." But Childs had "taken Frank under my wing." Childs was "jammed up with Frank, tight." DeLuca liked him, trusted him. White people, Childs said, had been "preying on us all our lives," but now it was his turn. When he got out, Childs intended to go to the state's attorney's office and make a deal to testify.

On cross, Baliunas tried to impugn Jackson-Bey by having him admit that he attacked—Jackson-Bey said "had an altercation with"—a jail officer named Hamilton, and also had tried to intimidate witnesses against him in his bank robbery trial by having dead rats mailed to them.

On redirect, Toomin asked if Jackson-Bey had been promised anything in return for his testimony. No. Did he expect anything from defendant DeLuca? "Nothing whatsoever."

Following Jackson-Bey, there came a series of witnesses who were called apparently to throw red herrings into the jury's pool.

Robert Rezzuto, under subpoena by the defense, was the son of Frank Columbo's sister Gloria. He had borrowed his Uncle Frank's family cars now and then, and on one occasion had seen a gun in the glove box of the Thunderbird.

Leroy Symanik was a self-employed home-improvement contractor who had done gutter and trim work on the Columbo home and been paid $1,815 in cash for the work.

Michael G. Doyle was a postal service letter carrier who delivered mail to 55 Brantwood, and during the early part of the week of May 3, 1976, had seen two men in the area of the Columbo house that he had never seen before. One was white, one black, both medium height, wearing work clothes; the black man wore glasses.

Georgia Brooks lived three doors east of the Columbo family and on the night of Tuesday, May 4, at about 10:15 or 10:30, had heard a loud noise like a car backfiring. She had gone to the window and seen a car going down the street in front of the Columbo house. The next morning when she left for work at 7:35, she noted the Columbo porch light on, which was unusual. (One wonders whether she noticed that porch light on Thursday and Friday mornings also, and if it was unusual why she did not check on her neighbors.) She also had seen a car in the Columbo driveway on the morning of Wednesday, May 5, between 7:30 and 8:30.

Clyde Brooks, Georgia's husband, testified that he returned home from a Southern Christian Leadership Conference meeting between 11:00 and 11:30 P.M. on May 4 and observed nothing unusual.

What did it all amount to? Nothing, really. Frank Columbo sometimes carried a gun in his glove box, and paid cash for large repair bills. A letter carrier had seen two strangers on his route. A neighbor heard a loud noise, saw a car going down the street, and noticed a porch light on. Her husband noticed absolutely nothing unusual. Unless the testimony was tied together and *explained* to the jury, it was meaningless.

Toomin would use some of it in his closing argument, but by then it would be worthless.

The first significant defense witness was John Norton, one of DeLuca's assistant managers. May 4 was his night to close. He got a call from DeLuca at 10:50 P.M. In a two-minute conversation, DeLuca verified that all was okay at the store and told Norton he was going to bed. Telephone records confirmed that the call came from the apartment that DeLuca and Patricia shared.

When the bodies were discovered three days later, Norton witnessed DeLuca in the store lunchroom "lamenting." He was "slumped in a chair ... hands on face ... ," but *not* crying. And, according to Norton, had *no* cuts, scrapes, scratches, scabs, or blood on his hands.

The next defense witness was Michael James Dunkle, twenty-two, of Omaha, Nebraska, the son of Mary Columbo's sister, and Patricia's first cousin. Dunkle was a contract driver who picked up and delivered cars, trucks, and buses for the Superior Bus Company of Omaha. On the morning of May 5 at 6:00 A.M.—a time when the Columbo family, according to Dr. Stein, had been dead at least five hours—Dunkle was changing buses in downtown Chicago on his way to Lima, Ohio. He had a one-hour layover, during which he ate breakfast and telephoned his Aunt Mary at 439–6949, the Columbo residence. The phone rang four times, *Mary Columbo answered it*, and Dunkle talked with her for five minutes. She sounded "nervous, jittery," but there was no doubt in Dunkle's mind that it *was* Mary Columbo; he had called her on at least twenty other occasions when changing buses in Chicago.

Bill Swano had Dunkle identify his bus ticket, which showed him leaving Omaha at 5:30 P.M. on May 4, arriving in Chicago at 6:00 A.M. May 5, leaving Chicago at 7:00 A.M., and arriving in Lima at 3:00 that afternoon.

Dunkle stated that he talked to his aunt sometime between 6:15 and 7:00 A.M.

John Leto, of 121 Spruce Street in Wooddale, was assigned the parking space directly next to the space where Mary Columbo's Oldsmobile was recovered five days after the murders. Leto testified that when he left for work at 5:10 A.M. on Wednesday, May 5, the Oldsmobile had not been there. When he returned home between 5:30 and 6:00 that evening, it *was* there. The implication, of course, was that the car had been abandoned there sometime during the day on Wednesday, May 5, when both defendants could account for their time.

Barbara Lefsky testified that she interviewed Patricia Columbo for a job with Central States Fund on Tuesday, May 4, from 1:30 P.M. until after 3:00 P.M., and noticed nothing unusual about her demeanor. John Malone, Michaeleen Straziota, and Bruce Trozak also interviewed her that afternoon, for shorter periods of time, and none of them recalled anything unusual in the comportment of this defendant that the state believed was planning to murder her family within hours.

Danielle McDonald, an employment manager at the Meyercord Company, recalled interviewing Patricia Columbo from 8:40 until 9:45 A.M. on Wednesday, May 5, for a job as purchasing secretary. This would have been mere hours *after* the carnage wrought at 55 Brantwood—*if* everyone was accurate about when it occurred. During this particular interview, Patricia was "calm, relaxed, conducted herself very well, answered questions intelligently," and was "pleasant and outgoing."

Roberta Walker of 140 South Whipple in Chicago, where Frank Columbo's Thunderbird was recovered, testified that the car was *not* in front of her house on Tuesday, May 4, Wednesday, May 5, or Thursday, May 6. She first noticed it around 11:00 A.M. on *Friday, May 7*, about four hours before the bodies were discovered. Dedilah English, who lived next door at 142, corroborated that testimony; the Thunderbird had not been there when she left for school at Marshall High that morning, but was there when she came home at 2:30 P.M.

Edward Burnett took the stand to repeat the story he had told Ray Rose about buying one of the Columbo CB radios at the Maxwell Street open market. The seller was a black man, six feet tall, two hundred pounds, and wore a little blue hat with a button on top of it.

Ronald R. Tross, the car salesman who loaned Lanny Mitchell his residence for sex parties, came to court with his attorney, John H. Bickley, Jr., and invoked the Fifth Amendment seventeen times rather than answer questions like, "Did you overhear Lanny Mitchell tell police you were present at sex orgies in your apartment in which Patricia Columbo, Roman Sobczynski, Lanny Mitchell, and yourself participated?"

Tross was excused, subject to recall.

Deputy Police Chief William Kohnke was a hostile defense witness testifying under subpoena. A former air force policeman and thirteen-year veteran of the Elk Grove department, he had been second in command of the ninety-eight-person force for one year.

The purpose of the defense in forcing Kohnke onto the witness stand was to dump more red herrings into the jury pool. Kohnke had made a number of somewhat imprudent comments to the press in the early hours and days immediately following the discovery of the murders, before his superior, Chief Harry Jenkins, had put a lid on *all* individual press statements. Kohnke was now publicly going to have to pay for his incautious conduct.

Toomin got Kohnke first. He made him admit comparing names in a Columbo personal telephone directory with names of known Mafia figures, and also admit to receiving an anonymous letter blaming the killings on the Mafia. Murphy then had Kohnke admit he knew that a CB radio taken from the Columbo home had been recovered early in the investigation (a clue that pointed toward a robbery motive).

It was then Toomin's turn again, but for his second attack on Kohnke, Judge Pincham had the jury removed in order to screen the testimony. Toomin now had Kohnke acknowledge stating that in his opinion the Columbos had been tortured in a "Helter-Skelter" type crime; that Frank Columbo may have been tortured in an effort to force him to open his safe; that Frank Columbo also was suspected of being a silent partner in trucking and labor firms, and that his death might be connected with *that*; and that the Columbo family life-style was far better than Columbo's salary at Western Auto would indicate.

After hearing those admissions, Judge Pincham ruled that they were personal opinions only and refused to let the jury hear them. Kohnke was excused, having admitted his poor judgment to everyone in the world except the panel of jurors.

In Judge Pincham's chambers, an attorney representing brothers Thomas and Edward Machek, and their bookkeeper

Virginia Stutz, asked that subpoenas for his clients be quashed on the ground that Frank Columbo's connection with the firm called Dock Help, Inc., was not relevant to the murder case.

Michael Toomin took the position that Frank Columbo was listed as one of five principals in the company, which had been formed specifically to provide workers for Western Auto. Frank Columbo received $250 per week as his share of the profits from that firm. Further, Toomin alleged, records in Columbo's safe showed that in one year he had also received $18,000 in salary from Mulvihill Cartage Company, a trucking firm that hauled for Western Auto and was also owned by the Machek brothers. Toomin's position was that Frank Columbo was receiving "kickbacks" in financial dealings that could have been involved in his murder (which is exactly what Toomin had criticized Bill Kohnke for saying).

Judge Pincham examined both Macheks in chambers and ruled to disallow their testimony (which would have been limited to invoking the Fifth Amendment anyway, according to their attorney), and not to permit the introduction of financial records of the two firms to the jury. This was probably for the best. A jury already called upon to figure out for itself the insidious nature of "conspiracy," and faced with the perplexing problem of what the DNA molecule had to do with the single hair on the front of Michael's T-shirt, should not have to decipher balance sheets as well.

Joseph Nicol, a University of Illinois professor in the Department of Criminal Justice who qualified as an expert on hair examination, testified that a single hair found on a dead boy's shirt, taken off and mounted on a slide, and eleven months later compared to hair samples taken from a sister six years older than he, with no comparison hairs from the dead boy himself, was a test of very low reliability. He did not think a conclusion could be drawn from it.

On cross, Patti Bobb had Professor Nicol admit that he had never seen either the hair taken from Michael's shirt nor samples from Patricia's head.

It was a draw.

Delores De Bartoli, a close personal friend of Mary Columbo's, whose husband, Art, had been a close personal friend of Frank Columbo's, all of them in the same bowling league, attending VFW dinner dances together, gave some rather peculiar testimony. Clifford Childs had said Frank DeLuca told him that to gain entry to the Columbo home, the doorbell had been rung, but that DeLuca had not said *he* did the ringing. Delores De Bartoli now said there *was no doorbell* at the Columbo home. Prior to April 1976, a month before the murders, Frank Columbo had changed all the locks and taken out the doorbell. He did not replace it.

Interesting.

At this point it was Friday, June 24, and as was Judge Pincham's custom during this trial, court would have reconvened on Saturday, but Bill Swano requested that they "not work" the following day. Patricia Columbo was in pain from a pinched nerve in her back, had lost ten pounds since the trial began, and—here Swano threw out an enticing appetizer to the prosecution—if she testified, he anticipated a very long cross-examination.

Pincham gave everyone the weekend off.

On Monday, June 27, with the jury out, Bill Swano told Judge Pincham that he was prepared to call the following:

Mr. and Mrs. Richard Nyquist, who had breakfast with the Columbos at the Around the Clock Restaurant on Sunday, May 2, two days prior to the murders, during which both Frank and Mary told them that Patty and Frank DeLuca were to be married in June.

Jack McCarthy, an assistant terminal manager at Western Auto, who was told of an "impending marriage" by Frank Columbo.

Thomas Lidwicki, a friend of Frank Columbo's, who was told the same thing.

And Carolyn Tygrett, another of Mary Columbo's sisters, who would testify that she had discussed wedding plans with Mary Columbo, that the family had finally given approval, and that the wedding was to be July 5. (This was probably a casual error, since July 5 was a Monday, and weddings were customarily held on Saturdays. *June 5 was* a Saturday, and everyone else who knew of the wedding plans believed them to be for June.)

It was all moot anyway, because Judge Pincham refused to let Swano call any of these witnesses. Their testimony, he ruled, would be irrelevant hearsay.

Swano immediately moved for a mistrial. It was denied.

Ron Tross was brought back to the witness stand, his attorney, John H. Bickley, Jr., once again in attendance. The jury was not in for this at first; Pincham wanted once again to screen the testimony.

Stanton Bloom immediately asked, "Did you ever have sexual intercourse with Patricia Columbo?"

"No," replied Tross.

"How long has your apartment been used for sexual trysts?" Bloom asked.

Al Baliunas objected.

"Sexual what?" the judge asked.

"Trysts," Bloom repeated.

Pincham sustained the objection, adding, "The witness may know, but I don't know what a sexual tryst is." Something else for the jury to wonder about, when it was called back in.

Ron Tross invoked the Fifth Amendment for most of the questions asked him, but finally did testify, with the jury present, that he had seen Lanny Mitchell carrying a gun, that he did lend Lanny the key to his apartment, but that he had never been present when the apartment was being used by anyone.

Father J. Ward Morrison, pastor of Queen of the Rosary Church in Elk Grove Village, testified that Patricia Columbo had called him the morning of Saturday, May 8, to "question him about cremation." Father Morrison told her that under extraordinary circumstances the Roman Catholic church allowed it. Patricia then said that the victims "had lived together and died together," and she would like to "have them buried that way."

Two days later, Father Morrison saw Patricia at the Columbo wake. He said he saw her "come in, go to each of three closed caskets"; he stated also that she was "crying." He observed her for an hour and a half that night, during which time she was "crying, upset."

Since her arrest, Father Morrison had visited Patricia between fifteen and twenty times in jail.

When Patti Bobb cross-examined, she elicited the surprising admission from the priest that he had *not* personally
known the Columbos prior to the murders. He had, however, known their "relatives and friends."

Bobb asked how he obtained permission to permit the victims to be cremated. Father Morrison said he had presented
the case to the Chancery Office of the Chicago Archdiocese
and it had been approved.

"Who approved it?" Bobb asked.

"I refuse to answer that," Father Morrison replied.

The court did not take issue with his refusal; it made no
difference to the case. Father Morrison was excused.

Next came perhaps the most paradoxical, poignant, and puz-
zling witness of the entire trial: Marilyn DeLuca.

A pretty woman with dark hair worn in bangs, she had
been married to Frank DeLuca for more than fifteen years
when their divorce became final the same month the Columbo family was murdered. She was also the mother of
DeLuca's five children. One had to wonder, after hearing Joy
Heysek's testimony, and with or without knowledge of how
DeLuca had conducted his affair with Patricia Columbo, what
kind of life this woman had with her longtime husband; how
much she knew; what she condoned; what she *participated* in
with the man that evidence was clearly showing to be a sexual psychopath, a sociopathic personality, and a cold-blooded
murderer. Particularly when in answer to one of the first
questions Michael Toomin asked her, regarding her current
status with respect to DeLuca, she replied, "We are presently
divorced"—as if it might be a temporary condition.

Marilyn testified that during the period between their separation and divorce, she had seen DeLuca twice a week, usually on Wednesdays and Sundays. He had, in fact, eaten
dinner with her and the children on Wednesday, May 5, the
evening after the murders, during which meal she noticed no
cuts or other unusual marks on his hands.

Then: Did she know Clifford Childs? Yes. She had met
Childs in the jail visiting area. Did she bail him out of jail?
Yes. Childs, she said, had signed a promissory note agreeing

to pay back five thousand dollars for a thirty-five-hundred-dollar loan, upon settlement of a civil disability claim he had pending. Marilyn admitted picking Childs up at the jail, driving him to her home, cooking dinner for him (a new fact not heard before), and giving him the keys to Frank DeLuca's car. (She was not questioned, by either side, about the envelope containing thirteen hundred dollars that Childs said she gave him.)

Did she know that Childs had been retained to kill two people? No.

Al Baliunas was surprisingly temperate in his cross-examination.

"Did you give Clifford Childs the last [money] you had?" Yes.

Did she then have to "go on" Aid to Dependent Children [state welfare]? Yes.

Had she subsequently had to take in other children to care for in order to earn money to support her own children? Yes.

Had she written to DeLuca in jail saying that she could not pay her bills and did not know what to do?

Before Marilyn could answer, Pincham decided in a sidebar not to allow the question. He instructed the jury to disregard it. Baliunas let the witness go without further cross-examination. His point to the jury had been made: Frank DeLuca took badly needed support money away from his five children and gave it to Clifford Childs. Would anyone in his right mind believe it was simply a loan?

Michael Toomin tried to make the jury believe it. On recross he asked, "Why did you go along with the loan?"

Marilyn shrugged almost helplessly and said, "For the fifteen hundred dollars profit."

"Have you done anything against the law in your own mind?" Toomin asked.

"No."

One more name to add to the list of people in this case who may or may not have been guilty of a crime, but who, if they *were* guilty, were getting away with it.

On Tuesday, June 28, in the morning, the defense attempted to call Jim Leary, the man to whom Roman Sobczynski had

introduced Patricia Columbo, and in the apartment of whose
secretary Roman and Patricia twice had sex.

Leary's attorney appeared with him and argued that only
innuendo, insinuations, and inferences of illegal activity
would result from putting Mr. Leary on the stand, and that he
would invoke a "blanket exercise" of the Fifth Amendment to
all questions.

Toomin, Murphy, and Swano all declined to call him under
those conditions.

During the noon break on this day, observers noted a great
deal of emotional turmoil on the part of the two defendants.
First Patricia Columbo was seen vehemently shaking her
head and someone on the defense team was heard to say, "We
can ask the judge to excuse her while he testifies."

The rumor immediately spread that Frank DeLuca was
about to be called to testify, and that Patricia did not want to
be in the courtroom when he did.

The prospect of DeLuca's imminent testimony was reinforced when the court did not reconvene on time and resump-
tion of the trial was delayed a little while because DeLuca
suddenly became nervously ill. Further rumors spread that he
had almost fainted from anxiety, and that he had vomited.

Then, just before the afternoon session finally began,
someone said Patricia Columbo was weeping and had
changed her mind, now begging to remain in the courtroom
while her lover testified.

It was all very dramatic; everyone had their own version of
what was going on—and their own evaluation of it. But
whatever had transpired, at 2:15 P.M. normality of a sort returned when Judge Pincham brought the proceedings back to
order with Patricia at her defense table and Frank DeLuca
about to be sworn in.

Before DeLuca's examination began, Pincham said to his
jury, "You are instructed that the testimony of Mr. DeLuca is
not being offered, and is not to be considered by you, as evidence as to the defendant Patricia Columbo."

Theoretically, DeLuca was testifying strictly for himself—
theoretically.

*　*　*

Stanton Bloom conducted the direct.

"What is your full name?"

"Frank John DeLuca."

"What is your age?"

"Thirty-nine."

"Date of birth?"

"June 28, 1938."

"In fact, today is your birthday, correct?"

"Yes."

Bloom went on to establish DeLuca's biography: his education, marriage, children, his football scholarship, and the history of his Walgreen's employment. Plus the fact that prior to the present charges, he had never been arrested for any offense.

Bloom then took DeLuca through his parking lot confrontation with Frank Columbo. "He called me at the store," the witness related, "and said he wanted to talk. I waited for him on the parking lot. At ten forty-five he pulled up and got out of the car with a rifle. He said, 'I'm going to blow your head off!' I said, 'Wait a second—' He swung the rifle and hit me in the face. I fell down. As I was trying to get up, he hit me in the stomach with the rifle and I fell down again. Then he said, 'You're dead, you motherfucker, you're dead!' And he drove away. Somebody who was driving by called the police."

Had a complaint been filed? Yes. Was it subsequently withdrawn? Yes.

DeLuca had no further contact with Frank Columbo, he said, between that incident, in July 1975, and the following April 1976. Then one night Frank Columbo telephoned Patricia and during that call talked to DeLuca. Columbo, the witness said, finally agreed to the marriage between him and Patricia, saying, "Then she'll be your problem, not mine."

Columbo allegedly even offered to buy them a washer and dryer for a wedding present. The date set for the wedding was June 5, because DeLuca's divorce became final the end of May.

Bloom moved on to Bert Green. DeLuca testified that Green had been one of his employees in the drugstore, and that he had promoted Green from manager of the liquor department to assistant store manager. He emphatically denied ever bringing a gun into the store or having Bert Green keep it for him. He denied ever having Green pick up Patricia at their apartment on three occasions and drive her anywhere, and he denied ever discussing "contracts" or "hits" with Green.

On to the night of the murders. DeLuca said he left work at 5:00 P.M. and stopped on the way home to buy a bucket of Kentucky Fried Chicken. After eating dinner in his apartment, he went out around 7:00 or 7:30 and drove to Yorktown Mall. He went window-shopping for a while, then bought a Coke and sat watching people as he drank it. He left the mall between 9:30 and 10:00 and on the way home stopped for two cartons of milk. He gave one of them to a neighbor in an adjoining apartment, repaying milk he had borrowed. Around 10:15 he had a cup of coffee and watched television. At 10:55 he called the store and checked with his assistant manager, John Norton, to ascertain that all was well. At 11:15 he went to bed. He slept until about 6:30 the next morning, Wednesday, May 5, then got up and went to work at 7:30.

"Do you have any personal knowledge of your own regarding these murders?" Bloom asked.

"No," DeLuca replied.

Bloom moved to Friday, May 7. DeLuca testified that he was assembling a floor display when he was paged for a phone call. An employee who lived three doors away from 55 Brantwood had called to say that Frank and Mary Columbo apparently had been murdered. DeLuca said he immediately telephoned the Elk Grove Village Police Department but could get no information.

"Were you upset?" Bloom asked gently.

"Yes," DeLuca replied softly.

DeLuca's testimony up to this point had been very good. All of his personal background was related sincerely, solidly. Even his movements on the night of the murders might have been believed. It was only at this point, regarding the phone call telling him about the murders, that his answers began to cause slight frowns, faint wonder, a hint of disbelief. *Were you upset? Yes.*

That was not enough. The two people who had finally accepted him as a fiancé to their only daughter, who were making wedding plans with them, whom he referred to as "Mom" and "Dad," who were going to give them a washer and dryer, were *murdered*, and he was only "upset." He should have been stunned, horrified, sickened. He could have driven to 55 Brantwood in *two minutes* to verify this terrible thing for himself. But he did not. Nor did he leave the store to rush to Patricia's side, to find his betrothed and be with her when she learned the tragic news. He did nothing that a normal person would have done. And everyone in that courtroom had to wonder why.

Bloom moved on mechanically in a stepladder style of rung-by-rung denials. "Did you ever have a conversation with Hubert Green regarding your alleged involvement in this crime?"

"No."

"Did you ever have a conversation with Joy Heysek regarding your alleged involvement in this crime?"

"No."

"Did you ever have a conversation with Clifford Childs regarding your alleged involvement in this crime?"

"No."

If that kind of staccato repetition was supposed to have a positive impact on the jury, it misfired. One-word denials by Frank DeLuca, after all the evidence presented against him, were not going to cut it.

DeLuca testified that he voluntarily went to the Elk Grove Village Police Department to "help" in any way he could. He was shown photos of the crime scene and the obscenely butchered bodies. (Perhaps he should have vomited *then*—but apparently he did not.)

On the day the search warrant was served, the apartment searched, and Patricia arrested, DeLuca said he was taken into "protective custody." During that period, the police "kept asking where [he] had been at 10:30 P.M. on the night of the murders," because "neighbors had heard shots" then. He also told Bert Green, when he had his friend and employee come to pick him up, that Deputy Chief Bill Kohnke had said to him, "You did it. You're going down for the count. Your fingerprints are all over the car. We know you did it." As Bert drove DeLuca to Addison to the house where Marilyn and the children still lived, they discussed the murders. The ubiquitous Bert Green, always around when something was being said about murder. Talking about it almost as if he were a working partner.

Bloom moved on to DeLuca's county jail time. He had become friends with Clifford Childs in jail, DeLuca said. When Childs asked to read DeLuca's "papers" regarding the crime and impending trial, DeLuca gave him permission. The testimony of Bert Green and Joy Heysek had already been given to the defense at that time under the discovery rule by which both sides must disclose to each other what evidence they had and how it would be presented. In other words, the direct testimony, or most of it, of Joy Heysek and Bert Green was already known to DeLuca. Clifford Childs, DeLuca said, was astounded by it.

"You got to be kidding," DeLuca testified that Childs said. "After all that careful planning, you turn around and supposedly tell these two people? It's never going to stand up. Nobody is going to believe that."

This was a peculiar line of examination. What was Stanton Bloom hoping to establish? That Frank DeLuca *did* "all that careful planning," but did *not* "tell these two people" all about it? It certainly seems so. What earthly good would that do DeLuca?

Regarding the hand-drawn map showing how to get to Joy Heysek's house, the diagram of the Grove Shopping Center area, and the handwritten physical descriptions of Bert Green and Joy Heysek, DeLuca said he drew them for his other defense attorney, Michael Toomin, so that Toomin could "drop in at the store" and pick them out. He did not say whether Toomin intended to "drop in" at Joy Heysek's residence. Clifford Childs, he said, must have "copied" them.

It was ludicrous testimony. If Childs "copied" them, why were they in DeLuca's handwriting? If by "copy," DeLuca meant using a Xerox or other means of mechanical reproduction, how did DeLuca's fingerprints get all over them? His testimony made absolutely no sense, yet he blithely gave it and expected it to be believed.

There is no literal definition of a sociopath; it is a word coined by the psychiatric community around 1944 as an offshoot of the word "psychopath." But the term is generally accepted to refer to someone whose behavior is characterized by asocial or antisocial habits. It has generally come to mean a person who knows right from wrong, doesn't care, believes he is somehow entitled to do *anything* he wants to, that whatever he does should be accepted and go unchallenged, unrebuked, unpunished; further, whatever he says should be believed without reservation.

Toward the end of his first session on the witness stand, Frank DeLuca was beginning to reveal subtle signs of his real personality. To think that the jury would believe he made those diagrams, maps, and descriptions for his attorney was not even reasonable, much less rational. Of course, if it *was* true, it would be easy enough to prove; Bloom could put Toomin on the witness stand, and Toomin could swear to it under oath. But that was not going to happen.

Just before court adjourned for the day, Stanton Bloom led DeLuca through another machine-gun litany of denials.

"Calling your attention to May fourth or May fifth or any other time, did you shoot or beat or kill Frank Columbo?"

"No, I did not."

"Calling your attention to May fourth or May fifth or any other time, did you shoot or beat or kill Mary Columbo?"

"No."

"Calling your attention to May fourth or May fifth or any other time, did you shoot or beat or kill Michael Columbo?"

"No."

It was good strategy on Bloom's part to try to end the day with strong denials for the jury to take out of the courtroom with them. However, the strategy did not fit his witness.

Wednesday, June 29. Al Baliunas cross-examined Frank DeLuca.

"When did you meet Patricia Columbo for the first time?"

DeLuca was nervous and had trouble with the date. At first, he said it was June 1967, which couldn't have been true because Patricia was only eleven years old. Then he collected his thoughts and corrected it to June 1972. He was, he said, thirty-four at the time; Patricia was sixteen, but said she was older. (This is close enough not to be objectionable. The actual date was May 26, 1972, twenty-six days *before* Patricia's sixteenth birthday. She was still only an impressionable fifteen-year-old when she began falling irreversibly in love with DeLuca and took her first tentative steps toward ruination.)

They met, DeLuca said, when he became manager of the Elk Grove Village store and "Patrish was already there, making sandwiches" in the fast-food section of the store.

When had they begun to date? "September or October of 1967." (Again the year was wrong, but no one bothered to correct it.) DeLuca admitted that at the time he began dating Patricia, he was living with his wife and five children.

In the summer of 1974, he said, when she really *was* eighteen, after obtaining permission from Frank Columbo, she left home and moved in with DeLuca and his family. (Here also the age is slightly off; Patricia was still seventeen when she left the Columbo home; and her parents did not give her permission, they simply did not try to prevent her leaving because it was so close to her eighteenth birthday.)

"Patrish" lived with his family for one year, DeLuca said, during which time she "did modeling and office work." Business cards were printed up, with the name "Trish Columbo—Model" on them, and DeLuca's name as her "agent." (There is no evidence anywhere that Patricia ever "modeled" for anyone—except DeLuca and whomever he had chosen for her sexual partner.)

Was he sexually involved with Patricia during this entire time she lived with his family? Baliunas inquired. Yes, DeLuca admitted, but they "did nothing at the house." (Fifteen years later, Patricia would discuss in detail with the author what actually went on in that house; as we have seen in part, it very definitely amounted to more than "nothing.")

Baliunas asked when Patricia had moved out of his home and DeLuca replied, "July 1976." Wrong again. By July 1976 the Columbos had been dead two months. He meant July 1975. He himself, he testified, moved out "two weeks later." (Patricia had surreptitiously been seeing Andrew Harper for several months before she moved out, but DeLuca did not know that. He may have suspected that her reason for leaving was another interest, but it was apparent that *his* reason for following two weeks later was that he was afraid he was losing her, this child-woman female counterpart whom he had spent more than three years forging and fashioning to his own twisted specifications. He chose Patricia over his wife and five children because, in his own depraved way, he loved her.)

His wife, DeLuca said, filed for divorce two months after he moved out. She did not charge adultery, but rather irreconcilable differences.

Was DeLuca's confrontation with Frank Columbo on the parking lot because Patricia had told her father that DeLuca was moving out and that he and she were to be married? It was. Was Patricia on the parking lot with DeLuca at the time? Yes. After Columbo hit DeLuca the second time, DeLuca said the enraged father turned to his daughter and said, "I'm going to kill you too!"

Did the attack by Frank Columbo make DeLuca angry? "No, I was just hurt and afraid. I was running very, very afraid."

Baliunas tried to dilute the fear factor. "You weren't afraid when you played football, were you?"

"No."

"Or when you skydived?"

"No."

"But you were afraid of Frank Columbo?"

"Yes, he pointed a gun at my head."

It was one of the few times that a line of questioning seemed to backfire on Baliunas. The jury believed that Frank DeLuca was afraid of Frank Columbo rather than angry at him. Which, of course, made little or no difference; anger *and* fear are strong enough emotions to generate the desperation needed to kill. And maybe Al Baliunas knew that; perhaps he realized that his questions worked no matter what the jury believed. But he poured a little more fuel on the anger theory anyway.

"The scars around your mouth are a result of the confrontation, aren't they?" Yes. And he had undergone oral surgery to have his teeth straightened and had one tooth replaced? Yes.

Baliunas moved on to October 1975. Did he know that Patricia had met Lanny Mitchell and Roman Sobczynski at that time? No. Had Patricia ever subsequently discussed meeting them? No.

Baliunas showed the witness People's Exhibits 165, 166, and 167—the floor plans and descriptions that Patricia had given to Lanny Mitchell. Had DeLuca ever seen them before? "Only in court," he replied.

Baliunas called his attention to the telephone conversations Roman Sobczynski had said he had with DeLuca. The first call, DeLuca testified, had come from "Patrish," who said she wanted him to talk to "someone very close" to her. Then a male voice said, "Hi, I'm Roman." That person, DeLuca said, had told him Frank Columbo had negotiated a hit contract on DeLuca but that Roman had "bought it off." When Patricia came home later that day, DeLuca claimed he had "questioned her at length" about the caller, whom he believed to be Patricia's godfather, Phil Capone, using "Roman" as a "street name."

The second call from Roman was also placed by Patricia, who again put Roman on the line. This time, DeLuca testified, he heard that Frank Columbo was "shopping for another hit man," and it looked like there was "only one way to stop him."

DeLuca admitted under questioning by Baliunas that he "finally agreed" to the murder—but "only regarding Frank Columbo." Mary and Michael Columbo, he declared, were "never mentioned." (This, of course, diametrically contradicts Roman Sobczynski's testimony that DeLuca, unnerved by Michael Columbo's staring routine in the drugstore, said, "Junior's got to go too.")

When Patricia got home after the second call, DeLuca said they "discussed" the matter and agreed to the murder "if it could be no other way."

Did DeLuca know Patricia was having sex with Lanny Mitchell and Roman Sobczynski? No. But hadn't he told the police that he didn't care if she was, that they had an "open" relationship? DeLuca denied the statement. "No. I did care."

Had Patricia been with him the evening of Tuesday, May 4, when he bought Kentucky Fried Chicken and later browsed in Yorktown Mall? Yes.

Baliunas now questioned DeLuca about his statements to the police that "Dad and Mom" Columbo had finally accepted him as a future son-in-law. The breakthrough, he said, had come on a Monday night in April, a month before the murders. Patricia had parked their car (the same Javelin that Marilyn DeLuca later gave to Clifford Childs) on the

Walgreen's parking lot, leaving the key under the floor mat. She had walked the three blocks to 55 Brantwood and had a long talk with her parents. They supposedly asked her if she was sure DeLuca was the man for her, and Patricia told them he was. Then she called DeLuca at the drugstore and told him to pick her up at the Columbo home. When DeLuca arrived, Frank Columbo went to the door and said, "Okay, come on in." The four of them then "talked almost all night."

Baliunas listened quietly until DeLuca had finished the story, then inquired, "This happened in April, a month prior to the murders?"

"Yes."

"On a Monday night?"

"Yes," DeLuca replied emphatically.

"Are you aware," Baliunas asked evenly, "that the Columbos bowled every Monday night?"

DeLuca's mouth dropped open. "No," he said, surprised.

Baliunas returned to the night of the murders, it now having been established that Patricia was with him all evening. What had the two of them done after DeLuca telephoned John Norton to check on the store? They finished their coffee, DeLuca said, went to bed, made love, then went to sleep.

Baliunas asked about the admissions Bert Green and Joy Heysek said he made to them the following morning; DeLuca denied them all. He admitted his sexual involvement with Joy Heysek from 1967 to 1972 (perhaps this is the significance of the year 1967, to which DeLuca twice erroneously referred in earlier testimony). He also admitted that he took explicit sexual photographs of, and with, Joy Heysek.

Baliunas led the witness to Thursday, May 6, nearly two days and two nights since the murders, with the crime still not discovered. DeLuca testified that he and Patricia left work at 5:00 P.M., ate dinner in the apartment, then went for a drive into Chicago, down around Damen and Chicago avenues, "where Patrish had lived as a child." They arrived back home at 10:30.

Wasn't the real reason for that drive, Baliunas inquired, to see whether Frank Columbo's Thunderbird had been recovered yet?

"No," DeLuca replied.

* * *

Baliunas continued his cross-examination after lunch, DeLuca's second afternoon on the stand.

Responding to an inquiry regarding his job, he testified that as a Walgreen's manager he was responsible for sales, inventory, and profit. His store had around $2.5 million in annual sales. He also had been a licensed pharmacist, but his license was now suspended pending the outcome of his trial.

Baliunas asked about Clifford Childs. "He conned me," DeLuca said bitterly. "He appeared to be a stand-up guy and I trusted him."

"Trusted him to kill Hubert Green and Joy Heysek?" Baliunas asked quickly, no doubt hoping.

But DeLuca wasn't *that* stupid. "No, to pay the money back," he said.

Did DeLuca know Clifford Jackson-Bey? "Yes, I saw him this morning at breakfast. I'm in cell six and he cells down in thirty-four or thirty-five on my tier [Jackson-Bey was actually in number 36]. After Jackson-Bey's testimony, DeLuca said, he had "thanked Bey for telling the truth."

Had DeLuca ever made loans to Bey? No.

Toomin gave the witness back to Stanton Bloom, who apparently now wanted to elaborate on the reconciliation between his client and the Columbos. How had it occurred?

"Patrish came into the store to pick me up. 'I've got a surprise for you,' she said. 'I bumped into Mom and Dad and they want to make up. Mom's not really enthusiastic, but Dad's willing to go along with it.' I then told her, 'You'd better call Roman and let him know we don't need protection anymore.' "

During the reconciliation with the Columbos, had Frank Columbo ever made comments regarding DeLuca's age? Yes, twice. "Once he said, 'If Patty wants to marry an old man, that's her problem, not mine.' Another time he said, 'You better not ever call me Dad.' "

On the morning after the murders, why had he gone into work so early when it wasn't his morning to open the store? "Because Patrish had a job interview at eight-thirty that morning" and he "had to drop her off."

Regarding Bert Green, DeLuca said Green had asked him many questions about prescription drugs: barbiturates, tranquilizers, others. DeLuca had told him the only way to avoid the strict controls on those drugs was to "short" each prescription one or two tablets and accumulate them that way.

DeLuca began to suspect, he said, that Bert was "stealing drugs. He was running around with Joy Heysek" but he "was wet behind the ears and she was very experienced." Green's wife "caught a note" to him from Joy and "left him."

Green also had been caught in a "sex act" with "a Mrs. Cooper" in the liquor storeroom, and had been transferred to Oak Brook (this was clearly hearsay testimony, since Green didn't leave the Elk Grove store until after DeLuca was in jail).

Regarding Joy Heysek, DeLuca stated she had told him, "No one walks out on me." Joy, he said, "hated Patrish and me."

Had she ever asked him to return the explicit photos they had taken together? Yes, she had, and he told her, "No problem, I haven't looked at them in two years anyway." Joy, he said, "got very mad" at that.

Bloom ended his recross with a simple but dramatic question. "Did you commit these murders, these atrocious murders?"

"No," DeLuca said, "I didn't."

That was the end of the defense's case in chief.

The prosecution offered one rebuttal witness, Frank Hamilton, a Cook County corrections officer, to impugn one of the defense witnesses. Hamilton had accompanied Clifford Jackson-Bey to the Cook County Hospital for medical reasons. Jackson-Bey was shackled to a wheelchair. While waiting to see a doctor, Jackson-Bey attempted to make a call on a hospital telephone, which Hamilton would not permit, saying it wasn't allowed. Jackson-Bey, Hamilton said, called him a "stupid motherfucker" and "lunged" at him from the wheelchair. Hamilton and another officer further restrained the prisoner by also cuffing his hands to the chair. Jackson-Bey then called Hamilton a "black son of a bitch" and a "stupid asshole," and threatened his life, saying he would kill Hamilton "at the first opportunity."

Toomin cross-examined. What was the reason for Jackson-Bey's being taken to the hospital? He had a fractured wrist. Had Officer Hamilton filed a complaint against him? No.

That was it. The last question and answer of the final witness. The jury had listened to testimony for thirty-seven days.

Including those at the pretrial hearing, fifty-eight people had testified, some of them more than once. Ray Rose had the record: he was on the witness stand four times—which seems appropriate, since he worked harder on the case than anyone, put in the longest hours, and perhaps was emotionally sickened more than anyone else by the appalling crime. To Rose, it was not just a case in which he was the chief investigator; because it happened in *his* community, where *his* family lived and worked and played and went to church and school, it transcended the simple category of another crime to solve—it became a crusade. If Rose had not found the Columbo murderers, he probably would have considered his entire law enforcement career a failure.

Ray Rose, Gene Gargano, and the other investigators who worked the case had done their jobs well. What remained was to see how well the prosecution and defense lawyers had done theirs.

44
July 1977

Final arguments.

Patti Bobb began for the state. She first thanked the jury for its dedication and attentiveness. Then she said that what they had heard during the trial had been "bizarre, gruesome, tragic." Patty Columbo and her lover, Frank DeLuca, had solicited Lanny Mitchell and Roman Sobczynski to kill her family. They "conspired together." But when Lanny and Roman did not follow through, Patty and DeLuca had "entered that house" themselves, and "massacred that family."

Their motives? "Hatred, greed, resentment."

For Lanny and Roman, it was "a bad joke that turned into a nightmare." (This was an astonishing statement by Patti Bobb. Lanny and Roman had not been playing a "joke." Theirs was a calculated victimization, committed for personal gain. Remove them from the picture, remove the encouragement they gave, the lies they told, the gun that was furnished, and perhaps Frank, Mary, and Michael *might* still be alive. Nothing about it was a "joke.")

When Bobb got around to the evidence, she reminded the jury that after DeLuca had called his assistant manager at 10:50 on the night of the murders, saying he was going to bed, Connie Larocco, the employment counselor, telephoned the apartment at 11:00 P.M. to query Patty about missing a job interview—and got no answer.

And at the Columbo home there was no forced entry. The killers were let in. "Do you think," Bobb asked the jury, "that Frank Columbo would have let Frank DeLuca into that house by himself?"

What happened, she said, was this: Patty and DeLuca entered. Frank Columbo turned and walked up the stairs. He was shot in the back of the head. He turned around and was shot again. Mary Columbo was on the toilet. She heard the shots, got up, rushed into the hallway, and was shot between the eyes. Michael, who was asleep, was stood up and shot once in the head.

"When you think about the question of Patty Columbo being in the house that night," the prosecutor said, "consider the ninety-seven wounds on Michael Columbo." (The count had increased again; the autopsy still showed 84.) Eight of the wounds were deep, but the others were "inflicted without a lot of force." (The implication was that they had not been made by an ex-football player, but by someone with considerably less strength.)

Patty Columbo and Frank DeLuca wanted the family killed. They had a "perfect plan." But they had not "thought about the physical evidence—the glass, the blood, the hand markings, the hair." (The prosecution apparently could not accept the fact that there *was* no hair evidence, except what had been contrived. But perhaps the jury thought there was.)

"Frank DeLuca," Bobb said scathingly, "had to brag about it. It was such a *perfect* plan." And, "Patty Columbo was in there that night. Evidence proves it." (Not quite, Ms. Bobb. She was in the house, all right, as we will see, but it was certainly never *proved*.)

But, Patti Bobb continued, "whether she helped inflict those wounds, or whether she stood by, or whatever she did in the house that night, she's guilty of those murders!"

This is probably the closest Patti Bobb came to pure truth in her entire summation.

Patty, Ms. Bobb said, "wanted to be there, to see them get what they deserved. She said that." (Only according to Lanny Mitchell. And one must remember the esteem in which Lanny held the truth, as well as the payment he received from the state for his testimony.)

"Frank DeLuca is guilty of murder," Bobb asserted. "He admitted it. To Hubert Green and Joy Heysek and Clifford Childs."

Bobb began to wind down, dramatically. "Three innocent people, three members of a family, are dead! Why? Because they stood in Patty Columbo and Frank DeLuca's way! No other reason. They stood in their way."

She faced the jury, stern, dedicated, undoubtedly convinced that she was right, that she stood for justice, that she was on the side of the angels.

"Judge the evidence," she all but ordered the jury. "Find them guilty."

Michael Toomin closed first for DeLuca.

After a rather dry and academic review of the history of the jury system, Toomin reminded the panel that "we"—the defense—"had told them about the mailman who saw two suspicious people on his route; the neighbor who heard a car backfire and saw it speeding away at ten-thirty on May fourth, the night of the murders; the woman who said the Thunderbird was abandoned in the ghetto neighborhood after the morning of May seventh; the man who told of the discovery of the Oldsmobile on May ninth; the fact that the murders were originally thought to have been committed at ten-thirty, but because the police couldn't place DeLuca there then, they changed the time.

"The state," Toomin accused, "conveniently overlooked evidence" (that might have shown his client's innocence).

The jury had also heard the neighbor who saw a car in the Columbo driveway at nine o'clock the morning after the murders; and the criminalist who admitted that only *one* in twenty-five fragments of glass found in the rented Buick *could* have come from the house.

And what about Michael Dunkle? He swore under oath

that he talked to his aunt from the bus station the morning *after* the state said the crime occurred—and the prosecution did not even bother to cross-examine him!

Lanny Mitchell? He was "a man who would lie, as he himself admitted, for sex, and to get a job—*but not to keep himself out of jail?*"

Roman Sobczynski? "Roman the thief, Roman the con, Roman the procurer, Roman the phony hit man—Roman, *who was never even arrested in this case!*"

Toomin became calm and understanding, a sane voice in the din and disorder of the case. "Consider the dilemma the prosecution and police are in," he quietly proposed. "Patty Columbo is locked up, charged *not* with solicitation, *not* with conspiracy, but with the *actual murders* of her family. But she has an alibi. Frank DeLuca. He is at home in his apartment in Lombard *twenty-five minutes* after [the police] believe the killings took place. What to do? *Two months later*, they arrest DeLuca! Why? Not because of Hubert Green! They didn't even *find* him until eleven days after DeLuca was arrested!" (Toomin was correct in that Bert Green made his formal statement eleven days after DeLuca's arrest, but the police certainly didn't "find" him at that late date. Ray Rose suspected Green's involvement the first time the assistant manager refused to cooperate with investigators, suspicions that were substantiated by Grace Mason's statement that Green had told her and her husband about DeLuca's admission to him the morning after the murders. Rose, however, knew he was dealing with legally inadmissible hearsay evidence at that point, so Bert Green was not pressed for a statement until Rose *knew* he could get one.)

Toomin hit on the fact that Green had not even been working on one morning when DeLuca allegedly said for the third time that "the hits had not gone down." Time cards proved it. So Green conveniently changed his statement and said he "just came into the store to make some purchases." (Apparently no one considered the possibility that Green was *involved* in the plan, caught up in the intrigue and the excitement of it, stimulated by hiding a murder weapon for his friend, captivated by the extramarital sex that the Walgreen's store provided; that, just possibly, he came in on his day off because he couldn't *wait* to find out what happened the night before.)

"Green," Toomin said, "stated that DeLuca told him he shot Frank Columbo twice. Frank Columbo was shot four times. Wouldn't DeLuca know that? (Of course he would. But that does not mean that *he* fired all four shots.)

Toomin went to Dr. Stein's testimony. The pathologist had said that one bullet, presumably the first one fired, entered the left rear of Frank Columbo's head. In order for Frank DeLuca to have fired the shot, he would have had to be holding the gun in his left hand because the stairway was so narrow that DeLuca could not have stepped to his left and fired with his right hand. And DeLuca, of course, could not have fired the gun with his left hand because that was the hand on which he was missing a trigger finger and part of another. (This was a lightweight argument, Perry Mason stuff. All DeLuca had to do—and it is an entirely natural move—was *turn* slightly to the left in order to have room to raise the gun. The killer was standing obliquely to his victim when he fired that first shot, which is probably why the bullet lodged in Frank Columbo's temporal lobe and did not kill him. That bullet, the first one fired but the *last* one removed during the autopsy, had the effect of a very hard blow to the head.)

But, Michael Toomin concluded from it all, "The incredible tale of Hubert Green was a lie."

Now for Joy Heysek. Toomin made short work of her. She was "a woman who would do *anything* to get even with" Frank DeLuca.

"The evidence of the state," Michael Toomin said, "was replete with doubts."

At any rate, that evidence, he told them, "warrants your returning to this courtroom to say that you find Frank DeLuca not guilty."

Anyone on the jury or in any other way involved in this case—judge, lawyers, court personnel, police officers, press, or mere spectators—who might have been expecting Michael Toomin to say that Frank DeLuca had made those diagrams and written the descriptions of Joy Heysek and Bert Green for *him*, would have a long wait. Toomin obviously was not about to touch that story.

*   *   *

Stanton Bloom now made *his* closing argument for DeLuca. He opened by assuring the jury that he was "only going to take half the time the others had taken." He then proceeded into a summation that filled fifty-nine pages of trial transcript, *more* than either of the two lawyers preceding him. This surprised no one; Stanton Bloom liked to talk. And, impressing many, he gave what may have been the best, or at least second-best, closing argument of the trial, and made what should have been the strongest legal points of all—providing the jury understood them.

First, Bloom said, regarding Lanny Mitchell and Roman Sobczynski: either they were or were not going to carry out the hits for Patricia Columbo. The state couldn't have it both ways. They claimed they were not. If they were not, there *was no conspiracy*. There are two primary legal elements that make up a crime: the act and the *intent*. If, in fact, Lanny and Roman never really *intended* to fulfill their part of the murder agreement with Patricia (in person) and DeLuca (on the telephone), then no conspiracy existed. A potent argument—but, considering the lack of verbal illustration regarding what legally constituted a conspiracy, how many jurors understood it? (Judge Pincham, of course, would cover that and other specific terms in his final instructions to the jury, but those too are framed in legalese not easily absorbed into an average vocabulary. If a judge like R. Eugene Pincham were permitted to sit down informally with his jury and explain things like conspiracy in his own words, juries would have a much easier job. But the law, for better or worse, does not permit that—probably because so many judges are not as competent as Pincham. Jury instructions are prewritten, numbered, approved, and uniform. All a judge can do is read them to his jury, and hope to God they understand.)

Emphasizing his absence of conspiracy theory, Bloom said that Lanny and Roman were "completely lacking in morals." Don't believe for a minute, he urged, that they "were just in it for the sex." Both of them were "capable and willing to commit murder." (Many at the trial believed that Stanton Bloom was at least half-correct in that theory.)

DeLuca, Bloom said, did not know about the sex *or* the murder plan. Patricia did not want DeLuca involved because "she loves him." But "they" told DeLuca on the telephone that there was "no other way." DeLuca "did not ask them to do it, did not solicit them, did not even encourage them. He just agreed," saying, "If that's the only way."

Of all the major witnesses who had testified in the case—Lanny Mitchell, Roman Sobczynski, Hubert Green, Joy Heysek, Clifford Childs—"all admitted to being liars." Only Frank DeLuca was "not impeached once."

Lanny and Roman claimed they weren't involved with Patricia after March. "So who, during the whole month of April," was Bert Green dropping Patricia off to meet? "If Lanny and Roman were out of the picture, who was *in*? I submit to you that these rides never occurred!"

Bloom then asked the jury to review what it knew about Frank DeLuca. "Think about Frank DeLuca," he appealed. A man who had worked for Walgreen's for seventeen years, worked his way through college, had a "degree in pharmacy," was thirty-nine years old, and had never committed a crime in his entire life. "Is he going to commit this kind of horrible, heinous crime?" (A sober thought. By all odds, no. And that was the second most tragic thing about the crime, next to the deaths themselves: *It never should have happened.* There was no *reason* for it.)

"Hubert Green?" Bloom said. A man interested in drugs, who "had an affair with one employee, was caught having sex with another." Hubert Green, "a liar."

Next, "Joy Heysek?" She admitted she "once cared for DeLuca." She was "jilted, offended." She had been in "sickening pictures," and told Bert Green she would "do anything to get them back." Joy Heysek, "a liar."

And both of them waited between two and three months "to tell what they knew!"

Now, what about "Frank and Patty"? He was thirty-nine, she twenty-one. "What's wrong with a thirty-nine-year-old man loving and wanting to marry a twenty-one-year-old woman?"

Bloom began to lambast the prosecution's case. "First the state says DeLuca planned this 'perfect crime.' Then he's running around telling people like Hubert Green and Joy Heysek, 'Look at me, I committed the murders and got away with it!' Does that make sense?" (Only if the person is a sociopath.)

The defense attorney finally got to Clifford Childs. "He

had all the smart answers." But he was a "pathological liar."
He admitted "he would lie right in a jury's face to keep out
of prison." Childs, Bloom reminded, "had been over in that
jail twenty-three months," facing three armed robbery charges, and "he gets a deal" to serve "a year and a day!" He was
a "five-time loser, a dope dealer"; he was "despicable!" And
the state "parades him up here and says he's *credible*" and
that "you've got to believe him!"

Clifford Childs "says DeLuca told him entry was gained to
the Columbo home by ringing a doorbell. There *was no doorbell*!" Childs said "the [bloody] clothes were burned in a
field; Hubert Green says they were burned in the [Wal-
green's] incinerator."

And who—*who*—did Michael Dunkle talk to (from the bus
station at six o'clock the next morning)? "Do you think
DeLuca and Patty just hung around for six hours?"

Frank DeLuca had submitted to five hours of cross-
examination and "was not impeached once!" (This was the
second time Bloom had used the word "impeached." The primary definition of "impeach," and the way most of us think
of it, is "to charge a public official with misconduct in office." Bloom could easily have said, "Not once did they
prove that DeLuca was lying." But lawyers, unfortunately,
talk like lawyers, and jurors hear and think like *people*.)

Bloom closed his argument by saying, "Frank DeLuca did
not commit these murders, did not commit the conspiracy,
was not involved in it, had withdrawn if he ever *was* involved
in anything, and the state has not proved their case against
him beyond a reasonable doubt. I ask you to return those verdicts."

That was it for Frank DeLuca. Nothing more could be said
in his defense.

There was, oddly, only *one* closing argument for Patricia.

Bill Murphy began by saying, "I will confine my remarks
and my arguments to the evidence the state introduced as to
my client, Patricia Columbo."

There were, Murphy said, "two ways for the police and
prosecutors to present a case." The right way was to look at
the crime, go out and obtain all the evidence, look where that
evidence logically proceeded, and make an arrest. The wrong

way was to "theorize who committed the crime, make an arrest, then gather evidence to support the theory." The "danger" in the wrong way was that police and prosecutors ignored evidence that led to "innocence."

The state knew, Murphy said, that Michael Dunkle "talked to Mary Columbo on the morning of May fifth." It knew that Mary's Oldsmobile had not been in the parking place next to John Leto's car in Wooddale on the morning of May 5. It knew that Patty Columbo had been interviewed for a job on the morning of May 5. And the state knew, subsequently, that one of the Columbo CB radios had been sold at the Maxwell Street open market (by a black man). All of those things, Murphy implied, pointed to Patricia's innocence.

And the state *claimed* it had not taken a hair sample from Michael Columbo (the implication being that it did not want a positive comparison made). Murphy found it inconceivable that the same man (evidence technician Robert Salvatore) who found the hair on Michael's T-shirt, who took all the fingerprints of the victims, and who got hair samples from Frank and Mary, did not get a hair sample from Michael. (This was a new, and most interesting, theory: the state did have a hair sample from Michael, but *did not use it* because they wanted to imply that the hair on his T-shirt came from Patricia, which was exactly what they did with the testimony of state criminalist Michael Podlecki. If the theory were true, however, it would have meant that Dr. Robert Stein, who had no law-enforcement interest in the case, had lied on the witness stand, which is absurd.)

The state, Murphy declared, wanted the jury to believe "because Patty Columbo used profanity, that she killed her parents"; that she committed some "sinister act" by having the bodies cremated—even though she "got permission from [her] church." The state was "clouding issues" because it could not "prove a case against her beyond a reasonable doubt."

Martin McCauley, who lived next door, Murphy reminded the jury, "got TV interference until one A.M. from . . . operation of a CB" (in the Columbo house).

Lanny Mitchell and Roman Sobczynski, the attorney declared, were "both admitted liars, both admitted thieves, both admitted con men." (This was a slight exaggeration; there was no evidence that Lanny Mitchell was a thief. He was certainly everything *else* that the defense attorneys said he was.) Both were "deceitful, self-indulgent" men who "carried guns to impress teenage girls." And even the teenage girls (Patricia, at least) tried to "ditch them." If Patricia had not been forced to go to that motel with them, why had Roman let the air out of her tires so that (the girls) couldn't get away?

And why hadn't the state called Nancy Glenn? *Because she wouldn't have supported one word of the Lanny Mitchell-Roman Sobczynski testimony.* (One had to wonder why the *defense* hadn't called her, either. She could have been subpoenaed as a hostile witness, just as Bill Kohnke was.)

Lanny and Roman, Murphy said, "tell so many lies under oath that they forget what they've told."

The state wanted the jury to believe that because Patty Columbo "used profanity, lived with an older man, had different sexual mores than some others" (sexual *habits*, in everyday language), she was "therefore guilty of killing her parents." The truth was that Lanny and Roman had come to Patty with a story of a contract on Frank DeLuca. Patty lived in "constant fear"—of her father, of Lanny and Roman, "of harm coming to the man she loved." She was "backed into a corner" until she agreed to a contract on her father. Then, when "she and her father reconciled, she tried to back out of it."

"Imagine," Murphy pleaded, "the state of this girl." (Was she a girl? A case could be made that she had, in fact, never grown up—even today, after sixteen years in prison.)

What about Patricia's so-called vision? Nothing more, Murphy dismissed, "than the ramblings of a grief-stricken and hysterical girl." (So much more could have been made of this; it is deplorable that the defense gave it so little consideration. The two officers who were there—one of whom did not even testify to that particular incident, but who should have been made to—might have been cross-examined relentlessly about Patricia Columbo's appearance, voice pattern, confusion, and many other aspects of her condition at that time. The jury could have been *shown* the subnormal state of the person, as corroborated by Dr. Cherian, and been allowed to weigh the alleged statements accordingly.)

Regarding Michael Dunkle, Murphy felt that his testimony

"standing alone" showed that "Mary Columbo and the Columbo family [were] alive at six A.M." (on May 5).

"More importantly," Danielle McDonald had interviewed Patricia at 8:30 A.M. on May 5, and found her to be "pleasant," with "good presence," and "energetic, career minded." Could a nineteen-year-old who had "just gotten done killing or participating in the killing, stabbing, and mutilation of her parents and brother, have gone into that interview and acted in that manner?"

The state's case, Murphy declared, was "full of mysteries. Of reasonable doubt." And, he reminded the jury, reasonable doubt "doesn't mean two or three or five or twenty" reasonable doubts, it "simply meant *a* reasonable doubt." And if there "is *a* reasonable doubt, the time to have it is during your deliberations. Next week, next month, next year, will be too late."

Bill Murphy faced Judge Pincham's jury with great humility and sincerity. The representation of Patricia Columbo had probably been more difficult for him than for anyone else on the dual defense team, and it showed in his face.

"If there is a reasonable doubt," he implored, "find Patricia Columbo innocent. Because she is. Thank you."

It was an odd final statement: *If* there is a reasonable doubt.

As with her lover, there would now be nothing further said to exonerate Patricia Ann Columbo.

Algis "Al" Baliunas, as is customary, would have the last word in the trial, because he represented "the people," and society must always have the last word over any individual. That is the law of the land.

Baliunas said he would respond first to Stanton Bloom, whose defense of DeLuca, the prosecutor said flatly, "was a fraud."

He started with Joy Heysek. Would she "come into this courtroom and fabricate a story like" the one she told? That was "utterly ridiculous." She told her story "out of fear. Of who? That man who sits there smiling at you right now. Look at him!"

Frank DeLuca was, indeed, smiling as Al Baliunas

summed up for the state. At what, probably only God knew. Or the devil.

Baliunas then defended Bert Green. "Why would he come into court and lie? He also was terrified of Mr. DeLuca. Wouldn't it put a chill in *your* spine to have DeLuca running around?" DeLuca had been in custody once and was "let go. It could have happened again." That, Baliunas pointed out, was what both Bert Green and Joy Heysek lived in fear of. (Perhaps they still do. Both have disappeared.)

On to Lanny Mitchell and Roman Sobczynski. "Granted, they are not pillars of our community." ("That," a reporter was heard to whisper, "is the understatement of the twentieth century.") They were both "low-life" individuals, "absolutely." But "would persons of any other caliber associate with a tramp like Patty Columbo? She is nothing more than that. Mr. Murphy would like you to think she's some poor innocent unblemished flower that was misled by the evil Mr. DeLuca. She is just as sinister as he is! It was not Frank DeLuca's father, mother, and brother!"

For someone who was supposed to be shooting at Stanton Bloom, Baliunas was certainly spreading the shell fragments to Bill Murphy. But he quickly came back to Bloom's defense of DeLuca.

Addressing DeLuca's story of having made the map and diagram and written the descriptions of Heysek and Green "for his lawyer, Martin Toomin," the prosecution said confidently, "They were for Clifford Childs. Mr. DeLuca in his twisted mind believed he could send this dummy out to do his dirty work for him. The man spends his last pennies to pay Clifford Childs, takes food from his children's mouths! For only one reason: to beat this case!"

Now, Baliunas would take aim on Bill Murphy, whom he had already wounded. He responded to Murphy's analogy of the right way and wrong way to prepare and present a criminal case. "Murder cases," he said, "had a tendency to destroy evidence." But some still remained. Why, for instance, were the contents of Mary Columbo's purse strewn around? "To get the keys to the Thunderbird. They already had the Olds." (But why look in Mary's purse, when the Thunderbird was *Frank's* car? Jack McCarthy, Frank Columbo's assistant at the Western Auto terminal, had told Ray Rose that he could only recall two occasions when his boss had *not* driven the Thunderbird to work. Baliunas, however, was correct. Frank Columbo's leather key case had been taken from the kitchen counter, where he customarily put it when he entered the house. It had been dropped and could not be found in the dark. The reason for emptying out Mary's purse was to find *her* key case, which had keys to both cars. The second set of Olds keys were being used by Patricia to drive the car she had already borrowed from her mother. Thus, of two sets of keys for each car, three left the house after the murders, and only Frank Columbo's keys to the Thunderbird were left behind—*accidentally dropped by whoever turned Michael's dead body over to inflict the eight deep puncture wounds.*)

The Thunderbird, Baliunas said, "*was* stolen" from where DeLuca had dropped it off, just as DeLuca had planned for it to be. Being the sharpest, sportiest of the two Columbo cars, it had probably been left by DeLuca somewhere around Patty's "old neighborhood." Then, whoever stole it, whoever "pulled" the ignition and vandalized the car (and presumably removed the CB and other items that DeLuca had put in it), subsequently abandoned it the morning of May 7 in front of Roberta Walker's home at 140 South Whipple in the Chicago ghetto, where it was recovered.

Baliunas directed his summation to the murder scene. "What had been found in the commode?" he asked, using an old-fashioned word for what most people now call a "toilet." Human excrement, Ray Rose had testified. That proved what Mary Columbo had been doing. And the Columbo bed was "turned back" but nobody "had slept in it yet." (Proving that if Michael Dunkle had spoken to his aunt the next morning, she had stayed up all night, and so had her husband.) Also, the porch light was on. Why? Because they were dead.

The scissors. "Mr. Purdue Football Player didn't stab" Michael "ninety-seven times. Ex-football players don't make superficial wounds!" (Nor do weak people make deep puncture wounds.) "Only one person in this courtroom had that kind of hatred. That is Patty Columbo."

Who got the bowling trophy out to hit the mother and brother? "DeLuca never talked about hitting anyone but 'the old man.'" Baliunas had the grimmest expression on his face that he had shown throughout the trial. "Markedly absent from what [DeLuca] said he did," the prosecutor intoned, "was what *she* did!"

Regarding Michael Dunkle, Baliunas was "not saying he lied. But weigh the possibility of him making a *mistake*, as opposed to all the other evidence. He *is* simply mistaken. He had called nineteen or twenty other times. Mistaken. No questions about it."

There had been, Baliunas said, "much to-do about no hair sample" being taken from Michael. It was "a mistake. Flat out and simple. There was no excuse for it. None. But—it couldn't be corrected by exhumation," because the bodies had been "conveniently cremated."

The defense, Baliunas asserted, wanted the jury to believe that Patty Columbo was "a little angel. A little nineteen-year-old." But Baliunas asked them to consider her and DeLuca's "life-style." It did not "take a genius" to figure out what Patty was. Baliunas repeated the profanity that had been imputed to Patricia in testimony: " 'Fuck you, asshole! Fuck you, jack-off!' That's her," the prosecutor told the jury.

He recalled the More cigarettes. "Everywhere Patty goes," there are More cigarettes. "The loan car, the Oldsmobile, the ashtray." (What point was *that* intended to make? Patricia had borrowed—or rented—the "loan car," borrowed her mother's Olds, and lived in the apartment where the ashtray was; why shouldn't her cigarette butts be in all those places?)

If "you say to yourself, well, maybe she *wasn't* there," Baliunas hypothesized, "how are you going to move those cars around?" (There was no doubt as to the answer to *that*. There had to be one other driver. *Or more.*)

But "assume she's *not* there." Assume that "DeLuca does all this stuff himself. Did she want it done? Did she ask him to do it? Did she conspire with him?" If so, there was "no difference under the law. If she participated in planning," if she "aided, encouraged, abetted, she's just as guilty." (This was true. The same might also have been said for Lanny Mitchell and Roman Sobczynski—but the state chose to make an exception in their cases.)

Baliunas considered "their conduct afterward." What else, he asked, could they have done? If Patty had canceled her job interview and DeLuca had stayed home from work, "Where are they at then?"

The letter carrier who had seen two strangers on his route—what had his testimony been? "Nothing."

Lanny and Roman—had they used Patty Columbo? "*She used them*—or tried to!" But she had "been fooled by these two idiots" who were "carrying guns, playing the big role, talking big stuff."

DeLuca, the prosecutor contended, was also a user. "He used Joy Heysek. Used Bert Green. Used Clifford Childs." But he "got outfoxed because old Clifford took DeLuca's money and ran." DeLuca had even "used his own wife and kids." (Baliunas left out one person—Patricia, whom DeLuca had begun using three months after her sixteenth birthday. Nearly everyone who dislikes Patricia Columbo disregards that fact.)

The Monday night rides that Bert Green testified he gave Patty three weeks in a row? "Patty Columbo *faked* the three dropoffs! No hit men were ever scheduled." It had been done to get DeLuca "progressively more nervous" until he finally said, "We've got to do it ourselves." (Here Baliunas is contradicting the evidence of his own witnesses. DeLuca did not "finally say" they would have to do it themselves; according to both Joy and Bert, he had been saying it for weeks, perhaps several months—almost as if he were relishing the idea. Every time he looked in the mirror and saw the scars on his lip and chin, he must have hated Frank Columbo more and more.)

The case, Baliunas allowed, had "lots of interesting little twists and turns, little things, that all mounted up."

Concluding, he said, "Don't let them use *you*, ladies and gentlemen. Don't let them sail out of this courtroom over the charred remains of Frank Columbo—Mary Columbo— Michael Columbo. Don't let them do that, ladies and gentlemen. Thank you."

On page 11,915 of the trial transcript, the hearing of witnesses, presentation of evidence, all the many squabbles between the lawyers, and the final summations by both sides ended.

Closing arguments had begun at nine o'clock that morning, and it was now well past the dinner hour. The date was July 1, 1977.

Frank, Mary, and Michael had been dead one year, one month, three weeks, and six days.

45
July to September 1977

PATRICIA COLUMBO, LOVER FOUND GUILTY

It took the jury only two hours to decide.

Everything happened in one long, sometimes seemingly interminable day—the same day that closing arguments were made by the lawyers on both sides. Following that, Judge Pincham read the appropriate prepared instructions to his jury. In formal, precise language, he covered the legal definitions of such words and terms as guilt; innocence; presumption of innocence; evidence; determination of facts; murder; conspiracy; and reasonable doubt. He cautioned the panel to give "separate consideration" to each defendant. He reminded them that they were to be the sole judges of the credibility of the witnesses they had heard. And he outlined for them the possible verdicts at which, under the law, they were allowed to arrive. Then, just before 9:00 P.M., he sent them into the jury room. The thinking of the court had been to let them work for three hours, while the summations were still fresh in their minds, and if they had not reached a verdict by midnight, send them to bed and let them begin fresh on Saturday morning.

But at 10:55 P.M., the jury foreman told the bailiff at the door that they had reached a verdict. The astonished bailiff hurried to tell Judge Pincham.

"The verdict came with surprising suddenness," the *Sun-Times* reported the next morning, "catching court personnel and attorneys out of the building. It was another forty-five minutes before the decision could be read."

As Patricia and DeLuca were brought back into the courtroom, DeLuca put his arm around her reassuringly. Some said he had almost an air of confidence about him, as if the quick verdict meant acquittal. One reporter shook his head in amazement and said, "Look at the guy. He actually thinks the jury *believed* him!"

When everyone was finally in place, at twenty minutes before midnight, Judge Pincham asked, "Mr. Foreman, has the jury arrived at a verdict?"

"Yes," came the reply.

The verdict was passed to the judge, studied, then passed to the court clerk to be read aloud. It was guilty.

Guilty on all counts. Guilty of everything. Guilty, guilty, guilty—the word was read again and again. Guilty of murder, three times for her, three for him. Guilty of solicitation to commit murder, three times for her, three for him.

Patricia appeared stunned at the verdicts. Blinking back tears, she slumped forward in her chair and Bill Swano quickly reached over to steady her. DeLuca, as the *Daily News* would report the next day, "wore the same faint smile he had displayed" throughout much of the trial.

Bernard Carey, the Cook County state's attorney for whom the prosecution team worked, and who attended the final day of the trial with his children, stated to the press that he had "predicted [the jury] would be back [by] 10:30." His reason: the case had been "so well presented that it was not difficult for jurors to reach a decision." When asked if the Columbo murders were "more vicious than the slaying of eight young nurses by Richard Speck," another infamous Chicago crime, Carey replied, "I would say so."

Bill Murphy said he would appeal the verdict on the basis that Judge Pincham should not have allowed sexually explicit testimony about a lewd photograph of Patricia and her dog, or the evidence regarding Patricia's use of profanity, both of which he felt, rightly, might have prejudiced the jury. Murphy also said that the state "ignored evidence and refused to contact witnesses" that would have shown his client's innocence. (Why didn't the *defense* contact those witnesses? The public defender's office has an investigative staff to track down people and evidence, just as the state's attorney does.)

Bill Swano said he would "definitely file an appeal based on [the judge's] denial of their severance motion."

Would separate trials have helped either defendant? Most of the jury, and others, thought not. "I don't think the outcome would have been any different," was an almost universal quote. Only one juror, Arlene Nettgren, who with her husband owned two retail piano stores and lived directly next to Elk Grove Village in Schaumburg, disagreed in part. "I think separate trials would have been better," she said. "Then it could have come out how it really did happen. As it was, one [defendant] couldn't say anything to implicate [the other], and it got a little confusing." Mrs. Nettgren added, however, that she was certain the defendants were guilty. She had not made a decision in the case, she said, until the last day, and "the closing arguments were a big factor . . . [they] seemed to round it all out, sum it all up."

Discussing Patricia Columbo, prosecutor Patti Bobb said, "She almost has two distinct personalities. One is a pleasant girl, a kind of actress type. Then she goes back to a hard self. It's kind of scary to watch her." Bobb was then quoted by the *Sun-Times* as saying that there was "evidence" not admissible in court because the two defendants were "tied together," but that there was no doubt "Miss Columbo is the one who stabbed her brother." Also, she said, "We know for sure DeLuca did the shooting and beat the father over the head with a lamp and probably a bowling trophy. We also know she and DeLuca were in the home the night of the murders." (That last statement seemed somewhat superfluous, given the ones that had preceded it. All in all, they were strange comments. If there *was* additional evidence that could have been presented in separate trials, then why not *have* separate trials? The defense certainly asked for them often enough; all the state had to do was second the motion. Why keep such compelling evidence from the court and the public?)

Regarding DeLuca, Patti Bobb said, "He's so scary. He's absolutely frightening."

Patricia's uncle, Mario Columbo, Frank's brother, seemed to blame everything that happened on DeLuca. "Patty was a normal little girl," he said. "This bit about the profanity, about the men in her life . . . there was nothing like that until she met DeLuca. I never saw her like they said she behaved. The change in her personality came when she moved in with DeLuca." Mario Columbo said he was certain "from all I heard in the courtroom" that the verdict was just. Then he shrugged helplessly. "She made the choice."

One of Mary's sisters, Carolyn Tygrett, said, "I think

DeLuca and Pat must have brought out the worst in each other."

Another sister, Myrtis Peterson, said, "I wanted to believe they weren't guilty. But I guess they are. I understand [Patricia] will get psychiatric help. Maybe someday she'll be all right."

Juror Linda Ollins, the twenty-one-year-old Roosevelt College science major, said that she was convinced of Patricia's guilt by the description of Michael's body. The way he was stabbed "had to be hate-involved." (Patti Bobb's summation, it appears, had hit a bull's-eye. But the general consensus, even among people who detest Patricia the most, is that she did *not* hate Michael. But *DeLuca* might have—because Michael had been tormenting him with his staring routine in the drugstore. "Junior's got to go too," he'd told Roman Sobczynski on the telephone.) Regarding DeLuca, Ms. Ollins pretty much voiced everyone's opinion. "He got up there [on the witness stand] and sank himself."

As far as Patricia was concerned, the Chicago newspapers, which would later remind their readers for nearly a decade of her alleged involvement in a prison "sex scandal," were not impressed at all by the prosecution's case. The *Sun-Times* said, "The main evidence against DeLuca did not directly implicate Miss Columbo." The *Daily News* said, "There was little evidence linking her to the actual murders, other than the state's contention that only she could carry enough hate to plunge a pair of scissors almost one hundred times into the chest and neck of her young brother." (How the story grows. From seventy-six incise cuts and eight puncture wounds in the back to the scissors being "plunged" into Michael's chest and neck "almost one hundred times.") The prosecution, continued the *Daily News,* "attempted to put her into the home by showing that a human hair about three inches long on the boy's body was 'similar' to Miss Columbo's shoulder-length tresses, but the testimony was inconclusive."

Judge R. Eugene Pincham, after praising his jury for "serving long and well," admitted to the press that, as a former defense attorney himself, he couldn't help thinking about how *he* would have defended Patricia Columbo if it had been up to him. But, being the ethical and high-principled individual he was, he declined to elaborate on what he might have done differently.

Sentencing, originally set for August 1, eventually took place on August 8. Judge Pincham's punishment of two hundred to three hundred years for each convicted defendant, plus lesser terms to run concurrently for solicitation to commit murder, were pronounced in a full courtroom that also heard DeLuca say, "Patty and I are innocent. I will stand on my testimony ... because that is the truth." And heard Patricia make her choked-up statement that her "father, mother, and baby brother" know that "it wasn't us in the house that night."

There were few if any real surprises at the sentencing. Al Baliunas said that if he had been able to, he would have asked for the death penalty. (Illinois did not have capital punishment at the time of the murders. The death penalty was signed back into law by Governor Bill Thompson on June 22, 1977, while the Columbo-DeLuca trial was still going on; the reinstated law would apply only to crimes occurring after that date. In the fifteen years since then, Illinois has sent one hundred forty-three men and two women to Death Row. It has executed only one condemned person, Charles Walker, who gave up his appeals and requested death by lethal injection.)

Defense attorney Bill Murphy told the press that he felt the sentence for Patricia was "pretty long for somebody who didn't do anything."

Judge Pincham was asked to allow Patricia to remain in the county jail to complete courses she had been taking to obtain a high school diploma. Pincham stayed her sentence for sixty days.

The only other conflict that arose in the trial was when the judge ordered the state to pay the fees of Michael Toomin and Stanton Bloom, who had been appointed by the court when DeLuca claimed that he was indigent. The state objected and presented evidence that DeLuca was enjoying an income of several hundred dollars a month from his Walgreen's pension and profit-sharing fund. (During the time Patricia was in the county jail, *her* inmate account averaged only ten to fifteen dollars a month, whatever her godmother, Janet Morgan, could afford. At that, she was still better off fi-

nancially than Marilyn DeLuca and the five children. Only
Frank somehow managed to remain relatively comfortable.)

The matter of the legal fees was subsequently resolved,
however, and DeLuca's attorneys were paid by the state.

The trial cost the taxpayers of Cook County a quarter of a
million dollars, with another hundred thousand being paid by
Elk Grove Village for the investigation of the crime. For a
time, Elk Grove Village considered a civil suit against
Patricia and DeLuca to recover its costs, but the matter was
not pursued after local authorities decided that legal expenses
for such an action would probably far outweigh what, if anything, the community got back.

On an overcast morning in September 1977, a caravan of four
cars left the Cook County Jail and headed downstate. In the
lead car were deputy sheriffs. In the second car were deputy
sheriffs and Frank DeLuca, handcuffed and shackled. In car
number three were deputy sheriffs, male and female, and
Patricia Columbo, handcuffed but not shackled. In car
number four were more deputy sheriffs.

Forty miles south of Chicago, on the northern edge of
Joliet, the caravan pulled up to the intake gate of the maximum security Illinois state prison for men, Stateville Correctional Center. DeLuca was taken out of the rear seat of the
car and without ceremony helped to hobble through the gate.
He did not look back at the car carrying Patricia.

In the Reception and Diagnostic Unit of Stateville, DeLuca
became Illinois convict number C-73216. He would subsequently be transferred to Pontiac Correctional Center, a
medium-to-maximum security facility farther downstate, but
within two years, because of his conduct, would be sent back
to Stateville, the "tough joint."

The car that had carried DeLuca to prison turned back toward Chicago. The other three continued thirty-two miles farther south to the Illinois state prison for women, Dwight
Correctional Center. There, Patricia Columbo was led inside
to become number C-77200.

She was twenty-one years old.

She hoped to God she would not live to turn twenty-two.

Part Three

Aftermath

46

May 1976

Family murder is always bizarre, always repellent. It revolts, disgusts, offends. Next to the wanton murder of a child, nothing disturbs the public more. Serial murder intrigues, but ultimately becomes statistical; robbery murder invariably is associated with drug addicts or habitual criminals. But family murder disrupts logical thinking, intrudes upon accepted values; family murder does not go away when the daily paper is put aside or the eleven o'clock news turned off. Family murder *persists*.

"How could he (or she, or they) do that to his (or her, or their) own flesh and blood?" the question goes. Everybody professes not to "understand" it. And in a family murder in which many questions go unanswered for many years, a murder truly inconceivable, wholly incomprehensible, totally unimaginable, the repugnance of the crime becomes steeped in controversy.

It would be difficult to find a murder case with more contradictions in it than the Columbo family killings. For every question there seem to be multiple answers, and the more scrutiny applied, the more complex the speculation becomes. Put almost any two people with more than cursory knowledge of the Columbo case into a room and within minutes they will argue at least one point. They may agree on 99 percent of their discussion, but they will *never* agree on everything. Even after fifteen years, mysteries still abound, discrepancies remain, inconsistencies linger intriguingly.

Some of the puzzles are minor—but still nag. Why, for instance, on the afternoon that the bodies were discovered, did Chicago policeman Joe Giuliano get only a ring and no answer when he dialed the Columbo house several times, but Western Auto employee Jack McCarthy got a busy signal? Not that it makes any real difference, but *why*?

Where did all the guns go? Frank Columbo's nephew Robert Rezzuto saw a gun in the Thunderbird's glove box. Frank told his nephew he had a second gun. A relative in South Carolina saw a gun in Mary Columbo's purse. Frank told another relative down there that he had bought a gun for Mary, and Michael told the same person that his father had a second gun. Frank DeLuca had a little derringer. Roman Sobczynski gave Patricia a .32 revolver. *None* of them have ever been found.

A stock argument concerns whether DeLuca and/or Patty really *believed* that Frank Columbo would do violence to either or both of them. Patricia, of course, must have known in her heart that her father would never have seriously hurt *her*—but it is preposterous to think that DeLuca supposed he had the same immunity. Why *wouldn't* DeLuca have believed that the threat was real? Frank Columbo unquestionably had a temper; Frank Columbo had smashed DeLuca's mouth in with a rifle butt; Frank Columbo was making ongoing threats to Patricia on the telephone and in person that he was going to "get" DeLuca. Only an idiot would not have taken him seriously.

Why did Patricia go out with Nancy Glenn to meet Lanny and Roman the first time? For one hundred dollars, as Lanny claims? Roman thought she had been paid for the evening. Patricia never received any money, but maybe she *had* agreed to go for that reason. She and DeLuca certainly weren't financially well off; Patricia could have used the cash. Lanny, of course, testified that Patricia told him in the lounge, shortly after the four met, that if Roman would "do favors" for her, she would "fuck his eyes out." Yet everyone agrees that within *an hour*, Patricia took the inebriated Nancy and tried to "ditch" the two men. So whether she was there for one hundred dollars or for unspecified "favors," Patricia Columbo obviously didn't consider either one important enough to voluntarily have sex with Roman Sobczynski. Not that night, anyway. Only when she was being forced to go to the motel did she try to get something out of it by talking Lanny into getting her some bullets for DeLuca's derringer. Later, of course, when by Lanny's own admission, Patricia became "afraid" of him, when the two men continued to flash their guns and talk about arranging "hits" and "contracts," Patricia had sex with both of them. But to say that she did it solely to arrange her father's death, and that she was not intimidated by those two individuals, simply is not realistic—no matter how much one dislikes Patricia Columbo. Lanny even admitted to police that he threatened to kill Patricia, though later, on the witness stand, the prosecution had him testify that he had lied. But who knows? For Lanny, by then, to admit lying was almost routine.

Did Frank DeLuca know about Roman and Lanny, or did he really believe, as he has maintained for fifteen years, that he thought Roman was Patricia's godfather, Phil Capone? His story, which he says came from Patricia, was that her godfather and Frank Columbo had a "falling-out," that her godfather "loved her like a daughter," and that he wanted to "protect" her and DeLuca. The godfather supposedly "bought off" a contract Frank Columbo had on DeLuca, but later told DeLuca that Frank Columbo was "shopping around" for another hit man. DeLuca testified that he then agreed to the killing of Frank Columbo "if it was the only way" to stop him. Up to that point it all makes sense; Patricia was fully capable of concocting a lie of that magnitude, and DeLuca, in a frightened state, "running very, very scared," certainly might have believed it. *Except* for the one statement that Frank DeLuca made to Roman Sobczynski on the telephone: "Junior's got to go too." If DeLuca really thought he was talking to Patricia's godfather, he would never have asked for Michael's murder. It is unthinkable.

Did Frank DeLuca kill the Columbos out of sudden desperation after the third Monday night meeting between Patricia and the "hit men" failed, or was he *actively* planning the crime himself? One has only to believe Joy Heysek for the answer to that. DeLuca's threat—that if she ever went to the police, he would have her son run down while riding his bike, her daughter kidnapped and raped, and Joy herself beaten until she was unrecognizable—was made a *full week* before the murders, a full week before Patricia's third meeting with the "hit men" was to take place. Frank DeLuca obviously knew at that time that the Columbos were not going to be killed by anyone but him. And if *he* knew it, did Patricia know it also? *No.* Because if she did, why continue the preposterous game of meeting "hit men?" Al Baliunas said Patricia "staged" the meetings to work DeLuca into

enough of an emotional turmoil that he would kill for her.
That was certainly possible. But wasn't it also possible that
DeLuca staged the meetings that never took place, or that Roman and Lanny set them up and then backed out on DeLuca,
as they had so many times on Patricia? It was clearly proven
that DeLuca *had contact with them* after Patricia had stopped
seeing and talking to them. Is it not conceivable that Roman
and Lanny would have been sorely tempted to work DeLuca
as they had worked Patricia? DeLuca, with ready access to
cash, drugs, quantities of liquor? DeLuca, frightened, vulnerable, ready to do anything to thwart the threat of Frank Columbo? At the trial, the prosecution was ready to believe that
Lanny and Roman at long last were going to tell the truth, the
whole truth, and nothing but the truth. But Lanny and Roman
had more cunning, more shrewdness, more down-and-dirty
smarts, than Al Baliunas, Patti Bobb, and Terry Sullivan all
put together. They would have known exactly how much they
had to tell in order to get immunity—and they would not
have told *one word more.* We must remember, except for the
telephone conversations Roman had with DeLuca, both men
were witnesses against *Patricia.* DeLuca didn't ask Clifford
Childs to kill *them.* He knew from the discovery evidence
that their testimony was directed primarily at Patricia.
DeLuca was the one who contrived master plans, plotted perfect crimes, was accustomed to moving people around like
chess pieces, controlling and manipulating. It is quite possible
that all Patricia did at this point was blunder along, just as
she had most of the past several years, making one mistake
after another, getting deeper and deeper into an adult world
that she simply did not have the intellect or instinct to handle.
Finally, there was no reason for Frank DeLuca to make his
threat to Joy Heysek a week before the murders unless he
was certain by then that she was going to have something to
go to the police *about.*

 Who wielded the scissors that cut and stabbed Michael Columbo? Someone so weak that the person could only make
superficial cuts on his tragic young body? Or someone strong
enough to grip the scissors so tightly that their handles and
tips were sprung, and strong enough to make the eight deep
puncture wounds? Or did *two* people swing those scissors?
Or was there *another* weapon—such as the pearl-handled

twelve-inch knife that Lanny Mitchell saw in Frank DeLuca's car when he met Patricia on the Elk Grove Village Bowl parking lot one time? That knife, like at least four known handguns, disappeared completely. It is curious that the state did not ask DeLuca about that knife when they had him on the stand for cross-examination, but they didn't—even though it was *their* witness, Lanny Mitchell, who had seen it in DeLuca's car. Butchered bodies at the crime scene, a knife in the accused's car—and no interest in it from the prosecution: *why*?

Contrary to Patti Bobb's summation, however, it is most unlikely that what was done to Michael was done out of any hatred on the part of Patricia. Fear and desperation—yes. As part of a "perfect crime" plan to make the murder look like a home invasion—maybe. Hatred by *DeLuca*—possibly. A complete and utter loss of all control, all rationality, all reason—probably. But the only way for the prosecution to put Patricia in the house was to put the scissors in her hands and hatred in her heart. Nothing else would make sense to a jury. And it worked.

Why would Frank DeLuca tell Bert Green and Joy Heysek about the crime the next morning? He had to; his personality dictated that he tell them. A sociopath never expects to have to take the responsibility or blame for anything—so why not brag about it? Particularly to two people whom he firmly believed he could control. DeLuca was accustomed to sharing personal secrets with both Joy and Bert. He thought Bert idolized him; after all, Bert had hidden the gun for him, driven Patricia to the three failed meetings with hit men, knew all about Frank Columbo's purported contract on him, knew that DeLuca was planning to commit the murders himself if no one would do them for him; so why not go all the way and tell Bert when it was *done*? Besides, Bert had caught him in the act of burning those bloody clothes. (That's what DeLuca *said* he was doing; Bert Green never *saw* what was in the incinerator—and Clifford Childs said the clothes were burned in a field—but all of that is just one more glitch in a case filled with glitches.)

And Joy Heysek? DeLuca still thought he owned Joy. He could threaten her and her children; he could try to use her as an alibi ("Go see *One Flew Over the Cuckoo's Nest* for me");

he had all those filthy photographs of her—black men, other
women, a dog. Could there be any doubt that DeLuca felt she
was *his*? And since he had bragged to Bert about it, why not
Joy also? Notice that he did not brag to John Norton or anyone else who worked for him. Just his confirmed sycophants.
Joy Heysek might have wanted everyone to think she didn't
care for DeLuca any longer, but she *had* transferred into his
store, and she had *not* told the police what she knew about
the murders until the day Ray Rose recognized her when she
walked into Corky's. If Rose had not confronted her that day,
can anyone say with any real conviction that Joy Heysek
would *ever* have told what she knew? Even if DeLuca had remained or again become a free man? Even if he was at large
to continue his sexual madness and manipulation? Even if it
led him to murder again? Never. Joy Heysek talked because
she *had* to talk. Just as much as Frank DeLuca, because of his
gigantic ego, *had* to talk.

Did DeLuca mention only himself when telling Bert Green
and Joy Heysek of the killings, or did he also mention
Patricia, and is *that* the wonderful evidence Patti Bobb mentioned so mysteriously after the verdict? Possibly. It is doubtful that DeLuca mentioned Patricia to Joy; he only spoke to
her briefly about the crime itself. He *might* have mentioned
Patricia to Bert, having spoken to him in greater detail, having taken Green into his confidence over a long period of
time and virtually *involved* him in the plans. Bert was the person DeLuca called to come get him when the police let him
go the first time; not Marilyn or his brother, Bill, but Bert
Green—another person who might have told police and prosecutors only *as much* as he had to. But if DeLuca did tell
Bert that Patricia had been with him, then Bert Green committed perjury in Judge Pincham's court; and if that *was* the
"evidence" Patti Bobb alluded to, then the prosecution *knew*
he committed that perjury. Because Michael Toomin asked
Bert Green on the stand, "Did DeLuca say he entered the Columbo house with anyone but himself?" Green replied, "No,
sir."

Should Patricia Columbo's statement to the Elk Grove police, made during the twelve hours she was being held without having a lawyer to represent her, have been used against
her at the trial? Absolutely not. It did not take a police officer

like Ray Rose, or an assistant state's attorney like Terry Sullivan, or even, two days later, a jail psychiatrist like Dr. Paul Cherian, to see that what they were dealing with was a nineteen-year-old adolescent role player with an addled mind. Anyone off the street could have seen that Patricia was confused, perplexed, bewildered. They had her separated from her one lifeline to security—DeLuca. And they had enough evidence against her, from Lanny Mitchell's statement and the floor plan and other material she gave him, to convict her of solicitation to commit murder. Her statement gave them no more than they already had.

Ray Rose, Gene Gargano, John Landers, Bill Kohnke, and Terry Sullivan made a joint assault on Patricia Columbo, and even brought in Lanny Mitchell to help them. Policemen are policemen, and they were dealing with cold-blooded murder, but Terry Sullivan should not have let it happen. Terry Sullivan should have telephoned for an on-call assistant public defender. Sullivan had taken an oath to protect the rights of "the people," and at that moment, like it or not, Patricia Columbo was one of "the people," with technically as much presumption of innocence due her as she had to be afforded by the jury. Of course, it is well documented that Patricia "gave up" her right to remain silent and to have an attorney present during her questioning—"I don't need no fucking lawyer," she told Janet Morgan on the telephone—but her reason for doing so was very clear: she knew the police were holding Frank DeLuca and she wanted them to let him go. Ray Rose was emotionally overwhelmed by the enormity of the crime; he would have chewed bullets to catch the killers. Bill Kohnke was running around spewing threats of the electric chair. John Landers was playing "good cop" to Rose's "bad cop." Terry Sullivan supposedly was there to "witness" Patricia's statement to Landers, but he actually participated in the questioning toward the end, even though the statement indicates it was taken by Landers, witnessed by Laura Komar, and Sullivan, who would later assist in the prosecution, did not sign it. It is unclear whether Judge Pincham knew Sullivan was present when the statement was taken or not; or, if he did, whether it would have made any difference in his ruling to permit it as evidence. Gene Gargano, that day, seemed to be the only police officer striving to stick strictly

to the rules. He could have secured a confession from
DeLuca if he had been willing to go under the table a little,
but he had not.

All that aside, it was not *necessary* to handle Patricia Columbo in the manner in which they did, and their collective
zeal to solve the horrible crime does not excuse this overkill.
The point at issue is not whether Patricia Columbo deserved
such treatment or not; the point is that it should have been
beneath the police officers and the assistant state's attorney to
participate in or permit it. The state could have meted out justice to Patricia Columbo without resorting to some of the tactics it used—and probably could have put Roman Sobczynski
away too, with Lanny Mitchell's help—and it is a pity that it
was not done that way.

The biggest unanswered question of all, of course, is: What
happened at 55 Brantwood on the night of May 4, 1976?

For fifteen years, DeLuca maintained he was not there, and
for fifteen years Patricia refused to talk about it, except at one
point to "accept responsibility" for the crime. That left only
one scenario: what the police and prosecution theorize happened. Although there is disagreement on *specifics* (Patti
Bobb, for instance, was quoted as believing that it was
DeLuca who used the bowling trophy to cave in the skulls of
Frank and Mary, while Ray Rose was quoted as thinking it
was Patricia), the broad law-enforcement scenario is this:

Patricia and DeLuca attempted to establish an alibi by returning to their apartment after visiting Yorktown Mall, paying back a neighbor for some milk previously borrowed, and
DeLuca telephoning the store to check with the assistant
manager who was scheduled to close up. Then they slipped
out again, Patricia driving the Olds she had borrowed from
her mother the previous Friday, DeLuca driving the 1968
Buick on loan (or rental) from Jack's Top and Trim. DeLuca
parked the Buick on Lancaster Avenue, around the corner
from the Columbo home, which was the third house down on
the other side of Brantwood. There were no houses on the
west side of Lancaster, only a narrow strip of open land; on
the east was the side of the corner house at 50 Brantwood,
which belonged to John and Ruth Payne. The couple had a
summer home on Lake Superior and had gone there to open

it up, leaving their Elk Grove house unoccupied. DeLuca could not have chosen a better spot to leave the Buick.

Patricia picked DeLuca up in the Olds and drove around the corner to her parents' house, parking in the driveway behind the Thunderbird. (To do this, Patricia would have had to park perpendicular to the Thunderbird, because the driveway at 55 Brantwood was not long enough to park two cars in a line without one of them being inside the garage. In effect, Patricia parked on the street, blocking her parents' driveway.)

They went to the front door. Patricia opened the unlocked storm door and knocked on the inside door. DeLuca, standing out of sight of the door to Patricia's right, pulled on what he would later tell Bert Green was a "stocking hat," which he drew down to cover his face; he was already wearing gloves, the left one "stuffed" with something to fill the index finger and part of the one next to it.

Frank Columbo opened the inner door and saw that it was his daughter. Patricia started to enter and her father turned and started up the seven stairs leading to the living room. Reaching out to keep the storm door open, DeLuca quickly stepped in behind Patricia. Instead of following her father up the stairs, Patricia went *down* the adjacent stairway, which led to the house's lower level. DeLuca closed the inside door, went up several stairs behind Frank Columbo, pivoted slightly to his left in the narrow stairway, raised the pistol, and shot Columbo once in the back of the head. Columbo was thrown forward against a wall that faced the stairway; he turned to the masked figure, using the wall for support, and said, "Who are you? Why are you doing this to me?" DeLuca said, "Fuck you!" and shot him a second time, in the face, sending him reeling off to his right, into the living room. At that moment, Mary Columbo rushed from the bathroom into the hall directly next to the wall where her husband had just been shot the second time, and had only a split instant to stare in wide-eyed shock at DeLuca before he shot her point-blank between the eyes. DeLuca then stalked down the hall past where Mary fell, entered Michael's bedroom, pulled him out of bed (he was lying in an open sleeping bag on top of his bed), stood him up, and shot him in the face.

Downstairs, Patricia opened her mother's sewing drawer and removed the gold-handled scissors, then grabbed the most convenient bowling trophy (from the very end of the lower shelf of a display containing more than a dozen others). By the time she hurried back upstairs, DeLuca had returned to the living room, found Frank Columbo still alive, floundering about on the living room floor. DeLuca put the gun down, picked up a heavy ornamental lamp, and beat Columbo about the head with it until he stopped struggling, shattering the lamp all over the room in the process. Then he picked the gun back up and shot the now still man twice more in the face.

By this time, there was blood everywhere—except on Patricia. Blood on the ceiling from the upward swings of the lamp; blood on the underside of a glass coffee table, spraying up from the prone Frank Columbo's face and head; blood all over the wall and hallway; and Columbo blood all over Frank DeLuca. His gloves were so slick with blood that he had to take them off to remove the stocking mask. Then when he started handling the large pieces of glass, using them to cut throats, he scratched and sliced his own hands. He cut his fingers some more collecting the glass to take with them, because he wasn't sure which pieces now had his fingerprints on them.

From this point on, details are speculative and argumentative. Someone used the scissors to stab Michael eight times, and the scissors or some other sharp instrument to cut him seventy-six more times. Someone used the bowling trophy to club Frank and Mary in the head, leaving clearly visible square indentations in their skulls that perfectly matched the trophy's base. Someone—DeLuca alone, or both of them—used the glass fragments to cut Frank's and Mary's throat.

When it was all over, one of them put a number of items taken from the house into the Thunderbird. (There is a school of thought that DeLuca did all, or most, of the butchering of the bodies, while Patricia, who would have known where everything was, went about collecting the CB, some jewelry, two fur coats, and other items to make the crime look like a home invasion or other kind of robbery, and that it was she who put them into the Thunderbird. That, of course, is no less conjectural than any other notion of what happened.)

At any rate, DeLuca drove the Thunderbird, Patricia the Olds, and they went into the inner city and left the Thunderbird somewhere in a lower West Side neighborhood where, with the CB and other items—perhaps the murder gun, other guns from the house; perhaps also the pearl-handled knife—lying tantalizingly in plain view, the car was almost certain to be stolen, robbed, vandalized, or, as it turned out, all three.

Returning to Elk Grove in the Olds, with Patricia still driving, DeLuca picked up the Buick on Lancaster Avenue and led Patricia to the parking lot of an apartment building in Wooddale, where they left the Olds. Then, presumably, they returned to their apartment.

The hypothesis of the police and prosecutors as to the murders themselves is very strong. Their theory begins to weaken only after DeLuca and Patricia leave the house. The movements of the cars, considering the quantity of blood DeLuca had to have on his clothes and body by then—Patricia too, if one accepts Patti Bobb's view of her work with not only the scissors but the trophy—has been a point of irritating uncertainty to Ray Rose for fifteen years. How could people with that much blood on them drive around for the better part of an hour, even at midnight, and not be noticed by someone? And why, if DeLuca drove the Thunderbird and rode in the Olds, was there no conspicuous evidence of blood in both cars when they were recovered?

DeLuca's story to Clifford Childs of burning the bloody clothes in a field was undoubtedly a lie. He would have been a fool to light, out in the open, a fire intense enough to consume bloody, wet clothes, particularly when he knew he had the convenience of the Walgreen's incinerator so handy. Since garbage had been dumped on the Columbo kitchen floor and the plastic bag containing it taken, and since DeLuca supposedly had earlier put a change of clothes in the Olds, he probably changed in the murder house, putting the bloody clothes and stocking mask into the plastic bag. Patricia may have brought his change of clothes in when she put the items taken from the house into the Thunderbird. Whatever the logistics, DeLuca had to have changed clothes before leaving the murder house. There is no other explanation for the absence of blood in the two Columbo cars.

Except the explanation Patricia gives.

* * *

Her mind, Patricia would recall fifteen years later, was so "fucked up" by May 4, 1976, that she considered herself fortunate just to get through a day without going stark, raving mad. Everything around her was, as usual, at odds with everything else. None of the pieces of her life *fit*. Nothing *worked* for her.

A month earlier, on April 10, a Saturday, she had dropped in unannounced at the Columbo home. It was Michael's thirteenth birthday. Because of the occasion, tension between Patricia and her parents had, for the moment, been put aside. Patricia stayed for several hours. The communication with her parents that day, she said, "was good." Her father, in particular, seemed to have "mellowed considerably" in the several weeks since she had last seen him.

That day had made her realize, Patricia recalled fifteen years later, that the single biggest mistake of her life had been leaving her father's house. That defiant act, almost two years earlier, she was now convinced, was when she began going completely out of control. When she broke the parental tie with her father and put herself totally under the control of Frank DeLuca, that was the point from which she slowly descended into the aberration and dementia that was Frank DeLuca's sick mind. The depths to which she sank in those two years astound her still: having sex with DeLuca in the house where his wife and five children lived; having sex, later in the apartment, with total strangers DeLuca picked out for her; drinking the liquor and taking the pills he provided; posing for him with the German shepherd; becoming convinced that her father was trying to kill him; having sex with Roman and Lanny to try to get them to kill her father first; staying with DeLuca as he became more paranoid, more deluded, more dangerous—even to the point of suspecting Michael of being part of a murder plot against him.

Madness, all of it. But every time she tried to turn her life around, she failed. She had broken off all contact with Lanny and Roman, but she suspected that DeLuca was still in touch with them. He wouldn't let her answer the telephone when he was at home; several times when he was out and she answered it, the caller hung up. At first, Patricia suspected it might be Joy Heysek; the woman was obviously still crazy about Frank. Gradually, however, Patricia decided that it was Lanny or Roman calling; she knew for sure when the bullshit started about meeting "hit men" on the church parking lot and helping them gain access to the Columbo home. The first time had been April 19, nine days after she began seeing her parents again. She had done it to indulge DeLuca; he was convinced that everything was arranged for the hits. Patricia didn't believe it for a moment; she had been down that road far too many times with Lanny and Roman to think they would ever do anything except *take*. But Frank, she feared, was so close to breaking down mentally—in addition to which he now had the gun she had obtained from Roman—that Patricia was afraid not to do as he asked. Besides, she had been doing Frank's bidding for so long now—all her life, it sometimes seemed—that it was almost a reflex action.

Patricia had seen DeLuca and Bert Green together in numerous private, whispered discussions for several weeks, but had no idea how involved Green might be in whatever Frank was doing. She knew that Bert had kept the gun for Frank after DeLuca became convinced that "the hits were going down," because "after it was over," DeLuca did not, as he had told Joy Heysek and Grace Mason, want the police to be able to "place [him] with a gun." Bert Green, in Patricia's estimation, was a "kid. He followed Frank around like a puppy, trying to be like him," wanting to be a "swinger."

Originally, the plan had been for DeLuca himself to drop Patricia off at the church parking lot, then for him to go on to the store for a few minutes; the car would be parked outside for Patricia to walk back to and meet him after she had helped the hit men enter the Columbo house. But at the last minute—Monday afternoon—Frank told her he had "changed the plan" to "cover" himself; he would work that night—and Bert Green would drive her. Being in charge of everyone's schedule, DeLuca could easily change shifts around to suit himself.

There was little conversation between Patricia and Bert Green that Monday night. At one point he asked her—somewhat awkwardly, she felt, "Doesn't this bother you?" As if he were having difficulty accepting her going to assist "hit men" in murdering her parents.

Patricia could hardly say, "No problem, these guys never *perform*, they only *plan*." Bert would have repeated it to his mentor, and DeLuca would have become furious at her disloyalty. So she responded, "Doesn't what bother me?" When she avoided answering his question, Bert Green had merely shrugged. Patricia actually felt a little sorry for him; he didn't seem to realize that, in his desire to please DeLuca, he had involved himself in some very serious business. But she realized that Bert Green was really no different from herself, or Joy Heysek, or even Marilyn DeLuca; once Frank started getting his way with anyone, about anything, he seemed to exert more and more control until he eventually had his way about everything. There was something about him that made people very uneasy having to say no to him.

After the three failed meetings when the "hit men" didn't show up, DeLuca was very tense, "like a coil ready to spring," wanting to "hurt somebody, anybody," to the point where Patricia herself felt threatened. As with her father, she could not really believe that DeLuca would hurt her, not seriously. DeLuca had, like her father before him, slapped her once after they began living together in the apartment, but Patricia admitted that she "initiated" it by pushing *him* during an argument over Michael. Patricia had again been trying to convince DeLuca that Michael's staring routine was juvenile bullshit, and that Michael was incapable of being part of a "plot" against DeLuca. The argument had escalated to the push and the slap. Patricia had walked out of the apartment. She went to Oliver's Pub alone, deliberately got friendly with one of the regulars, a young guy named Kirk, allowed him to pick her up, and went home with him. It was the only time she felt she really "cheated on Frank," the only time she had sex with anyone—she had, after all, never gone to bed with Andrew Harper—except at DeLuca's bidding, or in his interest, as with Roman and Lanny. It was her way of paying him back for the slap—but, she was also aware, it was symbolic, as was her renewed relationship with her parents, of the fact that she was slowly but clearly trying to move *out* of Frank DeLuca's sphere of influence.

Tuesday, May 4. DeLuca left work and stopped for a bucket of Kentucky Fried Chicken on his way home. Patricia was already at the apartment when he got there; using her mother's car, she had spent the previous Friday and the day before,

Monday, and that day, Tuesday, looking for a job. DeLuca had been somewhat put out, and not a little suspicious, of her borrowing the Oldsmobile; he wanted her to have nothing to do with her family, particularly her father. Patricia had to assure him several times that it was only her mother she was seeing, not her father or Michael, who were in the "plot" against him.

After they ate the chicken, DeLuca said, "I need to unwind. Let's go out and find somebody to party with." Patricia got the distinct impression that she was being tested. "Okay," she agreed without argument. That, she realized later, had probably been a mistake; Frank knew she didn't like that part of their relationship, and must have become even more suspicious of her obliging cooperation. It then became a war of nerves, with neither of them backing down.

They went to Yorktown Mall, where DeLuca casually propositioned a young man he picked out at random. DeLuca had extraordinary good luck with strangers that way—particularly after he pointed Patricia out to them; in bars, shopping malls, with vendors who serviced Walgreen's, he was charm personified. Of course, it must have helped that he was peddling prime merchandise.

On the way back to the apartment, DeLuca stopped to buy a fifth of whiskey, and Patricia bought a carton of milk to pay back their neighbor. Their new acquaintance, whose name Patricia doesn't recall at all, waited in the car for them.

It was not until they were back in the apartment, and DeLuca was pouring the Canadian Club, that Patricia silently admitted that, as usual, she had backed herself very tidily into a tight little corner. And, also as usual, she did not like it. On close inspection, it did not appear to her that the man Frank had picked was too clean. Not that he was filthy; but his fingernails were dirty, and Patricia suddenly, without clear reason, became certain that he had bad breath. Her nerve beginning to falter, she went into the bathroom and took several Valiums—"at least three, maybe four"—the strength of which she didn't know; all she knew was that by then two tablets no longer affected her. Back in the living room, she drank half of the cocktail Frank had fixed for her.

It was while she was waiting for the tranquilizers to alter her mood that Patricia decided she was not going to do it.

She could not say later that any one thing brought on that determination; most likely it was "the sum of many things," culminating perhaps in the way DeLuca and the pickup were smiling at each other like two adolescents sharing a porno magazine. Fucking vultures, she thought, waiting to devour her. Despite the pills, her anger began to rise.

"I better take Duke for a walk, honey," she said to DeLuca. "So he don't disturb us after."

"Good idea," DeLuca said.

In the bedroom, Patricia slipped her mother's car keys into her coat pocket. She couldn't take her purse, which was on the kitchen counter, because it would have alerted DeLuca to what she was doing. Getting the leash, she clipped it to Duke's collar and left. Outside the apartment door, she made the big dog lie down and whispered, "Stay."

Hurrying down the hall, Patricia pressed for the elevator. Duke, used to going in the elevator with her, ran down to her. Patricia had to drag him halfway back down the hall, then run to the elevator when it arrived. As it was, the door almost caught Duke's nose when it closed; then, as she started to descend, Patricia heard him bark several times. If Frank caught her, she thought, he would beat the shit out of her. She began to tremble.

Not caring who saw her, Patricia ran out of the building to where her mother's car was parked. She did not feel safe even after she had driven away.

Michael opened the door for her. "Hi, honey," Patricia said. "Where's Daddy?"

"Dad, it's Patty," Michael said as he went back up the stairs.

Inside the foyer, Patricia sat down on the stairs that led to the lower level. Her father, newspaper in his hand, looked down at her from the living room level. Mary, in her robe, came up beside him. Patricia began to sob.

"I'll handle this," Frank Columbo said, handing the paper to his wife. "You," he said to Michael, "go to your room and stay there."

Frank Columbo came down the upper stairs in his stocking feet and sat on the bottom step next to the foyer. Patricia was now bawling like a baby, wailing as she had in the back of the police car after her arrest for credit card fraud. Her father took one of her hands and held it, but didn't speak to her, possibly because she was crying so loudly that she "wouldn't have been able to hear him anyway." Her whole body, she said, was "heaving" with the intensity of her sobs.

The first thing her father said to her, after several minutes had passed, was, "Jesus, Patty Ann, your face is a mess—"

Her tears had streaked mascara and eyeliner down her cheeks, and she had smeared it "all over" when she buried her face in her hands to sob. Frank Columbo let go of her hand and stood up to climb the stairs; before he got to the top, Mary Columbo was there, handing down a box of tissues. Patricia only saw her mother's arm, but thinks she might have started to come down to the foyer, because she heard her father say, "I said I'd handle this." Then Frank Columbo returned to his daughter, handed her the box of tissues, and sat down again. Patricia wiped her eyes, cheeks, and mouth as best she could.

Patricia was not certain, after fifteen years, how long she and her father talked; it was not a very long time, however— probably, she estimated, thirty minutes at the most. (The killings, contrary to almost everyone's hypothesis, in all likelihood occurred not between 11:00 and midnight, but about five or ten minutes before 10:00 P.M. The car that Georgia Brooks heard backfire, then saw in front of the Columbo home around 10:30, was probably Frank in the 1968 Buick, which, despite the new radiator hose DeLuca had put on it the previous day, still ran very roughly.)

Although uncertain about the lapse of time, Patricia is clear about the conversation that took place. She asked—"begged and pleaded," she said—to be allowed to come home. And her father said no.

"You're too disruptive to this house," Frank Columbo told her. Patricia knew without thinking about it that the words he used were Mary Columbo's words, not his. "Too disruptive" wasn't a term Frank Columbo would have used unless he had picked it up from his wife. And Patricia and her father both knew that Mary was sitting very near the top of the stairs listening to their conversation. When her father refused to give her permission to return home, he wasn't doing it for himself, Patricia was certain, but for his wife. And, she decided, upon many years' reflection, it had not been a *final* decision, merely a temporary one until her father could work some compromise with her mother. She is convinced that her parents, given a few days to consider her sincerity, would have allowed her to come back and, at the "ripe old age of nineteen," begin her life anew.

But for the moment, the answer was no.

Frank Columbo's Thunderbird was parked on the drive, nearest the front door. Patricia had pulled the Olds up next to it; she had left the keys in the ignition. Now, as they sat there, both heard a third car pull up outside, a car that Frank Columbo must have thought sounded like his brother's car. He looked at his watch.

"What the hell's Mario coming over this time of night for?" he said, more to himself than to Patricia.

Frank Columbo stood and opened the inside front door. A moment later, Frank DeLuca opened the storm door.

Patricia says she froze. It was the first time the two men had been face-to-face since the confrontation on Walgreen's parking lot ten months earlier. She expected an immediate explosion. To her surprise, there was none.

"I've come to take Patrish home," DeLuca said.

Frank Columbo did not speak to him; instead, he said to Patricia, "Go clean yourself up. Then you'd better go with him."

Patricia could only stare dumbfoundedly at the two men. What was happening seemed like a dream, or a television program slightly out of focus. Everything suddenly "went into slow motion."

"Go on," her father said, "go clean yourself up. Then go with him. That's where you belong."

Mutely, Patricia rose and started down to the lower level, to the bathroom that had once been hers. On her way down, she heard her father speak again.

"Long as you've got a way home, leave the Olds here. Give me the keys."

"I left them in the car," Patricia said.

"I'll get them," she heard DeLuca say.

Patricia went into the bathroom. Looking at herself in the mirror, she saw that her father had been right; her face was a terrible mess: mascara was smeared into her hair and all the way back to her ear on one side, all the way down her neck on the other. She took off her coat, ran water, and washed her face.

She had just dried her face and hands and hung the towel back up, she says, when she heard two shots in quick succession. She remembers turning to stare at herself in the mirror, and she clearly remembers thinking: *Oh my God, Dad got him!*

Many years later, Patricia would guess that the reason for her thinking that, instead of thinking it the other way around, was probably because she and DeLuca, as well as Lanny and Roman, had engaged in so many conversations in which her father was depicted as someone trying to have DeLuca killed; that, along with the fact that he *had* threatened it on more than one occasion. "I guess I'd been programmed for it, or maybe programmed myself," she said. "It's the only reason I can think of. But whatever caused it, that was my very first thought: that Dad had shot Frank. It never entered my mind that Frank had shot Dad."

Patricia claims to have no idea how long she stood there, paralyzed by the thought that her father had shot Frank DeLuca. Two shots, she swears, is all she remembers hearing. When she finally got hold of herself enough to rush back to the stairs, DeLuca, coming down from the living room, met her in the foyer. He grabbed her roughly by the upper arm and forced her up the remaining stairs to the main level.

"Look what you've done now!" he shouted, turning her first to look at her father, lying on the living room floor, then at her mother, lying just inside the hall leading to the bedrooms. "Look what you've done now!" she says her enraged lover repeated over and over.

Finally he took her back down to the foyer and stood her in the corner where the inside door opened.

"I'll fix everything," DeLuca said. "Don't worry, I'll get you out of this."

Several minutes later, DeLuca came down and took her arm again. His hand on the sleeve of her blouse was wet. "Get in the Olds," he said, "and follow me." She felt him shake her. "You understand?"

Patricia nodded and DeLuca walked her out of the house and over to the Oldsmobile. He put her behind the wheel. The keys were still in the ignition, just as she had left them. For a flashing moment, it seemed to her that she had just arrived and hadn't been in the house yet. "Follow me, understand?" DeLuca repeated.

"Okay," Patricia said, vaguely aware that Frank did not have on his jacket anymore, and that he was wearing a very tight T-shirt that had a surfing design on it.

DeLuca got in the Buick. Patricia started the Olds and backed out to follow him. She does not remember either car backfiring. Nor does she know, independently, where she drove the Olds. She knows from the trial that the car was recovered one suburb south, from a Wooddale apartment house parking lot, but she cannot say whether or not she parked it there. All she recalls is that at some point DeLuca was at the Olds door again, helping her out, taking the car keys, and guiding her into the Buick. She remembers that she started trembling uncontrollably and tried "five or six times" to light a cigarette without success. She remembers DeLuca saying something like, "You're not going to be any good to me tonight," and for some insane reason she thought he was talking about sex. Her teeth began chattering and she couldn't stop them; they chattered so hard, she said, that her "face began to hurt."

The next thing she was aware of was that they had parked behind their apartment building, and DeLuca had her arm again and was marching her up the fire stairs, all the way up to the ninth floor, and that she could "barely breathe" by the time they got there. No one was in the hall on nine, so they entered the apartment without being observed.

Inside, DeLuca sat her on the couch and poured her a drink. He went into the bedroom and she heard the shower being turned on. She remembers going to her purse, which was still on the kitchen counter, and taking several more Valiums from a pillbox she carried. She realized that she had left her coat in the downstairs bathroom of her parents' home. Finishing the whiskey Frank had given her, she poured some more. One sleeve of her blouse was wet and sticky against her arm; she took the blouse off and wiped her arm with a paper napkin. Then she returned to the couch.

She thought she must have dozed off, because when she opened her eyes again DeLuca was back in the room, talking to someone on the telephone. She closed her eyes again. All she can remember after that is "going in and out" for the rest of the night. She woke up once just long enough to realize that she was in bed. And another time she was awakened by a noise and stood up out of bed to listen for it again. She was naked. The noise did not repeat itself and she got back in bed. She does not know if DeLuca was in bed either time she woke up.

She awoke the next morning with no hangover from the pills and whiskey, and was fresh and alert for a job interview she went on at 8:30 A.M. at Meyercord. Her coat was back in the apartment for her to wear.

An incredible story? Definitely.

Totally fabricated and untrue? Perhaps.

But—possible? *Yes.*

Little parts of it fit. In the "vision" story Investigator John Landers related, for instance, Patricia had "seen" Michael open the door for her. And, although she clearly described the appearance of her dead parents, she had not been able to say whether Michael even had clothes on or not. That agrees with her version of DeLuca showing her only the bodies of Frank and Mary.

Her story would also explain the absence of blood evidence in either Columbo car, because DeLuca would neither have ridden in nor driven either of the cars while he was blood-soaked.

Her story supports a theory that everything DeLuca told Clifford Childs was a lie. No doorbell had been rung. No bloody clothes had been burned in an open field. What was done in the murder house was not accomplished in a mere twenty minutes. And, if everything else was a lie, then the change of clothes was probably a lie too.

The car Georgia Brooks saw was in the right place at the right time. And the story of her husband, Clyde, who saw nothing unusual about the Columbo house when he came home between 11:00 and 11:30, also fit, because DeLuca wouldn't have been *back* there by then.

The T-shirt with the surfer design that DeLuca left the house in was Michael's; DeLuca had probably hastily grabbed it when he stripped off his bloody upper clothing.

That bloody clothing was left there; DeLuca knew he would be back. And the T-shirt was a missing item listed in Ray Rose's complaint for a search warrant.

If Patricia's time estimates are accurate, the telephone call she awoke to find DeLuca engaged in could have been the call to John Norton to check on the closing of the store. Or it could have been a call to someone to arrange for the help DeLuca was going to need to move the Thunderbird. Who would that person have been? Marilyn? She would have had to leave the children alone, but the oldest daughter was then thirteen, old enough to baby-sit her siblings. Would Marilyn have done it for her husband? (He *was* still her husband, their divorce not having become final at that point.) In light of everything she did after his arrest, there's not much doubt she would have helped him that night—particularly when all he wanted her to do was pick him up down in the city and bring him back to, say, the Walgreen's lot—three blocks from the Columbo home.

Or could it have been Bert Green? He lived even closer to Walgreen's than the Columbos. And by his own admission had been privy to the murder plan, the murder gun, the murder conspiracy, all along. Ingratiating as he always was to Frank DeLuca, the flunky assistant manager would have thought it was very "cool" to slip out of his apartment in the middle of the night and go pick up his mentor on some mysterious mission.

Whomever DeLuca chose to call for help, there was no doubt he could have found someone.

If Patricia's story is true, or even partly true, it means that DeLuca was in the Columbo house *twice* that night: once when the murders took place, which would have been around 10:00 P.M., and the other time after he cleaned up at his apartment, left Patricia there, and returned alone. If Patricia is only partially lying, they could have returned together, parked the borrowed Buick on the Walgreen's lot, walked the short distance to the Columbo home, and *both* gone in there again.

A second visit makes sense. Getting the CBs, the jewelry, the fur coats, the two Columbo guns, clubbing the adult bodies with the bowling trophy, stabbing and cutting Michael's dead body with the scissors (neither of which would by that time have produced much blood), messing up the house to make it look like a home invasion—all the things that Clifford Childs said DeLuca told him took "twenty minutes maximum." DeLuca might very well have meant that was how long he was in the house the first time.

Aside from the pieces of Patricia's story that fit into the over-all picture, there are elements of one other piece of evidence that lend support to DeLuca's committing most, if not all, of the savagery that went on that night. It is evidence that was not introduced at the trial because it probably would not have been allowed due to its hearsay nature. And it is information the defense team probably did not have, for they surely would have used it—Patricia's defense counsel anyway—in the cross-examination of Bert Green.

That piece of evidence is a statement, handwritten, given to police by someone who obviously knew a great deal about the Columbo murders. It contains details that apparently came from Bert Green. The statement may have been given by Green's wife, Peggy, who, curiously, is not mentioned *anywhere* in the official investigation. Or it may be the original *full* statement of Grace Mason—although it contains a great deal of information that was not included in the typed report Ray Rose prepared some nine months later for Assistant State's Attorney Terry Sullivan.

It has been established that on May 27, 1976, three weeks and two days after the murders, Bert Green told his wife Peggy about Frank DeLuca's admission to him that he had committed the crime. Peggy apparently had already known about Bert keeping the gun for DeLuca, and about Patricia's three trips to meet "hit men." It is unclear whether Peggy ever made a formal statement to the police, and if she did whether it was made before or after she left her husband. This statement *could* have come from her; it is written long-hand on the front and back of eleven sheets of seven-by-five-inch note paper, and is not dated. It is not until the very end of the statement that the contents become consequential, per-haps even crucial.

The statement, verbatim and with its own misspellings and parentheses, reads as follows:

"There were 3 times that Bert took Pat & dropped her off at the Lutheran Church on Arlington Heights rd. The first was April 19th. He worked all day Monday and that night we were supposed to go downtown to see his father who had a heart attack 2 weeks before. His sister & neice came in & we had plans that night. Bert had been on a weeks vacation and it was his first day as an assistant mgr. Frank said to Bert if you come back tonight for an hour and a half I'll give you all of Tuesday off. He was supposed to help out in the liquor dept. because the new liquor manager screwed things up." At this point a line is drawn to a note in the margin that reads: "But he really didn't."

The statement continues: "Bert didn't know he was to take Pat until she showed up to help out in liquor." This sentence is crossed out and a sentence is written in the margin to replace it: "He knew he had to pick her up in afternoon." Then it goes on: "Frank said not to tell anybody about dropping Pat off." In parentheses is added: "(He said she would be dressed down. Also he was to pick her up at the back door.)"

A new paragraph states: "Before we took our vacation Frank gave Bert a package (the gun.) He said would Bert hold it for him. It's nothing illegal or will get you in any trouble. He had it a week and Frank asked for it back— also he said don't tell Peggy or anybody else you have it.

"Frank again asked him to hold the package a few days to a week (about April 22 or so.) Frank showed Bert what was in the package—he thinks after he brought it back the 2nd time in the back room at work. It was a 32 revolver. Frank said he had it for protection against 'old man Columbo.'

"(Bert was supposed to be transferred to the Harlem & Foster store when he first became an assistant. Frank had it changed so Mr. Rivera went there instead of Bert)

"On the 2nd time Bert took Pat to the church (April 26th) I remembered Bert said she was nervous. On Friday or Saturday before Frank said he wanted Bert to pick her up again." The words "Friday or" are lined out. "ON AGAIN FOR MONDAY" is printed in capital letters between the lines. The paragraph continues without capitalization, "*the 2nd time Bert was late picking her up. On the first time he told Bert to stop at the store to get directions.*"

A new paragraph begins in parentheses without capitalization: "*(on the gun thing. He told Bert not to give it to anyone. Something about somebody coming in to pick it up. Don't let anybody have it. There might be a possibility of somebody wanting the package. Bert said 'how will I know.' He said the person will say 'Duke' sent me. Nobody came.)*"

"*Wednesday following*" is lined out to begin the next paragraph. Then: "*The first time he didn't know because he said to Pat do you need a ride home. She said no. I have a way, or Frank will pick me up or I'll go over to the store.*"

Another new paragraph without capitalization: "*the second time he knew of the setup. Frank told Bert 'old man Columbo' had a contract out on him & old man*"—the last "old man" is lined out—"*he had one out on him.*" The name "*Frank*" is written over "*he.*" Then a new sentence without capitalization reads, "*told sometime Wed or Thurs. 21st or 22nd.*"

"*Frank said he had some guys or people. Also that Columbo was going to frame Deluca with a thing about drugs through the pharmacy.*" It is curious to note that whoever gave this statement began, about halfway through it, referring to Frank DeLuca as "Deluca," with a small "l," instead of "Frank," as he was referred to up to that time.

"*Monday April 26th*" is lined out, and a new paragraph continues, "*told how Pat was to go into the house & set it up. Pat was to*"—the last three words are lined out, and it continues, "*Didn't know what she was setting up.*"

"*Monday April 26th. Pat*"—the name is lined out. "*Pick up 8:30.*" The "3" in 8:30 is written over darkly to change it to a zero, making the time 8:00. "*Left house at 7:30 or 7:45. On way stop at store Deluca said* hurry if you're gonna pick her up. Had to wait long time. tempted to leave. Sat & thought about anybody watching. Wondering if somebody was out to get Pat. Wondered if 'old man' crazy enough to have a hit out on Pat too. She comes down about 8:30. late & dark. Start driving. She is looking around and sloughing down in the seat." The "g" has been written over to make a "c" and change the word to "slouching." Then: "Bert didn't want to know what's going on. On 53—said I can't believe you're father would have a contract out on Deluca. also the bit about the drugs—Pat confirms it & says it's all true—Drop her off at church again—come back to A. Hts. rd. Wanted to get the 'Fuck' out of there.

"the first time why it didn't go down was ? One of the times the phone rang—Pat answered the phone & that blew it because she wasn't supposed to be there. A relative called. Another time the G'ma came over to visit." In a lined block between "she wasn't" and "supposed to" were the words "Always had to be Monday because every body was out of the house except Mr & Mrs Columbo."

New paragraph. "Monday morning May 3rd Bert considers not taking her (Pat). Bert tells Deluca something about getting out of the house." Between lines is written in much smaller script, "Not being able to" and "Deluca said get out"—then the sentence continues, "any way Bert can & put the blame on Deluca. 'You have to do it.' Things are going through his head that he has cindicate hit men & he is up to his neck in it." An "sy" is written over the "ci" to correct the spelling of "syndicate."

New paragraph. "again Pat makes him wait a long time. It's dark and he is really nev"—the latter lined out—"nervous. Pat tells him he is driving too fast. Pat talks about leaving home—went South—father pick her up—beat her up—ran away to California (?) he found her again & brought her back home.

"No going around the block. into the parking lot & right out then home.

"Tuesday May 4th. Might have had that fucking thing 3 times (gun) If the hit didn't go down, Bert got the gun back. Might have had it a couple of times? The day Copeck went to court I don't think he had the gun that time. He showed Bert where he hid it in the store—It was in the stock room on 2nd to top shelf under a box near the drug section off to the right. He thinks that tuesday he was off the whole day. Went to Woodfield to look for something. Had to be back by 3:30—Peggy baby sat. In the morning he says he was in the store—Joanne Hemmer saw you." The last name is written over to read "Emmer," and the name "Bert" is written above the "you" in "saw you." Then continues, "Thinks he told him to come in tuesday morning—to check with him."

New paragraph. "(In between times 'It didn't go down.' 1st time said 'didn't go down' 2nd time 'didn't go down.' A day lag or so. Said maybe I'll have to do it myself—very uptight—said it might not be going down because Columbo his hit people off. 3rd time doesn't go down—I'll have to do it myself—(possibility) short time spent there—In & out quick.

"tuesday night Lloyd & Grace down till 10:00 because we remembered what was on M.A.S.H.

"Wed morning. Into work at 8:30. Deluca was there— (Rarely is he ever there early in the morning.) OPen doors, lock doors—walks to 1st set of fuse boxes for lights. Doesn't realize—music & lights are one. Now he walks back past check out.

"Into door for lunch room lights are one usually off— Hears roar of incinerator. Turns corner & see Deluca." The following is then all lined out: "1) coming out of bathroom 2) Deluca coming out of stock room" Then, not lined out, "3) coming out of incinerator. Heard him close the door to it. Saw the glow of fire going. Comes up to Bert says 'I hit the old man last night'—or 'I did it last night' or 'I did the old man in.'

"Tells Bert he is burning the clothes—'That's the reason for the fire. I was covered head to foot in blood.' " In the margin is written "Bloody Mess." Then: " 'I haven't had any sleep. I didn't get home till 4:00 in the morning. then he said go into the lunch room and sit down with me. said

*punch in. Into lunch room & told how he killed them. the
1st shot didn't kill him—he was a tough old bird. then he
said he shot the old lady. the old man said—'Why are you
doing this to me?' Bert didn't think he knew it was Deluca
because Columbo said that—Deluca made the remark—
'That Mother fucker.' Bert remembers a stocking cap now.
'Stocking ski hat' didn't say articles of clothing but did say
ski hat.*

"1st shot (?)—said hit him point blank in forehead one
in back of head out mouth—shot Mrs. C.

"Bert said why the hell didn't you blow the house up—
release the gas—Bert was getting pissed. Thinks he said he
went into the kids room & shot him. Came back with lamp
& hit again 'tough old bird wouldn't go down.'

"Thursday morning—he wasn't there. Maybe
9:00–10:00 Deluca calls him in they haven't found the
bodies yet—getting uptight. keeps talking about how they
haven't found the bodies yet.

"Fri. Really uptight because they haven't found the
bodies—nobody has missed the old man, old lady—or
school hasn't missed the kid.

"Only contact on phone wanted Bert to go to wake Really insistant needed emotional support.

A line is drawn across this page, which is the reverse
of page 8, about two-thirds of the way down the sheet.
Below the line is a quote: "We told you this to see if we
could trust you." Below that: "Thurs. 5:00—Pat &
Frank leaving store—"

At the top of page nine: "After funeral acted as if Bert
didn't know shit."

Then a long paragraph: "When picked up Deluca police
station—waiting down street from police department. went
to wife's house criticized police & procedure—" Next is
"When go," which is lined out, and then it reads again,
"Went to wife's home—nobody home—went to apartment.
Acted as if Bert didn't know anything at all—acted as if he
was just giving him a ride—Relatively quite—talked about
how Pat didn't pay any bills—a whole list of checks (at one
time showed Bert whole pile of checks from Jewel with Pats

name—said Columbos were doing this & that somebody was forging signatures—Had checking account & she closed it out—She lost ½ of checks & checks were going through Jewel Check card—)

"Got to apartment—things were a mess. Started going through drawers—found overdue notices—took papers & bills with him.

"Drove back to wife's house—she was home—Had coffee—Got impression that Bert was 3rd party. Wife talked about attorney. Seems phony—Questions Why did Marilyn get $5000 to get guy out of jail if she knew it took $25,000 to get Frank out—maybe Scarlada."

A line is drawn across the page; this is the front of page ten. Below the line: *"Cuts on hand caused from lamp."* Another line all the way across, then: *"Gun powder—how to get it off."*

The reverse of page ten contains four separate quotes:

"Did some smart things to cover his tracks."

"Didn't," which is lined out, followed by *"try to find flash light couldn't—got a candle to pick up all the glass—on hands & knees—wasn't sure if he got all of it. Might have finger prints on it."*

"Gun & lamp pieces & dumped in river."

"Said he hadn't told Pat about Michael."

Page eleven has writing on the front side only. *"Police were talking through their hats."* Below that: *"May 27 told Peg. July 19 told Lloyd & Grace (day after he was arrested)"*

Obviously, the most unsettling part of this statement, whoever gave it, is the quote, *"Said he hadn't told Pat about Michael."*

Clearly, this indicates that DeLuca knew Michael was dead, but *Patricia did not.*

Again, this fits perfectly into Patricia's story that DeLuca showed her only the bodies of her parents, and fits as well into the Landers version of Patricia's "vision," in which she did not see Michael's body.

Where it does *not* fit is in the closing arguments of prosecutors Patti Bobb and Al Baliunas, both of whom accused Patricia of inflicting the numerous superficial cuts on Michael. The most sobering question this presents is: did the prosecution *know* about this statement? If so, did they check it out at all, disregard it, even conceal it?

Or was it known only to the Elk Grove police department? Did *they* conceal it, or ignore it, or did it simply get lost in the morass of reports that would eventually fill several file storage boxes?

Whatever happened to this information, it is undeniably something that should have been shown to the jury that found Patricia Columbo guilty of first-degree murder based on its belief that she participated in the actual crime by butchering her 13-year-old brother.

The rest of the statement also contains some interesting revelations.

There appears to be an attempt early on to protect Bert Green by modifying his involvement. "Bert didn't know he was to take Pat (to meet the hit men) until he showed up in (the) liquor (department)," was lined out, and then this included: "He knew he had to pick her up in afternoon."

Green had the murder gun at least twice, perhaps three times—and definitely knew what was in the package after keeping it for DeLuca the first time (which impugns Green's trial testimony, in which he related keeping the gun only once, with DeLuca showing him what it was only after he returned it).

DeLuca showing Bert Green where the gun was hidden in the drugstore, and telling him to give it only to someone using the phrase "Duke sent me" smacks of a possible arrangement between DeLuca and Roman Sobczynski, for Roman to retrieve the gun he gave Patricia. "Duke," of course, is DeLuca's by-now-infamous German shepherd, which is where DeLuca would have gotten the code name. But why brief Bert Green on the possibility of anyone coming to get that gun? Unless some kind of bargain had been made with someone? Patricia suspected (and it was established) that DeLuca was in contact with Roman Sobczynski *after* Patricia terminated all association with Roman and Lanny. Is it possible that DeLuca had agreed to give the incriminating weapon back to Roman after Roman (and perhaps Lanny) had carried out the hits? The gun was in the store every Tuesday morning; Frank gave it back to Bert Green to hold only when the "hits didn't go down" on Monday nights. Why was it there? So that after the hits, DeLuca could give the secret phrase to whoever did the job, and they could come into the store, say "Duke sent me," and pick up the gun from Bert Green— leaving DeLuca out of it completely? It has to be considered a definite possibility.

The statement appears to support again the position that DeLuca told Bert Green that possibly "I'll have to do it myself," not "we'll" have to do it, as he later testified in court. And DeLuca said to Bert, as well as to Joy Heysek, "*I* hit the old man last night," or words to that effect.

DeLuca's claim that he did not get home until four o'clock in the morning makes absolutely no sense if one believes the prosecution's case—but easily computes if DeLuca went back to the house, particularly if he waited until one o'clock or later to do so.

The statement seems to further implicate Bert Green. He was not shocked by what DeLuca told him; didn't even seem surprised. In fact, he asked DeLuca, "Why the hell didn't you blow the house up? Release the gas?" Green was clearly a far different person, the morning after the murders, from the nervous, Maalox-swigging trial witness who changed some critical dialogue and left out so much when he testified.

The statement also indicts Patricia. If she was with DeLuca on Thursday night after the murders, when DeLuca left the store at five o'clock, and DeLuca said to Bert, "We told you this to see if we could trust you," then Patricia, at least at that moment, knew her parents were dead, and had not repressed most of what happened after she heard the two shots. In separate statements detailing their movements for the week of the murders, both Patricia and DeLuca indicated that Patricia did pick DeLuca up at the store that day—but one or the other might be confused about *which* day it was, because they differ on what they subsequently did immediately afterward: Patricia said they stopped at an A&P to buy steaks, and DeLuca said they stopped for hot dogs on the way home. Patricia remembers neither fifteen years later.

A quote about the murder house, on the other hand, seems again to support Patricia's story. DeLuca is supposed to have said, "try to find flash light couldn't—got a candle to pick up all the glass—" It sounds as if this is DeLuca's second trip to the house, and he is alone. If Patricia was with him, if she had been participating *either* time, surely she would have known where a flashlight was kept. People usually keep flashlights in some convenient, permanent place. Patricia lived in the house for seven years. She would not have had to rely on a candle.

This handwritten statement, from *someone*, makes it very clear that there is much about the Columbo murders that Judge Pincham and his jury never got to hear; much that the prosecution should not have left out; much to which the defense teams should have had access.

And much that is still unknown, even after fifteen years.

C.H.
January 1992

The first time Patricia told me her version of what had happened on the murder night, I asked her the obvious question.

"Why haven't you ever told the story before?"

"For what?" she said. "Who would have believed it?" Then she challenged, "Do you even believe it?" Immediately both her hands shot up, palms out. "Never mind," she vetoed in the same breath, "I don't want to know."

I would not have answered her anyway. What I personally believe doesn't matter. My task was to maintain objectivity and to put in the book everything my research produced. If true-crime writers started culling out the material that made no sense to them, there would probably be no true-crime books. Researching murder is very precise business. It leaves no room for personal interpretation.

In researching a murder case, there is usually only one incontrovertible fact: the murder itself. Invariably, everything else about the case is conceptual, hypothetical, suppositional. Evidence is always interpretive. Opinions are always subjective. Appraisals, particularly of people by people, cannot avoid being personal. And convictions of the mind, once formed, nearly always become concrete.

Patricia Columbo is loathed and despised by so many people both involved in and removed from the Columbo murder case, I would not attempt even to list them, much less address their reasoning. Patti Bobb and Al Baliunas, I'm sure, will go to their graves convinced that Patricia hacked up Michael. Nothing would change their minds—not even a confession by DeLuca. Judge Pincham will go to his grave thinking she is, as he stated to the press, a "vicious, cunning, coy, mean, disruptive person," who should never be released even if she has reformed and been rehabilitated. It remains curious that in a case laced with thoroughly reprehensible people—Lanny Mitchell, Roman Sobczynski, Joy Heysek, Bert Green, Clifford Childs, Frank DeLuca himself—that Pincham's venom over the years seemed focused on Patricia. Perhaps it did not bother him that Lanny and Roman went free, and perhaps he does not care whether DeLuca is paroled. Perhaps, too, it is fortunate that he is no longer on the bench; the judicial system does not need a judge who is selective to the degree that Pincham seems to have become regarding the rehabilitative process. He seems to have forgotten that Patricia is serving her time at Dwight Correctional Center.

Because of Patricia Columbo's past life and her uncompromising personality, there are people who have become programmed not to believe a single word that she utters, or any positive word uttered about her. One female reporter for one of the suburban newspapers, whose only connection with Patricia Columbo has been writing recap stories of the case from time to time; who has never met, talked to on the telephone, or even corresponded with Patricia; and who certainly has never read the trial transcript, interviewed Sister Burke before the nun died, and learned from her that Sister Burke believed Patricia's story of her child abuse years. This reporter's evaluation of that interview was that Sister Burke "just fell for Patty's story." Sister Margaret Burke, with a master's and a doctorate in psychology from Loyola; a college president for twenty-two years, then for sixteen years after her retirement a counselor to homeless, abused, and incarcerated women; member of some of the most prestigious human rights committees in the nation—and *this reporter concludes that Sister Burke just fell for Patty's story.*

To be fair, it is not impossible that both a woman of Sister Burke's extraordinary background and credentials and an author with thirty years' experience writing in the fields of criminology and penology could both be "taken in" by a lie devised by Patricia Columbo, while a much less experienced general reporter for a small suburban newspaper would be astute enough to "see through" the fraud. It is possible—but the likelihood has to be considered remote, for three reasons:

First, Patricia was not trying to "use" Sister Burke in any way; she sought Sister Burke's counseling in confidence in order to help understand herself. She has never allowed her attorney, Peggy Byrne, to use the child abuse story as part of a parole plea, as mitigation of the terrible crime that was committed, or to gain sympathy in any other way.

Second, a point that is supported by studies in general on this subject, is that Patricia Columbo's experience falls into an almost classic psychological profile of a route that begins with early sexual abuse, is subsequently deeply repressed, and returns to the person's consciousness in her early thirties. There are legions of women just like Patricia Columbo, and the pattern of this common ordeal cannot be ignored.

Last, my primary reason for dismissing the reporter's conclusion is simply that I know Patricia now, know her very well, and where she might have a desire to fabricate a sexual abuse story of such complexity and rich detail, I am convinced that she lacks the creative ability to do so. Plain and simple, Patricia is one of the most inept liars I have ever encountered.

To be believable to another person, it naturally helps if one is likable—and Patricia, of course, does absolutely nothing to ingratiate herself to anyone. From the days of her trial when she would pass Ray Rose in the courthouse hall, glare at him, and say, "You motherfucker," through many long years at Dwight, where she wouldn't even condescend to attend her own parole hearings; long years in which she coldly ignored the members of the press, refusing to see any of them no matter who they represented or how far they had traveled; refusing to demand exoneration of year after year of unsupported newspaper allegations linking her name to the infa-

mous "sex scandal" at Dwight; and a general "fuck everybody" attitude, a determination that she could, and would,
take anything they could dish out. And if they kept her in
Dwight until she died, so be it.

So her rhetorical reply—"Who would have believed
it?"—to my question of why she had never told her version
of the murder night was not surprising. Reflecting back on all
the people I talked to about the case, I couldn't think of one
who would have admitted that her story was even possible,
much less probable.

"I would have told Sister Burke," Patricia said later. "She
would have believed me. And she would have helped me with
the rest of it, if there's anything I've repressed. But I lost
her."

Whether anybody ever believes Patricia's story or not, the
fact remains that she is entitled at last to tell it, just as she
is entitled to relate her long sessions with Sister Burke and
the child abuse repressions that she claims were brought to
consciousness as a result. If the child abuse story is a fabri-
cation, as many do believe, if in fact Sister Burke did simply
"fall for Patty's story," it must still be included along with everything else developed during the research.

After all, what will it hurt?

Who's going to believe it?

One night when my private line rang and I accepted a collect
call from Patricia, she said, "What are you doing, you bum?"

"I've been waiting for you to call again," I told her. "I
have some interesting news for you. Frank DeLuca has admitted the murders."

There was a long moment of silence on the line, then
Patricia asked, "What did you say?"

"DeLuca has admitted murdering your family," I repeated.

She was obviously as stunned as I had initially been.
Patricia and I had mutually felt all along that it was highly
unlikely that DeLuca would ever admit anything. My words to
Patricia early on had been that "he will probably stonewall
his innocence until the day he dies."

And, I had been convinced, he would die in the Illinois
state prison. "No parole board will ever let him out," I told
her, "as long as he maintains his innocence. Parole boards

dispense leniency only in the wake of repentance. No killer ever gets out without admitting, at least for the record, their guilt." For fifteen years, DeLuca had steadfastly maintained his innocence. At his very first parole hearing, he had been asked specifically, *"In regard to the murders, this is something you were directly involved in—you're not disputing that?"*

He had answered, *"Yes, I am. Yes, I am."*

"You are?" The questioner was Ann Taylor, a longtime Prisoner Review Board member. *"You're saying that you weren't there, that you were not involved?"*

"I was not *involved."*

"You did not make admissions *on May fifth of your guilt?"*

"No. No. That's what I'm saying."

"You did not say [of Michael], 'I just stood him up and shot him'?"

"No, I did not!"

"Where were you?" Ann Taylor asked. *"And where was Patty?"*

"We were at home. We were at home in bed."

For fifteen years, DeLuca had stuck to that lie.

"How do you know he finally admitted it?" Patricia asked. "It hasn't been in the papers or on the Chicago news."

"I have an audiotape of the parole hearing where he admitted it," I said. Illinois tapes its parole hearings instead of keeping a stenographic record. As for why the admission wasn't reported by the Chicago press, I had no idea. "If you want me to," I offered, "I can stretch a phone line to my stereo and let you listen to the tape—"

"Jesus Christ, no!" she snapped. "The last thing in the world I need is to hear that man's voice again. Just tell me about it."

"Basically," I said, "during routine questioning at his parole hearing, DeLuca's voice seemed to break and he said, 'I'm ashamed, okay? I'm ashamed of what I did.' After some further dialogue, he said, 'I—I shot the people in the—' The rest of his sentence," I told Patricia, "is unintelligible. I've tried to find out what it was, but Ann Taylor, the Prisoner Review Board member who was questioning him, won't return my calls. And when I spoke to Kent Steinkamp, the board's le-

gal counsel, he said she didn't have to talk to me if she didn't want to."

"But DeLuca did say he shot them?"

"Definitely. And the coroner testified at the trial that the cause of death was the gunshot wounds. So he's admitted murder."

"Did he admit anything else?" Patricia asked.

"No." I paused a beat, then added, "There's a good chance he won't."

"What do you mean?"

"Look, DeLuca's been in a tough prison for a lot of years," I told her. "He's got to have wised up. He's a con who probably knows every angle there is by now. He even refers to you as his 'rappy.'" That was convict vernacular for a rap partner, or co-defendant. "The excuse he's given the Prisoner Review Board for pleading not guilty, and for lying about his innocence all these years, is that he was protecting his rappy. He's implying that you've been the one to lead the way all along, since you were sixteen. He says you started the whole relationship with him by going to an assistant manager he had and asking to go to work in the cosmetics department so you could be near him, that it was never his idea at all, that he didn't charm you, seduce you, or cultivate you. The picture that he is giving the board is that he was a happily married man before you came along. One of the board members asked if he had any prior domestic trouble, or relationships with any other women, and he said no—"

"For Christ's sake," Patricia said incredulously, "aren't they aware of Joy Heysek's testimony? Don't they know about the things he did *before* he met me?"

"Apparently not. DeLuca was asked how long after he met you did he begin his relationship with you, and he said two or three years. I don't think the board knows he was having sex with you when you were barely sixteen. They obviously don't know about his sexual extremes before that. Ann Taylor is pretty good at leading questions; she asked if he befriended you because he felt you were in a bad home situation, and he said yes. Another member of the board was very surprised to find out you had lived in the DeLuca home with Marilyn and the five kids for a year."

"I can't believe this," Patricia said. "These are the people *who are going to decide whether to put Frank DeLuca on the street again? They don't know a goddamn thing about the case!"*

"At one point," I told her, "after DeLuca admitted the shootings, Ann Taylor asked him whether the victims were dead when he left. His reply was again partly unintelligible. He said, 'Well—they were—they were still breathing when Patty—uh—'—the words were mumbled from there until he says, '—uh—uh—the coroner said the wounds would have been fatal.' Notice," I said, "how carefully everything is worded. The coroner didn't say the gunshot wounds would have been fatal; he said they were fatal. DeLuca is implying that maybe the shots didn't kill them. Like I said, Frank has wised up in the joint. He's finally realized that the only way to walk is to cop to something. So he's trying to plant a seed of doubt about the shots being fatal, then he's copping to the shootings—and only the shootings."

"I guess that makes me the butcher," Patricia said evenly.

"It might, unless you deny it."

"I can't deny it," she said, her voice becoming very quiet. "I don't know if I did it or not." Patricia sighed a sigh that was barely audible over the telephone line. "I always knew I didn't fire the first two shots, because I heard them downstairs. And when Frank showed me my parents, I guess I subconsciously equated one bullet for each of them. It was not until later that I learned four more shots had been fired. It's a tremendous relief to know that I didn't fire them. I didn't think I did—but I never really knew for sure. As for the rest of it—I hope I never find out."

"You're afraid to know?"

"I'm terrified," she admitted.

I told her a little more about what was on the tapes: DeLuca praising his ex-wife, Marilyn, as being a "good woman"; the fact that two of his daughters were married now; that Frank Jr. was studying to become a pharmacist "just like me"; that DeLuca soon expected to be a grandfather; that if paroled he would live with his father or his brother, Bill; that he would look for work managing a retail drugstore. To the latter, Ann Taylor said, "You shouldn't have too much trouble with that." An incredible statement, given all that had gone before.

"*Do you think he'll get out?*" Patricia asked at last.

"*He's moving in the right direction,*" I said. "*He's ashamed, he's repentant, he was under the spell and direction of his rappy. Plus he has a lot of family behind him, and parole boards like that. You, on the other hand, are an orphan.*"

"*Oh, very fucking funny,*" she said icily.

"*I didn't mean it to be funny. I just meant that everybody in your family has abandoned you. The few friends you have, other than former Dwight inmates, are a decade or more older than you. Sister Burke has died; Sister Traxler and your godmother are probably twenty-five years your senior. As the years go by, you're going to be running out of friends. The only person who'll probably still be around to offer you any outside help will be Peggy; but since she's your attorney as well as your friend, the parole board won't give her much weight.*"

"*What about you?*" Patricia challenged.

"*I'm in it for the book,*" I reminded her. "*You've known that from the very beginning. When the book is finished, I move on to another one.*"

"*Kind of like a pimp,*" she said. "*Dropping one whore for the next.*"

"*Yeah, kind of.*" It was an interesting analogy. I certainly couldn't argue with it.

"*I don't care anyway,*" Patricia said. A familiar hardness returned to her voice. "*If they put DeLuca on the street again, I don't want to get out. I'll stay in here until I die.*"

"*It might turn out that way,*" I told her.

The last time I visited Patricia, she said, "*I don't think you should come back again.*"

"*All right.*" We were standing in a foyer on the prison side, waiting for an electronic door to open so that I could walk back through the main visiting room and out of the institution.

"*These talks of ours are becoming too intense for me,*" she said. "*I'm having trouble sleeping. It's nothing personal.*"

"*You don't have to explain,*" I told her. "*It's always been your call.*"

"*I never intended to tell you as much as I have,*" she said. "*All I was going to do is tell you about when I was a little*

*girl, about the child abuse thing. I felt I owed it to Sister
Burke to tell it, so all her work wouldn't have been for nothing. But the rest of it—I never meant to go this far." She
shook her head wryly. "You've got a way with you. You're
easy to talk to."*

"Someday you'll probably be glad you did," I said. But I
didn't say it very convincingly.

We shook hands. "Take care of yourself," I said.

"Sure," she replied, with the flicker of a smile. "You too."

*Patricia still calls me once in a while, late at night when she
feels like it. But we don't talk about the murders anymore.
Once when she called, she had been ill for several weeks; she
was losing weight and the prison medical staff could not determine the cause. First it was diagnosed as the flu, then
nerves. It turned out to be an inner-ear infection, and the next
time I heard from her it had cleared up.*

*Her life in Dwight, which at one time had provided such
positive reinforcement for her, has for the most part been neutralized by events and conditions over which she has no control. The decline began with Sister Burke's death. Then
Patricia's education came to an end when she received her
bachelor's degree and couldn't continue beyond that point because no master's program is offered to Illinois convicts. A
few months later, she learned that the teacher for whom she
had been an aide for eight years was retiring, and there was
some question as to whether "Columbo's Hoodlums" would
be allowed to continue. Then, just before Christmas of 1991,
in her sixteenth year of confinement, came the inner-ear infection that kept her sick through the holidays and suspended
the meager income she received for tutoring. Early in 1992,
one of her best friends, a forger, was transferred to another
institution to begin a work-release program. For the first time
in many years prison has, for Patricia, become punishment.*

*The long, cold winter on the flat plains of southern Illinois
would soon turn into the warm embrace of spring. But even
that was nothing for Patricia to contemplate with any degree
of pleasure. Spring was actually the worst time of all for her.*

That spring, Michael would have been twenty-nine.

Newlyweds Pam and Gregg Smart seemed like the perfect American couple. He was an up-and-coming young insurance executive, she the beautiful former cheerleader who now worked in the administration of the local school.

But on May 1, 1990, their idyllic life was shattered when Gregg was murdered in the couple's upscale Derry, New Hampshire townhouse—a single shot to his head. Three months later, the grieving widow was arrested and charged with the brutal crime.

In the dramatic trial that followed, a dark portrait of Pam Smart emerged—one of a cold manipulator who seduced a high school student with a striptease and then had a wild affair with him—until he was so involved with her that he was willing to do anything for her...even murder...

DEADLY LESSONS

BY EDGAR AWARD NOMINEE
KEN ENGLADE

When the sheriff of East Chatham, N.Y. first described the bloody scene—"Worse than anything I ever saw in Korea"—he was reduced to tears. Four people—a popular local businessman, his live-in girlfriend, his nineteen-year-old son, and his three-year-old orphaned nephew—had been brutally murdered in an isolated country cabin.

By the next day, a stunned community learned that the dead man's seventeen-year-old son, Wyley Gates—vice-president of his class and voted "most likely to succeed"—had allegedly confessed to the murders. What could possibly be the motive for such a grisly crime—and how could such an upright teenage boy explode with such lethal fury?

MOST LIKELY TO SUCCEED

ALAN GELB